C++ for Scientists, Engineers and Mathematicians

All trademarks found in this book are acknowledged. This acknowledgement
includes:

UNIX System Laboratories Inc:	UNIX
Microsoft Corporation:	MS-DOS
Symantec Corporation:	Zortech, FG

D.M. Capper

C++ for Scientists, Engineers and Mathematicians

Springer-Verlag

London Berlin Heidelberg New York
Paris Tokyo Hong Kong
Barcelona Budapest

Derek Capper
Eridge
Church Street
Wotton-under-Edge
Gloucestershire
GL12 7HB
UK

ISBN 3-540-19847-4 Springer-Verlag Berlin Heidelberg New York
ISBN 0-387-19847-4 Springer-Verlag New York Berlin Heidelberg

British Library Cataloguing in Publication Data
Capper, Derek
 C++ for Scientists, Engineers and Mathematicians
 I. Title
 005.13
 ISBN 3-540-19847-4

Library of Congress Cataloging-in-Publication Data
Capper, D. M. (Derek M.), 1947-
        The C++ programming language for scientists, engineers, and mathematicians / D.M. Capper.
          p.   cm.
        Includes bibliographical references and index.
        ISBN 0-387-19847-4 (acid-free paper)
        1. C++ (Computer program language)   I. Title.
     QA76.73.C153C36   1994
     005.13'3 - - dc20

93-47975
CIP

© Springer-Verlag London Limited 1994
Printed in Great Britain
3rd printing, 1996
4th printing, 1997

This book was prepared with LaTeX and reproduced by Springer-Verlag from camera ready copy supplied by the author.

Printed and bound at Bell & Bain, Glasgow, UK
34/3830-543 Printed on acid-free paper

Contents

List of Figures   xiii

List of Tables   xv

Preface   xvii

    Structure of this Book xviii

    Acknowledgements xx

1   Introduction   **1**

    1.1   Getting Started 1

    1.2   Solving a Quadratic Equation 3

    1.3   An Object-oriented Example 4

    1.4   Why Object-oriented? 6

    1.5   Summary 7

    1.6   Exercises 8

2   The Lexical Basis of C++   **9**

    2.1   Characters and Tokens 9

    2.2   Comments and White Space 9

    2.3   Identifiers 11

    2.4   Keywords 12

    2.5   Constants 13

        2.5.1   Integer Constants 13

        2.5.2   Floating Point Constants 14

        2.5.3   Character Constants 14

        2.5.4   String Constants 15

    2.6   Operators 15

    2.7   The Preprocessor 16

    2.8   Programming Style 16

    2.9   Summary 17

    2.10 Exercises 18

3 Fundamental Types and Basic Operators   **19**
  3.1 Integral Data Types 20
     3.1.1 Type `int` 20
     3.1.2 Integer Multiplication 23
     3.1.3 Integer Division 23
     3.1.4 Integer Modulus or Remainder Operator 24
     3.1.5 Increment and Decrement Operators 25
     3.1.6 Associativity and Precedence of Integer Operators 26
     3.1.7 Long Integers 29
     3.1.8 Short Integers 29
     3.1.9 Unsigned Integers 30
     3.1.10 Character Types 30
  3.2 Floating Point Data Types 31
     3.2.1 Type `double` 32
     3.2.2 Type `float` 34
     3.2.3 Type `long double` 34
  3.3 Changing Types 35
     3.3.1 Type Promotion and Conversion 35
     3.3.2 Casts 37
  3.4 Some Basic Operations 37
     3.4.1 The `sizeof` Operator 38
     3.4.2 Initialization 38
     3.4.3 Assignment Operators 39
  3.5 `const` 40
  3.6 `register` and `volatile` 41
  3.7 `typedef` 42
  3.8 Summary 43
  3.9 Exercises 43

4 Control Structure   **45**
  4.1 Relational Operators 45
  4.2 Logical Operators 47
  4.3 Equal and Not Equal Operators 49
  4.4 Blocks and Scope 50
  4.5 Branch Statements 51
     4.5.1 `if` Statement 51
     4.5.2 `if else` statement 54
     4.5.3 `switch` Statement 56
  4.6 Iteration Statements 59
     4.6.1 `while` Statement 59
     4.6.2 `for` Statement 60
     4.6.3 `do` Statement 62
  4.7 `break` and `continue` Statements 64

4.8 `goto` Statement 65

4.9 Comma Operator 66

4.10 Null Statement 67

4.11 Conditional Expression Operator 68

4.12 Order of Evaluation of Operands 68

4.13 The Preprocessor 69

    4.13.1 `include` Directive 70

    4.13.2 `define` Directive 70

    4.13.3 Conditional Compilation 72

4.14 Enumerations 74

4.15 Summary 76

4.16 Exercises 77

5 Functions   **81**

5.1 Introducing Functions 81

    5.1.1 Defining and Calling Functions 81

    5.1.2 Return Type 84

    5.1.3 Function Prototypes 86

    5.1.4 Functions Cannot Declare Functions 86

    5.1.5 Unused Arguments 88

    5.1.6 Default Arguments 89

    5.1.7 Ignoring the Return Value 91

5.2 Recursion 91

5.3 Inline Functions 93

5.4 More on Scope Rules 94

5.5 Storage Classes `auto` and `static` 95

5.6 Overloading Function Names 98

5.7 Function `main()` 100

5.8 Standard Library 101

5.9 Using Functions 104

    5.9.1 A Benchmark 104

    5.9.2 Root Finding by Bisection 106

5.10 Summary 110

5.11 Exercises 111

6 Pointers and Arrays   **117**

6.1 Memory, Addressing and Pointers 117

    6.1.1 'address-of' Operator 117

    6.1.2 Dereferencing or Indirection Operator 119

    6.1.3 Pointers 119

    6.1.4 Pointers Do Not Declare Memory 123

    6.1.5 Null Pointer 125

6.2 One-dimensional Arrays 125

6.2.1   Pointers and One-dimensional Arrays   127
6.2.2   Negative Array Indices   132
6.3   Type `void*`   132
6.4   Pointer Conversions   133
6.5   Multi-dimensional Arrays   133
6.5.1   Pointers and Multi-dimensional Arrays   135
6.6   Initializing Arrays   136
6.7   Size of Arrays   138
6.8   Arrays of Pointers and Multi-dimensional Arrays   139
6.9   Using Pointers and Arrays   141
6.9.1   Fitting Data to a Straight Line   141
6.9.2   Ragged Arrays   143
6.10   Summary   145
6.11   Exercises   148

7   Further Pointer Techniques   151
7.1   Strings   151
7.2   Pointers as Function Arguments   154
7.3   Passing Arrays as Function Arguments   156
7.3.1   One-dimensional Arrays   156
7.3.2   Multi-dimensional Arrays   158
7.4   Arguments to `main()`   160
7.5   Pointers to Functions   163
7.6   Dynamic Memory Management   169
7.6.1   Allocating Memory   169
7.6.2   Deallocating Memory   175
7.7   Pass by Reference and Reference Variables   177
7.7.1   Reference Arguments   177
7.7.2   Reference Return Values   179
7.7.3   Reference Variables   181
7.8   Using Pointers, Arrays and Strings   182
7.8.1   Matrix Addition   182
7.8.2   An Alphabetic Sort   187
7.9   Summary   191
7.10   Exercises   193

8   Classes   195
8.1   Declaring Classes   195
8.2   Class Access Specifiers   197
8.3   Accessing Members   198
8.4   Assigning Objects   200
8.5   Functions and Classes   201
8.6   Data Hiding   204

8.7   Returning an Object   206
8.8   Reference Arguments   207
8.9   Pointers to Members   208
8.10   Pointer-to-member Operators   210
8.11   Scope and Data Protection   213
8.12   Static Members   214
       8.12.1 Static Data Members   214
       8.12.2 Static Member Functions   216
8.13   Constructor Functions   217
8.14   Constant Class Objects and Member Functions   222
8.15   Friend Functions   223
8.16   Program Structure and Style   225
       8.16.1 Modules   225
       8.16.2 Header Files   228
8.17   Using Classes   230
       8.17.1 An Array Class   230
       8.17.2 A Weather Class   235
8.18   Summary   241
8.19   Exercises   244

9 Operator Overloading   245
9.1   Introducing Overloaded Operators   245
       9.1.1   Overloading the Assignment Operator   246
       9.1.2   The this Pointer   247
       9.1.3   Overloading the Addition Operator   249
       9.1.4   Overloading the Unary Minus Operator   251
9.2   User-defined Conversions   252
       9.2.1   Conversion by Constructors   252
       9.2.2   Conversion Functions   253
       9.2.3   Implicit Conversions   257
9.3   Operator Function Calls   259
       9.3.1   Binary Operators   260
       9.3.2   Prefix Unary Operators   262
       9.3.3   Postfix Unary Operators   263
9.4   Some Special Binary Operators   264
       9.4.1   Overloading the Subscript Operator   264
       9.4.2   Overloading the Function Call Operator   266
9.5   Defining Overloaded Operators   267
9.6   Using Overloaded Operators   269
       9.6.1   Complex Arithmetic   269
       9.6.2   Strings   274
9.7   Summary   280
9.8   Exercises   282

10 Constructors and Destructors   **283**
   10.1 More on Constructor Functions 284
      10.1.1 Dynamic Memory Management 284
      10.1.2 Assignment and Initialization 285
      10.1.3 Member Objects with Constructors 287
   10.2 Destructor Functions 289
   10.3 Creating and Destroying Objects 290
   10.4 Using Constructors and Destructors 295
      10.4.1 Singly Linked Lists 295
      10.4.2 Doubly Linked Lists 302
   10.5 Summary 307
   10.6 Exercises 307

11 Single Inheritance   **309**
   11.1 Derived Classes 309
   11.2 virtual Functions 314
   11.3 Abstract Classes and Pure virtual Functions 318
   11.4 Class Hierarchies 322
   11.5 Constructors and Destructors 327
   11.6 Member Access and Inheritance 329
      11.6.1 Access Specifiers 329
   11.7 Access Declarations 331
      11.7.1 Friendship and Derivation 333
   11.8 Using Single Inheritance 335
      11.8.1 A Bounds Checked Array Class 335
      11.8.2 A Menu Class 340
   11.9 Summary 347
   11.10 Exercises 351

12 Input and Output   **353**
   12.1 Introduction 353
   12.2 Generic Input and Output Classes 354
      12.2.1 Output 355
      12.2.2 Input 358
      12.2.3 User-defined Types 361
   12.3 File Input and Output 362
   12.4 Formatting 365
   12.5 Stream Condition 368
   12.6 In Memory Input and Output 370
   12.7 Using the I/O Library 372
   12.8 Summary 376
   12.9 Exercises 378

13 Bitwise Operations   **381**

13.1 Bitwise Operators 381

    13.1.1 Bitwise Complement 382

    13.1.2 Bitwise AND 382

    13.1.3 Bitwise Exclusive OR 382

    13.1.4 Bitwise Inclusive OR 383

    13.1.5 Shift Operators 383

    13.1.6 Bitwise Assignment Operators 384

13.2 Bit-fields 385

13.3 Unions 386

13.4 Using Bitwise Operators 388

    13.4.1 A Bit Array Class 388

    13.4.2 The Sieve of Eratosthenes 394

    13.4.3 Bit Representation of Integral Types 397

    13.4.4 Bit Representation of Floating Point Types . . 399

13.5 Summary 403

13.6 Exercises 403

14 Multiple Inheritance   **405**

14.1 Derived Classes 405

14.2 Virtual Base Classes 408

14.3 Constructors and Destructors 411

14.4 Member Access Ambiguities 412

14.5 Using Multiple Inheritance 414

14.6 Summary 424

14.7 Exercises 425

15 C++ Applications   **427**

15.1 Finite Difference Techniques 427

    15.1.1 Array Classes 429

    15.1.2 Grid Class 432

    15.1.3 Testing the Laplace Equation Solver 435

    15.1.4 Exercises 440

15.2 A Simulation 440

    15.2.1 Outline of Project 440

    15.2.2 Graphics 441

    15.2.3 Class Declarations 444

    15.2.4 Utilities 450

    15.2.5 Class Implementations 452

    15.2.6 Exercises 468

15.3 Projects 469

Appendix–A Templates   **471**

Appendix–B The ASCII Character Codes   **475**

Appendix–C Operator Precedence and Associativity   **477**

Appendix–D Differences between C and C++   **481**

Bibliography   **485**

Index   **489**

List of Figures

5.1 The structure of a typical function. 82
5.2 Root finding using bisection. 106

6.1 Labelled storage locations. 118
6.2 Relationship between memory and the address-of and dereferencing operators. 121
6.3 A pointer to a pointer. 123
6.4 Storage map for x[2][3]. 135
6.5 An array of pointers. 140
6.6 A ragged array. 145

8.1 Default assignment. 200

10.1 Singly linked list. 296
10.2 A stack. 298
10.3 Doubly linked list. 304

11.1 Classes derived from **shape**. 310
11.2 Assigning data for a **disc** object to a **shape** object. 311
11.3 Classes derived from **solid**. 318
11.4 A simple class hierarchy. 324
11.5 A complicated class hierarchy. 327
11.6 Classes for menus. 341
11.7 A typical menu system. 348

13.1 An example of bit-fields. 385
13.2 An example of a **union**. 386
13.3 Accessing an element of a **bit_array** object. 392
13.4 Using BIT_MASK to set a bit. 392
13.5 Using BIT_MASK to clear a bit. 392
13.6 The Sieve of Eratosthenes. 395
13.7 The bit structure for a **float**. 400
13.8 The bit structure for a **double**. 403

14.1 Multiple inheritance. 405

xiii

14.2 Derivation of a `space_time` class. 407

14.3 A repeated indirect base class. 408

14.4 A virtual base class. 409

14.5 An indirect base class which is both `virtual` and `non-virtual`. . 410

14.6 Controller classes. 415

15.1 Two-dimensional grid. 427

15.2 Red-black labelling of grid points. 428

15.3 Weather station display. 441

15.4 Graphics classes. 443

15.5 Classes used in the simulation. 444

List of Tables

2.1   Permissible Characters.   10

3.1   Some Common Operators.   28

4.1   A More Complete List of Operators.   46

9.1   Operator Function Calls.   282

10.1 Calling Constructors and Destructors.   294
10.2 Constructors and Destructors Invoked by a Function Call.   295

13.1 Bitwise Operators.   381
13.2 Bit Patterns Given by `print_bits(unsigned)`.   398
13.3 Bit Patterns Given by `print_bits(unsigned long)`.   399
13.4 Bit Patterns Given by `print_bits(float)`.   402

B.1 The ASCII Character Codes.   476

C.1 Operator Precedence and Associativity.   479

Preface

Computers are being used to solve problems of ever increasing complexity in science and engineering. Although some problems can be solved by means of 'off the self' packages, many applications would benefit greatly from using a sophisticated modern programming language. Without such a language, it is difficult to develop and maintain complex software and the difficulties are considerably worse for multi-processor systems. Of the many possible languages, C is being increasingly used in scientific applications, but it has some dangers and disadvantages owing to its system programming origins. These drawbacks have largely been overcome by the introduction of C++, an object-oriented version of C, which was developed at AT & T Bell Laboratories by Bjarne Stroustrup.

C++ has proved to be an enormously popular language, but most of the available books assume a prior knowledge of C. Unfortunately, most books on C (in common with those on C++) are not specifically intended for scientists or engineers and, for instance, often use manipulation of character strings as the basis for examples. To the scientist struggling to solve a non-linear differential equation, rather than writing a text editor, such examples may not be very illuminating. C programmers also seem to revel in writing very terse code, which can be difficult for the non-expert to penetrate.

This book is specifically intended for scientists, engineers and mathematicians who want to learn C++ *from scratch* by means of examples and detailed applications, rather than a formal language definition. The examples used are deliberately numerical in character and many other topics of possible interest (such as databases, computer algebra and graph algorithms) are left untouched. For someone with little or no programming experience there is much to be gained by learning C++ rather than C. Instead of becoming a good C programmer and then converting to an object-oriented language, the reader can progressively use those aspects of C++ that are both relevant and accessible. For instance inline functions instead of macros, together with function name overloading and data hiding by means of classes, are all useful programming techniques that can be introduced at an early stage. Another advantage is that in many ways C++ is a safer language than C and encourages better programming practices.

No prior knowledge of any programming language is assumed and the approach is to learn by means of relevant examples. The mathematical techniques

involved in these examples have been kept deliberately simple and are fundamental to any serious numerical application of computers. For any reader not
familiar with a particular technique, the explanations given in the text should be
sufficient and additional background material can be found in the bibliography.
This bibliography is annotated to provide the reader with a guide to parallel
reading whilst studying this book and to suggest pathways through the literature
for more advanced study. In particular, we do not dwell on those aspects of C++
that only provide backward compatibility with C. Such features of the language
may well be important to readers wishing to integrate existing C code into a
C++ program and help can be obtained from the bibliography. Since our approach is to learn by example, rather than by formal definition, the bibliography
(in particular [2]) should also be consulted if a precise definition of the language
is required.

Structure of this Book

It is very unlikely that any application will need every C++ feature described
in this book. However, with the exception of Chapter 12, the order in which
material is presented means that you can progress as far as necessary in order
to meet your particular needs, without working through the entire book. Even
if a fairly complete understanding of C++ is required, it is worth studying the
language in deliberate stages, interspersed with projects from your own field of
interest. The following stages are suggested:

1. Chapters 1 to 5 introduce the basics of C++, including control structures
   and functions. These features are common to most languages that have
   found numerical application and are essential for writing any significant
   program. Most applications would also need an understanding of Chapter 6,
   which introduces arrays. This stage is roughly equivalent to what you
   would have in a language such as FORTRAN 77. Most C++ programs
   make considerable use of pointers and, although this topic is introduced in
   Chapter 6, it is developed further in the following chapter. Here you will
   also find a description of strings and dynamic memory management.

2. Classes, objects, data hiding and member functions are introduced in Chapter 8. Although by themselves such techniques are not sufficient to constitute object-oriented programming, they should enable you to write safer
   code for fairly large applications. After working through this chapter you
   should also be able to use C++ class libraries, such as matrix algebra, complex arithmetic, strings etc., which are available on some systems. However,
   you will not be able to use inheritance to extend existing classes to meet
   any special needs of your own specific applications.

3. Chapters 9, 10 and 11 are devoted to operator overloading, constructors, destructors and inheritance. At this stage you can truly claim to be doing object-oriented programming with the ability to construct your own classes and to extend existing classes.

4. Chapter 12 describes input and output. In particular, file I/O is not introduced until this stage although you may have applications which lead you to consult this chapter before working through the preceding chapters. The reason for leaving details of the I/O library until Chapter 12 is that it involves classes, operator overloading, constructors, destructors and inheritance. However, if you do need facilities such as file I/O at an early stage, then you should be able to extract the necessary information without working through chapters 8 to 11.

5. Bitwise operations are described in Chapter 13. Such operations may not be central to your interests and you could decide to omit this chapter. However, an understanding of how numbers are stored in memory is very useful and you would miss the neat application to the Sieve of Eratosthenes.

6. Multiple inheritance is introduced in Chapter 14. Although many experts would claim that multiple inheritance is an essential part of object-oriented programming, you will probably be developing quite large applications before using such techniques. This chapter only gives a brief introduction and the bibliography should be consulted for further details.

The final chapter introduces no new features of the language, but rather uses C++ in several projects and also suggests some extended exercises. The appendices are mainly included for reference; the one exception being Appendix A. This appendix describes templates, which will certainly be important in numerical applications, but are currently only available on some systems.

If used as an undergraduate text, it is likely that the material contained in all fifteen chapters would be too much for a single course of lectures. Rather it is envisaged that chapters 1 to 8 would be used in a first course, with the following chapters being suitable for a subsequent course.

This book introduces some advanced features of C++ which could be omitted if a complete knowledge of the language is not required. The following techniques are used to identify such features:

1. Items which fit naturally into a particular chapter, but could reasonably be postponed until later, are marked by a single dagger (†). You would probably have to return to such sections in order to understand later chapters and you may have to postpone attempting some of the exercises. A typical example is Section 5.5 on `auto` and `static` local variables; you will probably need to use `static` variables sometime, but skipping this section on a first reading will not do any harm.

2. There are two kinds of section which are sufficiently self-contained that they can be omitted altogether without any loss of continuity and these are marked by double daggers (††). Some sections are only intended for reference. Other sections will only be of importance to particular applications; for example, bitwise operations could be crucial for a number theory application but of no relevance to solving a differential equation (Chapter 13).

Lack of space prevents the inclusion of a chapter on object-oriented design in the context of numerical applications. However, this is a topic which deserves an entire book to itself and some recompense may be obtained by consulting the bibliography ([1], [3] and [8]).

Acknowledgements

I would like to thank Helen Arthan for conscientiously working through the various drafts of this book and Mark Burton for removing many technical errors. Peter Dew and Ian Robson both provided inspiration for some of the applications. Above all I wish to thank my wife, Janet, for her constant support, without which this book would not have been completed.

Chapter 1

Introduction

1.1 Getting Started

Probably the most frustrating stage in learning any language is getting started. Our first steps should be modest and we start by simply sending a one line message to the output device. Very few assumptions are made in this book, but it is assumed that you have access to a C++ compiler[1] and that you know how to use an editor.[2] Suppose the following lines of code are entered into a file by means of an editor:

```
// A simple C++ program:

#include <iostream.hpp>

int main()
{
    cout << "This is our first C++ program.\n";
    return(0);
}
```

This complete C++ program must go through a two stage process before it can be run. First of all the code needs to be compiled in order to generate instructions that can be understood by our computer and then this collection of instructions must be linked with libraries.[3] The exact way in which the compilation and linking is carried out will depend on the details of the particular system.

---

[1] On some systems you may have to use a *translator* to first convert the C++ into C and then compile the C version. This situation is increasingly rare.

[2] Most word processors put undesirable characters in their output files. However, those that can be persuaded to output plain ASCII files could also be used to edit C++ code.

[3] A library consists of compiled code that performs tasks which are not intrinsic to the language. Typical examples are input, output and the mathematical functions (square root, logarithm etc.).

Typically, if this first program is in the file **example.cpp**, then both stages may be accomplished by entering:

```
c++ example.cpp
```

However, it may be conventional on your system to use a different extension for source code (such as **.cc**, **.cxx** or **.c++**) and the compile and link command may be different (perhaps **CC**). You may also have to change the **.hpp** extension on **<iostream.hpp>**; other possibilities are **.hxx**, **.H** and **.h**.

To run this program you should typically enter the command:

```
example
```

but the file in which the executable code is placed does not have a system independent name; it may be **example.exe** or even something unrelated to the original file name, such as **a.out**.

If you have overcome all of the system dependent hurdles, the following output should appear:

```
This is our first C++ program.
```

The lines of code that produce this output require a few words of explanation. The first line is a comment since any code following // on a line is ignored. A larger program would normally be introduced by a more significant comment. The third non-blank line is the start of a function definition. Every complete C++ program must contain a function called **main** and in our example, **main** is the only function. The function name is preceded by the type specifier, **int**, since **main** should return an integer. Parentheses, **()**, follow the name and are used to indicate that **main** is a function. In some circumstances these parentheses may contain variables, known as arguments.

The function, **main()**, contains two **statements**; the end of each statement being denoted by a semi-colon, sometimes known as a *statement terminator*. The first statement outputs a message and the second statement effectively returns control to the operating system. The standard output stream (usually the screen) is known as **cout** and the **<<** operator is used to send a string of characters to this stream, the group of characters between the double quotes, **" "**, being known as a string. In our example, the string ends with **\n**, which is used to denote a new line. This technique of sending character strings to the output stream is not actually defined by the C++ language, but is part of a library and is one of many standard functions that are available with any C++ compiler.

Since our program is compiled before it is linked to code for the output stream, we need to supply information about the interface to **cout**. This information is contained in the file, **iostream.hpp**, which is made available to the compiler by the instruction:

```
#include <iostream.hpp>
```

Files such as `iostream.hpp>` are usually known as *header files* and are described in more detail in Section 4.13.1. The `< >` notation is not part of the file system name, but rather an indication that the file exists in a special place known to the compiler.

1.2 Solving a Quadratic Equation

No doubt our interests are more numerical than simply outputting lines of text, so let's consider solving a quadratic equation:

$$ax^2 + bx + c = 0$$

The solutions are, of course, given by:

$$x = \frac{-b \pm \sqrt{b^2 - 4ac}}{2a}$$

which can be implemented by the following (not very robust) program:

```cpp
// Solves the quadratic equation:
//      a * x * x + b * x + c = 0

#include <iostream.hpp>
#include <math.h>

int main()
{
    double root1, root2, a, b, c, root;

    cout << "Enter the coefficients a, b, c: ";
    cin >> a >> b >> c;
    root = sqrt(b * b - 4.0 * a * c);
    root1 = 0.5 * (root - b) / a;
    root2 = - 0.5 * (root + b) / a;
    cout << "The solutions are " << root1 << " and " <<
        root2 << "\n";

    return(0);
}
```

This program introduces floating point variables, which can store numbers that include a decimal point, such as 0.5. Notice that we use 0.5, rather than divide by 2.0, since multiplication is usually faster then division. The variables `root1`, `root2`, `a`, `b` and `c` are defined to be floating point numbers by virtue of the type specifier, `double`.

The program first uses the `cout` stream to send text to the output device, instructing the user to input three coefficients. Values for `a`, `b`, and `c` are read from the input stream, `cin`, which is usually the keyboard. The code then makes use of the assignment, `=`, multiplication, `*`, addition, `+`, and subtraction, `-`, operators in self-evident ways.

In general, solving a quadratic equation involves finding the square root of a number. This is achieved by invoking the `sqrt()` function,[4] which is defined for us in a system-supplied mathematics library. Since our program is first compiled and then linked with compiled code for the libraries, we must also include the header file,`<math.h>` file, which contains a *prototype* for the `sqrt()` function, specifying the argument and return types (in this case `double`). Notice that we really do mean `<math.h>`, rather than `<math.hpp>`, since the `sqrt()` function is part of the C, rather than C++, libraries.[5]

On some systems it may be necessary to specify that this example requires the mathematics library for linking. A typical form of the compile and link command in such cases is:

```
c++ example.cpp -lm
```

but you may need to consult the compiler reference manual for your particular system.

1.3   An Object-oriented Example

The techniques illustrated by our examples so far have not differed much from other languages, such as FORTRAN, BASIC or Pascal. Now consider the following program, which multiplies two matrices and lists the result:

```
// Program to test matrix multiplication:

#include "matrix.hpp"

int main()
{
    int i, j;
    matrix A(6, 4), B(4, 6), C(6, 6);
```

---

[4]Within the text we write a function with an empty pair of parentheses following the name. This is to emphasize that we really do mean a function, but does not necessarily imply that the function takes no arguments. Within a segment of code, any necessary arguments are, of course, included.

[5]C++ is an extension of C, a language which was invented by Kernighan and Ritchie [6] and then adopted by ANSI (the American National Standards Institute). C++ is currently being considered by an ANSI committee. Files that would normally be included (that is copied) into C programs invariably have a `.h` extension.

```
    for (i = 1; i <= 6; ++i)
        for (j = 1; j <= 4; ++j)
            A(i, j) = i * j;

    for (i = 1; i <= 4; ++i)
        for (j = 1; j <= 6; ++j)
            B(i, j) = i * j;

    C = A * B;

    cout << C;

    return(0);
}
```

This program uses some features of C++ to perform operations on matrices. The statement:

```
    matrix A(6, 4), B(4, 6), C(6, 6);
```

defines matrices, A, B, C, which are of order 6×4, 4×6 and 6×6 respectively. The important point to notice about the next seven lines of code is that A(i, j) and B(i, j) are used to access the ij elements of the matrices A and B.

So far the program only assigns integers to the elements of two non-square matrices. However, the statement which multiplies these two matrices is wonderfully simple:

```
    C = A * B;
```

Notice how the code closely parallels the mathematics and is not obscured by function calls. Moreover, if we make a mistake and write:

```
    C = B * A;
```

which incorrectly attempts to assign a 4×4 matrix to a 6×6 matrix, then an error message results.

Finally, the statement:

```
    cout << C;
```

is all that is required to list the matrix, C:

30	60	90	120	150	180
60	120	180	240	300	360
90	180	270	360	450	540
120	240	360	480	600	720
150	300	450	600	750	900
180	360	540	720	900	1080

Matrices are not part of the C++ language, but are an example of a user-defined type, or class, which can be tailored to meet the exact needs of the application. For instance, some applications may be restricted to real matrix elements, whilst others may be complex. In some circumstances bounds-checking may be an intolerable overhead, whereas in others it may be essential. An application may even require that matrix elements are themselves matrices. We will learn how to construct such classes. We will also learn how to build on existing classes in order to create new classes, thus enabling us to reuse software *without* understanding its detailed design.

The three matrices, `A, B` and `C`, are instances of the `matrix` class and are known as *objects*. This example only skims the surface of object-oriented techniques, but the essential idea is that a matrix is considered as an entity on which we perform operations. A matrix object encapsulates details of how the data is stored, the value of each element, the numbers of rows and columns, etc. Moreover, the `matrix` class also shields the application programmer from details of how matrix operations, such as multiplication, are implemented.

1.4   Why Object-oriented?

Solving realistic problems can require programs of ten or even a hundred thousand lines. Such programs may be in use for many years and have been written by many different programmers. Three key requirements are that programs are *maintainable, reusable* and *efficient*.

A program must be maintainable because it may need modifying when hardware, software or requirements change, or when errors in the code are inevitably discovered. Developers of a program are frequently not involved in maintenance and, in any case, the changes may be made long after the program was written. Throughout this book you will therefore come across techniques which encourage maintainability: *readability, modularity, type-safe, self-documenting* ..., these techniques are in turn facilitated by object-oriented programming.

The code for a complicated application may involve many years of effort, so it makes sense to be able to reuse as much of this work as possible. Functions can aid reusability to a limited extent; instead of implementing a cosine every time it is required, we can use a function. But a function to perform other operations may be less straightforward. For instance, a function to invert a matrix needs information on how the matrix is stored, its size and type. It would be much easier to reuse a matrix inversion function if it simply operated on matrices as objects, which encapsulated details of storage, size etc. Also, rather than simply reusing the matrix class, we may want to modify it (perhaps to introduce bounds-checking) and ideally we should be able to make changes without tampering with the original code. Object-oriented techniques enable us to do all of these things.

Scientists and engineers are often working at the leading edge of what is computationally possible and are also well aware that inefficiency costs money. It might seem that efficiency is incompatible with the requirements of maintainable and reusable code. It is also true that object-oriented techniques usually introduce a slight run-time overhead when compared with traditional methods. However, the key to efficiency is identifying the *appropriate* objects. For example, if an application manipulates matrices, then it should be written in terms of matrix objects, rather than matrix elements. The details of matrix multiplication, addition, etc. are then hidden from the application programmer. Moreover, since the details are hidden, the implementation can be made as efficient as possible. Such increases in efficiency far outweigh any run-time overhead due to using object-oriented techniques.

1.5   Summary

- Every program must have one (and only one) function called **main()**.

- Compiling and linking a program is system dependent. Possibilities include:

```
c++ example.cpp
CC example.c
cc example.cxx
```

- **cout << x** sends the value of **x** to the output stream.

- **cin >> i** reads the value of i from the input stream.

- The object-oriented features of C++ enables us to write reusable code in a way which is natural for the particular application.

1.6   Exercises

1. Our program to solve a quadratic equation is not very robust. Try to make
   the program fail in as many different ways as possible. What would you
   like to do to improve the program? (We haven't learnt enough to actually
   carry out the necessary improvements yet.)

2. Using the quadratic equation program as a template, write a short program
   which reads a, b and c and lists the results for a+b, b*c and a/c. Again,
   you should be able to get your program to fail.

Chapter 2

The Lexical Basis of C++

The most basic study of any language is lexical; without knowing the rules for constructing words, we cannot begin to write books, or even to construct a single sentence. Communication is impossible. Likewise, before we can write a meaningful C++ program, we must learn the rules for constructing 'words', or more correctly *tokens*.

2.1 Characters and Tokens

A C++ program consists of one or more files, which contain a series of characters. The details of how characters are represented internally are dependent on the C++ compiler, but one byte per character is normal and one of the most popular representations, the ACSII character set, is given in Appendix B.[1] The allowed characters are shown in Table 2.1. A compiler resolves (or parses) the C++ program into a series of tokens. There are five types of token: identifiers, keywords, constants, operators and other separators.

2.2 Comments and White Space

Comments are an essential feature of good programming practice. In C++ there are two ways of denoting comments. Two forward slashes, //, indicate the start of a comment which continues until the end of a line:

```
// This is a comment.
x = 1;  // The first part of this line is not a comment.
```

---

[1] A byte is the smallest addressable element of memory and is usually eight bits. Indeed, throughout this book a byte is assumed to be synonymous with eight bits. A bit is the smallest element of memory and can only take the values 0 and 1. Bits and bytes are considered in more detail in Chapter 13.

upper case letters:	A B C D ... X Y Z
lower case letters:	a b c d ... x y z
digits:	0 1 2 3 4 5 6 7 8 9
special characters:	! " % ^ & * ( ) _ - + = |
	\ < , > . ? / ~ # : ; '
non printing characters:	blank, carriage return,
	new line etc.

Table 2.1: Permissible Characters.

An alternative technique is to use **/*** to indicate the start of a comment which continues until ***/** is encountered. Such comments can continue over many lines:

```
/* This is a comment */
/* This
is
a
longer
comment */
```

The **/*   */** technique may also include one or more **//** style of comments:

```
/* This is a comment. // This is a second comment
   and this is a continuation. */
```

However, the **/*   */** style of comments cannot themselves be nested:

```
/* /* This comment should not get past the compiler.
      If it does then the compiler does not conform with the
      proposed ANSI C++ standard.
      Such extensions are best avoided. */ */
```

This restriction is a minor nuisance, since commenting out sections of code by means of **/* */** is very convenient, but cannot be used if the code already contains **/* */** style comments. However, a viable alternative is demonstrated in Section 4.13.3.

Notice that blanks are not allowed within the tokens defining either style of comment:

```
/ *   This is not a valid comment. * /
/ /   Neither is this.
```

and that an incomplete **/* */** style of comment can lead to errors:

```
/* Get the coefficients of the equation:
   cout << "Enter the coefficients a, b, c: ";
   cin >> a >> b >> c;
/* Now find the roots: */
   root = sqrt(b * b - 4.0 * a * c);
```

In this example, everything between the first **/*** and ***/** is taken as a comment and, as a result, **a**, **b** and **c** have arbitrary values.

Comments, blanks, vertical and horizontal tabs, form feeds and new lines are collectively known as *white space*. White space is not allowed in any token, except in character or string constants. The compiler ignores any white space that occurs between tokens. Such white space is effectively a separator.

2.3 Identifiers

An identifier is a sequence of some combination of letters, digits and the underscore symbol, _. Both upper and lower case characters are valid and are distinct. On some systems such distinctions may not be implemented, but this is very rare. In any event, it is unwise to rely on the case being the only distinguishing feature between identifiers. In both C and C++ there is a tradition of using mainly lower case, except where some special significance is being highlighted, as with a global constant. This tradition makes for easily readable code.

There should be no limit on the number of characters in an identifier, although some compilers do impose a limit. One of the systems used to verify the code given in this book imposes a limit of 127 characters, but given a screen width of 80 characters, this is not a severe restriction!

An important restriction on identifiers is that they must start with a character or underscore rather than a digit. Some examples of valid identifiers are:

```
main
cout
position_1
initial_velocity
```

whereas invalid identifiers include:

```
velocity$         // $ is not a digit, letter, or _.
1velocity         // Identifiers cannot start with a number.
v e l o c i t y   // White space is not allowed.
initial-velocity  // Don't confuse - with _.
Oxygen_level      // Don't confuse 0 with o.
```

Identifiers can have a leading underscore:

```
_velocity
```

or embedded double underscores:

```
initial__velocity
```

Both of these combinations are best avoided, since leading and embedded double underscores are often generated internally by compilers or used in libraries. Likewise, it is worth avoiding trailing underscores:

```
velocity_
```

Apart from these minor restrictions, it is good programming practice to employ names which are meaningful in the context in which they are used, such as:

```
water_temperature
```

instead of:

```
T12
```

Meaningful names make the code self-documenting and avoid the need for excessive and distracting comments. While some programmers use an underscore to distinguish different parts of an identifier, others prefer to use an upper case letter:

```
waterTemperature
```

2.4 Keywords

Keywords are special identifiers which have a significance defined by the language rather than the programmer. A complete but, at this stage, rather impenetrable list is:

asm	auto	break	case
catch	char	class	const
continue	default	delete	do
double	else	enum	extern
float	for	friend	goto
if	inline	int	long
new	operator	private	protected
public	register	return	short
signed	sizeof	static	struct
switch	template	this	throw
try	typedef	union	unsigned
virtual	void	volatile	while

Further keywords which may be reserved for some compilers are:

ada	fortran	pascal	overload
huge	near	far	

and are best avoided as user-defined identifiers in order to ensure portability.[2]

Examples of the valid use of keywords are:

```
int i;       // The keyword int declares i
             // to be an integer variable.
char c;      // The keyword char declares c
             // to be a character variable.
```

However, the following are invalid:

```
int switch;  // Attempts to declare switch to be
             // an integer variable.
char class;  // Attempts to declare class to be
             // a character variable.
i n t i;     // White space is not allowed.
INT i;       // Keywords must be lower case.
```

2.5 Constants

Constants, which are also known as literals, can be integer, floating point, character or string. More details of these four types are given in the next chapter, but they are introduced here.

2.5.1 Integer Constants

Integer constants consist of a sequence of digits, such as

```
14768
```

but not:

```
14,768     // An embedded comma is not allowed.
14 768     // Embedded white space is not allowed.
-14768     // This is an integer expression.
```

Notice that a negative integer is actually an integer constant expression rather than an integer constant. Integer constants are usually given in decimal (base ten) notation, but octal and hexadecimal constants are also possible. Octal (base eight) constants start with 0 and cannot include the digits 8 or 9. An example of an octal constant is:

```
024
```

Hexadecimal (base sixteen) integer constants start with 0x (or 0X) and may include the letters a to f (or A to F, the case is not significant) as, for example:

```
0x7a1f
```

---

[2]For some compilers such keywords may have a leading underscore, as in _near.

2.5.2   Floating Point Constants

Floating point constants include a decimal point and/or an exponent, for example:

    2500.1   2.5001e3   25001E-1

where the value following e (or E) is the exponent. Negative floating point numbers, such as

    -2500.1   -2.5001e3   -25001e-1

are actually floating point constant expressions, rather than constants.

2.5.3   Character Constants

A character inside single quotes, such as:

    'a'   '1'   ' '

is a character constant and is usually represented internally by one byte. Note that '1' is not equal to the integer 1; for instance in the ASCII character set, '1' is actually represented by 49. (See Appendix B for more detail.) Notice also that a character constant has the form 'a', rather than `a`.

Certain hard to get at characters are represented by using an *escape sequence*, starting with a backslash; for instance '\n' signifies a new line. The complete list of all such sequences is given below:

new line	\n	backslash	\\
horizontal tab	\t	question mark	\?
vertical tab	\v	single quote	\'
backspace	\b	double quote	\"
carriage return	\r	octal number	\032
form feed	\f	hex. number	\x032
alert (bell)	\a		

The generalized escape sequence consists of up to three octal or as many hexadecimal digits as are required. For instance, '\61' and '\x31' both represent the character, '1'.

Exercise:[3]

To demonstrate that both '\61' and '\x31' represent the same character, try the following simple program:

---

[3]Occasionally we include simple, un-numbered exercises in the text. You should do these as you come across them. You are also expected to attempt the exercises at the end of each chapter!

```
#include <iostream.hpp>

int main()
{
    char a, b;
    a = '\61';
    b = '\x31';
    cout << a << ' ' << b << '\n';
    return(0);
}
```

and then modify it to sound your terminal bell by means of a suitable hexadecimal escape sequence.

2.5.4   String Constants

String constants are sequences of characters between double quotes, as in:

```
"Hello world"
```

Notice that the double quote is a single character, ", rather than, '', and that white space is significant in string constants; "Hello world" is not the same as "Helloworld". Internally a string is represented by an array of characters. "Hello world" is actually twelve characters since the escape sequence, '\0', is used after the last character to denote the end of a string. This means that 'C' is *not* the same as "C"; the first consists of one character whereas the second consists of two.

Adjacent string constants are concatenated, so that:

```
cout << "Hello" " World";
```

produces the output:

```
Hello World
```

2.6   Operators

An operator is a language defined token, consisting of one or more characters, which instructs the computer to perform some well defined action. An example is the assignment operator, =, used in the following:

```
i = 1;       // Assign 1 to the memory location
             // holding the value of i.
```

A complete list of operators is given below:

```
()          .          []          ->          ::          ->*         &           *
new         delete     !           ~           ++          --          -           sizeof
/           %          +           .*          <<          >>          <           <=
>           >=         ==          !=          ^           |           &&          ||
?:          =          +=          -=          *=          /=          %=          <<=
>>=         &=         ^=          |=          ,
```

Notice that three keywords are also operators and that multi-character operators form a single token. Once again it should be emphasized that white space is not allowed within a token, meaning, for instance, that `+ =` is not a valid operator, unlike `+=`. However, in contrast to some languages, two operators can follow in succession; for instance `x * -1` is equivalent to `x * (-1)`.

2.7   The Preprocessor

Before a C++ program is compiled it is normally passed through what is known as a preprocessor, which can be directed to make various substitutions, inclusions or omissions from the program. The `#` and `##` tokens are used by the preprocessor to control these operations. For instance:

```
#define PI 3.1415926535897932
```

instructs the preprocessor to substitute 3.1415926535897932 in place of `PI` in all subsequent lines of the file in which this `#define` directive appears. As might be expected, white space before the `#` is ignored. More details of the preprocessor are given in Section 4.13.

2.8   Programming Style

There is no enforced programming style in C++. White space is ignored (except within tokens), there is no restriction to typing statements in certain columns (as in Fortran), there is no required indentation (as in occam) and statements can flow across many lines. Consequently it is possibly to produce code which is very difficult to read, as in:

```
#include <iostream.hpp>
#include <math.h>
int main(){double x1,x2,a,b,c,root;cout<<"Enter the coeffic"
<<"ients a, b, c: ";cin>>a>>b>>c;root=sqrt(b*b-4.0*a*c);x1=
0.5*(root-b)/a;x2=-0.5*(root+b)/a;cout<<"The solutions are "
<<x1<<" and "<<x2<<"\n";return(0);}
```

However, it is up to the programmer to adopt a clear style which can easily be understood by others. There is no unique *good style*, but it is worth adopting something similar to that used in this book. In particular it is a good idea to keep to one statement per line (except in special circumstances) and to indent by one tab to denote blocks of code. Further hints on style will be given when more of the C++ language has been introduced.

There is one final point that should be made in this chapter. Very occasionally there may appear to be be an ambiguity as to how one or more lines of code are resolved by the compiler into tokens. For instance, given that both `--` and `-` are valid C++ operators, how should

```
x = y---z;   // x = (y--) - z; or x = y - (--z);
```

be read? The compiler resolves this ambiguity by adopting a *maximal munch* strategy;[4] the parsing stage of the compilation process bites off the largest sequence of characters that form a valid token. So the example above really does mean:

```
x = (y--) - z;
```

Such ambiguities can and in fact should be resolved by the use of white space.

2.9 Summary

- A C++ source file consists of a sequence of tokens which are made up of one or more characters.

- White space (including blanks, new lines, tabs etc.) is not allowed inside tokens.

- There are five types of token: identifiers, keywords, constants, operators and other separators.

- Use meaningful names for user-defined identifiers, such as `flow_rate`.

- Identifiers with language-defined significance are known as keywords, examples of which are `int`, `class`, `if`, etc. The significance of keywords cannot be altered.

- Constants can be integer, floating point, character, or string. Examples are: `10`, `2.01`, `'a'`, `"Hello"`.

- Operators are tokens representing operations, such as assignment, `=`, addition, `+`, multiplication, `*`, etc.

---

[4]See [4].

2.10   Exercises

1. How many different types of token are there? Classify the following tokens:

```
new    ->         -        >
()     ;          i        friend
int    pressure   14       *
1.4    '\n'       public   []
```

2. What is wrong with the following statements:

   (a)   `speed$of$light = 186000;`

   (b)   `initial velocity = 0.0;`

   (c)   `#zero = 10;`

   (d)   `180_degrees = 3.1415926535897932;`

   (e)   `-x = 360.0;`

   (f)   `void = 0;`

   (g)   `pressure := 760.0;              // in pascals.`

   (h)   `/* Perhaps this fix will work:`
   `            volume = 100.0;          /* in litres. */`
   `   */`

   (i)   `case = 2;`

3. Which of the following are valid constants:

   (a)   `27`

   (b)   `11,111`

   (c)   `'Hello world'`

   (d)   `'a'`

   (e)   `-3.1415926535897932`

   (f)   `'\t'`

   (g)   `25L4`

   (h)   `'\o32'`

Chapter 3

Fundamental Types and Basic Operators

C++ is a typed language; that is the variables and constants that occur in a C++ program each have a type which controls how they may be used and what storage is required. For example, variables of the `int` type, which are used to represent integers, may require two bytes of memory, whereas variables of the `float` type, which are used to represent floating point numbers, may need four bytes. Furthermore, the `float` and `int` types are represented in memory in entirely different ways. The language-defined types, which are used to represent integers, characters and floating point numbers, are known as *fundamental* types and are the concern of this chapter. It is also possible to define what are known as *derived* types in order to manipulate objects such as matrices, complex numbers or 3-dimensional solids. Techniques for creating derived types are described in later chapters.

The motivation for using a typed language is that the compiler can catch many programming errors by performing type-checking. For example, if an object is declared to be constant (by using the `const` keyword which is explained later in this chapter) then an attempt to assign a value to the object is a compile-time error since it has the wrong type for such operations.

In this chapter we examine all of the fundamental types defined by the C++ language, together with some of the basic operators. This will enable us to carry out the usual arithmetic operations and to manipulate characters. Compared with some languages, the fundamental types are rather limited; for instance, unlike Fortran, complex numbers are not defined. Although this may seem a bit restrictive for many applications, derived types can effectively extend the language indefinitely.

19

3.1   Integral Data Types

The integral data types consist of two groups: the integer and character types. The integer group contains the `short`, `int` and `long` types, all of which can be either `signed` or `unsigned`.[1] The integer types are used to store and perform arithmetic operations on 'whole' numbers (0, 1, -50 etc.). The character types are `char`, `signed char` and `unsigned char`. Since characters are actually represented internally by small integers, the character types can also be used for storing and operating on such integers.

3.1.1   Type `int`

The `int` data type is the most important of the integral types and can hold both positive and negative integers. For `int`s represented by two bytes (the minimum allowed by the ANSI C standard) the maximum number that can be represented is 32767 and the minimum is -32768. For some compilers these numbers may be 32768 and -32767 respectively. (Sixteen bits can hold $2^{16} = 65536$ different numbers, including 0.) The exact limits for all integral data types are given in a header file, called `<limits.h>`. It is worth examining this file at some stage to see the limits for your particular system.

If we wish to use the variables `i, j, k`, then they can be defined by:

```
int i;
int j;
int k;
```

It is also possible to define a list of variables:

```
int i, j, k;
```

We say 'define' rather than 'declare'; in C++ the distinction is both subtle and important. Defining an object, as above, not only specifies the type, but also reserves the appropriate amount of memory. As will be seen later, it is possible to make a declaration, such as

```
extern int i;
```

without reserving any memory (which must of course be done somewhere). In a complete program there must be one (and only one) definition of an object, even though there can be many declarations. It is worth emphasizing that, although an object may be defined in the sense of memory being allocated, its 'value' can still be arbitrary. An object must be defined or declared before it can be used in

---

[1]The integer types are `signed` by default. It is therefore very rare and completely redundant to have `signed int`, `signed long` or `signed short`.

a program, otherwise a compile-time error results. This is more restrictive than some other languages, but helps to eliminate errors such as mis-typed identifiers.

The operator, =, is used for integer assignment, so the following defines i, j, k and sets them to 1, 2, 3 respectively:

```
int i, j, k;
i = 1;      // Notice that every statement
j = 2;      // ends with a semi-colon.
k = 3;
```

Addition and subtraction of integers is carried out using the usual + and - operators, as in:

```
int i, j, k;
i = 1;
j = 2;
k = 3;
i = i + j;
k = k - i;
```

Notice that '=' is the assignment rather than equality operator, so the statement:

```
i = i + j;
```

means add the current values of i and j (1 and 2) and assign the result (3) to i. The fact that '=' is the assignment operator means that expressions such as:

```
i + 1 = 7;  // WRONG
```

which look mathematically respectable, are not correct C++ statements. Conversely, some expressions which are valid in C++, would make no sense as mathematical equations. For example, in the above code fragment,

```
i = i + j;
```

does not imply that j is zero; in fact j is 3. It is also worth pointing out that := is *not* a valid assignment operator, nor even an operator:

```
i := 10;    // WRONG:    := is not an operator.
```

Our short sequence of assignment statements does not form a complete C++ program but, following the examples in Chapter 1, we can easily rectify this situation with the following code:

```
#include <iostream.hpp>   // for cout
int main()
{
```

```
    int i, j, k;
    i = 1;
    j = 2;
    k = 3;
    i = i + j;
    k = k - i;
    cout << "i = " << i << "   k = " << k << "\n";
    return(0);
}
```

Notice that `main()` is a function which returns the `int` type and in this example we return the value 0. (More discussion of this `return` value is given later, but in some circumstances it may be important for the operating system to know whether or not the program has run successfully, as indicated by 0.) We also include a statement so that the program can actually display the result of the calculations by using the insertion operator to send the values of `i` and `k` to the output stream:

```
    i = 3   k = 0
```

Throughout this book short fragments of code, which are not complete programs, are frequently given. You should now be able to convert these code fragments into programs, by introducing `main()`, the appropriate `#include` directives and sending results to the output stream. Indeed, you are strongly encouraged to try out as many such programs as possible.

Exercise:

Enter the above program into a file on your system, making sure the file has the appropriate extension, such as `.cpp`. Then compile, link and run the program. Check that you get the expected result. Try modifying the program to add different combinations of integers.

Since the `int` type occupies a fixed and finite amount of memory, only a limited range of integers can be stored. Consequently it is possible to perform operations which mathematically would give results above the maximum value that can be represented or below the minimum value. Such invalid operations are known respectively as *integer overflow* and *integer underflow*:

```
    #include <limits.h>
    int i;
    i = INT_MAX + 10;   // Integer overflow.
    i = INT_MIN - 10;   // Integer underflow.
```

`INT_MAX` and `INT_MIN` are the maximum and minimum values that can be stored by the type `int` and are defined in the header file, `<limits.h>`. These values depend on the particular compiler, as does the result of underflow or overflow.

Exercise:

What values are given to i for these two statements on your system.

3.1.2 Integer Multiplication

As might be expected, the token, *, is used to denote integer multiplication. The usual rules of arithmetic are followed, as in:

```
int i, j, k, m, n;
i = 2;
j = -3;
k = -4;
m = i * j;        // Assigns -6 to m.
n = j * k;        // Assigns 12 to n.
i = 3 * 6;        // Assigns 18 to i.
```

Exercise:

Write a short program (similar to the previous exercise) to include the above code and check the results on your system.

3.1.3 Integer Division

The forward slash is used to denote the integer division operator, as in:

```
int k;
k = 3 / 2;
```

which means divide 3 by 2 and put the result in **k**. Since **k** is an integer and 2 does not exactly divide 3, there is a potential ambiguity as to whether **k** is set to 1 or 2. In fact, in common with most languages, the result in C++ is 1; integer division with both numbers positive always truncates. The same is true when both numbers are negative, so that -3/-2 yields 1 rather than 2. If only one number is negative, the result depends on the compiler; -3/2 could give either -1 or -2. To rely on a feature provided by a particular compiler is not good programming practice and should be avoided if possible (or if this is not possible all assumptions should clearly documented).

In mathematics, dividing any non-zero number by zero gives infinity and dividing zero by zero is undefined; in C++, any integer division by zero is undefined.

3.1.4   Integer Modulus or Remainder Operator

The **%** token is the modulus or remainder operator. If i and j are both positive
integers, then i **%** j (read as 'i modulo j') gives the remainder obtained on dividing i by j. For instance, 5 **%** 3 yields the value 2. If both i and j are negative
then the result is negative; that is -5 **%** -3 yields -2. If only one of i and j are
negative then the result is again dependent on the C++ compiler, but should be
consistent with the dependency for division. That is:

```
(i / j) * j + i % j
```

should give the value of i. Again, if j is zero the result of i **%** j is not defined
and may not be consistent with the (undefined) result of i **/** j. Notice that 0 **%**
j gives 0 for any (non-zero) integer, j.

Exercise:

Try out the following program for various values of i and j (positive,
negative and zero) and explain the output. What happens if you enter
a nonsense value, such as 'accidentally' hitting the **w** key instead of
2? Why?

```cpp
#include <iostream.hpp>
int main()
{
    int i, j, m, n, a, b;
    cout <<"enter an integer: ";
    cin >> i;
    cout <<"enter an integer: ";
    cin >> j;
    m = i / j;
    n = i % j;
    a = m * j;  // (i / j ) * j
    b = a + n;  // (i / j) * j + i
    cout << "i = " << i << "    j = " << j << "\n\n" <<
        "i / j = " << m << "      i % j = " << n <<
        "\n\nThe following result should be " << i <<
        ":\n" << "(i / j) * j + i % j = " << b << "\n";
    return(0);
}
```

In this example we use the C++ input stream, cin, so that the values of i and
j can be entered from the keyboard. The expression:

```
cin >> i;
```

extracts the value of i from the input stream. The operator, >>, is known as an *extraction* operator. It is possible to concatenate such operators so that the first few lines can be replaced by:

```
cout << "enter two integers: ";
cin >> i >> j;
```

but notice that the following is *not* equivalent, although the statement does compile:

```
cin >> i, j;          // WRONG!
```

since no value is assigned to j.

3.1.5 Increment and Decrement Operators

The value of a variable can be changed without using the assignment operator. Instead of:

```
i = i + 1;
```

we can use:

```
++i;          // Prefix increment operator.
```

or:

```
i++;          // Postfix increment operator.
```

In all three cases, i is increased by one. The prefix operator increments i by one before the value of i is used, whereas the postfix operator increments after the value of i has been used. In the above example either version of the increment operator has the same effect, but not for:

```
int i, j, k, m, n;
i = 2;
j = 2;
k = 3;
m = i++ / k;    // Assigns 0 to m.
n = ++j / k;    // Assigns 1 to n.
```

In this example, the expression for m is evaluated before i is incremented, whereas n is evaluated after j is incremented.

> **Exercise:**
>
> Write a short program, including the above code fragment, which reads i, j, k from the keyboard and outputs the values of m, n, i, j. Try inputting a few different values.

As might be expected, there are also prefix and postfix decrement operators:

```
--i;
```

and

```
i--;
```

are equivalent to

```
i = i - 1;
```

The prefix decrement operator decreases the value of i by one before it is used in an expression, whereas the postfix decrement operator decreases i after the value has been used.

Exercise:

Replace the increment by decrement operators in your program for the previous exercise.

The use of increment and decrement operators can lead to very compact code, but some restraint should be exercised to ensure that readability is not discarded. Also the order of evaluation of expressions involving the increment or decrement operators can depend on the compiler in some circumstances, as in:

```
k = ++i + i;      // A very trivial example.
```

As always, it is better to avoid writing compiler dependent code wherever possible. It may seem obvious, but constants cannot be incremented or decremented:

```
++3.142;          // WRONG!
10--;             // WRONG!
```

In any case, it is difficult to imagine what purpose could be served by such statements.

3.1.6 Associativity and Precedence of Integer Operators

Although only simple expressions have been considered so far, we have learnt how to use quite a few operators:

```
=    +    -    *    /    %    ++    --
```

The =, *, /, % tokens are all binary operators; that is they are defined for an operand on each side of the operator, such as in:

```
k = i * j;        // Valid C++.
```

rather than:

```
k = i *;          // WRONG: where is the second operand?
```

The `++` and `--` operators are both unary operators, that is they require a single operand:

```
++x;              // Unary - operator takes only one operand.
```

The `-` operator can be both a binary operator, as in:

```
k = i - j;        // Binary - operator.
```

or an unary operator, as in:

```
k = -j;           // Unary - operator takes only one operand.
```

The unary `+` operator is not expressly forbidden, but it serves no useful purpose, as in:

```
k = +j;           // Valid but useless unary + operator.
```

and we omit it from all future discussion.

In complicated expressions, such as:

```
k = i + j / m * n - k;
```

the two concepts of associativity and precedence are used to determine the order in which the evaluation is carried out. Operator precedence controls which operator in an expression is applied first; the associativity determines the order in which operators with the same precedence are applied. That is, the compiler first uses operator precedence to determine the order of evaluations in an expression and any remaining ambiguities are removed by using operator associativity. The properties of the operators introduced so far are given in Table 3.1. All operators shown in the same group have the same precedence and associativity, but a group higher up in the table has a higher precedence than one further down. For example, in the expression:

```
i = 1 - 2 * 3 + 4;    // * has higher precedence than - or +.
```

the multiplication operator has the highest precedence and is applied first, yielding:

```
i = 1 - 6 + 4;        // -, + have higher precedence than =.
```

The subtraction and addition operators have equal precedence, greater than that of the assignment operator, so the right hand side of the expression is evaluated left to right, giving the result of -1. Finally -1 is assigned to i. These rules, which are similar to those of many other languages, do not necessarily give the results that would be expected mathematically. For instance:

	Operator	Associativity	Section first defined
++	increment	right to left	3.1.5
--	decrement		3.1.5
-	unary minus		3.1.6
*	multiplication	left to right	3.1.2
/	division		3.1.3
%	modulus		3.1.4
+	addition	left to right	3.1
-	subtraction		3.1
=	assignment	right to left	3.1
+=			3.4.3
-=			3.4.3
*=			3.4.3
/=			3.4.3
%=			3.4.3

Table 3.1: Some Common Operators.

```
i = 3 / 4 / 2;
```

is evaluated as:

```
i = (3 / 4) / 2;
```

rather than:

```
i = (3 * 2) / 4;
```

due to the left to right associativity of the divide operator.

Any expression inside parentheses is evaluated first, which means that:[2]

```
i = (1 - 2) * (3 + 4);
```

is reduced to:

```
i = -1 * 7;
```

which assigns -7 to i. If you are in doubt about the precedence of any operator it is always possible to use parentheses.

Exercise:

Write a program to evaluate the following expressions:

---

[2]When describing the three different bracket types, the common terminology employed is: parentheses for ( ), braces for { } and square brackets for [ ]. Note that the various brackets must always occur in pairs.

```
i = 2 / 3 + 3 / 2;
i = 2 / 3 / 3;
i = 3 / 2 % 7;
i = 7 % + 2 * 3;
i = 7 / 2 * 3;
```

Are the results what you would expect?

3.1.7 Long Integers

Long integers have the same properties as integers, except that at least the same number of bytes must be used in their representation as are used for the int data type. Typically four bytes (the minimum acceptable for the ANSI C standard) are used and integers between -2147483647 and 2147483648 can be represented, as in:

```
long i, j, k;
i = 2140001111;      // Too big for 2 bytes.
j = -2140001111;     // Too small for 2 bytes.
k = i - j;
```

However, it is fairly common for a compiler to define both the int and long data types to have the same four byte representations.

Notice that the keyword, long, is used to define (and declare) long integers. The definition:

```
long int i, j, k;
```

is equivalent to that given above, but is less widely used.

The suffix L (or l) is used to distinguish a long constant:

```
long i = 1L;
```

3.1.8 Short Integers

The short type has the same properties as int, except that a particular C++ compiler should not use more bytes to represent short than are used for int. Typically the short type uses two bytes (the minimum acceptable for the ANSI C standard) and has a range of -32767 to 32768. This type can be useful for saving memory as in:

```
short i, j, k;
i = 1;            // Can easily be represented by 2 bytes.
j = 2;            // Can easily be represented by 2 bytes.
k = i - j;
```

but, if the representation is less than the natural size suggested by the hardware, there may be a performance penalty. It is best to avoid short integers unless there is a compelling reason to do otherwise.

Notice that the keyword, `short`, is used to define short integers. The equivalent definition:

```
short int i, j, k;
```

is again less widely used.

3.1.9   Unsigned Integers

The `short`, `int` and `long` types all have corresponding `unsigned` types. These occupy the same amount of memory as the `signed` type and obey the laws of arithmetic modulo 2^n, where n is the number of bits in the representation. For instance, if n is 16 (two bytes), then numbers between 0 and 65535 (that is $2^{16} - 1$) can be represented. Unsigned addition does not overflow and subtraction does not underflow; they simply wrap round:

```
unsigned int i;      // Suppose represented by 2 bytes.
i = 65535;           // Max. unsigned number for 2 bytes.
i = i + 1;           // The result is 0.
i = 1 - 2;           // The result is 65535.
```

It is not usually worth using an `unsigned` rather than `signed` integral type just to gain a higher upper limit on the positive integers that can be stored. An example of the resulting possible pitfalls is given in Exercise 2 of Chapter 4; an example where using an `unsigned` type *is* worthwhile appears in Section 13.4.1.

A `U` (or `u`) is used to denote an unsigned constant, as in:

```
unsigned int i = 1U;
unsigned long j = 1UL;
```

Any combination of `U,u` and `L,l` in any order can be used for an `unsigned long` constant.

3.1.10   Character Types

The type, `char`, is represented by a sufficient number of bytes to hold any character belonging to the character set for the particular compiler. This representation is usually one byte (the minimum allowed by the ANSI C standard). Rather confusingly C++ distinguishes three character types: `char`, `unsigned char` and `signed char`. The `signed char` and `unsigned char` data types obey the same rules of arithmetic as their integer counterparts. If the type is simply specified as `char`, then it is compiler dependent as to whether or not the high order bit is treated as a sign bit. This makes no difference when storing the standard printing characters, but if other data is stored as type **char** it may appear to be negative on one computer and positive on another. If the sign of such data is significant, then the type should be specified as either **signed** or **unsigned char**, as appropriate. Such distinctions may seem a bit obscure at present, but are raised as a possible portability problem which you could meet in the future.

Although the **char** types obey the corresponding rules of integer arithmetic, they are typically used to hold character data as in:

```
char c1, c2;
c1 = 'C';
c2 = '+';
cout << c1 << c2 << c2 << "\n";
```

Exercise:

What does the above fragment of code output? Verify the answer on your system.

Since characters are represented by numbers, it is possible to make assignments directly rather than by using the character constant notation. For instance an obscure way of rewriting the above code, for the ASCII character set, is:

```
char c1, c2, c3;
c1 = 67;
c2 = 43;
c3 = 10;
cout << c1 << c2 << c2 << c3;
// Does the output agree with the previous exercise?
// See the ASCII character set in Appendix B.
```

but such manipulations are rarely useful in scientific programming.

Another common use of character types, which is not introduced until Chapter 6, is to hold arrays of data of unknown type. For example, if we are copying data we may wish to copy a certain number of bytes but be unconcerned with how the bytes should be interpreted.

3.2 Floating Point Data Types

Floating point numbers, such as 3.142 and 2.9979×10^8, are essential to almost every scientific calculation. In C++ there are three floating point types: **float**, **double** and **long double**. The type **float** is typically represented by 4 bytes (the minimum acceptable for ANSI standard C), a **double** by 8 bytes and a **long double** by 10 or 12 bytes. However, all that is required is that a **double** uses at least the same number of bytes as a `float` and a `long double` uses at least as many as a `double`. We first consider the type `double`, since from many points of view it is the standard floating point type.

3.2.1   Type `double`

Identifiers of type `double` are defined by using the `double` keyword as in:

```
double pi, c;
pi = 3.1415926535897932;
c  = 2.997925e8;
```

where the floating point assignment operator is denoted by the token, `=`. The expression for `c` is typical of a floating point number and may be split into three parts:

2	the integer part
997925	the fractional part
8	the exponent.

A decimal point separates the integer and fractional parts, while `e` (`E` is also valid) separates the fractional part from the exponent. A floating point constant must contain a decimal point or an exponent or both, since otherwise there would be nothing to distinguish it from an integer. If there is a decimal point, then either an integer or a fractional part must be present. If there is no decimal point, then there must be both an integer part and an exponent (but there can be no fractional part of course):

```
double x, y, z;
x = 1.0;
y = 0.1;
z = 1e10;
x = 1.1e10;
y = 11e9;
z = .11e11;
```

The following are not valid `double` constants:

```
.e9          // WRONG: no integer or fractional part.
1,000.0      // WRONG: an embedded comma is not permitted.
1 000.0      // WRONG: an embedded space is not permitted.
1000         // WRONG: integer constant.
e10          // WRONG: no integer constant.
```

Apart from the use of e or E, all of this should be straightforward to anyone familiar with scientific notation.

We can perform all of the usual arithmetic operations of assignment, addition, subtraction, multiplication, division, increment, decrement and unary minus. In fact all of the operators we introduced for integers, except for the modulus operator, are also valid for `double` identifiers and constants:

```
double x, y, z;
x = 3.1416;             // Assignment.
y = -x;                 // Unary minus.
z = -3.1416;            // Unary minus.
++x;                    // Increment (prefix version).
y--;                    // Decrement (postfix version).
x = x - 1.0;            // Subtraction.
y = y + 1.0;            // Addition.
z = x * y;              // Multiplication.
z = z / 3.1416;         // Division.
```

All of these operators have the same precedence and associativity as for the corresponding integer versions. Notice that `-3.1416` is actually an expression involving an unary minus together with a `double` constant and that floating point division does not truncate to an integer, unlike integer division.

Exercise:

What is the final result for z in the above code? Verify your answer.

Only a finite subset of all floating point numbers can be represented by one of the defined types, such as `double`. There are many ways of representing a floating point number by a fixed number of bytes, but most C++ compilers conform to what is known as the IEEE standard. For such compilers a `double` of eight bytes gives a range of about 10^{-308} to 10^{308} and an accuracy of sixteen decimal places. More details of how floating point numbers are represented by a computer are given in Chapter 13. For the present it is worth pointing out that in numerical calculations it is very easy to attempt to generate a number whose absolute magnitude is too big to be represented (causing floating point overflow) or too small (causing floating point underflow). It is also possible to attempt to perform invalid operations, such as a divide by zero. For a C++ compiler conforming to the IEEE standard, all such meaningless results are flagged as NaNs (Not a Number). Once a NaN is created it propagates through the calculation, ensuring that any meaningless final answers are also suitably flagged. However, unless there is an appropriate compiler option, a NaN is not flagged when it is generated. Such an option is invaluable for numerical applications.

Unlike some other languages, such as FORTRAN, there is no operator for raising a number (either integer or floating) to a power. In C++ such operations are carried out by a function call. For small integer powers it is, in any case, usually much faster to use repeated multiplication, as in:

```
velocity = 0.5 * acceleration * time * time;
```

3.2.2   Type `float`

The type `float` should use at least four bytes (but not more than for `double`) to represent a floating point number. For compilers which conform to the IEEE standard this gives a range of about 10^{-38} to 10^{38} and an accuracy of seven decimal places. The type `float` has two advantages over `double`; it uses less memory and is usually significantly faster. In fact four byte floating point arithmetic is accurate enough for many scientific and engineering applications. This is one of the few occasions when one might be tempted to have reservations over using C++ for such applications. In C++ (as in C) there is a tendency to carry out calculations in `double` and then to convert back to `float`. For instance the standard library calculates all of the mathematical functions (sine, cosine etc.) using `double`. This can be wasteful, but as we will see, it is easier to overcome such problems in C++ than it is in C.

Variables of type `float` are defined by the keyword, `float`, as in:

```
float pi, c;
pi = 3.142f;
c = 2.9979e8f;
```

A `float` constant is distinguished from its `double` counterpart by means of the suffix `f` (or `F`). Omitting the `f` does not cause an error in the above examples, as the compiler inserts a conversion from `double` to `float`. Such omissions are quite common, although rather untidy, programming practice. Notice that the `f` is appended; it does not replace the `e` (or `E`):

```
c = 2.9979f8;        // WRONG: f is not legal.
```

The operators available for the types `float` and `double` are identical, as are their precedence and associativity.

3.2.3   Type `long double`

The type `long double` is defined by means of the `long double` keyword, as in:

```
long double pi, c;
pi = 3.14159265358979323846264643;
gamma = 0.577215664901532860606512; // Euler's constant.
```

A `long double` constant is distinguished from `double` and `float` by means of the suffix, L:

```
long double e_10;
e_10 = 2.20264657948067165169579e4L
```

The letter `l` is also valid, but is probably best avoided since `l` looks too similar to 1.[3]

The available operators for the types `float`, `double` and `long double` are identical. However, for some C++ compilers there may be no difference between the representations of `double` and `long double` (or even `double` and `float`).

3.3 Changing Types

The concept of type is needed in a language, such as C++, in order to be able to distinguish the different uses we make of different bytes of memory. Typing can help to prevent us carrying out incompatible operations on this memory. However, it is sometimes necessary to convert a value having one type directly into another. This may either be done automatically (and often silently) by the compiler, or we may have to force the change. Since typing, to some extent, exists in order to protect us from our own foolishness, we had better understand clearly what we are doing!

3.3.1 Type Promotion and Conversion

In many situations arithmetic binary operators have operands of different types:

```
double x;
float y;
int i;
long j;
x = 1 + 3.142;  // + operator has integer and double operands.
y = 3.142;      // = operator has float and double operands.
i = 2;
j = i;          // = operator has long and int operands.
```

Such statements can often be avoided by careful programming, but they are valid C++ since automatic conversions take place for arithmetic expressions containing mixed types. The rules for conversions are such that binary operations involving mixed types are performed using the type best able to handle the operands.[4] For instance in the expression, $1 + 3.142$, the right operand is of type `double` and the

---

[3]For the same reason, it is best to avoid using a single `l` as a user-defined identifier.

[4]More details are given in [2].

left is of type `int`, which therefore gets implicitly converted to a `double`. There is a hierarchy of conversions with the first match in the hierarchy being the one that is actually used. The hierarchy is as follows (with X standing for any type):[5]

1. A floating point conversion is performed:

   (a) `long double` *and* `X` $\longrightarrow$ `long double`

   (b) `double` *and* `X` $\longrightarrow$ `double`

   (c) `float` *and* `X` $\longrightarrow$ `float`

2. Integral promotions (which are also known as widenings) are performed on *both* operands. Whether the promotions are to the `int` or `unsigned int` type depends on the number of bytes used to represent these types by a particular C++ compiler. If the value of one of the following types can be represented by `int` then this type is used, otherwise a promotion to the `unsigned int` type is performed:

$$
\begin{array}{rcl}
\texttt{char} & \longrightarrow & \texttt{int or unsigned int} \\
\texttt{unsigned char} & \longrightarrow & \texttt{int or unsigned int} \\
\texttt{short} & \longrightarrow & \texttt{int or unsigned int} \\
\texttt{unsigned short} & \longrightarrow & \texttt{int or unsigned int}
\end{array}
$$

Subsequently, an integral conversion is performed:

   (a) `unsigned long` *and* `X` $\longrightarrow$ `unsigned long`

   (b) `long` *and* `unsigned` $\longrightarrow$ `long` or `unsigned long`
       The conversion is to `long` if this type can represent all values of the `unsigned` type, otherwise `unsigned long` is used.

   (c) `long` *and* `X` $\longrightarrow$ `long`

   (d) `unsigned int` *and* `X` $\longrightarrow$ `unsigned int`

This discussion may seem complicated and, indeed, there is the possibility of obscure conversion errors which depend on the particular C++ compiler being used. However, numerical applications mainly use either the `float` or `double` types, with `int` typically used as an iteration counter. As a result, mixed operand types are mostly: `double - int`, `float - int` and `double - float` and conversions between such types are straightforward.

Demotions may also occur, as in:

```
int i, j, k;
i = 3.142;          // double truncated to int.
j = -3.142;         // double truncated to int.
k = 2.9979e40;      // Undefined.
```

---

[5]This section almost merits a †(see page xix); there is no need to memorize the conversion hierarchy!

In the first case the `double` constant is truncated and 3 is assigned to `i`. In the second case the right operand is negative and the direction of truncation depends on the C++ compiler, the result could be either -3 or -4. The result in the third case is undefined since an integer cannot hold such a large value.

Exercise:

Why do

```
double x = (1.0 + 1) / 2;
```

and

```
double x = 0.5 + 1 / 2;
```

give different results?

3.3.2 Casts

An explicit conversion, known as a cast, can be performed by specifying the type, as in:

```
double x, y;
int i;
i = 4;
x = double(i);      // cast to double, preferred syntax.
y = (double)i;      // cast to double, older C style.
```

Used in this way, `double()` or `(double)` is actually a unary operator. In mixed arithmetic expressions casts are unnecessary since they are automatically inserted by the compiler. However, in later chapters we will come across situations in which we have to force a change of type by means of the cast operator.

3.4 Some Basic Operations

In this section we introduce a few basic operations. We first consider the `sizeof` operator, which is an essential part of the language. Then we go on to learn various new assignment operators and how to make an initialization in a definition; these features are all useful rather than fundamental.

3.4.1 The `sizeof` Operator

The number of bytes used to represent the fundamental types is dependent on the C++ compiler being used. However, it is frequently necessary to know the size of these types, for instance when copying an object between different memory locations. As an aid to writing portable code, there is an unary `sizeof` operator which, as its name suggests, gives the size of an object in bytes. To be precise, the result of the `sizeof` operator is an unsigned integer of type `size_t`, which is specified in the header file, `<stddef.h>`. So, if it is necessary to declare an identifier to hold the size of an object, we should really define it be of type `size_t`, as in:

```
#include <stddef.h>

size_t size1, size2;
double x;
int i;
size1 = sizeof(double);
size2 = sizeof(int);
size1 = sizeof(x);
size2 = sizeof(i);
```

This subtlety is not important for small objects, since the compiler will insert an implicit cast if necessary.

The `sizeof` operator actually gives the storage as a multiple of that required for the `char` type; that is the result of `sizeof(char)` is one by definition. However, throughout this book we assume that the `char` type takes one byte of memory.

Use of the `sizeof` operator is strongly encouraged since it is much more meaningful to see `sizeof(double)` in a program, rather than 8. The `sizeof` operator considerably aids portability and carries no performance overhead, since it is evaluated at compile-time.

3.4.2 Initialization

It is possible to combine a definition and assignment in a single statement, known as an initialization, as in:

```
int i = 1, j = 2, k = 3;
```

Such initializations are also possible for other fundamental data types. Now that the fundamental data types have been introduced, it is also worth pointing out that identifiers only need to be defined before they are used; there is no requirement to have all of the definitions at the start of a program:

```
int i = 1;
++i;
int j = i;
```

Readability is improved by collecting definitions in one place where possible. However, there is some advantage to be had from leaving the definition of an identifier until it can be initialized, since this technique avoids the common error of using uninitialized variables in expressions. In fact, in C++ it would be difficult to insist on collecting all definitions in one place, as for instance is done in FORTRAN, because the definition of objects is often a run-time decision. Some C++ programmers (such as [10]) go even further and advocate that objects should *not* be defined until they can be initialized.

Exercise:

Convert the quadratic equation program, given in Section 1.2, so that as far as possible variables are not defined until they can be initialized.

3.4.3   Assignment Operators

It is often necessary to carry out pairs of operations, such as:

```
int i, j;
double x, y;
i = i + 5;
j = j + i;
x = x * y;
z = z / x;
```

These pairs of operations can all be replaced by the following assignment operators:

```
i += 5;         // Equivalent to i = i + 5
j += i;         // Equivalent to j = j + i
x *= y;         // Equivalent to x = x * y
z /= x;         // Equivalent to z = z / x
```

In fact there are similar assignment operators corresponding to all arithmetic binary operators for all of the fundamental data types:

```
x -= y;         // Equivalent to x = x - y
i %= j;         // Equivalent to i = i % j
```

Such assignment operators are a convenient shorthand and may help the compiler to produce better code.

It is possible to carry out multiple assignments in one statement, as in:

```
i = j = k = 10;
```

In fact, we are not introducing anything new here. An assignment is an expression (which has a value) and as the assignment operator associates right to left, this example is equivalent to:

```
k = 10;
j = k;
i = j;
```

Multiple assignments can lead to compact code, but it is sometimes better to avoid the technique in order to improve readability.

While on the subject of assignments, it worth defining what is meant by *lvalue*, since you will probably get cryptic compiler messages of the form 'Must be lvalue'. An lvalue is an expression referring to a named region of storage; i, x and z are all lvalues in the following statements:

```
int i;
float x;
double z;

i = 20;
x = 1.2;
z = 1.222333444;
```

The terminology arises from the fact the left hand operand of an assignment operator must be an lvalue. An expression of the form:

```
2 = i;        // WRONG!
```

is incorrect because 2 is not an lvalue; we cannot assign the value of i to 2.

The analogous term, *rvalue*, is less widely used and refers to an expression on the right hand side of an assignment statement. An rvalue can be *read* but not assigned to. For instance, in the expression:

```
i = 2;
```

we cannot cannot assign a value to 2 since it is an rvalue.

3.5   const[†]

There are a number of keywords that can be used in conjunction with specifiers for the fundamental types (int, double etc.) in definitions and declarations. The type specifiers, const and volatile,[6] actually modify the fundamental types,

---

[6]In [6], but not [2], these are called type *qualifiers*.

whereas *storage class specifiers*, such as `register`,[7] change how data associated with a variable may be stored or accessed.

The `const` specifier is the most important type specifier. If we want to define a constant, the type is preceded by the `const` keyword, as in:

```
const int k = 27, i = 13;
const double pi = 3.1415926535897932, c = 2.9979e8;
```

Once such definitions are made, the compiler attempts to prevent any subsequent reassignments. It is possible to subvert this compiler checking, but foolish to do so; for some compilers, constants may even be placed in read only memory!

Using the `const` specifier can lead to much more readable code. Instead of the mysterious number `2.997925e8` appearing throughout the code, we can use:

```
const double speed_of_light = 2.997925e8;
```

Such definitions are usually placed near the start of a program, where they can be readily seen.

3.6   register and volatile[††]

The `register` specifier, as in:

```
register int i;
```

is a suggestion to the compiler that the code might execute faster if `i` were kept in one of the internal registers of the processing unit. This specifier is usually ignored by modern compilers, since they have very sophisticated techniques for making such decisions. The `register` specifier is not mentioned again in this book.

The `volatile` specifier, as in:

```
volatile int i;
```

is used to warn the compiler that the value of `i` may get changed (if, for example, there is memory mapped I/O) even though this change may not be apparent from the code. A possible use of the `volatile` specifier is for defining video screen memory. This specifier would only be used by very experienced C++ programmers (if then) and it only merits an occasional mention in this book.

---

[7]A complete list of storage class specifiers, some of which are discussed later, is: `auto`, `register`, `static` and `extern`.

3.7   typedef[†]

The **typedef** specifier simply introduces a synonym for a type. For example, if we make the declaration:

```
typedef double DISTANCE, TIME;
```

then instead of:

```
double x, t;
```

we can use:

```
DISTANCE x;
TIME t;
```

to define the variables **x** and **t**. Some programmers consistently use upper case letters for a **typedef**, but this is simply a matter of style. A **typedef** follows the standard rules for constructing any valid identifier and the name space is the same as for other identifiers (apart from labels, which are introduced in Section 4.8). This means that if we have introduced **DISTANCE** as a synonym for **double**, then:

```
int DISTANCE;        // WRONG!
```

is not allowed. It is important to realize that a **typedef** does not declare a new type. For example, although **x** and **t** are instances of a different **typedef**, the following assignment is valid, since there is no strong type checking:

```
x = t;      // O.K.
```

Common uses of the **typedef** specifier are as follows:

- A **typedef** can isolate compiler dependent parts of a program. For instance, the type used to represent a variable could be **short**, **int** or **long**, depending on the number bytes used in their representations. Examples are **size_t** and **ptrdiff_t** which are each declared as a **typedef** in the library header file, **<stddef.h>**. This technique has the advantage that, since the definition only appears in one place, changes are easily made.

- A **typedef** can be helpful for program documentation. The declaration:

```
DISTANCE x;
```

is more meaningful than:

```
double x;
```

Some authors (for example [1]) use this technique extensively. However, a valid alternative is to give meaningful names to variables, as in:

```
double distance, time;
```

- A `typedef` can clarify complicated declarations. An example is given in Section 7.5.

3.8   Summary

- The integral types are `short`, `int` and `long`. They all have `unsigned` variants.

- The character types are `char`, `signed char` and `unsigned char`.

- See Table 3.1 for the basic operators, together with their associativity and precedence.

- The floating point types are `float`, `double` and `long double`.

- An explicit cast (or conversion) can be performed, as in `int(3.142)`. For mixed arithmetic expressions, such conversions are automatically inserted by the compiler.

- The `sizeof` operator gives the size of an object in bytes.

- Use the `const` specifier wherever the contents of an object should not change.

3.9   Exercises

1. Using the `sizeof` operator, write a program that prints the number of bytes used to represent the `char`, `int`, `short int`, `long int`, `float` and `double` types on your computer. Work out the maximum and minimum values that can be represented by the integer types. Check your answers by examining the header file, `<limits.h>`. (You will need to consult your system documentation to discover the directory which contains `limits.h`.)

2. By examining the header file, `<float.h>`, find the maximum and minimum values which can be represented by the types `float` and `double` on your system. Check your answers by means of a program. What is the significance of other compiler dependent parameters given in `<float.h>`? (Again, consult your system documentation to find the location of `float.h`.)

3. Write a program which prompts for the base and height of a triangle and then outputs the area. Write one version that only uses the type int and a second that uses the type double.

4. Using the techniques learnt so far, sum the first four terms in the series:

$$e = \sum_{n=0}^{\infty} \frac{1}{n!}$$

Is the result a reasonable approximation to e?

5. The total relativistic energy, E, of a free particle is given by:

$$E = \frac{Mc^2}{\sqrt{1 - v^2/c^2}}$$

where:

$$M = \text{rest mass of the particle}$$

$$c = \text{speed of light} = 2.99725 \times 10^{10} \text{cm/s}$$

$$v = \text{speed of particle}$$

Write a program to calculate E for sufficient values of v to enable you to plot a graph of E as a function of v, where:

$$0 \leq v < c$$

and

$$M = 0.910954 \times 10^{-27} \text{g}$$

Chapter 4

Control Structure

In our program to solve a quadratic equation in Section 1.2, the user could enter values of a, b and c, which make:

$$b^2 - 4ac$$

negative. In such cases the program would fail, but there is nothing we can do to prevent this with the techniques we have learnt so far. All of our programs have a very simple control structure. In fact control just passes from one statement to the next, with no alternative pathway through a program. Our next task is to introduce iteration and branching techniques but before we consider these control structures a few preliminaries are needed; in particular, some new operators must be introduced. The precedence and associativity of all the operators that are introduced in this chapter are given in Table 4.1.

4.1 Relational Operators

There are four binary operators which can be used for comparing the values of arithmetic expressions. They are:

`<`	less than
`<=`	less than or equal
`>`	greater than
`>=`	greater than or equal

In each case a comparison of the left and right operands is carried out and the result is either true or false. Since there is no boolean type in C++, the `int` type is used to represent true or false; a non-zero value (usually one) denotes true and zero denotes false. Notice that although a single bit suffices to represent true or false, it is specifically the `int` type that is used, even though many compilers may represent an `int` by four bytes. The motivation for this is speed, since by definition an `int` is the natural integer type for the hardware. As an example, consider:

	Operator	Associativity	Section first defined
++	increment	right to left	3.1.5
--	decrement		3.1.5
-	unary minus		3.1.6
type()	cast		3.3.2
sizeof	size		3.4.1
!	logical negation		4.2
*	multiplication	left to right	3.1.2
/	division		3.1.3
%	modulus		3.1.4
+	addition	left to right	3.1
-	subtraction		3.1
>	greater than	left to right	4.1
>=	greater than or equal to		4.1
<	less than		4.1
<=	less than or equal to		4.1
==	equal	left to right	4.3
!=	not equal		4.3
&&	logical AND	left to right	4.2
||	logical OR	left to right	4.2
?:	conditional operator	left to right	4.11
=	assignment	right to left	3.1
+=			3.4.3
-=			3.4.3
*=			3.4.3
/=			3.4.3
%=			3.4.3
,	comma	left to right	4.9

Table 4.1: A More Complete List of Operators.

```
int i;
i = 2 > 1;          // Assigns 1
i = 2 < 1;          // Assigns 0
i = 2 >= 2;         // Assigns 1
i = 3.4 <= 2.4      // Assigns 0
```

where the variable, i, is assigned either 0 or 1, according to the results of the four relational operators.

From Table 4.1, we see that the relational operators associate left to right, so that:

```
i = a < b < c;
```

actually means:

```
i = (a < b) < c;
```

This associativity is rarely, if ever, of any use and can lead to some very obscure code. In the above expression a < b evaluates to 0 or 1, which is then compared with c. Depending on the result of this comparison, either 0 or 1 is assigned to i. In general this result is a lot different from that obtained by determining whether or not a < b and b < c.

Notice that <= and >= each constitute a single token, so that the following are invalid:

```
i = j > = k;        // White space is not allowed.
i = j =< k;         // =< is not a valid operator.
```

The operands of the relational operators can, of course, be expressions:

```
int i, j = 1, k = 2;
i = (j + 1) >= (k - 72);    // 2 is greater than -70,
                            // so 1 is assigned to i.
```

The parentheses used here and throughout most of this chapter are purely for clarity, since the rules for operator precedence make them unnecessary.

Exercise:

What values would you expect i and j to take in the following statements:

```
double x = 110.0;
int i = x > (x / 13.0) * 13.0;
int j = x < (x / 13.0) * 13.0;
```

Write a program to test your answer and try other values of x.

4.2 Logical Operators

The logical operators are:

```
!    negation
&&   AND
||   OR
```

These operators all give a result of type `int` and a value of zero or one. The logical negation operator, `!`, is an unary operator which acts on an operand of arithmetic type.[1] If the operand is 0 or 0.0, the result is one and if the operand is non-zero the result is zero. Like all unary operators, the logical negation operator associates right to left. A floating operand is valid, but not common; probably because it is rare for the result of a floating point calculation to be exact.

The logical `AND` operator, `&&`, is a binary operator whose operands are of arithmetic type. If both operands are non-zero, the result is one, otherwise the result is zero:

```
int i = 1, j = 0, k;
k = i && j;            // 0 is assigned to k
```

The evaluation is guaranteed to be left to right; consequently if the left operand is zero then the right one is never evaluated. This left to right evaluation can lead to compact code but there is also the possibility of insidious bugs:

```
int i = 0, j = 1, k;
k = i && j++;          // j is never incremented.
k = j++ && (i - j);    // j is incremented before i-j
                       // is evaluated.
```

The logical `OR` operator, `||`, is a binary operator whose operands are of arithmetic type. If either operand is non-zero then the result is one, otherwise the result is zero:

```
int i = 0, j = 1, k = 0, m;
m = i || j;            // 1 assigned to m
m = i || k;            // 0 assigned to m
```

Again the evaluation is left to right; if the left operand is non-zero then the right operand is never evaluated:

```
int i = 1, j = -1, k;
k = i || j++;          // j is never incremented.
k = j++ || (i - j);    // j is incremented before i-j
                       // is evaluated.
```

Exercise:

What values are assigned to `a`, `b`, `c` and `d` by the following statements:

---

[1] The expressions in any of the three logical operators can also involve pointers, which are introduced in Chapter 6.

```
int i = 0, j = 10, k = 0;
int a = i || j && !k;
int b = !i && k || j;
int c = !(j || k);
int d = !(j && !k);
```

Check your answers by means of a program.

4.3 Equal and Not Equal Operators

The binary operators to be considered in this section are:

```
==   equal
!=   not equal
```

Both operators are used to test operands of arithmetic type, with the result being of type int. The *equality* operator, ==, gives a result of one if both operands are identical and zero otherwise. Some valid examples are:

```
int i = 0, j = 10, k;
double x = 10.0, y = 2.0, z = 5.0;
k = i == j;              // Assigns 0 to k
k = k == i;              // Assigns 1 to k
k = z * y == x;          // Assigns either 0 or 1 to k.
k = z == 5.0;            // Assigns 1 to k
```

It is rare that we can anticipate the exact result of a floating point calculation and this means that using the equality operator in this way is dangerous and a frequent cause of numerical application programs that fail to terminate.

The following are invalid or not what was intended:

```
k = (i = = j);   // White space is not allowed.
j == 10;         // Valid but does nothing, j = 10; intended.
k = (z = 5.0);   // Assigns 5.0 to z and k, z == 5.0 intended.
```

The binary *not equal* operator, !=, takes arithmetic operands. The result is zero if the two operands are identical and one otherwise, as in:

```
int i = 1, j = 10, k;
double x = 10.0, y = 2.0, z = 5.0;
k = i != j;              // Assigns 1 to k.
k = k != i;              // Assigns 0 to k.
k = z * y != x;          // Assigns either 0 or 1 to k.
k = z != 5.0;            // Assigns 0 to k.
```

The following are invalid or not what was intended:

```
k = i ! = j;      // White space not allowed.
k = i =! j;       // =! is not a valid operator (!= intended).
```

Exercise:

What is the result of i =! j in the above code fragment?

4.4   Blocks and Scope

A pair of braces, { }, can be used to group statements, definitions and dec-larations into a *compound statement* or *block*, as it is more commonly known. Any definitions made within a block are only valid within the block and hide definitions made for the same identifiers outside:

```
int variable = 10;      // variable has type int, value 10
// some code
{
    double variable;    // variable has type double
    // more code
    variable = 1.7724532925;
    cout << variable << "\n";
}
cout << variable;       // variable has type int, value 10
```

Notice that there is no semi-colon after the second (terminating) brace of the block.[2]

Some compilers issue helpful warnings when a definition hides a previous definition. The parts of a program where a particular identifier is valid (that is where it is visible) are known as the *scope* of that identifier.

Notice how the two braces in the above code have the same indentation and the enclosed statements are all indented by one tab. This layout is not a requirement of C++, but is generally adopted and improves readability.

Blocks can be both nested and parallel; the following code illustrates how definition hiding works in such circumstances:

```
{
    int i = 1;
    double x = 1.111;
    cout << i << "    " << x << "\n";
```

---

[2]A block can be empty. An example of this is when a function needs to be defined but does not perform any operation.

```
        {
            int x = 2;
            double i = 2.222;
            cout << i << "    " << x << "\n";
        }
        cout << i << "    " << x << "\n";
        {
            char i = 'i';
            char x = 'x';
            cout << i << "    " << x << "\n";
        }
    }
```

Exercise:

Explain the output from this code segment.

A block can appear anywhere that a single statement is permissible and often occurs in the context of branching and iteration, both of which we consider next.

4.5   Branch Statements

There are three branch statements: the `if`, `if else` and `switch` statements.

4.5.1   `if` Statement

The `if` statement takes the form:

```
    if (expression)
        statement
```

where the expression is any valid arithmetic expression.[3] The expression is evaluated and, if it is non-zero, the statement is executed:

```
    if (i == 0)
        x = 100.0;  // 100.0 is assigned to x if i is zero
```

This code fragment can alternatively be written (perhaps more obscurely) as:

```
    if (!i)
        x = 100.0;
```

---

[3]The expressions in any of the three branch statements can also involve pointers, which are introduced in Chapter 6.

It is, of course, possible for the if statement to involve a block:

```
if (!i) {
    x = 3.142;        // If i equals zero, all three
    y = 100.0;        // statements are executed.
    z *= x;
}
```

Notice that the closing brace has the same indentation as the if statement. The opening brace is also on the same line as the if statement. Although not a requirement of C++, this style is widely adopted.

The following are invalid examples of attempts to use the if statement:

```
if !i                 // WRONG: parentheses omitted.
    x = 100.0;
if (i == 0)
    double x = pi;    // WRONG: cannot have a declaration
                      // (except in a compound statement).
if (!i) {
    double w;
    w = x * y;
}                     // Scope of w does not extend beyond
                      // the block and w cannot be accessed.
```

There is also a common error involving the equality operator which is notoriously difficult to detect:

```
if (i = 0)
    x = 1000.0;
```

The code is syntactically correct, but is equivalent to:

```
i = 0;
x = 1000.0;
```

whereas the programmer almost certainly meant to write:

```
if (i == 0)
    x = 1000.0;
```

In general the result of the two code fragments is very different; in the first case zero is assigned to i, the expression always evaluates to true and hence 1000.0 is always assigned to x. Some programmers avoid such errors by writing any constant first, as in:

```
if (0 == i)
    x = 1000.0;
```

If we accidentally write:

```
if (0 = i)                    // WRONG
    x = 1000.0;
```

then a compiler error occurs. However, care is needed to do this in every case. Some helpful compilers issue a warning if an assignment occurs as the outermost operator in the expression for an `if` statement.

Another common error is to omit the braces for a compound statement following an `if`. The following statements:

```
if (!i)
    x = 3.142;
    y = 100.0;
    z *= x;
```

look like (the programmer's intention):

```
if (!i) {
    x = 3.142;
    y = 100.0;
    z *= x;
}
```

but execute as:

```
if (!i)
    x = 3.142;
y = 100.0;
z *= x;
```

Since non-zero and zero are used to represent true and false, the readability of code involving branch statements is improved by defining `TRUE` and `FALSE` identifiers, as in:

```
const int TRUE = 1;
const int FALSE = 0;
// some code
if (last_entry == FALSE)
    x = pi;
if (last_iteration != FALSE)
    y = beta;
```

Notice the traditional use of upper case letters so as to distinguish `TRUE` and `FALSE` from other identifiers. It is normal practice to make such definitions at the start of a file so that they are valid for the entire file. The last `if` statement may appear to be equivalent to:

```
if (last_iteration == TRUE)      // RISKY!
    y = beta;
```

However, `last_iteration` could be non-zero but not have the value 1. It is therefore safer to test against `FALSE`.

4.5.2   if else statement

The `if else` statement takes the form:

```
if (expression_1)
    statement_1
else if (expression_2)
    statement_2
// more else ifs
else
    statement_n
```

where the expressions are of arithmetic type. If `expression_1` is non-zero, `statement_1` is executed and control passes beyond `statement_n`. By contrast, if `expression_1` is zero then `expression_2` is tested. The sequence continues until one of the statements (which may be the last one) is executed. In fact, there is no requirement to have the final `else` statement: there may be no default action to be taken, in which case it is possible for all of the expressions to evaluate to zero and for none of the statements to be executed. A valid example of the `if else` statement is:

```
if (i == 0) {
    x = pi;
    y = 2.0 * pi;
}
else if (i == 1) {
    x = 2.0 * pi;
    y = 0.0;
}
else {
    x = 0.0;
    y = 0.0;
}
```

The `if else` statement has one pitfall awaiting the unwary, known as the *dangling else* trap:

```
if (i == 0)
    if (j == 0)
```

```
            cout << "Both i and j are zero\n";
    else {
        cout << "i is non-zero\n";
        x = pi;
    }
```

The intention of the programmer is apparent from the indentation; if i is non-zero then the code in the braces should be executed, whatever the value of i. But the **else** is dangling; in other words there is an ambiguity as to whether it is associated with the first or second **if**. In fact the dangling **else** is always really associated with the previous **if**, so an indentation which expresses better the logic of the code is:

```
if (i == 0)
    if (j == 0)
        cout << "Both i and j are zero\n";
    else {
        cout << "i is non-zero\n";
        x = pi;
    }
```

This is presumably not the programmer's intent, but such mistakes can be very difficult to find since the indentation has a very powerful effect on code readability, even when the indentation is wrong! The dangling **else** problem can be overcome by the use of pairs of braces:

```
if (i == 0) {
    if (j == 0)
        cout << "Both i and j are zero\n";
}
else {
    cout << "i is non-zero\n";
    x = pi;
}
```

As an example of the **if else** construct, we can now rewrite our quadratic equation program so that complex roots are trapped:

```
#include <iostream.hpp>
#include <math.h>
int main()
{
    double a, b, c;
    cout << "Enter the coefficients a, b, c: ";
    cin >> a >> b >> c;
```

```
    double temp = b * b - 4.0 * a * c;
    if (temp > 0.0) {
        double root = sqrt(temp);
        double root1 = 0.5 * (root - b) / a;
        double root2 = 0.5 * (root + b) / a;
        cout << "There are two real solutions:  " <<
            root1 << " and " << root2 << "\n";
    }
    else if (temp < 0.0) {
        double root = sqrt(-temp);
        double real_part = -0.5 * b / a;
        double imag_part = 0.5 * root / a;
        cout << "There are two complex solutions: " <<
            real_part << " + i * " << imag_part << " and "
            << real_part << " - i * " << imag_part << "\n";
    }
    else {
        cout << "Both solutions are: " <<
            -0.5 * b / a << "\n";
    }
    return 0;
}
```

This is our first complete program with any control structure; the `if else` s-
tatement enables us to trap all three possible cases resulting from any values of
`a`, `b`, `c`. Notice how variables, such `root1` and `real_part`, are defined in (and
only have scope within) different blocks; this enables us to use more appropriate
variables. Notice also how there is only one `return` statement. It is tempting to
put a `return` at the end of each block, but such *alternative returns*, as they are
sometimes known, are best avoided if possible. The reason for this is that it is
easy to miss a `return` statement in some deeply embedded inner block.

Exercise:

Try out our improved quadratic equation program for various values
of `a`, `b` and `c`. You should be able to cause the program to fail, in
which case, make appropriate further modifications.

4.5.3   switch Statement

Although the `switch` statement takes the general form:

```
switch (expression) {
case constant_1:
```

```
        statement_1;
case constant_2:
        statement_2;
// more case, statement pairs
case constant_n:
        statement_n;
default:
        last_statement;
}
```

our discussion will be clearer if we consider a specific example. Suppose we have a program to solve a differential equation by a variety of iterative methods and we want to be able to choose which one to use; that is we want a menu. A suitable piece of code achieving this is:

```
int option;
cout << "menu:\n" <<
    "\t1 Jacobi\n" <<          // Note \t for horizontal tab.
    "\t2 Gauss-Seidel\n" <<
    "\t3 Red-black Gauss-Seidel\n" <<
    "Enter a number to choose the required technique\n";
cin >> option;

switch (option) {
case 1:
    // Jacobi code
    break;
case 2:
    // Gauss-Seidel code
    break;
case 3:
    // Red-black Gauss-Seidel code
    break;
default:
    cout << option << " is not a valid option\n";
    break;
}
```

Notice that there is no terminating semi-colon.

In this example, the value of option is tested in turn against the constants appearing after each **case** keyword. When one of these constants is found to be equal to the value of option, then the subsequent code is executed. The **break** statement, which we have not met before, causes control to pass to whatever follows the **switch** statement. The important point to realize is that it is the

break statement which *alters* the flow of control, rather than the **case** or **default** statements.[4]   If there is no **break** corresponding to a particular **case** statement, then the flow of control is unchanged. This drop-through behaviour is both an advantage and a curse; it sometimes permits elegant code:

```
cout << "Do you want to continue (Y or N): ";
cin >> reply;

switch (reply) {
case 'Y':
case 'y':
    // Code for Yes.
    break;
case 'N':
case 'n':
    // Code for No.
    break;
default:
    // Code to recover from invalid reply.
    break;
};
```

but it is easy to miss out a **break**, with potentially disastrous results. For instance, in the menu example, if the first **break** were omitted, then entering menu item 1 would cause both the Jacobi and Gauss-Seidel code to be executed.

If none of the constants match the **switch** expression, then control passes to the statement following the **default** label (if there is one). It is possible for the **break** before the **default** label to be omitted, in which circumstances the final **case** would also lead to the **default**. Such circumstances are usually mistakes!

The final **break** statement after the **default** label in the example is redundant, but is worth including as it is so easy to subsequently add another **case** without including a desired **break**. The keywords **case** and **default** can never appear outside of a **switch** statement and there can be at most one **default** label. The **case** and **default** labels can appear in any order.

Exercise:

Turn the above code fragment into a small program which sends messages identifying the three possible replies to the output stream.

For large programs, the switch statement can often be avoided by using the object-oriented aspects of C++, resulting in code which is more elegant and maintainable. The key concepts involved are classes, inheritance and polymorphism, which are introduced in Chapter 11.

---

[4]The **case** and **default** are actually special types of statement labels which can only appear in a **switch** statement. Labels are described later in this chapter.

4.6 Iteration Statements

In a program it is often necessary to execute one or more statements many times. It is tedious to repeat the statements and, in any case, it is often impossible to predict how many times the execution should be repeated. Such circumstances are handled by the three iteration statements: `while`, `for` and `do`.

4.6.1 `while` Statement

The `while` statement takes the general form:

```
while (control)
    statement
```

and has two distinct parts, which we have called `control` and `statement`. A typical example is

```
int n = 5;
double gamma = 1.0;
while (n > 0) {
    gamma *= n;
    --n;
}
```

The control expression, which is of arithmetic type,[5] is evaluated before each execution of what is in this particular case a compound statement. This statement is executed if the expression is not zero and then the test is repeated. If the test never fails, then the iteration never terminates:

```
int n = 1;
double gamma = 1.0;
while (n > 0) {
    gamma *= n;      // Presumably a mistake somewhere!
    ++n;
}
```

Notice that there is no `do` associated with the `while` (unlike some other languages) and that there is no terminating semi-colon:

```
while (n > 0) do {  // WRONG: 'do' is not allowed.
    gamma *= n;
    --n;
};              // ; is unnecessary, but does no damage here.
```

---

[5] The expressions in any of the three iteration statements can also involve pointers, which are introduced in Chapter 6.

Exercise:

Use a while loop to sum the first twenty terms in the series:

$$1 - \frac{1}{2} + \frac{1}{3} - \frac{1}{4} \cdots$$

The result should be an approximation to $\ln 2$.

4.6.2   `for` Statement

The `for` statement has the general form:

```
for (initialize; control; change)
    statement
```

and can be seen to consist of four separate parts, which we call `initialize`, `control`, `change` and `statement` in order to indicate their respective roles. The `initialize` expression is evaluated first and if `control` is non-zero, `statement` is executed. The `change` expression is then evaluated and if `control` is still non-zero, `statement` is executed again. Control continues to cycle between `control`, `statement` and `change`, until the `control` expression is zero. Control then passes beyond the `for` statement. A typical example is:

```
factorial = 1;
for (i = 1; i <= n; ++i)
    factorial *= i;
```

Notice that `initialize` is only evaluated once and, as the name given to the expression suggests, it performs an initialization. It is possible for the final `statement` part of the `for` statement not to be executed at all:

```
n = 0;
factorial = 1;
for (i = 1; i <= n; ++i)      // 1 <=0 is FALSE so
    factorial *= i;           // factorial is unchanged.
```

It is also possible for any (or even all) of the expressions (but not the semi-colons) to be missing:

```
int factorial = 1, i = 1;
for (; i <= n; ++i)
    factorial *= i;
```

or

```
int factorial = 1, i = 1;
for (; i <= n; )
    factorial *= i++;
```

If the second (`control`) expression is missing then it is taken as evaluating to one (`TRUE`) and the loop continues for ever unless there is some way of breaking out.

It is often convenient to define the loop variable in the `initialize` expression. However, don't be misled into imagining that the scope of the variable is confined to the loop since a `for` loop with a block is equivalent to a single statement:

```
for (int i = 1; i < 10; ++i) {
    sum_1 += i;
    sum_2 += i * i;
}                       // O.K. so far.
double i = 10.0;        // WRONG: the i of type int is still
                        // in scope. This is a redefinition.
```

The scope of an identifier defined by the `initialize` expression in a `for` statement is the same as if the definition occurred before the `for` loop:

```
int i;
for (i = 1; i < 10; ++i) {
    sum_1 += i;
    sum_2 += i * i;
}
double i = 10.0;        // WRONG: Now the error is obvious.
```

It is worth noting that, unlike some other languages, there is nothing special about the variable that controls the iteration in a `for` statement. For instance, the controlling variable (in this case, `i`) can be assigned to:

```
for (i = 0; i < 10; ++i) {
    x *= 24.0 + pi;
    if (x > 17.0)
        i = 9;
}
```

and can be of floating type:

```
for (double x = 0.0; x != 10.0; ++x)      // VERY RISKY.
    total += x;
```

A test for equality of a floating type is very risky since it is likely that the finite machine precision will mean that the condition never occurs and the iteration continues for ever. For this reason it is very unusual to have a loop counter which is a floating type, although it is possible to use a relational expression, as in:

```
for (double x = 0.0; x < 9.5; ++x)        // SAFER.
    total += x;
```

As example of using **for** loops, we can find some integer solutions to the equation:

$$k^2 = i^2 + j^2$$

by means of the code:

```
#include <math.h>

int i_max = 40;       // Change this value as required.
for (int i = 1; i < i_max; ++i) {
    for (int j = i; j < i_max; ++j) {
        int i_j = i * i + j * j;
        int k = sqrt(i_j);
        if (k * k == i_j)
            cout << "A solution is: i = " << i <<
                " j = " << j << "  k = " << k <<
                "\n";
    }
}
```

Exercise:

Turn this code into a complete program and find the first 100 solutions. Your program should prompt for a value of **i_max** and include a test so that integer overflow cannot occur.

Since the conversion from **double** to **int** truncates rather than rounds, there is a small possibility that your program may miss a valid solution. Remedy this defect.

4.6.3   do Statement

The do statement has the form:

```
do
    statement
while (control);
```

Notice that the semi-colon is a necessary part of the **do statement**. The statement is executed and then, if the **control** expression evaluates to zero, control passes to the next statement. If the **control** expression is non-zero, control passes back to the **do statement** again. As an example, we could improve our code in Section 4.5.3 to read:

```
do {
    cout << "menu:\n" <<
        "\t1 Jacobi\n" <<
        "\t2 Gauss-Seidel\n" <<
        "\t3 Red-black Gauss-Seidel\n" <<
        "Enter a number to choose the required " <<
        "technique\n";
    cin >> option;
} while (option < 1 || option > 3);
// The same switch statement as before.
```

As before, the menu is sent to the output stream and the user enters an integer. If the integer has the wrong value then the menu is repeated until a correct value is entered.

It is worth including the pair of braces in a do statement, even if a compound statement is not required. If this isn't done then the code may look like a while loop with an empty statement.

With some contortions it is possible to interchangeably use any of the three iteration statements; which one is the most appropriate depends on the particular circumstances. In C++ programming (as in C) the for loop seems to be the most common iteration statement. This is probably because the syntax conveniently collects the initialization, loop control and increment all in one place. It is also helpful to read the control expressions before a large block statement is encountered. The while statement is often appropriate when initializations have been performed by the preceding statements. The iteration counter in a while statement is often changed by using an increment or decrement operator, resulting in very compact code:

```
while (i < 10)
    sum += i++;
```

The do iteration statement appears rarely in C++ (or C) programs. However, if there is a requirement for a statement to be executed at least once (as in our menu example) then the do statement is a very appropriate construct, since neither the for nor while loops have this property.

Exercise:

Turn the menu code, given above, into a program which uses a switch statement to output a message identifying the chosen option. Write versions using each of the three types of iteration statement.

4.7   `break` and `continue` Statements

The `break` statement can only occur inside a `switch` or iteration statement. We have already met the `break` statement in the context where it causes control to exit from the enclosing `switch` statement. The `break` statement can also supply an exit from the three iteration statements, such as:

```
while (1) {
    cout <<"Enter an integer > 0 and < 10 ";
    cin >> i;
    if (i > 0 && i < 10)
        break;
}   // A do statement would be more appropriate.
```

In the above example, the `while` loop does not necessarily terminate. However, if i satisfies $0 < i < 10$, then the `break` causes control to pass to the first statement after the end of the `while` loop. Notice that, since we can only break from a single enclosing loop, the `break` statement does not directly provide a way of exiting from inside deeply nested loops:

```
for (i = 0; i < 10; ++i) {
    for (j = 0; j < 10; ++j) {
        for (k = 0; k < 10; ++k) {
            x += i * a + j * b + k * c;
            // More code.
            if (x > max_x)
                break;
            // More code.
        }               // The break leaves us inside
    }                   // the i and j loops.
}
```

The `continue` statement can only occur inside an iteration statement and causes control to pass directly to the next iteration. For instance in the following trivial example:

```
for (i = 0; i < 10; ++i) {
    ++x;
    if (i == 5)
        continue;
    ++y;
}
```

x and y are both incremented on each pass through the loop, except for when i is five. In this case x is incremented, but then control passes directly to the next iteration (i is six). The `continue` statement can play the same role in the `while` and `do` iteration statements.

4.8   goto Statement††

C++ even possesses the infamous goto statement. This is an unconditional jump, or transfer of control, to a labelled statement, such as:

```
const double max_error = 0.00001;
for (i = 0; i < 100; ++i) {
    for (j = 0; j < 100; ++j) {
        for (k = 0; k < 100; ++k) {
            // Some code.
            if (delta_x < max_error)
                goto leap;
            // Perhaps more code.
        }
    }
}
leap:   cout <<"The iteration has converged\n";
```

Here we have used the identifier, leap, as a label. If delta_x is less than 0.0001, then control is transferred out of all three loops to the output stream statement which is labelled by leap. Any valid identifier is acceptable as a statement label, but the same label can only be used once in the same function, since a label has the scope of the function in which it is declared. A label can only be used by a goto statement and is the *only* identifier whose scope is not local to the block in which it is declared. The following demonstrate valid labels:

```
label9999:  x = y + z;
label1: label2: label3: x = y + z;  // Multiple labels.
a:  a = y - z;      // Labels have their own name space.
```

whereas

```
100error:   x = y + z;  // Label must start with letter or _
error 100:  x = y + z;  // White space is not allowed.
```

are invalid.

Use of the goto is strongly discouraged in current programming practice, since it makes the flow of control very difficult to follow and in general its use indicates poor program design. In the example given previously, a break statement, together with an extra condition added to the first two controlling expressions, has the same effect:

```
const double max_error = 0.00001;
for (i = 0; i < 100 && delta_x >= max_error; ++i) {
    for (j = 0; j < 100 && delta_x >= max_error; ++j) {
```

```
for (k = 0; k < 100; ++k) {
    // Some code.
    if (delta_x < max_error)
        break;
    // Perhaps more code.
  }
 }
}
```

However, there is clearly a trade-off between writing elegant structured code and using the more efficient goto.

4.9   Comma Operator

The *comma* operator can be used to separate a sequence of two or more expressions. The expressions are evaluated from left to right, with the result of each evaluation being discarded before the next expression is evaluated. The main use of the comma operator is in for statements, as in:

```
for (i = 0, j = 0, x = 0.0; i < 10 && j < 10; ++i, ++j)
    x = x * i + j;
```

In this example, the initialization is equivalent to:

```
i = 0;
j = 0;
x = 0.0;
```

and the end of each pass through the loop amounts to:

```
++i;
++j;
```

The type and value of a series of expressions, separated by comma operators, are those of the right-most expression, although these facts are rarely significant. It is clearly possible to use the comma operator to overburden the control part of the for statement with expressions. However, it is a good idea to restrict the comma operator to expressions closely related to loop control. Although the following is valid code, it is not regarded as good style:[6]

```
root=sqrt(b*b-4.0*a*c), x1=0.5*(root-b)/a, x2=-0.5*(root+b)/a;
```

Spurious comma operators can give rise to errors which are hard to find. The statement:

---
[6]Hopefully, the reasons are obvious!

```
x = y, + 10;
```

is valid C++, whereas the programmer probably intended:

```
x = y + 10;
```

It is also worth pointing out that most commas appearing in C++ programs, such as in definition lists and function arguments, are separators rather than operators.

4.10 Null Statement[†]

A statement that does nothing is occasionally useful, often redundant and sometimes disastrous. The *null* statement is useful if the syntax requires a statement, but there is nothing to do, as in:

```
while (cin >> x, x > 0)
    ;           // Put the null statement on a separate line.
                // It makes our intention more obvious.
```

The null statement is often a mistake:

```
for (i = 0; i < 10; ++i) {
    x *= i;
    y += i;
};              // This semi-colon is a mistake, but does nothing.
```

Sometimes, as above, the null statement is harmless, but occasionally the result is a disaster, as in:[7]

```
while (i < 10);             // This loop never ends.
    sum += i++;
```

where the semi-colon on the first line is actually a null statement. Since nothing is evaluated in this `while` loop, once started it can never finish. A similar mistake can occur with the `if` statement:[8]

```
if (i == 0);               // This statement does nothing.
    x = initial_velocity;  // This statement is always
                           // executed.
```

Such mistakes are unlikely with compound statements, if a sensible layout style is followed.

---

[7]See Section 4.6.1.
[8]See Section 4.5.1.

4.11   Conditional Expression Operator

The conditional expression operator, ?:, is the only ternary operator defined in C++ and takes the form:

```
control ? result_1 : result_2
```

control is evaluated and, if non-zero, then the whole expression evaluates to result_1, otherwise it evaluates to result_2. For instance, in the statement:

```
max = (i > j) ? i : j;
```

if i is greater than j, then i is assigned to max, otherwise j is assigned. This is equivalent to:

```
if (i > j)
    max = i;
else
    max = j;
```

which some programmers may prefer. However, the conditional expression operator produces terse code and often avoids introducing a temporary variable:

```
cout << "Max. pressure = " << (p1 > p2 ? p1 : p2);
```

Notice that the parentheses are necessary because the precedence of << is higher than the conditional expression operator. (See Appendix C.)

Exercise:

Write a program which prompts for pairs of floating point numbers and uses the conditional expression operator to send 1 to the output stream if $x^2 + y^2 \leq 1$ and 0 otherwise.

4.12   Order of Evaluation of Operands

The order of evaluation of operands is undefined for most operators. As mentioned in the previous chapter, the value of k in the expression:

```
k = ++i + i;
```

is dependent on the particular C++ compiler because either operand of the binary + operator may be evaluated first. Since we have now met the only four operators which are exceptions to this rule, it is worth summarizing them here. In each case the operands are evaluated left to right:[9]

---

[9]Do not confuse the order of evaluation of operands with the precedence of operators. The former concerns the order in which the operands of *one* operator are evaluated, whereas the latter determines the order in which *several* operators are applied.

- The logical AND operator, &&, does not evaluate the right operand if the left one evaluates to zero (FALSE).

- The logical OR operator, ||, does not evaluate the right operand if the left one evaluates to one (TRUE).

- Only one of the second and third operands of the (ternary) conditional expression operator is evaluated, as detailed in the previous section.

- The left operand of the comma operator is evaluated before the right operand.

In the first two cases one of the operands *may* not be evaluated; in the third case one of the operands is *certainly* not evaluated and in the fourth case both operands are *always* evaluated.

4.13 The Preprocessor

In addition to the control statements that are recognized by the C++ compiler, there is a control structure associated with the C++ *preprocessor*. Before a program is compiled, it is passed through a utility known as a preprocessor.[10] This is capable of performing various transformations on a C++ program, but it knows nothing about the syntax of the language and simply makes textual changes as directed. The preprocessor *directives*, or commands, are denoted by a # as the first non-blank character in a line and this # is followed by a directive. Blanks and horizontal tabs can precede the directive as well as the #, but more than one directive on the same line is not permitted. The # is a preprocessor operator.[11]

There are many preprocessor directives; the complete list is:

```
#define  #else    #elif    #endif  #error  #if
#ifdef   #ifndef  #include #line   #undef  #pragma
```

However, not all of these directives will be described in detail; the two most important ones are #define and #include. The #if, #elif, #else and #end are also common. Some of the other directives are introduced later; when they are needed.

---

[10]A single command usually invokes the preprocessor, compiler and linker, with special compiler options being used in order to omit any of these stages.

[11]There is another preprocessor operator, ##, which is used for concatenation but is not considered in this book. This operator can be used to implement class templates for those compilers that do not do so directly. (Class templates are described in Appendix A.)

4.13.1   include **Directive**

The include directive takes the form:

```
#include <filename>
```

or

```
#include "filename"
```

Both forms of the directive cause the line containing the directive to be replaced by the entire contents of the named file. Exactly how the search for the file is carried out is dependent on the C++ compiler. All that can be stated with certainty is that if a search specified by the second form fails, then another search is carried out as if the first form had been given. Usually directives of the first form are used for system files and the search is carried out in a standard place, as in

```
#include <math.h>        // Declarations for
                         //     maths functions.
#include <string.h>      // Declarations for string
                         //     and memory functions.
#include <float.h>       // Definitions of constants
                         //     for floating types.
```

The second form generally means that the search is initially carried out in the directory of the source file and is the method by which user-defined files are included:

```
#include "my_program.h"
```

Such files, which are often called *include files*, are particularly useful for large programs which are split up into separately compiled files, otherwise known as *modules*. Consistency, throughout the modules, of any constants and function declarations can be ensured by each module using the same include file. Include files that are used like this are called *header files*. Those system provided header files which are common with the C language have a .h extension, while those peculiar to C++ may either have a .h extension or something similar, such as .hpp. There is no restriction on user-defined file extensions, but it is advisable to conform to the accepted conventions, as this helps to identify how a file is to be used.

4.13.2   define **Directive**[†]

We mainly introduce the **define** directive because it is common in library header files that are shared with the C language, such as **<float.h>** and **<math.h>**. The **define** directive takes the form:

```
#define identifier tokens
```

and causes all subsequent occurrences of `identifier` to be replaced by `tokens`. This directive can be used to give global constants meaningful names, as in:

```
#define SPEED_OF_LIGHT 2.997925e8
```

It is traditional, but not obligatory, to use upper case letters for constants in order to distinguish them from variables. Notice that there is neither a semicolon (or statement terminator) nor an assignment operator. Such definitions have no run-time overhead and increase the readability of programs. However, it is actually preferable to use the `const` specifier, together with an initialization, as in:

```
const double SPEED_OF_LIGHT = 2.997925e8;
```

With the `const` specifier there is again no run-time overhead, but this technique has the advantage of type-checking and scoping.

The define directive can also take the form:

```
#define identifier(identifier, ...., identifier) token_string
```

with no space between the first identifier and the opening parenthesis. Such use of the define directive is a *macro definition*; that is, it acts like a function, but without the associated call overhead. The preprocessor searches subsequent lines for occurrences of the first identifier and substitutes `token_string`, with the identifiers in parentheses replaced by actual arguments. An example should make this clear. If we have

```
#define SQUARE(X) ((X) * (X))
```

then a subsequent statement of the form:

```
y = SQUARE(4.0);
```

is expanded to

```
y = ((4.0) * (4.0));    // Equivalent to y = 4.0 * 4.0;
```

The apparently excessive use of parentheses is because macros perform purely textual substitutions and, without these parentheses, unexpected expansions may take place. For instance:

```
#define SQUARE(X) (X * X)
y = SQUARE(u + v);
```

is equivalent to:

```
y = u + v * u + v;
```

which is very different from:

```
y = (u + v) * (u + v);
```

If necessary, any preprocessor directive can be continued to the next line by a
\, followed immediately by a carriage return. It is therefore possible to write quite
complicated macros which are many lines long. However, we do not pursue the
topic of macros further; in C++ it is possible to define `inline` functions, which
can be inserted directly into the code by the compiler. Such functions have the
same advantages as macros, but are also type-checked and have no possibility of
unexpected expansions. Inline functions will be discussed in detail in Chapter 5.

4.13.3   Conditional Compilation[†]

It is often convenient to be able to have two versions of the same program; for
instance there might be a test version, which gives diagnostic messages, and
a production version, which omits such messages. Simultaneously maintaining
more than one version of the same program is not easy; it is much better to be
able to compile the same program in different ways. Such conditional compilation
can be achieved by means of the following sequence of directives:

```
#if condition_1
    // First code segment goes here.
#elif condition_2
    // Second code segment goes here.
#else
    // Third code segment goes here.
#endif
```

The interpretation of these directives is similar to the `if else` statement given in
Section 4.5.2. The constant expression, `condition_1`, following the `if` directive
is checked to determine whether it evaluates to zero; if it does not then the
first code segment is included. If `condition_1` does evaluate to zero, then the
constant expression following the `elif` (else if) directive is evaluated and, if it is
non-zero, the second code segment is included. If all of the constant expressions
are zero, then none of the code is included. The `endif` directive signifies the end
of a sequence of conditional directives, although there may be many sequences in
one program. In a given sequence there cannot be more than one `else` directive
(there may be none), although there may be any number (including zero) of `elif`
directives. There are some restrictions on the constant expressions; they must
evaluate to an integral type and cannot contain a cast, `sizeof()` or enumeration
constant.

So far we have not really considered programs of sufficient length to justify the use of conditional compilation, but as an example we might rewrite our quadratic equation solver of Section 1.2:

```
// Solves the quadratic equation:   a * x * x + b * x + c = 0

#include <iostream.hpp>
#include <math.h>

#define TEST 1

int main()
{
    double root1, root2, a, b, c, root;

    cout << "Enter the coefficients a, b, c: ";
    cin >> a >> b >> c;
#if TEST
    double temp = b * b - 4.0 * a * c;
    cout << "temp = " << temp << "\n";
    root = sqrt(temp);
    cout << "square root of temp = " << sqrt(temp) << "\n";
#else    // TEST
    root = sqrt(b * b - 4.0 * a * c);
#endif   // TEST
    root1 = 0.5 * (root - b) / a;
    root2 = - 0.5 * (root + b) / a;
    cout << "The solutions are " << root1 << " and " <<
        root2 << "\n";

    return(0);
}
```

The test version of this program could be used to discover why incorrect results are obtained for certain values of a, b, c. Because the preprocessor merely makes textual changes, this is a situation where it is essential to use **#define** rather than the **const** specifier:

```
const int TRUE = 1;      // Not useful for preprocessing.
```

Notice that it is useful to include comments to indicate which **#if** directive goes with each **#else** or **#endif**. Moreover, it is worth trying to keep conditional compilation simple since the *dangling else* trap is always awaiting the careless programmer.

In Section 2.2 we mentioned that the `/*  */` style of comments cannot be used to comment out segments of code that already contain such comments. The `#if` directive provides a solution to this problem. If we surround the unwanted code with `#if 0` and `#endif`, as in:

```
#if 0
for (int i = 1; i < 10; ++i) {
    sum_1 +== i;
    sum_2 += i * i;
}                      // O.K. so far.
double i = 10.0;    /* WRONG: the i of type int is still
                       in scope. This is a redefinition. */
#endif  // 0
```

then it is excluded by the preprocessor.

4.14   Enumerations[†]

An *enumeration* is a distinct integral type with a set of named constants. The constants are named by means of an enumeration declaration, which is a list of the constants following the keyword, `enum`, as in:

```
enum day {Sunday, Monday, Tuesday, Wednesday, Thursday,
    Friday, Saturday};
```

In this example, `day` is the enumeration type and `Sunday` has the value 0, `Monday` has the value 1 etc. An individual member of the list (such as `Tuesday`) is known as an *enumerator*. Enumerations are a way of giving meaningful names to integral constants and are a useful alternative to the `#define` directive, which merely performs a textual substitution. An enumeration has the advantage of compiler checking. It is also easy to generate numerical values by using an enumeration; the above example does not explicitly specify any values, in contrast to:

```
#define Sunday  0
#define Monday  1
#define Tuesday 3
// etc.
```

Identifiers in an enumeration list can be assigned a particular value, in which case subsequent identifiers increase by one, going from left to right. In the enumeration:

```
enum traffic_light {red = 1, amber, green};
```

`amber` and `green` have the values 2 and 3 respectively.

It is also possible for two or more enumerators to have the same numerical value, as in:

```
enum day {Saturday, Sunday = 0, Monday, Tuesday, Wednesday,
    Thursday, Friday};
```

An equivalent but preferable technique is to use the statement:

```
enum day {Sunday, Monday, Tuesday, Wednesday, Thursday,
    Friday, Saturday = Sunday};
```

In both cases, Saturday and Sunday have the value 0 and Monday, Tuesday, Wednesday, ... have the values 1, 2, 3, ...

Enumerators, the enumeration type and ordinary variables in the same scope must all be distinct. The following sequence of statements is incorrect:

```
enum colour {red, blue, green};
enum traffic_light {red, amber,
    green};            // WRONG: red, green redefined.
int colour;           // WRONG: colour redefined.
```

It is possible to define *enumeration variables*, as in:

```
day today;
// Put assignment to today here.
if (today == Monday)
    cout << "Today is Monday\n";
```

The only valid operation that is defined on an enumeration variable is assignment. For any other operation (such as equality in the above example) the enumeration variables and constants are converted to integers and an integer operation performed. This implies that operations, such as:

```
if (today == 1)
    cout << "Today is Monday\n";
```

are valid. But mixed operations, as in:

```
today++;        // WRONG!
today = 8;      // WRONG!
```

are not defined. It is always possible use a cast:

```
today = today + day(1);
today = day(8);
```

but such explicit casts defeat the purpose of an enumeration as a distinct integral type.

There is no need to actually provide a name for the enumeration. For example, the statement:

```
enum {red, green, blue} colour;
```

defines colour to be an enumeration variable which can take the values red, green or blue, but does not define an enumeration type. Of course, this syntax does not enable us to subsequently define more enumeration variables of the same type, although the original statement can define a list of such variables:

```
enum {red, green, blue} colour1, colour2;
```

It is even possible to omit both the enumeration type and the variable list, as in:

```
enum {FALSE, TRUE};
```

Exercise:

Define an enumeration for the months of the year. Given a month enumeration variable, what methods could you use to 'increment' it to the following month? Try out your ideas in a short program.

4.15   Summary

- The relational operators are: `<`, `<=`, `>`, `>=`. They are binary operators, returning zero if the relation is false and one if it is true.

- The negation operator, `!`, returns one if the operand is zero, otherwise the operator returns zero.

- The logical AND operator, `&&`, returns one if both operands are non-zero, otherwise the operator returns zero.

- The logical OR operator, `||`, returns zero if both operands are zero, otherwise the operator returns one.

- The equality operator, `==`, returns one if both operands are equal and zero otherwise.

- The not equal operator, `!=`, returns zero if both operands are equal and one otherwise.

- A compound statement, or block, is denoted by a pair of braces, `{ }`.

- There are three branch statements: `if`, `if else` and `switch`.

- Watch out for the *dangling else* trap.

- There are three iteration statements: `while`, `for` and `do`; use whichever is most natural for a particular problem.

- The `break` statement is used to exit from an iteration, whereas a `continue` statement causes control to pass to the next iteration.

- The comma operator separates a sequence of expressions and is mainly used in `for` statements.

- The conditional expression operator, `?:`, is the only ternary operator and is useful for writing compact code.

- Files can be included by using the `#include` preprocessor directive:

```
#include <filename>      // For system filenames.
#include "filename"      // For user-defined filenames.
```

- Constants can be given meaningful names by using the `#define` preprocessor directive:

```
#define SPEED_OF_LIGHT 2.997925e8
```

but the `const` specifier is a better alternative:

```
const double SPEED_OF_LIGHT = 2.997925e8;
```

- An enumeration declares a distinct integral type and can also give meaningful names to integral constants:

```
enum colour {red, green, blue};
```

4.16 Exercises

1. π can be calculated from the series:

$$\sum_{n=1}^{\infty} 1/k^4 = \pi^4/90.$$

Write a program which uses the first ten terms of this series to obtain an approximation for π. Compare your result with that given in a standard table of mathematical constants. Try increasing the number of terms in the series.

2. Why may the iterations in the following code segments never terminate?

   (a)   ```
          int sum = 1;
          for (unsigned i = 10; i >= 0; --i)
              sum *= 2 * i + 1;
          ```

   (b)    ```
          double i = 10, sum = 1;
          while (i != 0)
              sum *= 2 * i-- + 1;
          ```

   (c)   ```
          int i = 0;
          double sum = 1.0;
          while (1) {
              sum *= 2 * i++ + 1;
              if (i = 10)
                  break;
          }
          ```

3. Why doesn't the following program compile:

   ```
   #include <iostream.hpp>

   int main()
   {
       for (double sum = 1.0, int i = 1; i <= 10; ++i)
           sum *= 2 * i + 1;
       cout << "sum = " << sum;
       return 0;
   }
   ```

4. Consider the sequence of *integers*: $u_1, u_2, u_3, \ldots$, where $u_1 = 1, u_2 = 1$ and $u_n = u_{n-1} + u_{n-2}$ for $n \geq 3$. These integers constitute what is known as the Fibonacci sequence. Write a program which prompts for a positive integer, **n**, and lists the first **n** members of the sequence. Notice how u_n increases very rapidly with **n** and soon exceeds the largest integer that can be represented as a standard type on your computer.

   Verify your results by modifying the program to check that:

   (a) $u_1 + u_2 + \cdots + u_n = u_{n+2} - 1$

   (b) $u_n^2 - u_{n-1} u_{n+1} = (-1)^{n-1}$.

   (If you want to learn what all this has to do with rabbits and number theory, it is well worth consulting [12].)
   ```

5. If we define $f(x) \equiv x^n - c$, then solving $f(x) = 0$ is equivalent to finding $c^{1/n}$ for $n > 0$. Given an approximate value of x, the Newton-Raphson method consists of calculating a new approximation, x_{new}, by:[12]

$$x_{new} = x - \frac{f(x)}{f'(x)}.$$

In our case, this reduces to:

$$x_{new} = \frac{(n-1)x}{n} + \frac{c}{nx^{n-1}}.$$

Write a program to find $c^{1/n}$ for positive n and c. The program should prompt for n (as a positive integer), the initial value of x (as a positive double) and c (also a positive double). Incorrect entries should be trapped and a prompt for a new value issued. Use the above formula for x_{new} to iterate towards an approximate value of x and hence $c^{1/n}$. The program should terminate if the number of iterations exceeds a reasonable limit or the difference between two successive iterations is *small*. For instance, you might try a limit of twenty iterations and a limit close to the machine precision. Try different values of n and c, listing the approximations to the root.

6. A very naive way of numerically integrating a function in one dimension is the trapezoidal formula,[13] which splits the integration region into strips. The sum of the areas gives an approximation to the integral:

$$\int_{x_0}^{x_m} f(x)\, dx \approx h[f_0/2 + f_1 + \cdots + f_{m-1} + f_m/2]$$

where

$$h = (x_m - x_0)/m.$$

Write a program which uses the trapezoidal formula, with $m = 20$, to evaluate:

$$\int_0^{\pi} \sin x\, dx$$

and compare your result with the exact answer. Experiment with different values of m and also try to evaluate different integrals.

---

[12]See [17]

[13]For a description of better methods, again see [17].

Chapter 5

Functions

5.1   Introducing Functions

In the previous chapter we introduced the control structures of C++. Although these structures enable us to write very powerful programs, they do not give us a means of controlling this power, nor do they encourage reusable code. The introduction of functions is an essential first step in the writing of modular, maintainable and reusable code. In particular, testing can be carried out on each function in isolation, rather than on the whole program. This is important as the number of different pathways through even a modest program is often very large indeed. Functions provide a way of encapsulating relatively self-contained segments of code. A function typically carries out some well-defined action, such as returning a random number, performing numerical integration or inverting a matrix.

5.1.1   Defining and Calling Functions

In general, a function definition takes the form:

```
return_type function_name(type argument, ..., type argument)
{
    // function body
}
```

However, it is more instructive to start by considering a simple example:

```
int factorial(int n)     // calculates n*(n-1)*(n-2)*...*1
{
    int result = 1;
    if (n > 0) {
        do {
            result *= n;
```

```
        --n;
    } while (n > 1);
}
else if (n < 0) {
    cout << "Error in factorial function:\t" <<
        "argument = " << n << "\n";
}
return result;
}
```

This function calculates the factorial function ($n(n-1)\ldots 1$ or $n!$ in the usual mathematical notation) and its structure is shown in Figure 5.1. Notice that there

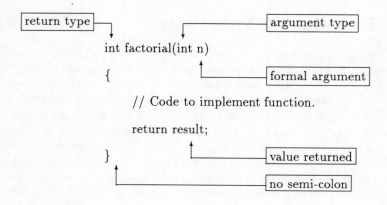

Figure 5.1: The structure of a typical function.

is no terminating semi-colon. The first line, sometimes known as the *function header*, declares that the function returns the type **int** and defines the name of the function to be **factorial**, which is the identifier used to invoke this particular function. The identifier, **n**, is known as a *formal argument* and is again declared to be of type **int**. A function can have any number of formal arguments, including zero, and these arguments can be a mixture of types. The arguments in a list are separated by commas. In this context the comma is a separator, rather than an operator (in contrast to Section 4.9).

The outermost set of braces contains what is known as the *function body*; it is here that we find all of the code that implements the function. The body of the function contains a **return** statement, which terminates the function. In this particular case the statement also causes a value to be returned to the calling environment. The value being returned can optionally be enclosed by parentheses, as in:

```
    return (result);
```

If the result of evaluating an expression is returned directly, parentheses can help to make the statement more readable; compare:

```
    return (a * a + b * b + c * c);
```

with:

```
    return a * a + b * b + c * c;
```

A function is called (*invoked* or *executed*) by including its name, together with appropriate arguments within parentheses, in a statement, as in:[1]

```
    sum = 0.0;
    for (i = 0; i < 10; ++i)
        sum += 1.0 / factorial(i);
```

The arguments to the function being called are known as *actual arguments*, distinguishing them from the formal arguments of the function definition. The identifiers used in both cases may or may not be the same; this has no significance since the values of the actual arguments are copied to the formal arguments. The scope of the formal arguments is limited to the function body and changes made to these arguments are not propagated back to the calling program. For instance, in the body of our factorial function, the formal argument, n, is decremented, but this has no effect on the actual argument, i. This process of copying the value of the actual argument to the formal argument is known as *pass by value*. Some languages, such as FORTRAN, use *pass by reference*, in which case any changes to a formal argument that are made by a function are indeed propagated back to the calling environment. As we will see in Chapter 7, C++ functions can also use pass by reference, but pass by value is the usual technique. The reason for this is that pass by value encourages more modular, safer code and helps to prevent unexpected changes in the value of variables.

Exercise:

Write a program which calculates an approximation to:

$$e = 1 + \frac{1}{1!} + \frac{1}{2!} + \frac{1}{3!} + \cdots$$

by invoking the `factorial()` function. (Remember that integer division truncates!)

It is worth pointing out that although function arguments can be expressions:

---

[1] The parentheses in the function call should be regarded as an operator.

```
int j = factorial(2 * i + 1);
```

the order of evaluation of expressions in argument lists is not defined. Therefore a function call of the form:

```
double x = too_clever_by_half(++i, (i+5));
```

is likely to give different results with different compilers.

5.1.2 Return Type

The return statement causes a function to terminate, but in many cases the statement also causes a value to be passed back to the calling environment. The type returned by a function must agree with that specified in the function header. Any attempt to return a type differing from that declared should be trapped by the compiler. However, implicit type conversions are allowed so the following return is valid:

```
double sum(int n)
{
    int result = 0;
    for (int i = 1; i <= n; ++i)
            result += i * i;
    return result;
}
```

In the above return statement, result is of type int and is converted to a double. But the following is not valid since the first return does not return a value:

```
double sum(int n)
{
    int result = 0;
    if (n < 0)
        return;                         // WRONG!
    for (int i = 1; i <= n; ++i)
            result += i * i;
    return result;
}
```

In this example the compiler prevents an arbitrary value being returned as an apparently valid result. We should, of course, replace the incorrect return statement by some action which recognizes that if n is less than zero then an error has occurred. Something should also be done to limit the consequences of the error; one possible course of action is suggested later in this chapter (in Section 5.8).

It is quite common for there to be no requirement for a function to return a value, in which case a special type, called `void`, should be used to specify the return type in the function header:

```
void print_welcome()
{
    cout << "Welcome to the interactive C++ tutorial\n" <<
        "There are twenty lessons which will take " <<
        "about half an hour each.\n";
    // And so on...
    return;      // This statement can be omitted.
}
```

If no value is returned by a function (as above) then the `return` statement at the end of the function body can be omitted.

If no function return type is specified, then it is taken to be `int`, rather than `void`:

```
print_welcome()
{
    cout << "Welcome to the interactive C++ tutorial\n";
    // etc.
    return;     // WRONG: should return an int.
}
```

However, it is a good idea to always specify the return type explicitly.

If a function has no arguments, then `void` may be used, as in:

```
int rand(void)
{
    // Generate a pseudo-random integer.
}
```

The use of `void` is preferable to empty parentheses, since it is emphasizes the programmer's intention that the function takes no arguments. Apart from this equivalence to an empty argument list, `void` cannot be used as an argument type, nor can an identifier of type `void` be declared:

```
int factorial(int n, void)   // WRONG: what would
                             // be the purpose?
{
    void empty;              // WRONG: cannot declare a
                             // variable to have type void.
                             // What would be the purpose?

    // Same function body
}
```

It is also invalid to have **void** as the operand of the **sizeof** operator.

Notice that even if a function takes no arguments, the calling program must use parentheses, as in:

```
print_welcome();
```

rather than:

```
print_welcome;        // This does nothing useful.
```

which does nothing useful.

5.1.3   Function Prototypes

A function can be declared without specifying how it is implemented:

```
int factorial(int n);
```

Such a statement is known as a *function prototype*. Notice that, unlike a function definition, a function prototype must end with a semi-colon and has no function body. A function with an empty body is *not* a prototype, but rather defines a function which does nothing:

```
int lazy_function(int n) { }
```

Any argument names given in the prototype are ignored by the compiler, but can be a useful documentation technique. For complicated programs, possibly involving use of the same functions in different modules, function prototypes considerably aid program maintenance and modularity. This is because the code implementing a function may be compiled independently to code using it. Such prototypes are often collected together in a header file and since a function is only known to the compiler after it has been declared, it makes sense to include the header file at the start of all files which either use functions or implement them. As we will see when we come to the specifically object-oriented aspects of C++, prototypes have a fundamental role to play in defining classes and therefore objects. In fact, C++ requires that all functions are either prototyped or else the definition is seen before each function is invoked.

5.1.4   Functions Cannot Declare Functions

In some languages, such as Pascal, it is possible to declare functions within other functions. It is important to realise that this feature is not available in C++. So a program to print out the first ten factorials is:

```cpp
#include <iostream.hpp>

int factorial(int n)
{
    int result = 1;
    if (n > 0) {
        do {
            result *= n;
            --n;
        } while (n > 1);
    }
    else if (n < 0) {
        cout << "Error in factorial function\t" <<
            "argument = " << n << "\n";
    }
    return result;
}

int main()
{
    for (int i = 0; i < 10; ++i)
        cout << i << "!  =  " << factorial(i) << "\n";
    return 0;
}
```

rather than:

```cpp
#include <iostream.hpp>

int main()
{
    int factorial(int n)      // WRONG: cannot declare here.
    {
        // Body of function as in previous example.
    }
    for (int i = 0; i < 10; ++i)
        cout << i << "!  =  " << factorial(i) << "\n";
    return 0;
}
```

Since every program must have a function called **main()** and a function cannot be defined inside another function, the general structure of a program is a list of function definitions. We might expect the relationship between the functions to look like a tree with the function **main()** as the root. Unfortunately programs can be much more complicated than this, being general graphs, complete with cycles. For some problems, functions are a very effective way of controlling complexity. However, for really complicated problems it becomes difficult to control the relationship between the functions and more powerful techniques are needed. It is by encapsulating related functions and the data they operate on into a single class, that C++ can bring some order to these more complicated problems. You are probably wondering why we don't go directly to these more powerful methods. There are really two reasons: firstly, there is no point in attacking a small problem with all the latest techniques; secondly, classes at their most fundamental level are partly built from functions and so we do need a good understanding of how to use functions before we can progress to object-oriented techniques.

5.1.5 Unused Arguments[†]

There is no requirement for all of the formal arguments in a function declaration to be used, in which case an identifier does not have to be specified:

```
void print_error(int)
{
    cout << "An error has occurred\n";
}
```

But notice that the function cannot be called without an argument, even though the argument is not used:

```
print_error(1);     // O.K.
print_error();      // WRONG: incorrect number of arguments.
```

Unused arguments may serve to reserve a place in the argument list for future use. For instance, in the previous example we might want to have a list of the various possible errors:

```
void print_error(int error_number)
{
    cout << "An error has occurred:\n";
    switch (error_number) {
        case 1:
            cout << "\tThe matrix is too large for " <<
                "the available memory.\n";
            break;
        case 2:
            cout << "\tThe matrix is singular.\n";
            break;
        case 3:
            cout <<"\tThe iteration is not converging.\n";
```

```
                        break;
                default:
                        cout << "\tUnknown error.\n";
                        break;
        }
        // Perhaps some code to handle the error.
}
```

An argument type without an identifier can also be useful when an argument has been made redundant by a changed function implementation, but the calling functions have not yet been brought up to date.

5.1.6 Default Arguments

A function declaration can specify expressions which are to be used as the default values for one or more arguments. For instance, if we define a function to return the area of a rectangle, with defaults for the height and width:

```
double rectangle(double height = 1.0, double width = 10.0)
{
        return height * width;
}
```

then we could make the following function calls:

```
area1 = rectangle();          // 1.0 * 10.0 = 10.0 is assigned.
area2 = rectangle(5.0);       // 5.0 * 10.0 = 50.0 is assigned.
area3 = rectangle(2.0, 3.0);  // 2.0 * 3.0 = 6.0 is assigned.
```

Notice that it is the trailing arguments that are assumed to be missing, which means that default arguments must be supplied right to left in the declaration. For instance, we can make the declaration:

```
double rectangle(double height, double width = 10.0);
```

but not:

```
// The following declaration is WRONG!
double rectangle(double height = 10.0, double width);
```

A default argument cannot be redefined by a subsequent declaration, not even to the same value. A common error is to give the same default arguments in a function definition, as in the corresponding prototype:

```
double rectangle(double height = 1.0, double width = 10.0);

// Perhaps some other code.

// The following function header is WRONG:
double rectangle(double height = 1.0, double width = 10.0)
{
    return height * width;
}
```

However, a subsequent declaration can introduce one or more additional default arguments:

```
double disc_area(double radius);

// Some other code.

double disc_area(double radius = 10.0)
{
    return PI * radius * radius;
}
```

Notice that default arguments *must* be provided for any arguments that are omitted in the function call:

```
double rectangle(double height, double width = 10.0)
{
    return height * width;
}

int main()
{
    double rect1 = rectangle(5.0);   // Correct.
                                     // Default width = 10.0
    double rect2 = rectangle();       // WRONG: insufficient
                                     // function arguments.
    // More code.
}
```

Since default arguments do not need to be named in a function prototype, we could use the following for the rectangle function:

```
double rectangle(double, double = 10.0);
```

However, omitting argument names it not a good idea since they are far too valuable as a method of self-documenting code. Also, notice the distinction between prototypes and definitions; names cannot be omittted from function definitions, even if they do have default arguments:

```
double rectangle(double height, double = 10.0)       // WRONG!
{
     return height * width;           // Where is width defined?
}
```

Since default argument values are a feature of the function interface, rather than the implementation, it is normal practice to put the defaults in the header (`.hpp`) file rather than the source (`.cpp`) file.

> **Exercise:** Implement and test a function which has the base and height of a triangle as arguments and returns the area. If the function is called with a single argument, then the value of the base should default to 1.0. In the case of no arguments, the function should return a result of 1.0.

5.1.7 Ignoring the Return Value

The calling function can ignore the value returned by a function. For instance, some libraries include a function to create a file system directory. In general it is important to know whether a directory is successfully created or not, so such a function should return an integer to indicate success (usually zero) or failure (non-zero). A program might contain the following:

```
int status = mkdir("test"); // Creates directory called test.
if (status)
     cout << "Failed to create directory 'test'.\n";
else
     cout << "Directory 'test' created.\n";
```

However, we may be willing to ignore the risk that the directory creation could fail and to simply use:

```
mkdir ("test");       // Return status is ignored.
```

In general it is wise to program defensively; assume that anything which may fail is worth testing, at least in the development phase.

5.2   Recursion

A function can call another function, as in:

```
double binomial_coef(int n, int k)
// calculates binomial coefficient:   n!/(k! (n-k)!)
{
    return factorial(n) / double(factorial(k) *
        factorial(n - k));
}
```

(The cast to `double` in this function is necessary to force floating point rather than integer division; otherwise integer truncation would occur.)

A function can also call itself; this is known as *recursion*. For example, we could rewrite our factorial function as:

```
int factorial(int n)
{
    int result;
    if (n == 1 || n == 0)
        result = 1;
    else if (n < 0)
        cout << "Error in factorial function:  " <<
            "argument = " << n << "\n";
    else
        result = n * factorial(n - 1);
    return result;
}
```

A recursive function invariably follows the same pattern; it has a base case and always calls itself. In this example the base case occurs when n is one or zero; the function then returns without calling itself. When the function does call itself, then the value of the argument is different and must in some sense be changing in the direction of the base case. Care should be taken to trap any possible call errors (such as n less than zero in this example) otherwise the function may call itself for ever. It is also possible to have a set of mutually recursive functions, but the general ideas are the same.

Recursion should be used with care; it is sometimes a very effective way of solving problems which are otherwise difficult. However, every use of a function carries a call overhead and if the recursion depth is large and little calculation is done on each call, then recursion can be very inefficient. Another disadvantage is that each function call makes temporary use of a fixed quantity of memory, known as the stack.[2] If the depth of a recursive function call is large, it is possible to use up all of this memory, in which case the program may stop with a 'STACK OVERFLOW' message. However, if the compiler does not enforce stack checking by default (or an option is set to disable it) the stack will overflow without

---

[2]We will describe stacks in more detail in Section 10.4.1.

warning. Memory belonging to other parts of the program, or even the operating system, may be overwritten and the results will probably be disastrous. The compiler/linker may have an option to increase the amount of memory allocated to the stack, but if the recursion depth is unknown it is difficult to anticipate how much memory is needed.

Exercise:

Implement a function, with the prototype:

```
double u(int n);
```

to recursively generate the Fibonacci sequence defined in Exercise 4 of Chapter 4. Check that the results given by the two exercises are consistent.

5.3 Inline Functions

It is often desirable to write short functions in order to improve the readability of a program, but the call overhead may not justify the use of a function definition. In such cases it is possible to define *inline* functions by means of the `inline` keyword:

```
inline int min(int i, int j)
{
    return((i < j) ? i : j);
}    // Returns the minimum of i and j.
```

The `inline` keyword is a suggestion to the compiler that the body of the function should be substituted directly in the code, instead of the program making a run-time function call. The suggestion may be ignored and probably will be if the function is complicated. A recursive function could be declared `inline`, but even a simple function would not be completely expanded, since the recursion depth is not known at compile-time.

Inline functions usually (but not always) increase the size of the generated code and decrease the execution time. For most functions, the call overhead is insignificant compared with the time taken to execute the body of the function and these functions should not be declared inline. In general it is only very short functions, consisting of one or two statements, that are worth declaring inline. Such functions are common when implementing the data hiding techniques associated with classes, as described in Chapter 8.

Functions declared `inline` should be *defined* in a header file, rather than a `.cpp` file, since the definition (in contrast to the declaration) must be seen before

every use of the function. This is particularly important when a program is split
into separately compiled files (modules) as each file using an `inline` function
needs the definition and files `#include` the `.hpp` (not the `.cpp`) file.

Exercise:

Try changing some of your previous programs to declare `inline` functions (for example, any programs using the `factorial()` function).

5.4   More on Scope Rules

Now that we have introduced functions, it is worth considering the concept of
scope in more detail. There are three kinds of scope: local, class and file. Classes
will not be introduced until Chapter 8, but any member of a class has class scope.

A variable defined within a function has *local scope* and each function has
a distinct scope. Such variables hide definitions made outside. (In fact, as we
noted in Section 4.4, the same is true of any block.) For instance, suppose we
define a function to calculate the sum of the squares of the first n integers and
that this function is called from `main()`:

```
#include <iostream.hpp>

int sum(int n)
{
    int i, result = 0;
    for (i = 1; i <= n; ++i)
        result += i * i;
    return result;
}

int main()
{
    for (int i = 1; i <= 10; ++i)
        cout << "sum of the first " << i << " squares is " <<
            sum(i) << "\n";
    return 0;
}
```

The declarations of i in the two functions are hidden from each other; this is true
whatever the relative positions of the functions within a single file.

Reuse of the same identifier in different scopes in the same file should be done
with some restraint as it can lead to programs that are very difficult to read.
The reuse of nondescript identifiers such as i (which may typically be used as a

generic loop counter) is quite acceptable. But consider a file using square matrices which contains an identifier called `matrix_size`. In one function it could mean the number of rows (or columns) of a matrix; in another, the total number of elements in a matrix and in a third, the total number of bytes needed to store a matrix. The possibility of errors would be greatly reduced if we used three different and more descriptive identifiers.

Any object not having local or class scope has *file* (or *global*) *scope* and is visible throughout the file. This visibility is both useful and dangerous, which means that global variables should be kept to a minimum. Since any function has access to a variable with file scope, it is well worth using the **const** specifier if at all possible. A simple example of file scope is:

```
#include <iostream.hpp>

const int i_max = 10;          // i_max has file scope.

int main()
{
    int sum = 0.0;
    for (int i = 1; i <= i_max; ++i) {
        sum += i;
        cout << "sum of the first " << i <<
            " numbers is " << sum << "\n";
    }
    return 0;
}
```

5.5 Storage Classes auto and static[†]

In the following simple function:

```
int sum(int n)
{
    int i, result = 0;
    for (i = 1; i <= n; ++i)
        result += i * i;
    return result;
}
```

the variables `i`, `result` and `n` are all *automatic*. That is each time control passes to the body of this function, memory is allocated for these variables and deallocated when control leaves the function. There is no guarantee that the same memory will be allocated each time control passes to the function body and that the memory won't be used to store something else when control passes elsewhere. All local initializations are performed each time control passes to a block; in this example result is set to zero each time the function is invoked. If no explicit initialization is performed, then the value of an automatic variable is initially arbitrary:

```
int sum(int n)
{
    int i, result;
    for (i = 1; i <= n; ++i)
        result += i * i;
    return result;              // WRONG: result is arbitrary.
}
```

Identifiers that are local to a block (which includes a function body of course) have automatic storage by default; for this reason you will rarely, if ever, see the keyword auto, even though most variables in a program are usually automatic:

```
auto int i; // Rarely seen.
```

Sometimes it is convenient to have a variable which retains its value when control leaves the block where the variable is defined; this can be achieved by declaring the storage class to be static:

```
int sum(int n)
{
    static int grand_total;     // Implicitly
                                // initialized to zero.
    int i, result = 0;
    for (i = 1; i <= n; ++i)
        result += i * i;
    grand_total += result;
    cout << "Total so far = " << grand_total << "\t";
    return result;
}
```

In this example, the static variable, grand_total, accumulates the values returned by sum(). A static variable retains its value even when it goes out of scope. By default, grand_total is initialized to zero, but the initialization is only performed once. Any explicit initialization is also only performed once, so in the following example grand_total correctly accumulates the values returned by sum:

```
int sum(int n)
{
```

```
    static int grand_total = 0;      // Initialized once.
    int i, result = 0;
    for (i = 1; i <= n; ++i)
        result += i * i;
    grand_total += result;
    cout << "Total so far = " << grand_total << "\t";
    return result;
}
```

An initializer for a `static` variable does *not* need to be a constant expression and can involve any previously declared variables and functions:

```
static int grand_total = total_for_last_week *
    weighting_factor(current_week);
```

It is a good idea to keep such initializers simple since the order in which initializations are performed may not be obvious; a local `static` variable is initialized when the function is first invoked and a `static` variable with file scope is initialized before any functions or objects are used.

Global variables (that is variables having file scope) have `static` storage by default and are therefore initialized to zero, unless an explicit initializer is given:[3]

```
#include <iostream.hpp>
int grand_total;     // Static variable, initialized to zero.

int sum(int n)
{
    int i, result = 0;
    for (i = 1; i <= n; ++i)
        result += i * i;
    grand_total += result;
    return result;
}

int main()
{
    for (int i = 1; i <= 10; ++i)
        cout << "sum of the first " << i << " squares is " <<
            sum(i) << "\n";
    cout << "The sum of the sum of the first 10 squares " <<
        "is " << grand_total << "\n";
```

---

[3]The keyword, `static`, has several distinct meanings. More details are given in Section 8.16.1.

```
        return 0;
}
```

Exercise:

Why is the use of `grand_total` in the above program considered to be bad style? How could you improve the program?

5.6   Overloading Function Names

In C++ it is possible to use the same function name for functions that actually have different function bodies. This is known as *function overloading*. The functions must be distinguished by having different numbers of arguments or different argument types, such as:

```
double norm(double a, double b, double c)
{
    return sqrt(a * a + b * b + c * c);
}           // Returns the norm of a 3-dimensional vector.

double norm(double a, double b)
{
    return sqrt(a * a + b * b);
}           // Returns the norm of a 2-dimensional vector.

float norm(float a, float b)
{
    return (a * a + b * b);
}           // Correct but confusing. See below.
```

but not:

```
float norm(double a, double b, double c)     // WRONG!
{
    return (a * a + b * b + c * c);
}
```

The fourth function does not correctly overload the first, since functions must be distinguished by their argument types and not by their **return** types. The third function is correct, but confusing; the square root has been omitted and therefore what the function actually does is different from the first two examples. Remember that floating constants are of type **double** by default, so we might typically have the following (distinct) function calls:

```
double norm2 = norm(3.0, 4.0);          // Assigns 5.0
double norm3 = norm(3.0f, 4.0f);        // Assigns 25.0
```

It is clearly possible to write very confusing code by overloading the same function name with functions that perform completely different actions. However, there are circumstances in which overloaded functions are very useful. For instance we might want to have both `float` and `double` versions of the mathematical functions, such as sine, cosine, square root etc. The `float` version would be used where speed is more important than accuracy. We could then have function prototypes of the form:

```
float log(float x);
double log(double x);
float sin(float x);
double sin(double x);
```

Typically these functions are approximated by power series expansions and the `float` version would use fewer terms in the series.

Exercise:

Implement overloaded functions to calculate an approximation to:

$$e^x = \sum_{n=0}^{\infty} \frac{x}{n!}$$

One version should have an argument and return type of `double` and a second version should use the `float` type. The number of terms used in each function should be appropriate for the type. Test the functions either against the library function, `exp()`, which is prototyped in `<math.h>`, or by calculating $e^x e^{-x} - 1$. Check that the test program really does invoke the two different functions.

Ambiguity Resolution[††]

The rules used by a C++ compiler to resolve which overloaded function is invoked by a particular function call are quite complicated. The resolution is done entirely by comparing the type of each argument in the function call with the corresponding argument in the function prototypes that have the same function name. Functions with default arguments can be considered as a set of overloaded functions, so that:

```
double rectangle(double height = 1.0, double width = 10.0);
```

is equivalent to:

```
double rectangle(double, double);
double rectangle(double);
double rectangle(void);
```

The compiler constructs the *intersection* of the sets of functions that 'best' match each argument (that is the match is done on an argument by argument basis). In order that the function overloading is resolved, this intersection must have one (and only one) member. It is the interpretation of the adjective, 'best', which gives rise to some complication. A full description of the rules is given in [2], but briefly, the fewer promotions and conversions that are needed to achieve a match, the better. As a very simple example, suppose we have the following function prototypes:

```
void f(float x);
void f(double x);
```

Then the statement:

```
f(2.0f);
```

invokes the first, rather than the second function; there is an exact match for the first function whereas the second requires a promotion from `float` to `double`.

5.7   Function `main()`

We first encountered the function `main()` in Chapter 1, but now that we have introduced the general features of functions it is worth making some further comments. As far as the user is concerned, this function is where the program actually starts. There are some restrictions on what we can do with `main()`; in particular `main()` cannot be declared inline, cannot be overloaded and cannot call itself. Every C++ program must have one and only one function called `main()`. The body of `main()` is entirely defined by the programmer, but the function prototype (including the return type) depends on the compiler. Usually a definition of the form:

```
int main()
{
    // code
}
```

is allowed, where the return value is used to indicate the termination status of the program.

There is a second form of `main()`, involving function arguments, which is considered in Chapter 7.

5.8   Standard Library

Many numerical application programs make frequent use of mathematical functions, such as sine, cosine, square root etc. These functions are not part of the C++ language, but are provided in a standard library. This library usually contains all of the functions specified for the ANSI C standard, together with some others, which are more hardware dependent, and the C++ streams library. The available functions extend far beyond the obvious mathematical ones and it is not intended to describe the functions in any detail; entire books have been written on the ANSI C standard library. Rather, a brief description of what is available is given, in order to encourage you to look through the function manual for your own system and to indicate the extent of the library. Some of the functions will be introduced during the course of this book.

All library functions require the inclusion of a header file, which typically contains function prototypes, constant definitions and macros. The header is normally included near the top of the file in which the function is used:

```
#include <math.h>            // for sqrt()
#include <stdlib.h>          // for EXIT_SUCCESS
#include <iostream.hpp>

int main()
{
    for (int i = 1; i <= 20; ++i) {
        cout << "square root of " << i << " is " <<
            sqrt(double(i)) << "\n";
    }
    return(EXIT_SUCCESS);
}
```

In this example `<math.h>` is required for the `sqrt()` function and `<stdlib.h>` is required for the definition of the `EXIT_SUCCESS` constant. This constant is used to tell the operating system that the program has terminated normally, whereas `EXIT_FAILURE` indicates that an error has occurred. Rather than returning 0 or 1, it is more meaningful, as well as being less system dependent, to use named global constants (such as `EXIT_SUCCESS` and `EXIT_FAILURE`).

As a further example, `<stdlib.h>` also contains a prototype for the `exit()` function, which terminates a program and returns control to the operating system, after doing any necessary tidying up (flushing output buffers etc.). The `exit()` function takes an `int` argument which can be used to indicate how a program has terminated. By convention, either `EXIT_SUCCESS` or `EXIT_FAILURE` is used for this argument.

We can use `exit()` to improve our `factorial()` function:

```cpp
#include <stdlib.h>            // for exit()

int factorial(int n)           // calculates n*(n-1)*...*1
{
    int result=1;
    if (n > 0) {
        do {
            result *= n;
            --n;
        } while (n > 1);
    }
    else if (n < 0) {
        cout << "Error in factorial function:  " <<
            "argument = " << n << "\n";
        exit(EXIT_FAILURE);
    }
    return result;
}
```

Now if we call the `factorial` function with a negative argument, the program terminates cleanly, rather than continuing an invalid calculation.

The `exit()` function can likewise be used to improve our function to sum squares in Section 5.4:

```cpp
#include <stdlib.h>            // for exit()

double sum(int n)
{
    int result = 0;
    if (n < 0) {
        cout << "Error: sum(n) called with n = " <<
            n << "\n";
        exit(EXIT_FAILURE);
    }
    for (int i = 1; i <= n; ++i)
        result += i * i;
    return result;
}
```

This modified function terminates the program if we call `sum()` with a negative argument since there would not be much purpose in continuing with an invalid return value.

The same header file is often required for different but related functions in the standard library; for instance `<math.h>` is needed for the trigonometric, hyperbolic, square root, logarithmic and many other such functions. For this reason it is convenient to group the functions by their header files. The more useful groups of standard functions are briefly described below.

ctype.h These functions are for character manipulation. There are functions to determine whether a character is upper or lower case, a digit, a letter etc. and to convert between upper and lower case.

float.h This file contains definitions of constants which give the compiler dependent limits of the floating point types.

limits.h This file contains definitions of constants which give the compiler dependent limits of the integer types.

math.h Here are all of the mathematical functions that are provided by the standard library, including trigonometric, hyperbolic, logarithmic and exponential functions.

stddef.h This file defines some commonly used types. Our main use of this header file is for the definition of `size_t`, which is the type returned by the `sizeof` operator.

stdio.h Although this file is relevant for buffered input and output functions, of which there are many, we make use of the streams library since it provides object-oriented techniques.

stdlib.h Here are defined a few types, such as `size_t` (which is also defined in `<stddef.h>`) and prototypes of many commonly used functions, such as `exit()`, `rand()` (an integer random number generator), `system()` (to call a system function) etc.

string.h The prototypes for many useful functions which manipulate strings and memory are contained here. These functions can copy, concatenate, compare and determine the length of strings. They can also copy, compare and search areas of memory.

time.h The functions associated with this header are all connected with time and, apart from returning the current time, can be used to suspend a process for a specified period.

All the above groups of functions are directly taken over from C in order to provide compatibility. C++ is itself an excellent language for writing library functions. There are many commercially available libraries, some of which are really application packages,[4] but there are not yet any standard C++ libraries apart from the I/O streams library. This library provides a comprehensive set of input and output facilities, of which we have already used a small selection, and is described in more detail in Chapter 12.

---

[4]A description of useful packages for scientists and engineers is contained in [9].

Exercise:

What mathematical functions are prototyped in `<math.h>` on your system? Write a program which evaluates:

$$\cosh^2 x - \sinh^2 x - 1$$

for 1,000 different values of x. Explain any unexpected results.

5.9   Using Functions

Now that we have introduced functions in some detail, we can use them to write more interesting programs, rather than just having the single function called `main()`.

5.9.1   A Benchmark

There have been a large number of attempts to find programs, commonly called *benchmarks*, which can be used to compare the performance of different computers. One of these programs, called the Savage benchmark (after its author[5]), tests the speed and accuracy of the common mathematical functions. A version of the test is given below and you should try it on whatever systems you have access to.

```
// The Savage benchmark: tests the speed and accuracy
// of some common mathematical functions.
#include <iostream.hpp> // for cout
#include <math.h>        // for tan(), atan(), exp(),
                         // log(), sqrt()
#include <time.h>        // for clock(), CLOCKS_PER_SEC
#include <stdlib.h>      // for EXIT_SUCCESS

int main()
{
    double a = 1.0;
    clock_t start_time = clock();
    for (int i = 0; i < 2499; ++i)
        a = tan(atan(exp(log(sqrt(a * a))))) + 1.0;
    clock_t stop_time = clock();
    cout << "a = " << a << "\n";
    cout << "2500 - a = " << 2500.0 - a << "\n";
```

---

[5]See: B. Savage, Dr. Dobb's Journal, 120, September 1983.

```
        cout << "Time taken = " <<
            (stop_time - start_time) / CLOCKS_PER_SEC <<
            " secs.\n";
        return(EXIT_SUCCESS);
    }
```

The program starts with a simple comment about what it actually does. As far as possible code should be self-documenting through the use of well-chosen identifiers since too many comments are distracting. Of course, a balance should be kept between too few and too many comments, since either extreme can lead to unreadable code. Typical circumstances in which comments are useful are:

- giving references to books, algorithms and maintenance manuals:

  ```
  // See Press et al., Numerical Recipes in C, page 255.
  ```

- explaining the purpose of a function where the function name is insufficient:

  ```
  // Finds roots of a polynomial using Newton-Raphson.
  ```

- drawing attention to any compiler dependent or particularly tricky segment of code:

  ```
  // Assumes the int type is at least 32 bits.
  ```

The required header files follow the comment. These are all system supplied files so the names appear inside < > pairs. We have noted which of the constants and functions, prototyped in these files, are used in this program. It is not usual to include such comments, but you may find them helpful until you are familar with the contents of the standard library. Also, although the only requirement is that the `include` directive must appear before the associated functions or constants are first used, it is normal practice to collect all such directives at the start of the file.

In this program there are no user-declared functions; if there were, then the appropriate function definitions would be next.[6] Inside the body of `main()` we adopt the style of defining variables as they are first used. The type `clock_t` is defined in `<time.h>` and its use avoids needing to know the type returned by the `clock()` function for a particular compiler. Likewise, use of the `CLOCKS_PER_SEC` constant, to convert the result of `clock()` to seconds, hides compiler dependent details.

---

[6]If all functions are prototyped, no restriction is placed on the order in which functions are defined.

The program tests for speed and accuracy by making repeated calls to the tangent, inverse tangent, exponential, natural logarithm and square root functions. In fact, it is easy to show that the final result would be 2500 for infinite precision arithmetic. Notice how the function calls can be nested quite deeply.

Our final statement returns a *normal termination* flag. This may not be necessary on some systems, but others may actually care whether a program fails or not! Again, the EXIT_SUCCESS constant avoids having to know the numerical value of the flag.

5.9.2   Root Finding by Bisection.

A frequent requirement in numerical analysis is to find the roots of a function of a single real variable; specifically to solve

$$f(x) = 0$$

for x in the interval

$$x_1 \le x \le x_2$$

If $f(x_1)$ and $f(x_2)$ have opposite signs, then at least one zero or singularity must lie between these limits, as shown in Figure 5.2. The method of bisection

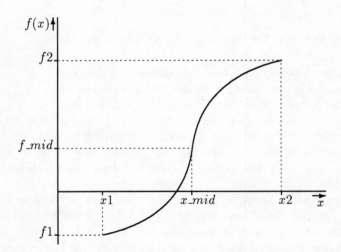

Figure 5.2: Root finding using bisection.

consists of finding the value of $f(x)$ at the mid-point of the interval. The segment of the interval for which $f(x)$ changes sign again brackets a zero (or singularity) and this interval can again be bisected. The procedure continues until the zero is known to be within a sufficiently small interval. What constitutes a sufficiently small interval can be quite subtle, but in the example below this stopping criterion is kept deliberately simple.[7]

A zero can be distinguished from a singularity by evaluating the function at the midpoint of this final interval. The method of bisection is not the fastest technique for finding a root, but it does have the advantage of simplicity.

Recursion is clearly a natural way to implement the bisection algorithm and this is done in the code listed below:

```cpp
#include <iostream.hpp>
#include <math.h>          // for exp(), pow(), cos()
#include <stdlib.h>        // for exit()

// Function prototypes:
double f(double x);
double root(double x1, double x2, double f1, double f2);
double find_root(double x1, double x2);

double f(double x)  // We want to find a root of f(x) = 0.
{
    return (exp(x) + pow(2.0, -x) + 2.0 * cos(x) - 6.0);
}

double root(double x1, double x2, double f1, double f2)
// Finds a root of f(x) = 0 using bisection.
// Assumes that x2 >= x1 and f1 * f2 < 0.0
{
    const int max_depth = 50;
    const double x_limit = 1e-5;
    static int depth;
    double estimated_root;
    double x_mid = 0.5 * (x1 + x2);
    if (x2 - x1 <= x_limit) {
            cout << "Root found at recursion depth = " <<
                depth << "\n";
            estimated_root = x_mid;
    }
    else if (++depth > max_depth) {
        cout << "WARNING: maximum limit of " << max_depth <<
            " bisections reached\n";
        estimated_root = x_mid;
    }
```

---

[7]A more detailed discussion is given in [17].

```cpp
        else {
            double f_mid = f(x_mid);
            if (f_mid == 0.0) {
                // Zero at x_mid.
                estimated_root = x_mid;
            }
            else if (f(x1) * f_mid < 0.0) {
                // Zero in first segment.
                estimated_root = root(x1, x_mid, f1, f_mid);
            }
            else {
                // Zero in second segment.
                estimated_root = root(x_mid, x2, f_mid, f2);
            }
        }
    return estimated_root;
}

double find_root(double x1, double x2)
{
    double f1 = f(x1);
    double f2 = f(x2);
    if (f1 * f2 > 0.0) {
        cout << "Error in find_root():  " <<
            "end-points have same sign\n";
        exit(EXIT_FAILURE);
    }
    if (x2 - x1 > 0.0)
        return root(x1, x2, f1, f2);
    else
        return root(x2, x1, f2, f1);
}

int main()
{
    double x;

    x = find_root(1.0, 2.0);
    cout << "Root is " << x << "\nf(x) at root = " <<
        f(x) << "\n";
    return(EXIT_SUCCESS);
}
```

The overhead incurred by using recursion for this algorithm is probably reasonable since for most functions the calculation will be dominated by the evaluations of `f(x)`.

In this example, we use bisection to search for a zero of $f(x)$, where

$$f(x) = e^x + 2^{-x} + 2\cos x - 6$$

in the range

$$1 \leq x \leq 2.$$

The function, $f(x)$, is implemented by the first function in our program. Three library functions are used, which are all prototyped in the file `<math.h>`. The `exp()` and `cos()` functions are self-explanatory; `pow(x,y)` returns x^y.

The analysis of the remainder of this program starts at the function `main()`. As usual `main()` is kept very simple and calls the function `find_root()`, which returns the calculated value of the root. This value is assigned to `x`.

The function, `find_root()`, takes as its arguments the interval limits and the maximum recursion depth. It would be useful if we could specify `f(x)` as a fourth argument to `find_root()`, in order to facilitate root finding for other functions. However, we must wait until Chapter 7 to learn how to do this.

Examining the body of `find_root()`, we see that the current depth is set to zero and the maximum recursion depth is set to the user-defined value. If `find_root` were called with only two arguments, then the maximum recursion depth would be set to a default value (in this case 100). The function, `find_root()` also checks that `f(x)` has opposite signs at the two end points.

The function `root()` has the prototype:

```
double root(double x1, double x2, double f1, double f2);
```

where `x1`, `x2` are the end-points of the interval and `f1`, `f2` are the corresponding values of `f(x)`. The implementation of `root()` assumes that `x2` is not less than `x1` and that `f1` and `f2` have opposite signs. Both of these assumptions are enforced by `find_root()`. The function, `root()`, first finds `x_mid`, the mid-point of the interval. If `(x2 - x1)` is less than the required accuracy, or the maximum recursion depth has been reached, then the value `x_mid` is returned. Next, `f_mid`, the value of `f(x)` at the mid-point, is evaluated. If `f_mid` is zero, a root has been found and `x_mid` is returned. Finally, if none of the previous cases has occurred, then the value of `root()` is returned for the segment of the interval which shows a sign change for `f(x)`. It is this call of the `root()` function which constitutes recursion.

It is worth pointing out that this program can only find the root of a single function since there is no way of resetting the value of `depth`. This restriction is removed in Section 7.5.

5.10   Summary

- A function definition implements the function:

```
double f(int n)
{
    // Code implementing function.
}
```

- Functions are executed (called or invoked) by statements such as:

```
x = f(m);
```

    or

```
f(m);
```

- If a function is declared to return a value it must do so:

```
double f(int n)
{
    // Code.
    return;              // WRONG!
}
```

- The order of evaluation of expressions in argument lists is not defined:

```
x = f(++i, (i + 5));    // Compiler dependent.
```

- A function prototype defines the function interface:

```
double f(int n);
```

- A function cannot be declared inside another function:

```
int main()
{
    int f(int n);              // WRONG!
    // Code.
}
```

- Functions can have default arguments, which are supplied right to left:

```
double rectangle(double height, double width = 10.0);
```

and can be called by either:

```
z = rectangle(x);
```

or

```
z = rectangle(x, y);
```

- Simple functions may be worth declaring inline:

```
inline int theta(int i)
{
    return((i > 0) ? 1 : 0);
}
```

- Function names can be overloaded:

```
float sqrt(float x);
double sqrt(double x);
```

- Consult the standard library; it may have the function you are about to write!

```
#include <math.h>
x = cosh(y);            // Returns hyperbolic cosine of y
```

5.11 Exercises

1. Using a suitable function from the standard library supplied with your system, write a program which measures how long it takes to evaluate the factorial function. Use various function arguments and compare the times for both the recursive and iterative versions of the function. It is worth using at least four byte integers for this example, since the factorial function grows rapidly with the magnitude of its argument.

2. Repeat the previous exercise for both recursive and iterative functions that sum the first n positive integers.

3. Write a function which converts degrees Celsius to degrees Fahrenheit and a second function which converts degrees Fahrenheit to Celsius. Both functions should take a `float` argument and return a `float`. They should also trap impossible values of the arguments.

   Check your functions by listing some temperatures using both scales. Also try one function with the other as its argument; do you get the original temperature?

4. Use the power series expansion:

$$\sin x = x - \frac{x^3}{3!} + \frac{x^5}{5!} - \frac{x^7}{7!} + \frac{x^9}{9!} - \cdots$$

   for $|x| < \infty$ to implement a *sine* function with the prototype:

   ```
   float sin(float x);
   ```

   (You should truncate the series and only consider arguments satisfying $|x| \le \pi/2$.)

   Compare the accuracy and time taken to evaluate `sin(x)` with the standard library function in `<math.h>` for $|x| \le \pi/2$. Make sure that you really do invoke the two overloaded `sin()` functions. (Beware of implicit conversions!)

   Try to make your version of `sin(x)` as accurate and efficient as possible. For instance:

   (a) Don't evaluate unnecessary terms in the power series.

   (b) Don't evaluate the factorials for every function call; use pre-calculated values for the inverses. In fact, for a truncated power series, more accurate values of the coefficients are given in standard mathematical tables such as [11].

   (c) Reduce the number of multiplications by using nested parentheses (Horner's method) as in:

$$\sin x \approx ((((a_8 x^2 + a_6) x^2 + a_4) x^2 + a_2) x^2 + 1) x$$

5. Rewrite our root finding by bisection program (Section 5.9.2) so that an iterative, rather than recursive technique, is used. Compare the time taken for both methods.

6. The Monte Carlo technique is often used to evaluate multi-dimensional integrals. As an illustrative example, we can generate random points in the region of the x-y plane given by $0 \le x \le 1$ and $0 \le y \le 1$. If we count those

points satisfying $x^2 + y^2 \leq 1$ as 'hits', then the hits divided by the total number of points should be an approximation to the area of a quadrant of a disc with unit radius. Since the total area of such a disc is π, this gives us a (rather inefficient) way of actually calculating π.

The random number generator, `rand()`, prototyped in `<stdlib.h>`, returns random integers in the range 0 to `RAND_MAX`, which is also given in `<stdlib.h>`. Use this library function to write a Monte Carlo program which calculates π and lists deviations from the tabulated value as the number of points increases. (For example, give the deviation for every 1000 points.) Try to explain any pattern you find in the deviations. (The constant, `PI`, is conveniently defined in `<math.h>`.)

7. Write a function that tests whether a positive integer is prime.[8] The function should have the prototype:

   `int test_prime(unsigned n)`

   where n is the integer to be tested and the function returns `TRUE` if n is prime and `FALSE` if n is not prime.

   Write a second function, with the prototype:

   `void list_primes(unsigned m)`

   which uses `test_prime()` to list all prime numbers up to m. Write a program, using the `test_prime()` and `list_prime()` functions, which prompts for a positive integer and then lists all primes less than or equal to this integer. Check your results against a table of prime numbers.

8. Calculation shows that $f(i)$, given by

   $$f(i) = i^2 + i + 41$$

   generates prime numbers for $i = 0, 1, 2, 3, 4, 5, 6$. Write a simple function that implements $f(i)$ and use `test_prime()` from the previous exercise to check whether or not primes are generated for larger values of i.

9. The $J_0(x)$ Bessel function is given to at least seven decimal places by:[9]

   $$J_0(x) = 1 - a_1(x/3)^2 + a_2(x/3)^4 + a_3(x/3)^6 + a_4(x/3)^8 + a_5(x/3)^{10} + a_6(x/3)^{12}$$

   where:

---

[8]Straightforward division by successive integers is sufficient for this exercise.
[9]See [11].

$$a_1 = 2.2499997 \quad a_4 = 0.0444479$$
$$a_2 = 1.2656208 \quad a_5 = 0.0039444$$
$$a_3 = 0.3163866 \quad a_6 = 0.0002100$$

and:

$$|x| \leq 3.$$

Write a function which returns $J_0(x)$ and show that $J_0(x)$ changes sign for $0 < x < 3$.

Modify the bisection program given in Section 5.9.2 to find a solution of

$$J_0(x) = 0$$

within the stated range of x. You should check your result by directly evaluating the function.

10. Legendre polynomials, $P_n(x)$, can be defined by:

$$P_n(x) = \sum_{k=0}^{[n/2]} \frac{(-1)^k (2n - 2k)! x^{n-2k}}{2^n k! (n - 2k)! (n - k)!}$$

where n is an integer, with:

$$n \geq 0$$
$$-1 \leq x \leq 1$$

and:

$$[n/2] = \begin{cases} n/2 & \text{if } n \text{ is even} \\ (n-1)/2 & \text{if } n \text{ is odd.} \end{cases}$$

Write a function, taking n and x as arguments, which returns the value of $P_n(x)$.

Legendre polynomials satisfy many identities, including the so-called *pure recursion relation*:

$$(2n + 1)x P_n(x) = (n + 1)P_{n+1}(x) + n P_{n-1}(x)$$

for $n = 1, 2, 3, \ldots$

Use this relation to write another function which tests your Legendre polynomial function. (Notice that if we were given $P_0(x)$ and $P_1(x)$, then this relation could be used to recursively generate $P_n(x)$.) You are likely to come across two problems in this example; the factorial function given earlier in this chapter suffers from integer overflow for values of n which are not very large and, secondly, you may encounter rather large rounding errors for x close to zero. You could solve the first problem by converting the factorial function to return a `double` and the second by ignoring it, once you have convinced yourself that the cause really is rounding error!

11. The logistic map, defined by

$$x_{n+1} = cx_n(1 - x_n)$$

where

$$0 \leq x_n \leq 1$$

and

$$0 < c \leq 4,$$

can be used to model a simple biological population at successive time intervals. x_n is the population, normalized so that the maximum sustainable population is one. The motivation for the equation is that as x_n is increased from zero, the next generation will be larger since there are more parents. However, as the normalized population approaches one, survival is less likely and the size of the next generation actually decreases. The variable, c is the control parameter for both of these effects.

Starting from some initial population, the logistic map can be used to generate successive populations. Write a function that implements the logistic map. The function should have c and x as its arguments and return the value of x after a large number of generations, such as 150.

Write a second function which has c as its argument and uses the first function to list the final values of x for a selection of initial values of x. Using these two functions, write a program which continues to prompt for a value of c and then lists a number of final populations.

For c between 1 and 3 you should find that the population tends to a single value. In fact, if you plot these *fixed points* against the values of c you should get a smooth curve. (It would be convenient if a C++ program could plot the curve, but this is beyond the techniques that we have covered so far.)

Study of the logistic map has given rise to an enormous number of research papers. If you investigate successive iterations for the two regions

$$3 < c < 3.449499$$

and

$$3.449499 < c < 3.544090$$

you should get some glimpse of the complex structure that arises from this simple map.[10]

---

[10]There is a large literature on the logistic map. A good start is [14].

Chapter 6

Pointers and Arrays

It is difficult to imagine performing many scientific calculations without the ability to manipulate arrays of one or more dimensions. Arrays are needed for vectors, matrices and the convenient storage of related data. In this chapter we introduce a simple picture of the way memory is organized, together with powerful methods for using contiguous areas of memory.

6.1　Memory, Addressing and Pointers

The memory of a computer can be regarded as a collection of labelled storage locations, as shown in Figure 6.1. In our discussions we assume that we can access these memory locations in any order. A very simplified picture is to visualize memory as a linear sequence of storage locations, one byte in size, which are labelled 1, 2, 3 ... etc. A particular label is known as the address of the corresponding memory element. The two operations of interest are to read what is stored at a particular address and to write data to the memory labelled by an address.

6.1.1　'address-of' Operator

In C++ the address of any variable can always be found by preceding the variable with the *address-of* operator, denoted, **&**. The address-of operator has the same precedence and right to left associativity as other unary operators. Several new operators are defined during the course of this chapter; their precedence and associativity are given in Appendix C. In the present context, the **&** operator simply means 'return the address of the variable to the right'. The following example illustrates the difference between values stored by variables of various types and their corresponding addresses:

```
int i = 1;
double x = 3.0;
```

```
float z = 4.0;
cout << "Address of i is " << &i <<
    " whereas the value of i is " << i << "\n";
cout << "Address of x is " << &x <<
    " whereas the value of x is " << x << "\n";
cout << "Address of z is " << &z <<
    " whereas the value of z is " << z << "\n";
```

Exercise:

Run the above code on your system. You may notice that the memory
locations given by the above code differ by the size of the various
types. (Whether or not this occurs depends on how the compiler
allocates storage.)

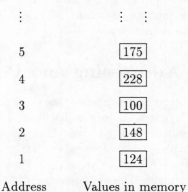

Address   Values in memory

Figure 6.1: Labelled storage locations.

There are a few things that we cannot do with the address-of operator. It is
illegal to take the address of a constant:

```
&10;        // WRONG: cannot take the address of a constant.
&3.142;     // WRONG: cannot take the address of a constant.
```

It is also illegal to take the address of an expression:

```
float x = 302.8;
&(x + 73.6);              // WRONG: cannot take the address
                         //        of expressions.
```

6.1.2 Dereferencing or Indirection Operator

Given an address, there is an operator, known as the *dereferencing operator*, denoted by *, which returns the value stored at that particular address. The phrase, *indirection operator*, is often used in place of dereferencing operator. In some sense the address-of and indirection operators are inverses of each other; if j is a variable of type int, then &j is the address in memory where that variable is stored. The value stored at the memory location, &j, is given by, *&j; in other words, j:

```
int i, j = 1;
i = *&j;      // This is an over-complicated way of writing:
i = j;
```

Notice that the address-of and indirection operators are only inverses in a limited sense; for example, &*j would be meaningless in this context since j is not an address and so cannot be dereferenced.

The indirection operator, *, should not be confused with the multiplication operator, *; the first is a unary operator, whereas the second is a binary operator; their meanings are completely unrelated. Both the compiler and human reader can unambiguously distinguish the operators by their context.

6.1.3 Pointers

So far we have come across many different types of variables. In general, the value of a particular variable in one of our programs is held at a location in memory with some specific address. It is the *starting address* that is significant; the actual number of bytes used varies with the variable type and the C++ compiler. For instance a char may be stored in one byte and a double in eight bytes. It is useful to have variables which can hold the address of a storage location. For instance we may have many large contiguous areas of memory, each one storing a large amount of data concerning observations on galaxies. If we know the addresses of these areas of memory, we can efficiently sort the data by manipulating addresses rather than copying the data itself. Variables for storing memory addresses are known as pointers. There is a special pointer type corresponding to each variable type. The different pointer types are needed because it is usually necessary to know how much memory is being pointed to (the size of the type) and how the bits stored in memory are to be interpreted.

Pointers may be declared as follows:

```
int *p1;          // p1 is a pointer to the type int.
double *p2;       // p2 is a pointer to the type double.
float *p3;        // p3 is a pointer to the type float.
```

The notation for pointer declarations may seem peculiar, but it can be understood by recalling that * is the dereferencing operator. This operator returns the value stored at the address held by its (right) operand. Since the dereferencing operator acting on p1 gives an int type, p1 must have the correct type for storing the address of an int; that is p1 is a pointer to an int. Remember that white space is ignored so the above could be rewritten as:

        int*p1;

or

        int * p1;

or

        int* p1;

but all of these variations are unusual.

In order to define a number of integer pointers we might be tempted to use:

        int *p1, p2, p3;   // WRONG: p2, p3 are not pointers.

But the indirection operator, like all unary operators binds to the right, not the left. In the above case the indirection operator binds only to p1, leaving p2 and p3 defined as having type int. To correctly implement our intention we need:

        int *p1, *p2, *p3;

A related error can occur if a #define is used to rename a type and for this reason a typedef is preferable. For example, if we make the declaration:

        typedef char * STRING;

then

        STRING message1, message2;

correctly declares message1 *and* message2 to be of type char*, whereas:

        #define STRING char *

would only declare message1 to be of type char*.

If we do indeed wish to use a single statement to simultaneously declare both identifiers of a type and pointers to that type, then we can do so and the order of the declarations is not significant:

        int x, y, *pt_x, *pt_y;   // pt_x and pt_y are pointers.

However, it is best to avoid mixing declarations like this, since it is so easy to make mistakes.

Dereferenced pointers can be used anywhere that an identifier of the corresponding type would be valid:

```
int i, j, k;
int *pt_i, *pt_j;

pt_i = &i;            // Assigns the address of i to pt_i.
pt_j = &j;            // Assigns the address of j to pt_j.
i = 1;
j = 2;
k = *pt_i + *pt_j;    // 3 is assigned to k.
*pt_i = 10;           // 10 is assigned to i.
```

Notice that a dereferenced pointer can appear on the left of the assignment operator; that is assignments can be made to the object that the pointer points to. The indirection operator has the highest precedence of any operator we have introduced so far, apart from the function call operator; the precedence of the indirection operator is the same as the `sizeof`, address-of (`&`) and logical not (`!`) operators. Therefore the assignment to `k` is equivalent to:

```
k = (*pt_i) + (*pt_j);
```

In this example `pt_i` and `pt_j` are assigned the addresses of the memory where i and j are stored. The values stored in these memory locations can then be accessed by using i and j or `*pt_i` and `*pt_j`, as shown in Figure 6.2. Again,

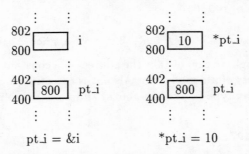

Figure 6.2: Relationship between memory and the address-of and dereferencing operators. (The addresses are decimal and do not refer to any particular computer.)

recall that white space is ignored so that:

```
pt_i = &i;
```

could equivalently be written as:

```
pt_i = & i;
```

although this style is quite unusual.

Exercise:

Rewrite the quadratic equation program, given in Section 1.2, so that
as many operations as possible are performed by using dereferenced
pointers. Since there is considerable scope for mistakes, you may find
it worthwhile to work in stages, modifying a small part of the original
program at a time. (Note that this is purely an exercise and is *not*
advocated as a style of programming.)

A pointer can point to a `const` type, but the pointer definition must also
include the `const` specifier:

```
const int w = 100;
const int *pt_c;
int *pt_i;
pt_c = &w;          // O.K.
++pt_c;             // O.K.
pt_i = &w;          // WRONG: a non-const pointer
                    //        cannot point to const.
```

The fact that it is illegal to assign the address of a `const` type to an unqualified
pointer makes it non-trivial to modify a `const` object. Of course, a malicious
programmer can always use a cast:

```
const int w = 100;
int *pt;
pt = (int*)&w;       // O.K. but not a good thing to do.
```

Notice that, although we cannot take the address of a constant (such as 3.142), we
can take the address of a `const` type. Also, it is essential to distinguish between
a pointer to a `const` type (described above) and a `const` pointer, an example of
which is as follows:

```
double x = 127;
double *const pt = &x;

++*pt;      // O.K:   x is not constant.
++pt;       // WRONG: pt is constant.
```

A pointer is simply a variable which is used to hold the address of another
variable, so it is also possible to store the address of a pointer. A variable used
to store the address of a pointer is known as a pointer to a pointer:

```
double x;           // Memory defined to store a double.
double *pt;         // Memory defined to store the
                    // address of a double.
double **pt_pt;     // Memory defined to store the address
                    // of a pointer to a double.

pt = &x;
pt_pt = &pt;
x = 11.11;
// Try dereferencing pt_pt to access x:
cout << "x = " << **pt_pt << "\n";
```

The value stored by `pt` can be accessed by dereferencing `pt_pt`, whereas to access `x` we need to dereference `pt_pt` twice. The relation between the three storage locations is shown in Figure 6.3. In numerical applications, pointers to pointers

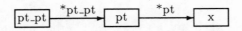

Figure 6.3: A pointer to a pointer.

usually occur when we have multi-dimensional arrays. The chain of pointing can continue indefinitely (pointer to pointer to pointer to ...). This is one effective way of implementing linked lists, although it is rare to see explicit dereferencing of the form `***pt`.

Exercise:

Try out the above code on your system. Modify it to multiply two numbers using pointers to pointers and check that you get the correct result.

6.1.4   Pointers Do Not Declare Memory

We make considerable use of pointers throughout this book and you will come to appreciate that pointers are an extremely powerful tool. However, like most powerful tools, pointers can also be abused. One problem is that you may make a programming error which results in an incorrect address being used. For instance suppose we mis-typed the last example:

```
int i, j, k;
int *pt_i, *pt_j;
pt_j = &j;
```

```
i = 1;
j = 2;
k = *pt_i + *pt_j;              // WRONG: pt_i is arbitrary.
*pt_i = 10;                     // WRONG: pt_i is arbitrary.
```

We have not assigned the address of i to pt_i and hence pt_i stores some
arbitrary address, not necessarily zero. When we use *pt_i in:

```
k = *pt_i + *pt_j;
```

an integer is read from whatever area of memory pt_i happens to point to. The
memory may not be storing an int; it could be a double, part of an executable
program or even part of the operating system. Nevertheless the bit pattern will
be interpreted and returned by *pt_i as an integer. A mistake of this kind may
well be fatal to your program, but is no worse than many typical programming
errors in C++, or other languages.

The real disaster is the final statement:

```
*pt_i = 10;
```

Since we don't know where pt_i points, some arbitrary area of memory gets
assigned the value 10. This may mean that your program fails at some apparently
unrelated statement and the cause of the error may be very difficult to find. You
may even attempt to write to an area of memory which doesn't exist. On some
computers you may actually write over the operating system, causing the entire
system to 'crash'. It cannot be overemphasized that when using pointers you
must make certain you get them right!

A related and quite common error is to forget to allocate any memory for the
pointer to point to:

```
int *pt_k;
*pt_k = 10;                 // WRONG: pt_k is arbitrary.
```

In this example pt_k is again the address of some arbitrary area of memory, to
which we attempt to assign the value 10. Here the mistake is readily apparent,
but analogous mistakes are often made in complicated programs; typically the
indirection takes place in a function which may be several nested function calls
removed from where the memory should have been defined.

Exercise:

Try running the above code, which manipulates i, j and k, on your
system. You should output the values of k and *pt_i so that the
results can be checked. If, by good fortune, no disaster occurs, try
incrementing the value of pt_i before it is used; you should be able
to produce something like a 'memory error' or else crash your system.
Now modify the code so that it runs and gives the correct results.

6.1.5 Null Pointer

There is a special constant pointer, known as the *null* pointer, which is guaranteed not to be a valid memory address. The constant NULL, defined in <stdio.h>, is normally used as the value of the null pointer. Assigning zero to a pointer is the same as assigning NULL, although strictly the zero is converted to the null pointer, which may not have the same bit pattern as 0.[1] Since the null pointer cannot be a valid address, we have a very useful way of signalling certain error conditions involving memory locations and we will make frequent use of this technique.

6.2 One-dimensional Arrays

One-dimensional arrays use a single integral parameter to access contiguous areas of memory. A square bracket pair is used to declare a one-dimensional array:

```
int i[10];              // Defines an array of 10 ints.
double x[100];          // Defines an array of 100 doubles.
char c[80];             // Defines an array of 80 chars.
```

In this example, ten contiguous memory locations, each large enough to hold one int, are allocated for the array named i. The individual values that are stored in the memory are known as *elements*. The array named i has 10 elements, x has 100 elements and c has 80 elements. The number of elements in an array is known as the *size* of the array. The array size can be specified by a constant expression; that is an expression which evaluates to an integral constant at compile-time, as in:

```
const int MAX_DATA = 100;
double data[3 * MAX_DATA];
```

but not:

```
int MAX_DATA = 100;
double data[3 * MAX_DATA];  // WRONG!
```

The array elements can be accessed (that is assigned to and read from) by specifying an *index* (also known as a *subscript*). The same square bracket notation (the *subscripting operator*) is used, but the context is slightly different:

```
int i[10];          // Defines an array of 10 ints.
int j;

i[6] = 24;          // Assigns 24 to the element with index 6.
j = i[6];           // Assigns i[6] (that is 24) to j.
cout << "j = " << j << "\n";
```

---

[1] Any integer, floating point or pointer type can be assigned 0. An appropriate zero will be assigned, which typically, but not necessarily, has all bits set zero.

The array index must be of integral type (apart from a rather bizarre exception demonstrated in Section 6.2.1):

```
double x, y[20];

x = 10;
y[x] = 42.0;            // WRONG: x is not of integral type.
```

In contrast to some languages, such as FORTRAN, the indexing starts from zero, so that the array defined by i[10] has elements i[0], i[1], i[2], ... i[9]. A very common mistake is assigning to an element with an index equal to the size of the array:

```
int i[10];
i[10] = 24;             // WRONG: i[10] is not an element
                        //        of the array.
```

or

```
double x[5];
for (int i = 0; i <= 5; ++i)
    x[i] = double(i);   // WRONG: x[5] is not an element
                        //        of the array.
```

The result of such mistakes is exactly the same as assigning to a dereferenced pointer which points to an arbitrary address. In the first example, 10 is assigned to the area of memory just beyond that used for storing the array. There is no array bounds checking in C++ and this memory could well be used by another part of your program or even the operating system. The results are likely to be unpredictable and erratic, with the cause difficult to trace.

One-dimensional arrays have many obvious uses in engineering and science. For instance:

```
double pressure[1000];
```

could be used to store pressure measurements at 1,000 different time intervals and the array defined by:

```
double velocity[3];
```

could be used to hold the components of a 3-dimensional velocity vector. However, it should be noted that the C++ definition of an array is simply a sequence of contiguous memory locations; there is no concept of adding or multiplying arrays, unlike the vectors of mathematics. However, since C++ allows us to define our own types, it is possible to impose more structure on the idea of an array and to create types closer to what we want in many applications. We return to this theme in Chapter 8, but for the present, if an array represents a vector, then vector operations must be performed element by element. An example demonstrating vector addition, followed by calculating a scalar product is:

```
#include <math.h>          // for sqrt()

double velocity_1[3], velocity_2[3], total_velocity[3];
// Assign values to velocity_1[i] and velocity_2[i].
for (int i = 0; i < 3; ++i)
    total_velocity[i] = velocity_1[i] + velocity_2[i];
double temp = 0.0;
for (i = 0; i < 3; ++i)
    temp += total_velocity[i] * total_velocity[i];
double velocity_norm = sqrt(temp);
```

Exercise:

Run the above code on your system. Check the calculated value of
`velocity_norm` for various assignments to elements of the arrays,
`velocity_1[]` and `velocity_2[]`.

6.2.1   Pointers and One-dimensional Arrays

The concept of an array in C++ is very primitive and directly related to pointers.
If we define an array by:

```
int a[20];
```

then `a[i]` means:

```
*(&a[0] + i)
```

and nothing more. Let's explain this in more detail. The expression, `&a[0]` is
the base address of the array, so `(&a[0] + i)` is the address of the element i
locations up from the base address. This is the address of element `a[i]`; the
dereferencing operator gives the value stored in this element.

In C++ it is both possible and very useful to be able to perform arithmetic
on pointers. The arithmetic that can be done is necessarily very restricted and
consists of the following:

1. Addition of a pointer and an integral type or subtraction of a pointer and
   an integral type:

   ```
   double *pt;
   double a[10];
   pt = &a[0];    // pt points to element 0 in the array.
   ++pt;          // pt points to element 1.
   pt += 4;       // pt points to element 5.
   pt = pt - 2;   // pt points to element 3.
   ```

Exercise:

Use the standard subscripting notation to assign the values 1, 2, 3 . . . to the elements of a[] in the above code. By adding integers to the pointer, pt, list these elements. Also list the elements in reverse order by subtracting integers from pt.

Notice that these expressions don't involve the number of bytes used to represent a double; pt is declared to be a pointer to double and the compiler does the necessary calculations to ensure that when using pointer arithmetic, appropriate allowance is made for the storage requirements of the different types. Essentially, if pt is a pointer to an element of an array, then pt+1 is a pointer to the next element in the array. All of these expressions are only valid provided we stay within the memory allocated to the array:

```
double *pt;
double a[10];
pt = &a[0];
pt += 100;          // WRONG: pt attempts to point
                    //        outside of the array.
```

Pointing outside of the array is undefined, even if we don't attempt to access the memory location. One obvious way in which such operations may fail is if a small number of bytes are used to store pointers; going beyond the end of an array may cause the value of the pointer to wrap round. It is permissible to point one element beyond the high end of the array, but it is still incorrect to dereference such a pointer:

```
double *pt;
double a[10];
pt = &a[0];
pt += 10;                   // O.K.: pt points to one
                            //       element beyond a[9].
*pt = 3.14159265358979;     // WRONG: cannot dereference
                            //        this address.
```

The memory outside of an array may well be allocated for some specific purpose and the result would be the usual symptoms of a pointer error.

2. Subtraction of two pointers of the same type. The type of the result is dependent on the C++ compiler, but is defined as ptrdiff_t in the header file <stddef.h>. The result is a signed integer representing the number of elements separating the two pointers:

```
#include <stddef.h>

double *pt_1, *pt_2;
double a[10];
ptrdiff_t diff;

pt_1 = &a[1];
pt_2 = &a[4];
diff = pt_2 - pt_1;     // Assigns 3 to diff.
cout << "Difference is " << diff << "\n";
diff = pt_1 - pt_2;     // Assigns -3 to diff.
cout << "Difference is " << diff << "\n";
```

The result of subtracting pointers is undefined if the pointers do not point to elements within the same array, except that it is again permissible to point one element beyond the end of the array:

```
#include <stddef.h>

double *pt_1, *pt_2;
double a[10], b[20];
ptrdiff_t diff;

pt_1 = &a[10];
pt_2 = &a[9];
diff = pt_1 - pt_2;     // Correctly assigns 1 to diff.
cout << "Difference is " << diff << "\n";
pt_1 = &b[19];
diff = pt_1 - pt_2;     // WRONG: undefined.
cout << "Difference is " << diff << "\n";
```

3. Relational operations. It is possible to compare pointers, but the elements pointed to must again be in the same array or one element beyond the high end of the array:

```
double *pt_1, *pt_2;
double a[10];

pt_1 = &a[10];
pt_2 = & a[5];
cout << "pt_1" << pt_1 << "  " << "pt_2" << pt_2 << "\n";
if (pt_2 > pt_1)
    cout << "pt_2 > pt_1\n";
```

```
    else
        cout << "pt_2 <= pt_1\n";
    if (pt_1 != pt_2)
        cout << "pt_1 != pt_2\n";
    if (pt_1 == pt_2)
        cout << "pt_1 == pt_2\n";
    else
        cout << "pt_1 == pt_2 is false\n";
```

All other arithmetic pointer operations are illegal; for instance multiplying, adding and dividing two pointers are not allowed. In any case, such operations would not be particularly useful!

One consequence of the relationship between pointers and arrays is that operations on arrays can always be rewritten directly in terms of pointer arithmetic. Suppose we have an array of size ten and type **double**; the following would provide the sum of the values stored by the array:[2]

```
    double sum = 0.0, x[10];

    // Assignments to x[i]

    for (int i = 0; i < 10; ++i)
        sum += x[i];
```

This summation can be rewritten in terms of pointers as:

```
    double sum = 0.0, x[10], *pt, *pt_end;

    // Assignments to x[i]

    pt = &x[0];
    pt_end = pt + 10;   // Points one element beyond the array.
    while (pt < pt_end)
        sum += *pt++;
```

which is more efficient, since incrementing i and performing an address calculation is replaced by the single pointer operation. This code also demonstrates why the pointer one element beyond the high end of an array is defined, even though the pointer cannot be dereferenced. The pointer is needed for comparison in a loop termination condition.

---

[2]Notice once again that the terminating condition is $i < 10$. A common error is to write $i <= 10$, which uses the value held in memory after the high end of the array.

Exercise:

Using the above code, assign the values 10, 20, 30 ... to the elements of `x[]` and check that the correct value of `sum` is calculated.

For an array, `x[ARRAY_SIZE]`, a notational convenience is that `x` is defined to be the base address of the array. So we could rewrite the above example as:

```
double sum = 0.0, x[10], *pt, *pt_end;

// Assignments to x[i]

pt = x;
pt_end = pt + 10;
while (pt < pt_end)
    sum += *pt++;
```

This notation is one which we employ frequently. Notice that, since `x` is an unmodifiable lvalue, we cannot do anything which attempts to change its value:[3]

```
double x[10], y[10];
double **pt;
x = y;       // WRONG: cannot assign to a constant.
++x;         // WRONG: cannot increment a constant.
```

There is an interesting curiosity which results from the fact that an array, such as

```
double x[10];
```

can be accessed by `x[i]`, which is directly equivalent to:

```
*(x+i)
```

Since the order of `x` and `i` is irrelevant in this expression (addition commutes), `x[i]` can be validly written as `i[x]`. The latter looks like an array of integers which is indexed by the value of a `double`. This bizarre expression will be correctly interpreted by the compiler, but seems to serve no useful purpose for human readers!

---

[3]Recall that an lvalue is an expression referring to an object or function. An lvalue is unmodifiable if it is an array or function name or if it is declared `const`.

6.2.2   Negative Array Indices[††]

It may seem surprising, having stated that array indices in C++ run from zero to one less than the size of the array, that we should now be considering negative indices. However, we could do the following:

```
double a[10];
double *pt = a + 5;
pt[-5] = 2.976;              // Assigns 2.976 to a[0]
```

Provided we don't manipulate memory outside of that allocated to the array, negative indices are perfectly valid. To understand this we must recall that a[i] means nothing more than *(a+i). So pt[-5] is actually *(a+5-5) or, more explicitly, a[0]. This technique could be used to make array indices start from one, rather than zero:[4]

```
double a[10];
double *pt = a - 1;
pt[1] = 2.976;              // Assigns 2.976 to a[0]
```

except that the evaluation of a - 1 *does* assume pointer arithmetic outside of the allocated array memory. Moreover, it seems less confusing to either remain with the standard notation of arrays starting at element zero, or to use the full power of C++ to construct self-describing arrays with specified and fully checked ranges.

6.3   Type void*

Suppose we want to store a memory address, but we don't know what type of object will be stored at that address. In such cases the type void* should be used as a generic pointer type. As was emphasized in Chapter 5, an object cannot be declared to be of type void. (One reason is that the compiler would not know how many bytes to allocate for such an object.) However, a pointer can be declared to be of type void*, as in:

```
int i, a[10];
double v[20];
void *pt;
pt = &i;
pt = a;
pt = v;
```

The address of any type can be assigned to a pointer of type void*, but arithmetic operations are not allowed on such pointers:

---

[4]See [17].

```
void *pt;
double a[10];
pt = a;
++pt;           // WRONG: cannot increment a pointer to void.
```

This restriction is perfectly reasonable; pt simply holds an address, but the compiler has no information on the type of object stored at that address, so it has no way of calculating the address of the next element in the array.

6.4 Pointer Conversions

A pointer of any type can be assigned to a pointer of type void*, but the converse is not true.

```
int a[10];
int *pt_i;
void *pt;
pt = a;                 // O.K.
pt_i = pt;              // WRONG!
```

Such prohibitions are for our own protection. If pt holds an address and we don't know what type of object may be stored there, then assigning that address to a pointer to a type other than void would be risky; we might, for instance, dereference that pointer. If it is necessary to get round these prohibitions, then we can use an explicit cast, but we had better understand what we are doing:

```
int a[10];
int *pt_i;
double *pt_d;
void *pt;
pt = a;
pt_i = (int*)pt;
*pt_i = 2;              // O.K.
pt_d = (double*)a;
*pt_d = 1.1;            // Do we really mean this?
```

Notice that int* (or equivalently int *) is used to indicate the type 'pointer to int' in a cast. Casts to other pointer types are made in a similar way.

6.5 Multi-dimensional Arrays

C++ also supports *multi-dimensional arrays*, which are defined by repeated square brackets, as in:

```
double x[3][5];      // Defines a 3 x 5 array of doubles.
float y[2][3][4];    // Defines a 2 x 3 x 4 array of floats.
```

Notations typical of some other languages are not valid:

```
double x[3, 5];              // WRONG!
float y(2, 3, 6);            // WRONG!
```

The definition of a multi-dimensional array, such as:

```
int a[4][2];
```

allocates sufficient contiguous memory to store the array. In this example, eight values of type int could be stored. Each array index runs from zero to one less than the size specified for that index:

```
int a[4][5];
a[0][0] = 1;     // Low end of the array.
a[3][4] = 25;    // High end of the array.
a[4][5] = 100;   // WRONG: outside of the allocated memory.
```

For a two-dimensional array, it is conventional to regard the first index as labelling rows and the second as labelling columns; this is consistent with the standard notation for matrices.

Multi-dimensional arrays can be used to represent matrices and tensors, but arithmetic operations must be done element by element. For example, we can add two 4×5 matrices A and B:

```
double A[4][5], B[4][5], C[4][5];
for (int i = 0; i < 4; ++i)
    for (int j = 0; j < 5; ++j)
        C[i][j] = A[i][j] + B[i][j];
```

and multiply a 4×5 matrix, X, by a 5×6 matrix, Y:

```
double X[4][5], Y[5][6], Z[4][6];
for (int i = 0; i < 4; ++i)
    for (int j = 0; j < 6; ++j) {
        double temp = 0.0;
        for (int k = 0; k < 5; ++k)
            temp += X[i][k] * Y[k][j];
        Z[i][j] = temp;
    }
```

The equivalent mathematical equations are much simpler:

$$C = A + B$$

and

$$Z = X * Y$$

but it is only by introducing overloaded operators (in Chapter 9) that we can truly manipulate matrices, rather than matrix components, as objects.

Exercise:

By assigning appropriately chosen integers to the elements of A[][], B[][], X[][] and Y[][], check the correctness of matrix addition and multiplication as implemented above.

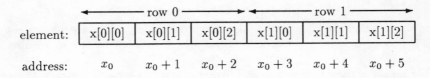

Figure 6.4: Storage map for x[2][3]. (x_0 represents &x[0][0].)

6.5.1 Pointers and Multi-dimensional Arrays[†]

Since a memory location is specified by a single address, the two or more dimensions of a multi-dimensional array must be mapped into the linear address space of physical memory. This mapping is often known as a *storage map*. In C++, two-dimensional arrays are stored by rows and a typical storage map is shown in Figure 6.4.

An array defined by:

```
int x[2][3];
```

is accessed via x[i][j], which is equivalent to:

```
*(&x[0][0] + 3 * i + j)
```

In fact, two-dimensional arrays have no more significance than this equivalence. In this example, x[0][0] is the element at the low end of the array and therefore &x[0][0] is the base address of the array. Great care should be exercised when using pointers to access multi-dimensional arrays. The constant, x is also the base address of this array, but

```
*(x + 3 * i + j)
```

is not equivalent to x[i][j] since (x + i) is actually the base address of row i; for instance, (x+1) is the base address of the row 1. A correct way of using x, rather than &x[0][0], to access an array element is:

```
(*(x + i))[j]
```

The outer parentheses are required because [] binds tighter than the dereferencing operator. In fact, by studying the above expression, we can see how the notation for two-dimensional arrays arises. The expression, *(x+i), is the same as x[i], the base address of row i, so the whole expression is directly equivalent to x[i][j]. There are two other, equally devious, ways of rewriting x[i][j]:

```
*((*(x + i)) + j)
```

and

```
*(x[i] + j)
```

It is worth convincing yourself that these expressions really are equivalent to x[i][j], although in practise it is usually best to stick to the more obvious notation.

For arrays of three dimensions and higher, the storage map is a straightforward extension of the two-dimensional case. For instance, if we make the definition:

```
float y[2][3][4];
```

then an element, y[i][j][k], can equivalently be accessed by:

```
*(&y[0][0][0] + 3 * 4 * i + 4 * j + k);
```

Needless to say, there are devious ways of rewriting this expression in terms of y rather than &y[0][0][0].

We don't need to know how arrays are stored in order to use them, but doing so can help us to understand (and even reduce) the overhead caused by indexing into multi-dimensional arrays. For instance, if a calculation involves going down columns, one step at a time, then it may be faster to rearrange the code so that the stepping is done along rows. In Section 7.3.2 we show how knowledge of the array storage map can speed up a typical numerical application.

6.6   Initializing Arrays

One-dimensional arrays can be initialized by a comma-separated list between a pair of braces, known as an *initialization list*, as in:

```
int x[] = {1, 2, 3};
float y[4] = {1.1, 2.2};
```

If the array size is not specified, then it is taken as the number of elements between the braces. In this example, x[] can store three elements and the initialization of x[] is equivalent to:

```
x[0] = 1;
x[1] = 2;
x[2] = 3;
```

If the size specified is greater than the number of values given, then the low end of the array is initialized with these values and the remaining elements are set to zero (of an appropriate type). The initialization of `y[]` is therefore equivalent to:

```
y[0] = 1.1;
y[1] = 2.2;
y[2] = 0.0;
y[3] = 0.0;
```

It is illegal to have more members in the list than the specified array size:

```
double z[2] = {1.1, 2.2, 3.3};   // WRONG: size specified
                                 //          is too small.
```

Multi-dimensional arrays are initialized by comma-separated, nested, braces:

```
int w[4][3] = {{1, 2, 3}, {4, 5, 6}};
```

This two-dimensional array is initialized row-wise, with the last two rows being filled with zeros; that is, the initialization is equivalent to:

```
w[0][0] = 1;  w[0][1] = 2;  w[0][2] = 3;
w[1][0] = 4;  w[1][1] = 5;  w[1][2] = 6;
w[2][0] = 0;  w[2][1] = 0;  w[2][2] = 0;
w[3][0] = 0;  w[3][1] = 0;  w[3][2] = 0;
```

As discussed in the previous section, two-dimensional arrays are actually stored row-wise, so the above initialization is equivalent to:

```
int w[4][3] = {1, 2, 3, 4, 5, 6};
```

Incomplete rows can also be initialized, as in:

```
int w[2][3] = {{1}, {2, 3}};
```

which is equivalent to:

```
w[0][0] = 1;  w[0][1] = 0;  w[0][2] = 0;
w[1][0] = 2;  w[1][1] = 3;  w[1][2] = 0;
```

Nested, comma-separated braces can also be used to initialize arrays of more than two dimensions in a completely analogous way.

Exercise:

Verify the initialization of the 2×3 array, `w[][]`. Achieve the same initialization by using a single, rather than nested, comma-separated list.

6.7   Size of Arrays††

So far we have used the `sizeof` operator to determine the size of fundamental types, such as `int`, `double`, `char` etc. This operator can also give the size of an array, but we must make a clear distinction between the size of one element in an array and the size of the entire array. If we specify a particular element, then, as expected, we obtain the size of just a single element:

```
double x[10], y[5][10];
cout << "The size of a single element of x[10] is " <<
    sizeof(x[0]) << "\n";
cout << "The size of a single element of y[5][10] is " <<
    sizeof(y[0][0]) << "\n";
cout << "For comparison, the size of a double is " <<
    sizeof(double) << "\n";
```

Notice that in general the size of a type can be obtained by using the type name, rather than a specific variable.

Specifying the name of the array as the argument of the `sizeof` operator gives the size of the entire array. There is a minor inconsistency here, since in most circumstances **x** and **y** are the (unmodifiable) base addresses of the arrays x[] and y[][]:

```
double x[10], y[5][10];
cout << "The size of the array x[10] is " <<
    sizeof(x) << "\n";
cout << "The size of the array y[5][10] is " <<
    sizeof(y) << "\n";
cout << "The size of an element of the array y[5] is " <<
    sizeof(y[0]) << "\n";
cout << "For comparison:\n\tThe size of a pointer to " <<
    "a double is " << sizeof(double*) <<
    "\n\tThe size of a double is " <<
    sizeof(double) << "\n";
```

Exercise: What sizes are given by running the above code on your system?

On a particular computer we obtain the following output:

```
The size of the array x[10] is 80
The size of the array y[5][10] is 400
The size of an element of the array y[5] is 80
For comparison:
    The size of a pointer to a double is 2
    The size of a double is 8
```

Notice that `sizeof(x)` gives the size of the entire array, `x[10]`, and not the size of a pointer to an element of `x`; the meaning of the array name when used as an argument to the `sizeof` operator is not the same as when the array name is used in pointer arithmetic. Similarly, `sizeof(y)` gives the size of the entire 5×10 array and `sizeof(y[0])` gives the size of row 0, that is $10 \times$ `sizeof(double)`.

6.8   Arrays of Pointers and Multi-dimensional Arrays

It is possible to define arrays of pointers, as in:

```
double *pt_a[5];
float *pt_b[4][10];
```

Since the array index operator, `[]`, has higher precedence than the indirection operator, `*`, the two statements do indeed each define an array of pointers, rather than a pointer to an array (which will be discussed shortly). The first definition is an array of size 5, which can store addresses of type `double`, whereas the second is a 4×10 array, which can store 40 addresses of type `float`. It must be clearly understood that these arrays can only store addresses. They do not themselves define any memory for storing values of type `double` or `float`. Such memory must be defined separately:

```
double a, b;
double *pt[2];
pt[0] = &a;
pt[1] = &b;
```

The distinction between an array of pointers and a pointer to an array is worth emphasizing. In the definitions:

```
double *p_d[3];
int (*p_i)[3];
```

`p_d` is an array of three pointers to type `double` and can therefore store three addresses:

```
double x, y, z;
p_d[0] = &x;
p_d[1] = &y;
p_d[2] = &z;
```

whereas `p_i` is a pointer to an array of three integers and can therefore only store one address:

```
int a[2][3];
p_i = a;
```

The usefulness of a pointer to an array stems from the fact that pointer arithmetic automatically allows for the size of the array. In this particular case, `p_i` points to the base address of row 0 of the array, but `(p_i+1)` points to row 1.

The following example uses an array of pointers, in addition to pointers to pointers:

```
double x, y, z;
double *pt[3], **p, **p_end;

pt[0] = &x;
pt[1] = &y;
pt[2] = &z;
x = 1.11;
y = 2.22;
z = 3.33;
p = pt;
p_end = p + 3;
while (p < p_end)
    cout << "data = " << **p++ << "\n";
```

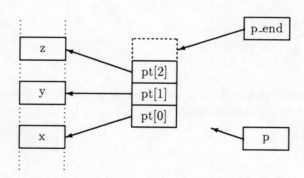

Figure 6.5: An array of pointers. (p scans the addresses of the elements of `pt[]`.)

As shown in Figure 6.5, x, y, z are stored in some arbitrary memory locations and it should not be assumed that these locations are either contiguous or ordered in any particular way. The addresses of x, y and z are stored in `pt[0]`, `pt[1]` and `pt[2]` respectively and these array elements must therefore be declared to be of type pointer to `double`. The address of pt[2] is stored in `p_end` and p scans the addresses of the array, `pt[]`; both `p_end` and p are of type pointer to pointer to `double`. Dereferencing `p` twice gives the data stored in **x**, **y** or **z**. In this simple example, using pointers to pointers is not an improvement on manipulating the array elements directly, but such techniques are useful for manipulating large amounts of data, where copying the data would be very inefficient.

6.9 Using Pointers and Arrays

In this section we consider two examples which employ some of the techniques introduced in this chapter. The first example uses one-dimensional arrays, rather than explicit pointers, and highlights some of the deficiencies with the techniques learnt so far. In the second example we use an array of pointers to construct a ragged two-dimensional array.

6.9.1 Fitting Data to a Straight Line

A common task in science and engineering is to fit a set of data points to a straight line. More specifically, if we are given data x_i and y_i, where $i = 1, 2, \ldots n$, then we must find **a** and **b** such that:

$$y = a + bx$$

We suppose that the x_i's are known exactly, but that there is a error, σ_i, associated with each measurement, y_i. It can be shown that **a** and **b** are given by the following definitions and equations:[5]

$$S_x \equiv \sum_{i=1}^{N} \frac{x_i}{\sigma_i^2}$$

$$S_y \equiv \sum_{i=1}^{N} \frac{y_i}{\sigma_i^2}$$

$$S \equiv \sum_{i=1}^{N} \frac{1}{\sigma_i^2}$$

$$t_i \equiv \frac{1}{\sigma_i}\left(x_i - \frac{S_x}{S}\right)$$

$$S_{tt} \equiv \sum_{i=1}^{N} t_i^2$$

$$b = \frac{1}{S_{tt}} \sum_{i=1}^{N} \frac{t_i y_i}{\sigma_i}$$

---

[5]We use *exactly* the same notation as [17] so that background reading for this example is readily accessible.

$$a = \frac{S_y - S_x b}{S}$$

A program which prompts for data points and then computes the values of a and
b is as follows:

```
// source:      fit.cpp
// use:         Does straight line fitting.

#include <iostream.hpp>
#include <stdlib.h>        // for EXIT_SUCCESS

int main()
{
    const int max_points = 100;
    int i, points;
    double x[max_points], y[max_points], sigma[max_points];
    do {
        cout << "How many points (less than " <<
            max_points << ") do you want to fit?\n";
        cin >> points;
    } while (points < 1 || points > max_points);
    cout << "\nEnter " << points << " data points in the " <<
        "form:\n   x coordinate  y coordinate  error:\n\n";
    for (i = 0; i < points; ++i) {
        cin >> x[i] >> y[i] >> sigma[i];
    }

    double s = 0.0, s_x = 0.0, s_y = 0.0;
    for (i = 0; i < points ; ++i) {
        double temp = 1.0 / (sigma[i] * sigma[i]);
        s += temp;
        s_x += temp * x[i];
        s_y += temp * y[i];
    }
    double s_x_s = s_x / s;
    double s_tt = 0.0, b = 0.0;
    for (i = 0; i < points ; ++i) {
        double t = (x[i] - s_x_s) / sigma[i];
        s_tt += t * t;
        b += t * y[i] / sigma[i];
    }
    b /= s_tt;
    double a = (s_y - s_x * b) / s;
```

```
        cout << "The " << points <<
            " points fit the equation: y = a + b * x\n" <<
            "with:    a = " << a << " b = " << b << "\n";
        return (EXIT_SUCCESS);
    }
```

Exercise:

Try this program with your own data.

This line-fitting program exposes a number of limitations with the techniques learnt so far:

- The maximum points that the program can handle is fixed at compile-time and can only be altered by editing and recompiling. Techniques for removing this difficulty are given in the next chapter.

- The data must be entered directly in response to a program prompt, rather than read from a file. This is particularly tedious with large data sets and infuriating if you make a typing mistake! How to read data from a file is explained in Chapter 12.

- Since we have not learnt how to pass arrays as function arguments, the entire program consists of the single function, `main()`. This makes it difficult to reuse our line-fitting code as part of a larger program. Passing arrays as function arguments is introduced in the next chapter.

6.9.2 Ragged Arrays

One use of an array of pointers is to define a *ragged array*, in which the rows have different lengths. For instance, suppose we make some astronomical observations on seven different nights. One night is very cloudy and we only manage 5 observations, whereas another is exceptionally clear and we carry out 2,000 observations. On the remaining nights we make various numbers of observations between these two extremes. We could define a $7 \times 2,000$ two-dimensional array to store the data. However, a more efficient approach is to use a ragged array as shown in the following code:[6]

```
    // Define arrays of just sufficient size to
    // store the observations made each night:
    double Sunday[500];
    double Monday[100];
    double Tuesday[10];
```

---

[6]`Sunday`, `Monday` ... mean the nights of Sunday-Monday, Monday-Tuesday ...

```
double Wednesday[1000];
double Thursday[20];
double Friday[5];
double Saturday[2000];

// Define an array of pointers to the data arrays:
double *data[7];
data[0] = Sunday;
data[1] = Monday;
data[2] = Tuesday;
data[3] = Wednesday;
data[4] = Thursday;
data[5] = Friday;
data[6] = Saturday;

// Enter data in each array.

// Average element one of each array:
double average = 0.0;
for (int i = 0; i < 7; ++i)
    average += data[i][1];
average /= 7;
cout << "Seven day average of data element 1 = " <<
    average << "\n";
```

The observations for each night are stored in a one-dimensional array of the appropriate length, named Sunday, Monday etc. An array of pointers, data[ ], then stores the base address of each array holding the observations. The result is a ragged array as shown in Figure 6.6. With care, we can now use data as if it were the name of a two-dimensional array. As a simple example we have averaged the second observation (that is element one) for the seven nights. Of course, it is entirely our responsibility to avoid attempting to access elements beyond the end of a defined row. In practise, an integer array holding the length of each row would help to prevent such disasters. Notice that in our interpretation of data as the name of a (ragged) array, the first index does indeed label rows and the second index labels columns. The essential step in understanding data[i][j] is to recall that the array subscripting operator, [ ], associates left to right, so that data[i][j] is equivalent to (data[i])[j]. For example, since data[2] is the base address of the array Tuesday[], data[2][j] reduces to the one-dimensional array, Tuesday[j], which is accessed in the usual way. There is, of course, no equivalence to a storage map as described in Section 6.5.1:

```
*(&data[0][0] + row_length * 2 + j)
```

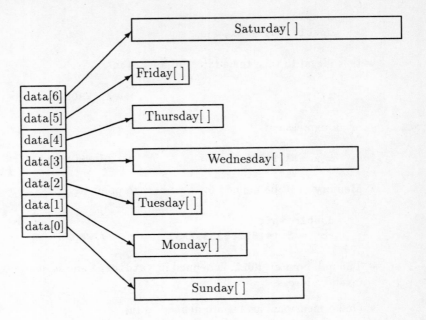

Figure 6.6: A ragged array.

since memory for the entire array is not necessarily contiguous and the rows have different lengths.

Exercise:

Make this ragged array example into a complete program. You should define an array which stores the length of each row and test the program by generating random data and finding the average for each night.

6.10 Summary

- A pointer is a variable that can be used to store an address:

  ```
  double *pt;
  ```

- The address of an object can be found by using the address-of operator, **&**. A particular address is accessed by means of the dereferencing or indirection operator, *****:

```
double x;
double *pt = &x;
```

- It is illegal to take the address of a constant:

```
&10;                              // WRONG!
```

or an expression:

```
&(x + 3.142);                     // WRONG!
```

- Memory must be defined for a pointer to point to:

```
double *pt;
*pt = 3.1415926535897932;         // WRONG!
```

- The null pointer, NULL, is defined in **<stdio.h>** and is guaranteed to be an invalid address.

- One dimensional arrays are defined as in:

```
double x[10];
```

Individual elements are accessed by specifying an index:

```
double y = x[5];
```

Notice that this array starts at x[0], has 10 elements and the element, x[10], is undefined.

- Pointer arithmetic is only valid for restricted operations, such as:

```
++pt_x;
pt_z = pt_x - pt_y;
if (pt_x < pt_y) { ... }
```

- For a one-dimensional array, an element a[i] means nothing more than *(&a[0]+i).

- The generic pointer type is **void***:

```
void *pt;
```

The address of any type can be assigned to **pt**:

```
double x[100];
pt = x;
```

but pointer arithmetic on `pt` is illegal:

```
++pt;                    // WRONG!
```

as is assigning `pt` to a pointer to a standard type:

```
double *pt_x = pt;   // WRONG!
```

unless a cast is used:

```
double *pt_x = (double*)pt;
```

- Multi-dimensional arrays are defined as in:

```
double x[2][4];
int i[2][5][4];
```

Indices are used to access such arrays:

```
y = x[0][1];
```

This means nothing more than successive applications of the subscripting operator and implies that two-dimensional arrays are stored by rows; an element, `x[i][j]`, is equivalent to:

```
*(&x[0][0] + 4 * i + j)
```

- Arrays can be initialized by comma-separated lists:

```
int i[] = {4, 5, 6};
double x[4] = {10.1, 10.5};
int w[3][2] = {{1, 2}, {0, -3}, {7, -5}};
```

- If an array is defined by:

```
double a[10];
```

then `sizeof(a)` gives the size of the entire array, whereas `sizeof(a[1])` gives the size of a single element.

- The statement:

```
double *pt_a[5];
```

defines an array of pointers, whereas:

```
double (*pt_a)[5];
```

defines a pointer to an array.

- The precedence and associativity of all C++ operators are given in Appendix C

6.11   Exercises

1. Given a set of real numbers, $x_1, x_2 \ldots, x_N$, the mean, $\bar{x}$, is defined by:

$$\bar{x} = \frac{1}{N} \sum_{i=1}^{N} x_i$$

the variance by:

$$variance(x_1 \ldots x_N) = \frac{1}{N-1} \sum_{i=1}^{N} (x_I - \bar{x})^2$$

and the standard deviation, σ, by:

$$\sigma(x_1 \ldots x_N) = \sqrt{variance(x_1 \ldots x_N)}.$$

Write a program which calculates these three values from a list of numbers stored as a one-dimensional array. For test purposes you can use the `rand()` function, prototyped in `<stdlib.h>`, to generate the list, in which case the mean should be approximately 0.5. Try lists of increasing length. Is there any point in generating more than `RAND_MAX` random numbers?

2. A χ^2 test is often used to check the validity of binned data and consists of evaluating:

$$\chi^2 = \sum_i \frac{(N_i - n_i)^2}{n_i}$$

where N_i is the number of observed items in bin i and n_i is the number of items expected in bin i. Write a program which has an integer array representing ten bins and uses the library function, `rand()`, to generate a sequence of random numbers. If the generated number is in the range 0 to 99, then increment bin 1, if the number is in the range 100 to 199, then increment bin 2, and so on. Your program should send the value of χ^2 and the total number of items to the output stream.[7]

---

[7]An introduction to the χ^2 test is given in [17].

3. Polynomials in x and y are given by:

$$P = \sum_{i,j=0}^{3} p_{ij} x^i y^j \quad \text{and} \quad Q = \sum_{i,j=0}^{3} q_{ij} x^i y^j$$

where p_{ij} and q_{ij} are integers. Use two-dimensional arrays to add P and Q for various values of p_{ij} and q_{ij}. The output should be given in terms of a polynomial, rather than a list of coefficients.

4. Write a program which *initializes* the int array a[2][3][4], with values corresponding to:

$$a_{ijk} = (1 - i)(2 - j)(3 - k)$$

by using nested, comma-separated lists. Elements which have the value zero should be initialized by default and *not* explicitly. Check your program by comparing the initialization actually achieved with the expected values of a[i][j][k].

The following exercises require an understanding of Section 6.5.1:

5. The results of an experiment are stored in a five-dimensional array:

```
float data[SIZE_1][SIZE_2][SIZE_3][SIZE_4][SIZE_5];
```

One requirement is to find the average of all elements. Write two programs to calculate this average; one version should use the standard array notation, whereas the other should use a pointer. Compare the times taken by the two programs for various values of SIZE_1, ... SIZE_5. Can you make the pointer version any faster?

6. Use nested, comma-separated lists to initialize the array, a[2][3][4], so that it corresponds with:

$$a_{0ij} = \begin{pmatrix} 1 & 2 & 3 & 4 \\ 5 & 6 & 7 & 8 \\ 9 & 10 & 11 & 12 \end{pmatrix}$$

and

$$a_{1ij} = \begin{pmatrix} 13 & 14 & 15 & 16 \\ 17 & 18 & 19 & 20 \\ 21 & 22 & 23 & 24 \end{pmatrix}$$

Using only pointer arithmetic and the array name (that is a, but *not* a[0][0][0] or a[i][j][k]), list the array elements and hence verify your method of access.

The following exercise requires an understanding of Sections 6.5.1 and 6.7, which you may have decided to omit:

7. If the definition of an array is:

```
double y[2][3][4];
```

what is the type of `y[2]`? Verify your answer by assigning `y[2]` to a suitable pointer. What is the result of `sizeof(y[2])`?

Chapter 7

Further Pointer Techniques

Pointers are fundamental to many aspects of C++. In this chapter we introduce a number of different topics concerning pointers. In particular, we consider strings, pointers as function arguments, pointers to functions, dynamic memory allocation and reference arguments.

7.1   Strings

A *string* is simply a one-dimensional array of type `char`, with the character constant `'\0'`, indicating the end of the string.[1] This string terminator is the crucial feature that distinguishes a string from a general `char` array; if the terminator is omitted, functions that manipulate strings usually fail disastrously.[2] Recall that a string constant (or string literal) consists of a sequence of characters enclosed by double quotes, as in:

```
"This is a string constant (or string literal)."
```

There is a special way of initializing a `char` array with a string constant:

```
char message[] = "Hello world";
```

which avoids the equivalent, but more tedious alternative:

```
char message[] = {'H', 'e', 'l', 'l', 'o', ' ',
    'w', 'o', 'r', 'l', 'd', '\0'};
```

---

[1] `'\0'` is the null character which is represented by zero in the ASCII character set. The null character differs, of course, from the character, `'0'`.

[2] The disaster occurs through attempting to interpret a perfectly valid `char` array, such as `char c[3] = {'C', '+', '+'}`, as a string. The absence of a string terminator causes string manipulation functions to access memory beyond the end of the array.

As can be seen, this array actually has 12 elements, since the last element is '\0'. The empty pair of square brackets signifies that the compiler should allocate an array of sufficient length to store the given string constant, together with the '\0' terminator. An alternative strategy is to define a `char` array of sufficient size to hold at least the required number of characters:

```
char message[80] = "Hello world";
```

Notice that the array need not be initialized with the maximum number of characters.

Now suppose we want to assign a new string to `message[]`. It is tempting, but futile, to use:

```
message = "Hello";                    // WRONG!
```

We cannot assign anything to `message` since it is an unmodifiable lvalue (the base address of the array). However, we can assign characters to individual elements of the array:

```
char message[80];
message[0] = 'H';
message[1] = 'e';
message[2] = 'l';
message[3] = 'l';
message[4] = 'o';
message[5] = '\0';
cout << message;
```

Notice how `cout` recognizes the '\0' string terminator and simply sends the first five characters to the screen, even though the array can hold up to 80 characters. (What happens if the '\0' terminator is omitted?) This example shows us a lot about the structure of strings, but a much easier technique is to use an appropriate string manipulation function, prototyped in `<string.h>`. The function, `strcpy()`, has the prototype:

```
char *strcpy(char *string1, const char *string2);
```

and copies a string (including the terminator) from `string2` to `string1`. (Notice the direction in which the copy is made. It may not be what you would expect!) The function, `strcpy()`, also returns the destination address of the string (that is `string1`). As usual, it is up to the programmer to ensure that `string1` is the address of sufficient allocated memory to hold the required characters, together with the '\0' terminator. The penalty for failure is to write over some arbitrary, but possibly important, area of memory.

We can now assign values to the array, `message[]`, as follows:

```
#include <string.h>
char message[80];
strcpy(message, "Hello");
cout << message;
```

Again notice that we don't add the '\0' terminator, since it is part of the double quotes or string constant syntax.

There are many functions in the `<string.h>` group. For instance:

```
char *strcat(char *string1, const char *string2);
```

appends `string2` to the end of `string1`, as in:

```
#include <string.h>
char message[80];
strcpy(message, "Hello");
strcat(message, " world.");
strcat(message, "\nHave a nice day.");
cout << message;
```

Again `strcat()` takes care of any subtleties involving the '\0' terminators and the result is:

```
Hello world.
Have a nice day.
```

Exercise:

Does this code give the same message on your system?

What functions are prototyped in `<string.h>`? Modify your code for the first part of this exercise so that it uses at least one additional function from this part of the standard library.

Now consider the following code:

```
char *pt;
pt = "Hello world.";
```

or, equivalently:

```
char *pt = "Hello world.";
```

and compare it with:

```
char pt[] = "Hello world.";
```

It is tempting to think that the *pt and pt[] definitions are equivalent. However, in the first case memory is allocated to hold the string constant, a pointer is declared and the base address of this string is assigned to the pointer. The only new assignment that we can make, is to change the address held by the pointer, since we cannot assign to the string constant, "Hello world.". In the second case, we have an array, of just sufficient length to hold the given string and which is initialized to that string. It is possible to copy another string to the array, exactly as we have done previously.

Any temptation to use a pointer assignment to a string constant as if it were an array definition should be resisted. Suppose we had the following:

```
char *string1 = "Hello world";
char *string2 = "world";
```

then a clever compiler could simply make string2 point to the appropriate place in the "Hello world" string. A programmer making assignments to the memory pointed to by string1 or string2 would be rather surprised by the result.

Scientists, engineers and mathematicians don't usually spend a lot of their time performing complicated string manipulations; they are more interested in inverting matrices than writing word processing programs. The places where you are likely to want to use strings are creating filenames for various storage media and annotating output. Moreover, with more advanced C++ techniques it is possible to implement a string class with the advantages of safer and more natural string manipulations.[3]

7.2   Pointers as Function Arguments

As we discussed in Chapter 5, function arguments in C++ are normally passed by value; the function makes a copy of the value of each argument and then manipulates these copies. The return value of a function can be used to change a single variable in the calling environment, but often we want to change several or even many variables. For instance, suppose we need to write a function that swaps two integers. One way of doing this is to use function arguments to pass the addresses of the integers, since once a function has the addresses, it can directly manipulate the values in memory. Of course, this is just the kind of potentially disastrous situation which we discussed previously, so we must be careful to get such pointer manipulations exactly right. Here is a possible swap() function:

```
void swap(int *pt_x, int *pt_y)
{
    int temp;
```

---

[3]See Section 9.6.2.

```
        temp = *pt_x;
        *pt_x = *pt_y;
        *pt_y = temp;
    }
```

In this example `pt_x` and `pt_y` are of type pointer to `int`; in other words they can store the addresses of variables of type `int`. When calling the function `swap()`, the two arguments must also be the addresses of objects of type `int`:[4]

```
    int i = 10, j = 20;

    swap(&i, &j);
    cout << "i = " << i << " j = " << j << "\n";
```

When the `swap()` function is invoked, the addresses of `i` and `j` are passed as arguments and 10 (the value stored at the address of `i`) is assigned to `temp`. The value currently stored at the address of `j` (that is 20) is then assigned to the memory location of `i`. The final statement in the swap function assigns 10 (the value of `temp`) to the memory location of `j`. Hence the values stored in `i` and `j` are interchanged.

Notice that the statement:

```
    *pt_x = *pt_y;
```

has a totally different effect from:

```
    pt_x = pt_y;
```

The latter is valid C++, but simply assigns one pointer to another. In this context, the address of `j` (which bears no relation to 10) would be assigned to `pt_x`. Since the scope of `pt_x` is limited to the function body and nothing further is done with `pt_x`, this syntactically correct statement would achieve nothing.

The technique of using pointer arguments to change values in the calling environment can clearly be extended indefinitely. The main disadvantage is that function modularity is eroded. Once the address of a variable is passed to a function, that variable may be changed in a way that can only be discerned by examining the function body. For this reason, pointers should only be used as function arguments when it is really necessary. No purpose is served by using pointers as function arguments just to save trivial quantities of memory.

Exercise:

Write a program to try out the `swap()` function implemented in this section.

---

[4]Now that you understand more about strings, you may wish to use '\n' rather than "\n" However, the space saved is at best minuscule.

7.3 Passing Arrays as Function Arguments

As has already been pointed out, arrays are of vital importance in many numerical applications and functions are an essential technique for controlling the complexity of programs. It should therefore come as no surprise to learn that functions frequently need to access the elements af arrays.

7.3.1 One-dimensional Arrays

It is straightforward to pass one-dimensional arrays as function arguments. The basic point to remember is that accessing an element of a one-dimensional array simply involves dereferencing a pointer. The array size is needed for the array definition, which allocates the memory. Thereafter, it is entirely the programmer's responsibility to ensure that a pointer really does point to the allocated memory. Therefore, to pass a one-dimensional array as a function argument, it is only necessary to pass an address, since the array size is not relevant for accessing array elements, although it may be necessary in order to ensure that an element is a member of the array.

Suppose we want to write a function to return the sum of a sequence of elements of an array. A suitable function is:

```
double sum(double pt[], int n)
{
    double temp = 0.0;
    for (int i = 0; i < n; ++i)
        temp += pt[i];
    return temp;
}
```

The argument, n, in the function prototype is the number of elements that we want to sum. The following illustrates using the sum() function to find the total value of all elements of an array:

```
double height[100], total_height;
// Assign values to heights.
total_height = sum(height, 100);
```

However, there is no need to start the summation at the low end of the array:

```
double height[100], total_height;
// Assign values to heights.
total_height = sum(&height[10], 24);
```

This example sums 24 heights, starting with height[10]. Notice that we must pass an address as the first argument to sum; height[10] would merely pass a double precision floating point number, which would tell sum() nothing about where the array is stored (and would also be a compile-time error).

Exercise:

Assign 1, 2, 3 ... to the elements of `height[]` and then verify that `total_height` has the expected value.

In the function prototype for `sum()` we omitted the size of the one-dimensional array; even if we did insert the size it would be ignored by the compiler. In fact we could simply use a pointer:

```
double sum(double *pt, int n);
```

It is worth remarking that we can only omit the array size in a function header or prototype; elsewhere a compile-time error occurs:

```
double height[];    // WRONG: array size not specified.
```

It is also important to understand that, although in the above example we can access `pt` as if it were an array, it is actually a pointer, rather than an array name. We can even assign an address to `pt`:

```
double sum(double pt[], int n)
{
    double temp = 0.0, *pt_end;
    pt_end = pt + n;
    while (pt < pt_end)
        temp += *pt++;                    // Increments pt.
    return temp;
}
```

Exercise:

Replace the `sum()` function used in the previous exercise by this pointer version. Does your program give the same result for `total_height`?

Using the array notation for function arguments can lead to confusion, as in:

```
double sum(double pt[1000])
{
    double temp = 0.0;
    int n = (int)sizeof(pt) / sizeof(double); // WRONG!
    for (int i = 0; i < n; ++i)
        temp += pt[i];
    return temp;
}
```

In this attempt at a `sum()` function, `n` is actually assigned the size of a pointer to a `double` divided by the size of a `double`, rather than 1000. The two values are very different!

7.3.2   Multi-dimensional Arrays

An Introduction

Passing multi-dimensional arrays as function arguments is fairly straightforward. The only feature to note is that a function needs access to the values of all sizes associated with the array indices (apart from the first) in order to generate the correct storage map. Details of storage maps for mult-dimensional arrays were given in Section 6.5.1, which you may have decided to skip for the moment. The essential idea is that a multi-dimensional array is mapped by the compiler into a one-dimensional array corresponding to the computer memory. In order to generate this mapping, the compiler must have available the sizes corresponding to all array indices apart from the first. For instance, in the case of a two-dimensional array, a function needs the number of columns in order to index into the correct row. As an example, a function which returns the trace of a 5×5 array (regarded here as representing a matrix) is:

```
double trace(double y[][5])
{
    double sum = 0.0;
    for (int i = 0; i < 5; ++i)
        sum += y[i][i];
    return sum;
}
```

The function `trace()` could be invoked by:

```
double x[5][5];
for (int i = 0; i < 5; ++i)
    for (int j = 0; j < 5; ++j)
        x[i][j] = (i + 1) * (j +1);
cout << "Trace = " << trace(x) << "\n";
```

Notice that it is the base address of the array which is passed as the argument to `trace()`. We could have used:

```
cout << "Trace = " << trace(&x[0][0]) << "\n";
```

but not:

```
cout << "Trace = " << trace(x[0][0]) << "\n";    // WRONG!
```

More Advanced Features[†]

The declaration in the `trace()` function header of the previous section could equivalently be written:

```
double trace(double (*y)[5]);
```

which says that y is a pointer to an array of 5 doubles. However, this declaration is probably more obscure and there is the danger of writing:

```
double trace(double *y[5]);
```

Since the square brackets have a higher precedence than the dereferencing operator, this declares an array of 5 pointers to the type double, which is not what is required in the trace() function header. The reason for using:

```
double trace(double (*y)[5]);
```

rather than:

```
double trace(double *pt);
```

is that the former enables us to employ the standard array subscripting notation. Since y points to an object with size $5 \times$ sizeof(double), array subscripting automatically does the correct pointer arithmetic. For instance, (y+1) is the base address of row 1 of the array, rather than element 1 of row 0.

Sometimes, knowledge of how arrays are stored can considerably improve the speed of calculations. As an simple example, suppose we want to sum two matrices represented by 100×100 arrays:

```
double a[100][100], b[100][100], c[100][100];
// Values are assigned to a[i][j] and b[i][j]
sum(a, b, c);
```

A suitable sum() function is:

```
void sum(double a[][100], double b[][100], double c[][100])
{
    for (int i = 0; i < 100; ++i)
        for(int j = 0; j < 100; ++j)
            c[i][j] = a[i][j] + b[i][j];
}
```

The disadvantage of this implementation is that a considerable amount of unnecessary arithmetic is done in calculating the address of each element since, for matrix addition, there is no advantage in scanning over rows and columns. A faster, but more devious, implementation is:

```
void sum (double *pt_a, double *pt_b, double *pt_c)
{
    double *pt_end = pt_c + 100 * 100;
    while (pt_c < pt_end)
        *pt_c++ = *pt_a++ + *pt_b++;
}
```

This version simply steps from one element in memory to the next. The function should be called as in:

```
double a[100][100], b[100][100], c[100][100];
// Values are assigned to a[i][j] and b[i][j]
sum(&a[0][0], &b[0][0], &c[0][0]);
```

since the function prototype differs from the previous version. For high dimensional arrays, the increase in speed obtainable through using such techniques can be considerable.

Exercise:

Write a program which assigns values to the elements of b[][] and c[][] and then verifies the result given by the sum() function.

7.4   Arguments to `main()`

It is fairly common for a program to require user-defined parameters. For instance we could have a program to list all primes up to some maximum, entered by the user. So far our programs have all prompted the user to enter any necessary values. However, an alternative would be to have a command line argument, so that we could enter the required values at the same time as typing the program name. For example:

```
prime 100
```

could generate all prime numbers less than 100. This technique can be achieved by using arguments to main().

Although strictly dependent on the C++ compiler, a function of the following form is usually acceptable:

```
int main(int argc, char *argv[])
{
    // Code.
}
```

Since the two arguments are *formal* arguments, they could be given any names, but argc and argv[] are established conventions. The number of command line arguments, including the program name, is given by argc. For our prime example, argc would be 2. The second argument, *argv[], is an array of char pointers. These pointers actually point to strings, terminated in the usual way by '\0'. The first element of the array is rather special since argv[0] points to the program name as a string. For instance, in the above example the string would

be "prime". Subsequent elements of the argv array point to the command line
arguments; argv[1] is the first command line parameter as a string, argv[2] is
the second and so on. In this example argv[1] points to the string "100". The
following program does no more than print the command line arguments. Try it
for different arguments:

```cpp
#include <iostream.hpp>
#include <stdlib.h>                    // for EXIT_SUCCESS

int main(int argc, char *argv[])
{
    cout << "The program name is: " << argv[0] << "\n\n";
    cout << "There are " << argc << " arguments\n\n";
    for (int i = 0; i < argc; ++i)
        cout << "Argument " << i << " is " <<
            argv[i] << "\n\n";
    return(EXIT_SUCCESS);
}
```

Notice that the arguments are strings rather than integers; in our prime
example we must convert "100" to the integer, 100. Fortunately, a library function exists which converts a string to an integer. The function prototype is in
<stdlib.h> and is:

```cpp
int atoi(const char *pt);
```

So if we supply a string as the argument to this function, the result is the corresponding integer.

Exercise:

Try the following:

```cpp
#include <stdlib.h>                        // for atoi()

int i = atoi("12345");
cout << "The integer is " << i << "\n";
```

and find out what happens if the string is not an integer.

Using the answer to Exercise 7 in Chapter 5, we can now write a prime
program to take a command line argument:

```cpp
#include <iostream.hpp> // includes <stdio.h>
#include <math.h>       // for sqrt()
#include <stdlib.h>     // for exit(), atoi()
```

```cpp
const int TRUE = 1;
const int FALSE = 0;

// Function prototypes:
int test_prime(long n);
void list_primes(long n);

int test_prime(long n)
{
    int prime;

    if (n == 0L || n == 1L)
        prime = FALSE;
    else if (n == 2L)
        prime = TRUE;
    else if (!(n % 2L))
        prime = FALSE;
    else {
        // add 0.5 to ensure round up:
        long i_end = 0.5 + sqrt(double(n));
        prime = TRUE;
        for (long i = 3L; i <= i_end; i += 2L) {
            if (!(n % i)) {
                prime = FALSE;
                break;
            }
        }
    }
    return prime;
}

void list_primes(long n)
{
    cout << "Primes up to " << n << " are:\n\n";
    if (n >= 2)
        cout << "2\n";
    for (long i = 3L; i <= n; i += 2L)
        if (test_prime(i))
            cout << i << "\n";
}

int main(int argc, char *argv[])
```

```
    {
        if (argc != 2) {
            cout << "Usage:  prime <max>\n";
            exit(EXIT_FAILURE);
        }
        long n = atoi(argv[1]);
        list_primes(n);
        return(EXIT_SUCCESS);
    }
```

If, after compiling and linking this program, the executable file is **prime.exe** (or whatever extension is required on your system) then, to list all primes up to 100, enter the command:

```
prime 100
```

Exercise:

Run the **prime** program with various values for the command line parameter. Does **test_prime()** deal appropriately with all possible arguments? If not, make suitable modifications.

7.5   Pointers to Functions

It is fairly common to want to pass a function as an argument to another function. For instance, suppose we want to write a function, called **sum()**, which sums the first n values of another function:

```
double f(int m)
{
    // Definition of f().
}

double sum(int n)
{
    double temp = 0.0;
    for (int i = 0; i < n; ++i)
        temp += f(n);
    return temp;
}
```

This approach does work, but now suppose we want to do the summation for a number of different functions. The problem is that we would really like to specify

the function as an argument to `sum()`, rather than embedded in the function
body. We now explain how to achieve this.

In C++ it is possible to have a pointer to a function. As an example, a pointer
to a function that returns a `double` is defined by:

```
double (*g)();
```

The slightly bizarre notation is necessary because the function operator, `()`, binds
tighter than the indirection operator, `*`. So if we wrote:

```
double *g();
```

this would actually declare a prototype for a function that takes no arguments
and returns a pointer to a `double`. Apart from the fact that this declaration is
not our intention, the compiler would not allow us to do this inside a function
body; we cannot prototype a function inside another function.

So our `sum()` function can be rewritten as:

```
double sum(double (*g)(int m), int n)
{
    double temp = 0.0;
    for (int = 0; i < n; ++i)
        temp += (*g)(i);
    return temp;
}
```

In the function header, `g` is declared to be a pointer to a function which takes an
argument of type `int`. (The identifier, `m`, could be omitted.) Notice that since `g` is
a pointer it must be dereferenced when it is used in the body of `sum()`. However,
the usual function notation:

```
        temp += g(i);
```

is also permitted in this situation as the two forms are defined to be equivalent.
This is consistent with the name of a function being that function's address.

A complete program which invokes several different functions by means of a
pointer is as follows:

```
#include <iostream.hpp>
#include <math.h>          // for pow()
#include <stdlib.h>        // for EXIT_SUCCESS

// Function prototypes:
double f2(int i);
double f4(int i);
double sum(double (*g)(int m), int n);
```

```
double f2(int i)
{
    return 1.0 / (i * i);
}


double f4(int i)
{
    double temp = i * i;
    return 1.0 / (temp * temp);
}


double sum(double (*g)(int m), int n)
{
    double temp = 0.0;
    for (int i = 1; i < n; ++i)
        temp += (*g)(i);
    return temp;
}


int main()
{
    cout << "Approximations to the Riemann Zeta " <<
        "functions are:\n\n";
    cout << "Zeta(2) = " << sum(f2, 40) <<
        "\nA better approx. is " << PI * PI / 6.0 << "\n\n";
    cout << "Zeta(4) = " << sum(f4, 40) <<
        "\nA better approx. is " <<
        pow(PI, 4) / 90.0 << "\n\n";
    return(EXIT_SUCCESS);
}
```

In this example, **pow()** is a library function, which has the prototype:

```
double pow(double x, double y);
```

and returns the value of **x** raised to the power **y**. Unlike some other languages, C++ has no built-in operator which raises a number to a power.

Exercise:

Compile and run this program (which evaluates the Riemann Zeta function, $\zeta(n)$, for $n = 2$ and 4).[5] Try summing other functions, such as $\frac{1}{i!}$. If necessary, modify the **sum()** function.

---

[5] The Riemann Zeta function is defined by $\zeta(s) = \sum_{k=1}^{\infty} k^{-s}$. See [11] for further details.

Notice in the above example that we need to pass the address of the appropriate function as the first argument to **sum()**; **f2** and **f4** (without the usual function call operator, **()**) are the function addresses. This syntax is analogous to **x** being the base address of an array, **x[]**.

We can now improve our root program, given in Section 5.9.2 by using a pointer to a function:

```cpp
#include <iostream.hpp>
#include <math.h>          // for exp(), pow(), cos()
#include <stdlib.h>        // for exit()


// Function prototypes:
double f(double x);
double root(double x1, double x2, double f1, double f2,
    int &depth);
double find_root(double (*g)(double), double x1, double x2,
    int &depth);

double f(double x)         // We want to find a root of f(x) = 0.
{
    return (exp(x) + pow(2.0, -x) + 2.0 * cos(x) - 6.0);
}


double root(double x1, double x2, double f1, double f2,
    int &depth)
// Finds a root of f(x) = 0 using bisection.
// Assumes that x2 >= x1 and f1 * f2 < 0.0
{
    const int max_depth = 50;
    const double x_limit = 1e-5;
    double estimated_root;
    double x_mid = 0.5 * (x1 + x2);
    if (x2 - x1 <= x_limit)
            estimated_root = x_mid;
    else if (++depth > max_depth) {
        cout << "WARNING: maximum limit of " <<
            max_depth << " bisections reached\n";
        estimated_root = x_mid;
    }
    else {
        double f_mid = f(x_mid);
        if (f_mid == 0.0) {
            // Zero at x_mid.
```

```
                estimated_root = x_mid;
            }
            else if (f(x1) * f_mid < 0.0) {
                // Zero in first segment.
                estimated_root = root(x1, x_mid, f1, f_mid,
                    depth);
            }
            else {
                // Zero in second segment.
                estimated_root = root(x_mid, x2, f_mid, f2,
                    depth);
            }
        }
        return estimated_root;
}

double find_root(double (*g)(double), double x1, double x2,
    int &depth)
{
    double f1 = g(x1);
    double f2 = g(x2);
    if (f1 * f2 > 0.0) {
        cout << "Error in find_root():  " <<
            "end-points have same sign\n";
        exit(EXIT_FAILURE);
        }
    else if (x2 - x1 > 0.0)
        return root(x1, x2, f1, f2, depth);
    else
        return root(x2, x1, f2, f1, depth);
}

int main()
{
    int depth = 0;
    double x;

    x = find_root(f, 1.0, 2.0, depth);
    cout << "Root is " << x <<" recursion depth = " <<
        depth << "\n";
    cout << "f(x) at root = " << f(x) << "\n";
    return(EXIT_SUCCESS);
}
```

The function whose root is required is passed as an argument to `find_root()`, rather than being embedded in the body of `find_root()`. This means that it is now straightforward to implement root finding for a number of different functions. A further improvement on the original program is that since `depth` is defined in `main()` (rather than as a `static` within the body of `root()`) its value can be reset to zero. This would enable a single program to use the `root()` and `find_root()` functions to discover multiple roots.

Exercise:

Compile and run this root-finding program for a variety of different functions. Some suggestions are:

1. $f(x) = e^{2x} - x - 2$

2. $g(x) = 1000x^3 - x - 1$

3. $v(r) = (5.67 \times 10^6)e^{-21.5(r/\sigma)} - 1.08(\frac{\sigma}{r})^6$ where $\sigma = 4.64$.

   ($v(r)$ is an approximation to the potential energy between two helium atoms.)

Declarations involving pointers to functions often look quite complicated, as in:

```
double f(double (*p1)(double), double (*p2)(double),
    double (*p2)(double));
```

but a typedef can provide some simplification. For instance, we could declare a `typedef` for a pointer to a function taking a single `double` argument and returning a `double`:

```
typedef double (*PT_FUNC)(double);
```

in which case the declaration for `f()` could be rewitten as:

```
double f(PT_FUNC p1, PT_FUNC p2, PT_FUNC p2);
```

After working through this section you should understand our remark in Chapter 5, that to invoke a function, the syntax is:

```
f();
```

rather than:

```
f;
```

The latter statement, without any parentheses, achieves nothing since `f` is the address of the function; an analogous error for an array, `x[]`, is:

```
x;
```

7.6 Dynamic Memory Management

At the time of writing a program, the sizes of arrays needed in many scientific applications are often unknown. For instance, the sizes might depend on how much data we manage to collect or how much memory is available on the particular computer running our program. One way of coping with these situations is to define array sizes by means of global constants:

```
const int MAX_DATA_POINTS = 100;

double pressure[MAX_DATA_POINTS];
double height[MAX_DATA_POINTS];
double temperature[MAX_DATA_POINTS];
double humidity[MAX_DATA_POINTS];
```

If the complete program consists of more than one module, then the array size definition is best placed in a header file so that modifying the header file automatically adjusts the array size throughout the modules. However, each change necessitates re-compiling and re-linking the program, both of which can be very time-consuming processes. Also, it may not be clear whether an array is needed until the program is actually running. A further difficulty is that the useful lifetime of an array may not be obvious at compile-time.

Fortunately C++ it is possible to allocate and deallocate memory while a program is running; such techniques are often known as *dynamic memory management*. The program has access to an area of memory, commonly known as the *heap* or the *free store*. Requests can be made to allocate contiguous portions of this memory and, when no longer required, the memory can be returned to the heap. The operators which allocate and deallocate memory are called **new** and **delete** respectively. These operators hide the necessary book-keeping from the user; it is not necessary to calculate the number of bytes of memory required to store a particular object.

7.6.1 Allocating Memory

The **new** operator returns the address of sufficient memory to store the specified fundamental or derived type. If we want to allocate memory to store a single object, then the syntax is demonstrated in the following examples:

```
int *pt_i = new int;        // *pt_i can store an int.
float *pt_f = new float;    // *pt_f can store a float.
double *pt_d = new double;  // *pt_double can store a double.
int *pt = new(int);         // *pt can store an int.
                            // (Alternative syntax.)
```

Notice that in the last line of this example we have used a function-like syntax; in general there is little to choose between the two alternatives, although occasionally the function-like syntax can be useful to override operator precedence. We could, of course, define the pointer and invoke the **new** operator in two separate statements:

```
double *pt;
pt = new double;
```

Accessing dynamically allocated objects is straightforward, except that since we have a pointer to an address, we need to dereference the pointer:

```
float *pt = new float;
*pt = 100.14;        // O.K. Assigns 100.14 to *pt.
float x = pt;        // WRONG: pt is a pointer not a float;
```

In the above examples, the **new** operator allocates memory, but does no initialization. It is possible to allocate and initialize with the same statement, by enclosing the initializing expression in parentheses:

```
float *pt_pi = new float(3.142);  // 3.142 assigned to *pt_pi.
cout << "pi = " << *pt_pi << "\n";
```

Notice that it is the memory pointed to by `pt_pi` that is initialized, rather than `pt_pi`, which stores the address of the allocated memory. It is possible for the initializing expression to be missing; this is equivalent to omitting the parentheses and consequently the memory stores an arbitrary initial value:

```
float *sum = new float();  // O.K.
for (int i = 0; i < 10; +i)
    *sum += i;                 // WRONG: the initial value of
                               //        *sum may not be zero.
```

It is not possible to use the **new** operator to allocate memory for a function, but memory for a pointer to a function can be allocated. Recall that:

```
double (*g)(void);
```

or

```
double (*g)();
```

defines a pointer to a function, having no arguments and returning a `double`. The following allocates memory for such a pointer:

```
double (**g)() = new(double (*)());
```

which can be accessed via ***g**. Notice that we have used the function-like syntax for **new**. The statement:

```
double (**g)() = new double (*)();          // WRONG!
```

is incorrect because this is actually equivalent to:

```
double (**g)() = (new double)(*)();          // WRONG!
```

which is not as intended.

Sometimes, if there is insufficient free store available, the **new** operator cannot allocate memory. In such cases no error message is output, but the pointer returned is the null pointer. Since it is guaranteed that the null pointer does not point to valid memory, we can always test for a memory allocation failure:

```
#include <stdlib.h>          // for exit()
#include <stdio.h>           // for NULL

float *pt = new float(3.1415926);

if (pt == NULL) {
    cout << "Failed to allocate memory for pt\n";
    exit(EXIT_FAILURE);
}
```

If there is any possibility of running out of free store, it is worth testing the pointer in this way. If no test is made and a null pointer is returned, the cause of the error may be very hard to trace.

For fundamental types, such as **int**, **float**, **double** etc., there is usually little, if anything, to be gained by using the **new** operator to allocate memory for single objects. But derived types, such as arrays and class objects, may require a lot of memory and then the **new** operator can prove to be very useful. A class is a rather special derived type which will be described in Chapter 8. Here we consider dynamic memory allocation for arrays of the fundamental types.

The syntax for allocating memory for arrays is demonstrated by:

```
int *pt_i = new int[10];          // Array of 10 ints.
double *pt_d = new double[100];   // Array of 100 doubles.
char *pt_c = new char[10];        // Array of 10 chars.
int *pt = new(int[10]);           // Alternative syntax.
```

In each case, the base address of the array is assigned to the pointer. To access the array we can either explicitly dereference or, equivalently, use the standard array subscripting notation:

```
int *m = new int[10];
*(m+2) = 4;                    // Assigns 4 to element m[2].
m[9] = m[2];                   // Assigns 4 to element m[9].
```

Notice that square brackets are used to enclose the expression specifying the number of elements required in each array. For example, the following is not correct:

```
int *pt = new int(10); // Initializes *pt to 10, instead of
                       // requesting an array of 10 ints.
for (i = 0; i < 10; ++i)
    pt[i] = i;         // WRONG: for 0 < i < 10 we are outside
                       //        of the allocated memory.
```

The new operator can also be used to allocate an array of pointers:

```
double **pt;              // pt is a pointer to a pointer.
pt = new(double *[20]);

int i;
// Assign to i.
float **pf = new(float *[i]);
```

In the first example, the base address of memory, sufficient to store twenty pointers to type double, is assigned to pt. In the second example, the new operator dynamically allocates memory to store i pointers to type float, using the run-time value of i.

Exercise:

Modify the program which used ragged arrays (in Section 6.9.2) so that all arrays are allocated dynamically.

Multi-dimensional arrays can also be allocated dynamically:

```
int i;
// Assignment to i.
float (*x)[10][20] = new float[i][10][20];
```

This example allocates memory for an $i \times 10 \times 20$ three-dimensional array of type float. The sizes associated with all array indices, apart from the first, must be positive constants since the compiler needs to create a storage map, but the value of i need only be known at run-time. A dynamically allocated multi-dimensional array can be accessed by means of the standard notation (in this case x[i][j][k]), since x is actually a pointer to an array.[6]

---

[6]Notice that x is *not* an array of pointers, but rather a pointer to an array. See Section 6.8.

Memory can also be dynamically allocated for an array of pointers to functions. The following returns the base address of an array of ten pointers to functions, where each function returns a `float` and takes no arguments:

```
float (**g)() = new(float(*[10])());
```

There are several features that are worth noting for dynamically allocated arrays:

- If we define an array by:

```
int m[10];
```

then m is an unmodifiable lvalue and we cannot assign to m:

```
int m[10], *pt;

// Address assigned to pt.

m = pt;           // WRONG: cannot assign to a constant.
```

However, if the array is dynamically allocated, then m is of type pointer to int and can be used to hold any int address:

```
int *m, *pt;
m = new int[10];

// Address assigned to pt.

m = pt;           // O.K. (but probably unwise).
```

Such assignments may be misguided; the base address of a dynamically allocated array should not be lightly discarded, since without this information we cannot deallocate the array.

- Dynamically allocated memory remains allocated even when control passes out of the function where the **new** operator was invoked:

```
double *f(void)
{
    double *a;

    a = new double[20];    // Allocates memory.
    for (int i = 0; i < 20; ++i)
```

```
        a[i] = i;              // Assigns to elements.
    return a;                  // Returns base address of
                               // array. a goes out of scope.
}

void g(void)
{
    double *pt;

    pt = f();                  // Assigns base address of
                               // allocated array to pt.
                               // (a is not in scope.)
    for (int i = 0; i < 20; ++i)
        cout << "a["<< i << "] = " << pt[i] << "\n";
}
```

- When the new operator is used to allocate an array, initializers cannot be specified:

```
    int *pt = new int[3](1,7,28);  // WRONG: initializer
                                   //        is not valid.
```

The elements of dynamically allocated arrays have arbitrary initial values:

```
    float *velocity = new float[10];

    // Assignments to velocity[i].

    float *total_velocity = new float[10];
    for (int i = 0; i < 10; ++i)
        total_velocity[i] +=
            velocity[i];     // WRONG: total_velocity[i] may
                             //        not be initially zero.
```

- For large dynamically allocated arrays there is much to be gained from testing whether or not the allocation has been successful; the overhead involved is comparatively small and the probability of failure is greater than in programs where only limited memory allocations are made:

```
    #include <stdlib.h>                // for exit()
    #include <stdio.h>                 // for NULL

    double *pt = new double[100000];
```

```
    if (pt == NULL) {
        cout << "Failed to allocate memory for pt.\n";
        exit(EXIT_FAILURE);
    }
```

Rather than terminating the entire program, techniques can be used to recover from such failures. For instance, it may be possible to deallocate other objects and then to try allocation again. Such techniques depend on details of the application and are not discussed further in this book.

One minor restriction on the **new** operator is that the type cannot include `const` or `volatile` specifiers:

```
const int *pt_i = new const int[10];   // WRONG: const not
                                        //          allowed.
volatile char *pt_c;
pt_c = new volatile char *pt_c[1000];  // WRONG: volatile
                                        //     not allowed.
```

7.6.2   Deallocating Memory

Once memory is allocated dynamically, the allocation is valid until the program terminates, unless we explicitly deallocate the memory. The **delete** operator is used to perform this deallocation:

```
float *pt_f = new float;
int *pt_i = new int(10);

// Code accessing *pt_f and *pt_i.

delete pt_f;
delete pt_i;
```

The same notation is used for deleting arrays of the fundamental types:

```
int *pt_i = new int[10];
double *pt_d = new double[100];

// Code accessing pt_i[i] and pt_d[i].

delete pt_i;
delete pt_d;
```

Notice that we don't specify the number of elements to be deleted since the the
C++ compiler keeps track of the array size.[7]

Incorrect attempts to use the `delete` operator may not be detected by the
compiler. If you are lucky, you may get a run-time error message, such as 'COR-
RUPTED HEAP'. At worst, the consequences of a bad deletion will only show
up at some later point in the program execution and the cause of the failure will
be difficult to locate. Typical errors, some of which will be trapped by a good
compiler, are:

- Deleting memory that was not allocated by `new` is undefined:

```
int a[10];
// Code accessing a[i].
delete a;              // WRONG: a[10] was not
                       //        allocated by new.
```

- Since a `const` object cannot be allocated by `new`, such objects cannot be
  deleted:

```
const int a[4] = {100, 200, 300, 400};

// Code accessing a[i].

delete a;              // WRONG: a[] was not
                       //        allocated by new.
```

- Deleting memory that has already been deallocated has undefined consequences:

```
int *p = new int[10];

// Code accessing int[i].

delete p;              // O.K.

// More code.

delete p;              // WRONG: memory already
                       //        deallocated.
```

- A deleted object must not be accessed; the consequences are undefined and
  the values stored in memory may have been changed by the deletion:

---

[7]A slightly different syntax is used for deleting an array of class objects and this is introduced
in Section 8.3.

```
int *p = new int[20];

// Code accessing p[i].

delete p;
cout << "p[0] = " <<
    *p << "\n";        // WRONG: memory deallocated.
```

However, applying the `delete` operator to the null pointer is harmless since it does nothing.

Exercise:

Use the `delete` operator to deallocate memory in the ragged array program developed for the exercise on page 172.

7.7 Pass by Reference and Reference Variables

7.7.1 Reference Arguments

The use of pointer arguments to change values in the calling environment is notationally rather cumbersome. For example, in our `swap()` function (Section 7.2) we had to use the dereferenced variables `*pt_x` and `*pt_y`. It is possible to overcome this inconvenience by specifying that some or all of the function arguments are to be passed by reference, as in:

```
void swap(int &x, int &y)
{
    int temp;

    temp = x;
    x = y;
    y = temp;
}
```

In this context the token, `&`, is known as the *reference declarator* and simply means that the function arguments are to be passed by reference.[8] There is no direct connection with the address-of operator and in no sense does taking the address of `x` give the `int` type. The way in which our new `swap()` function is invoked is rather different from and certainly more convenient than using the pointer notation:

---

[8]Notice that in this context the & token is *not* an operator but rather is used in the declaration of a type.

```
int i = 10, j = 20;
swap(i, j);
cout << "i = " << "j = " << j << "\n";
```

As with pointers, pass by reference erodes the modularity of functions; in order to find out how (if at all) variables are changed in the calling environment, we need to examine the function body. There is even more chance of unexpected changes, since in the calling environment there is no indication that the arguments are actually passed by reference, as in:

```
int sum = 0;
for (int i = 0; i < 10; ++i)
    sum += dark_sheep_function(i);
```

The `dark_sheep_function()` may have very unpleasant consequences; the following would cause the above loop to continue for ever:

```
int dark_sheep_function(int &i)
{
    --i;
    return i * i;
}
```

Due to the possibility of such effects, it is only worth using pass by reference when it is really necessary, such as when a function needs to access large amounts of data or to change variables in the calling environment.

One restriction on functions which use pass by reference is that they cannot be invoked with a temporary as an argument. For example, the following is illegal for our `swap()` function:

```
swap(10, 20);
```

In this case swapping 10 and 20 is clearly futile, but even a function which does not modify the value of a reference argument cannot be invoked with a temporary as argument.

If a function argument that is passed by reference does not get modified by that function, then it is worth using the `const` specifier. You will find that you are forced to be consistent and to introduce the specifier at a lower level. For instance, the following code segment:[9]

```
void g(float &x);
void h(float *pt);
```

---

[9]This example is only for illustration since it is not actually worth using pass by reference for a `const` fundamental type. More realistic examples involve class objects, which are introduced in Chapter 8.

```
void f(const float &x)
{
    g(x);              // WRONG!
    h(&x);             // WRONG!
    float *pt = &x; // WRONG!
    // Use pt here.
}
```

does not compile and should be replaced by:

```
void g(const float &x);
void h(const float *pt);

void f(const float &x)
{
    g(x);
    h(&x);
    const float *pt = &x;
    // Use pt here.
}
```

One advantage of the **const** specifier for functions using pass by reference is that invoking such functions with a temporary as an argument *is* legal; for instance:

```
f(1.414);
```

is valid with the above prototype for **f()**.

Exercise:

Use pass by reference to implement and test a function which interchanges the values of three variables, **x**, **y** and **z**, so that $x \leq y \leq z$. The three variables should have the type **double**.

7.7.2 Reference Return Values

It is also possible for functions to return a reference. For instance:

```
double &component(double *vector, int i)
{
    return vector[i];
}
```

returns the reference, **vector[i]**. The reference return type is specified by the **&** in the function header. We can invoke this function by:

```
double x[10], y;
x[4] = 72.3;
y = component(x, 4);                // Assigns 72.3 to y
```

which is no different from our previous use of functions. However, what is new is that we can also put the function on the left hand side of an assignment statement:

```
component(x, 5) = 34.7;            // Assigns 34.7 to x[5]
```

which is something we can only do by returning a reference.

So far, our `component()` function is too much like the C++ array element to be useful, but suppose we define

```
double &component(double *vector, int i)
{
    return vector[i-1];
}
```

We can now access the components by indexing from 1 rather than 0:

```
double x[10], y;
component(x, 10) = 72.3;   // Assigns 72.3 to x[9].
y = component(x, 10);      // Assigns value of x[9] to y.
```

By using more advanced C++ techniques, it is possible to write a version of `component()` which uses a less cumbersome notation. Such techniques are introduced in Chapter 9.

Some caution must be exercised when returning a reference, since effectively an address is passed back to the calling environment. This means that you must return something that has scope outside the function; it is no good returning a reference to an object which is defined inside the function, since that memory may well be reused when control leaves the function:

```
double &new_component(double *vector, int i)
{
    return 2 * vector[i]; // WRONG: cannot return a reference
                          //        to an expression.
}


double &square(double x)
{
    double temp = x * x;
    return temp;              // WRONG: temp goes out of scope
                             //        outside the function body.
}
```

Equivalent remarks apply if a pointer to a local array is returned:

```
double *array(int i)
{
    double x[10];
    return &x[i];         // WRONG!
}
```

except that in such cases the error is probably more obvious.

7.7.3 Reference Variables

Use of the reference declarator is not restricted to functions. Consider the following:

```
int x;
int &y = x;
x = 10;
cout << "y = " << y << "\n";
```

In this example, y is known as a reference variable. The statement:

```
int &y = x;
```

means, in effect, that y is an alias for x. There is one memory location which is allocated by the statement:

```
int x;
```

The value for x and y is held in this same memory location and changing the value of one changes the other:

```
int x;
int &y = x;
x = 10;
cout << "y = " << y << "\n";
y = 200;
cout << "x = " << x << "\n";
```

This use of the reference declarator is consistent with its use in function arguments. In our swap() function example, x and y are reference variables or aliases for the actual variables supplied when the function is called (i and j in the example given). Indeed, there does not seem to be much purpose in having reference variables, except in the context of function arguments and return statements. In the above example, the way in which changing the value of x changes y (and vice versa) is confusing; it would be far better to remove the redundant variable.

There are a few restrictions on what we are allowed to do with reference variables:

- A reference variable must be initialized at the time of declaration and cannot subsequently be changed to refer to a different object:

```
int x, y, z;
int &a = x; // O.K.
int &w;      // WRONG: no initializer.
&a = y;      // WRONG: attempt to re-initialize reference.
```

- Pointers to references, and consequently arrays of references, are not defined in C++. References to references are likewise not allowed:

```
int x;
int &y = x; // O.K.
int &z = y; // WRONG: reference to reference not allowed.
```

- Memory cannot be allocated for reference variables by means of the **new** operator. Given that we are not permitted to have a pointer to a reference, this restriction is not surprising.

7.8   Using Pointers, Arrays and Strings

In this section, we develop two programs which demonstrate most of the ideas introduced in this chapter. The design technique used in both cases is to start by developing a function, `main()`, which invokes various other functions. Initially we know what we would like these functions to do, but we don't actually implement them until we are satisfied with `main()`. This *top-down* approach is adequate for small and medium sized projects, although there is some debate as to whether it is appropriate for those that are large and use object-oriented techniques [1].

7.8.1   Matrix Addition

Suppose we want to add two matrices, A and B, whose elements are real numbers:

$$C = A + B$$

The elements of C are given by:

$$c_{ij} = \sum_{ij=1}^{n} a_{ij} + b_{ij}$$

In C++ we could obviously store the matrices as two-dimensional arrays:

```
double a[MAX_ROWS][MAX_COLS];
double b[MAX_ROWS][MAX_COLS];
double c[MAX_ROWS][MAX_COLS];
```

However, with this approach we are forced to decide on the maximum sizes of the matrices before the program is compiled. Moreover, code to implement matrix addition might be something like the following:

```
for (int i = 0; i < m; ++i) {
    for (int j = 0; j < n; ++j) {
        c[i][j] = 0;
        for (int k = 0; k < w; ++k)
            c[i][j] += a[i][k] * b[k][j];
    }
}
```

This is not a very efficient implementation since each access of a two-dimensional array, a[i][j], implicitly uses pointer arithmetic of the form:

```
*(&a[0][0] + i * MAX_COLS + j)
```

whereas it would be more efficient to use pointers directly. It is also worth noting that array indices in C++ take the values 0, 1, 2 ..., rather than 1, 2, 3 ... as is often more natural for scientific applications.

So our project is to write a program which we can use to try out matrix addition. A suitable program is:

```
#include <iostream.hpp>
#include <stdlib.h>      // for exit()

// Function prototypes:
double *create_matrix(int rows, int columns);
double &element(double *pt_matrix, int columns, int row,
    int column);
void add_matrices(double *pt_result_matrix, double
    *pt_matrix_a, double *pt_matrix_b, int rows, int columns);
void print_matrix(double *pt_matrix, int rows, int columns);

int main(int argc, char *argv[])
{
    if (argc != 3) {
        cout << "Usage:  mult <rows> <columns>\n";
        exit(EXIT_FAILURE);
    }
    int rows = atoi(argv[1]);
    if (rows < 1) {
```

```
        cout << "Rows in matrix = " << rows <<
            ".\nMust have:  0 < rows.\n";
        exit(EXIT_FAILURE);
    }
    int columns = atoi(argv[2]);
    if (columns < 1) {
        cout << "Columns in matrix A = " << columns <<
            ".\nMust have:  0 < columns.\n";
        exit(EXIT_FAILURE);
    }

    // Create matrices:
    double *pt_a = create_matrix(rows, columns);
    double *pt_b = create_matrix(rows, columns);
    double *pt_c = create_matrix(rows, columns);

    // Fill matrices:
    for (int i = 1; i <= rows; ++i) {
        for (int j = 1; j <= columns; ++j) {
            element(pt_a, columns, i, j) = i * (j + 1);
            element(pt_b, columns, i, j) = (i + 2) * (j + 3);
        }
    }

    // Print matrices:
    cout << "Matrix A:\n";
    print_matrix(pt_a, rows, columns);
    cout << "Matrix B:\n";
    print_matrix(pt_b, rows, columns);

    // Add matrices:
    add_matrices(pt_c, pt_a, pt_b, rows, columns);

    // Print results:
    cout << "Result of adding matrices:\n";
    print_matrix(pt_c, rows, columns);

    // Destroy matrices:
    delete pt_a;
    delete pt_b;
    delete pt_c;

    return(EXIT_SUCCESS);
```

```
}
```

As promised, `main()`, is the only function that has actually been implemented so far. Command line parameters are passed to `main()` by using the function arguments. If the compiled program is in a file called `add.exe` (or whatever extension is required on your system) then:[10]

```
add <rows> <columns>
```

causes the program to start executing; an example is:

```
add  4  5
```

The first thing that `main()` does is to check that `argc` is equal to three; if it is not, then the correct syntax has not been used and there is no point in proceeding further. We then read in the two parameters. The ANSI C library function, `atoi()`, is used to convert the `argv[]` strings to integers, which are then checked to ensure they have appropriate values. Next, we dynamically allocate three contiguous areas of memory with sufficient size to store data for the three matrices. In order to test addition, two matrices are filled with data corresponding to:

$$c_{ij} = i(j + 1)$$

and

$$c_{ij} = (i + 2)(j + 3)$$

by using the `element()` function and the results are sent to the output stream. Then the matrices are added and the result is also sent to the output stream.

Having given an overall picture of what the program actually does, we now need explicit code for the functions. The `create_matrix()` function returns the address of dynamically allocated memory for a `rows` ×`columns` matrix:

```
double *create_matrix(int rows, int columns)
// Dynamically allocates matrix.
{
    double *pt = new double[rows * columns];
    if (pt == NULL) {
        cout << "Failed to allocate matrix.\n";
        exit(EXIT_FAILURE);
    }
    return pt;
}
```

The `element()` function uses a reference return statement so that assignments can be made to matrix data:

---

[10]Throughout this book, command parameters are delimited by <>.

```
double &element(double *pt_matrix, int columns, int row,
    int column)
{
    return *(pt_matrix + (row - 1) * columns + column - 1);
}
```

Notice that indices take the values 1, 2, 3 ..., rather than 0, 1, 2 ....

The function to add matrices is very simple:

```
void add_matrices(double *pt_result_matrix, double
    *pt_matrix_a, double *pt_matrix_b, int rows, int columns)
{
    double *pt_end = pt_result_matrix + rows * columns;
    while (pt_result_matrix < pt_end)
        *pt_result_matrix++ = *pt_matrix_a++ + *pt_matrix_b++;
}
```

since we can iterate through the one-dimensional memory space rather than the two-dimensional space of matrix rows and columns.

Finally, the function to print the matrix data makes straightforward use of the `element()` function:

```
void print_matrix(double *pt_matrix, int rows, int columns)
{
    for (int i = 1; i <= rows; ++i) {
        for (int j = 1; j < columns; ++j) {
            cout << element(pt_matrix, columns, i, j) << " ";
        }
        if (columns != 1)
            cout << element(pt_matrix, columns, i, columns) <<
                "\n";
    }
    cout << "\n";
}
```

There are many improvements that can be made to this program by using techniques which are introduced in subsequent chapters. Such improvements include:

- defining a matrix by the statement:

    ```
    matrix a(rows, columns);
    ```

- assignment to the ij'th matrix element by statements such as:

```
a(i, j) = i * (j + 1):
```

- printing a matrix, a, by:

```
cout << a;
```

- adding matrices by:

```
c = a + b;
```

Exercise:

Compile and link the program described in this section. Check that the correct answers are given for various rows and columns. Also check the answers when other values are assigned to the matrix elements.

7.8.2 An Alphabetic Sort

Earlier in this chapter, we remarked that engineers and scientists don't usually spend much time manipulating strings. But suppose you want to write a book, perhaps even one on C++. Using a document preparation system, such as LATEX [16], makes it fairly easy to generate an index, but the ordering of the entries is arbitrary. So our project is to develop a program to sort a list of index entries. Initially we will just consider an alphabetic sort of lower case words, later you will have to decide what to do about entries, such as **#define**, || and ~.

Our program should accept the number of words, followed by a list of words, entered on separate lines. The words must be converted to lower case and listed alphabetically. Also, the program should not be unreasonably restricted in either the number or length of these words. As an example, if we enter:

```
10
Inheritance
new
delete
class
object
overload
address
Constructor
inline
private
```

the result should be:

```
address
class
constructor
delete
inheritance
inline
new
object
overload
private
```

A suitable program is:

```cpp
#include <iostream.hpp>
#include <stdlib.h>       // for exit(), atoi()
#include <string.h>       // for strlen(), memcpy()
#include <ctype.h>        // for tolower()

// Function prototypes:
void get_words(char **pt_words, int words);
void list_words(char **pt_words, int words);
void words_to_lower_case(char **pt_words, int words);
void word_to_lower_case(char *word);
void bubble_sort(void **pt_data, int elements,
    void (*order)(void**));
void order_strings(void **pt);

int main(int argc, char *argv[])
{
    if (argc != 2) {
        cout << "Usage:  sort <number of words>\n";
        exit(EXIT_FAILURE);
    }
    int words = atoi(argv[1]);
    if (words < 1) {
        cout << "Cannot enter " << words << " words\n";
        exit(EXIT_FAILURE);
    }
    char **pt_words = new char *[words];

    get_words(pt_words, words);
    cout << "\nOriginal list:\n";
    list_words(pt_words, words);
```

```
        words_to_lower_case(pt_words, words);
        cout << "\nLower case list:\n";
        list_words(pt_words, words);

        bubble_sort(pt_words, words, order_strings);
        cout << "\nOrdered lower case list:\n";
        list_words(pt_words, words);

        return(EXIT_SUCCESS);
    }
```

After checking the command line parameters, `main()` gets the words from the input stream, lists the words, converts them to lower case and lists them again. Next, the list is sorted using a *bubble sort* and the sorted list is displayed.

First consider the `get_words()` function:[11]

```
    void get_words(char **pt_words, int words)
    {
        char buffer[128];
        for (int entry = 0; entry < words; ++entry) {
            cin >> buffer;
            int length = 1 + strlen(buffer);
            pt_words[entry] = new char[length];
            memcpy(pt_words[entry], buffer, length);
        }
    }
```

In order to allow for an arbitrary number of arbitrary length words, we store the characters in a ragged array. (See Section 6.9.2.) The **new** operator is used to allocate an array of pointers, just sufficient to store all of the base addresses of strings, which in turn store the entered words. Each word is first copied into a temporary buffer, which can store a word of up to 127 characters. The C library function, `strlen()`, returns the length of a string, excluding the '\0' terminator, which enables us to dynamically allocate sufficient memory for the string. We then copy the string from the buffer into this memory, using the library function, `memcpy()`.

The `list_words()` function is straightforward:

```
    void list_words(char **pt_words, int words)
    {
        cout << "\n";
```

---

[11]This implementation is not very robust since it does not properly handle cases where the value of **words** is inconsistent with the number of words actually in the list. Techniques for overcoming such limitations are considered in Chapter 12.

```
    for (int i = 0; i < words; ++i)
        cout << pt_words[i] << "\n";
}
```

as is `words_to_lower_case()`:

```
void words_to_lower_case(char **pt_words, int words)
{
    for (int i = 0; i < words; ++i)
        word_to_lower_case(pt_words[i]);
}
```

which in turn invokes the function, `word_to_lower_case()`:

```
void word_to_lower_case(char *pt)
{
    while (*pt) {
        *pt = tolower(*pt);
        ++pt;
    }
}
```

This function uses the ANSI C library function, `tolower()`, to convert any upper case character to lower case.

We use a bubble sort to arrange the words in alphabetical order, although our code is sufficiently general to cope with any kind of data:

```
void bubble_sort(void **pt_data, int elements,
        void (*order)(void**))
{
    int n = elements - 1;
    for (int i = 0; i < n; ++i)
        for (int j = n; j > i; --j)
            order(pt_data + j - 1);
}
```

A bubble sort sweeps through an array, comparing successive pairs of elements. If a pair is out of order, then the elements are swapped. Here we use a pointer to a function (called `order`) to do the comparison and reordering. This allows us to invoke different functions for different data types, ensuring that we can reuse the `bubble_sort()` function in other programs. To be sure of getting all of the elements in the correct order, we must sweep through the array n times, where n is one less than the number of elements. As a result, a bubble sort is very inefficient, the time taken being $\mathcal{O}(n^2)$.

In the `main()` function, `bubble_sort()` is invoked with the address of a function called `order_strings()` as the third argument. This function has the following implementation:

```
void order_strings(void **pt)
{
    void *temp;
    if (strcmp((char*)pt[0], (char*)pt[1]) > 0) {
        temp = pt[0];
        pt[0] = pt[1];
        pt[1] = temp;
    }
}
```

The library function, `strcmp()`, is used to compare two adjacent words and returns a value greater than zero if the words are out of order. Notice that the amount of copying is reduced by swapping the addresses of the strings within the `pt_words[]` array, rather than the strings themselves. The argument of `order_strings()` is the address of the element in `pt_words[]` which gives the address of the first word of the pair to be sorted.

Exercise:

A bubble sort is so-called because elements of an array are 'bubbled' into the correct order. Modify the above program so that you can observe this happening as the sort proceeds, by sending the partially sorted lists to the output stream.

7.9   Summary

- A string is a one-dimensional array of type `char` and is terminated by the `'\0'` character. A `char` array can be initialized by a string constant (a sequence of characters inside double quotes):

  ```
  char message[] = "Hello world";
  char big_message[80] = "Hello";
  ```

  Notice the difference between a string constant and an array of type `char`.

- Use the string functions, prototyped in `<string.h>`, to carry out manipulations such as string copying:

  ```
  strcpy(message, "Bye");
  ```

  but make sure that you allocate enough memory. (Don't forget to allow for the `'\0'` terminator.)

- Declaring functions with pointer arguments:

```
void swap(int *pt_x, int *pt_y);
```

enables a function to change values in the calling environment. This is both useful and potentially dangerous.

- Arrays can be passed as function arguments:

```
double sum(double a[], int n);
double trace(double a[][5]);
```

All array sizes, apart from the first, must be known at compile-time.

- Command line arguments are implemented by using arguments to `main()`:

```
int main(int argc, char *argv[]) { // ... }
```

- For a function, `f()`, `f` is the address of the function. A pointer to a function can be defined by:

```
int (*pt)();
```

- Memory is dynamically allocated by using the `new` operator:

```
int *pt_i = new int;
```

and returned to the heap by the `delete` operator:

```
delete pt_i;
```

- The reference declarator, `&`, has three related uses:

  - A function can change variables in the calling environment by using pass by reference, as in:

    ```
    void swap(int &x, int &y);
    ```

  - Returning a reference:

    ```
    double &component(double *vector, int i):
    ```

    enables a function to be the *left* operand of an assignment operator:

    ```
    component(x, 5) = 550.0;
    ```

  - Reference variables create aliases to the same storage location:

    ```
    int data[100];
    double &header = data[0];
    ```

    but such aliases are confusing and should be avoided.

7.10 Exercises

1. Modify the program developed in Section 7.8.1 so that it implements and tests a matrix multiplication function.

2. Implement a function to transpose a matrix. The transposition should overwrite the original matrix.

3. Modify the sort program developed in Section 7.8.2 to sort at least some of the more esoteric entries that appear in the index to this book (such as `<stdlib.h>`, `#define` and `operator+=`).

4. Modify the sort program so that it sorts a list of integers into ascending order.

5. The bubble sort in Section 7.8.2 continues comparing values even if an array is in order after the first few passes. Write a version without this inefficiency.

6. Write a program that accepts a single word as a command line parameter and then linearly searches an array that stores lower case words, just as in our sort program. The program should print:

   ```
   <n> OCCURRENCES OF <word>
   ```

   or

   ```
   NO OCCURRENCES OF <word>
   ```

   depending on the result of the search. (You may wish to write a function which generates a list of words for test purposes. In practise the list would be read from a file.)

   Modify your program so that the list is sorted before being searched and the search is terminated as soon as possible.

7. A bubble sort is *very* inefficient. A much better method, invented by C. A. R. Hoare is known as *Quicksort*[12] and is typically $\mathcal{O}(n \log n)$ rather than $\mathcal{O}(n^2)$. Quicksort is part of the ANSI C library, where it is implemented by a function called `qsort()`. Use `qsort()` to sort a list of random integers. Compare the time taken to sort the same list, using both a bubble sort and Quicksort. Do the times have the expected dependency on the list size?

---

[12]The method is too complicated to describe in an exercise, but an explanation is given in [17].

8. The Newton-Raphson technique was described in Exercise 5 of Chapter 4, but now that we have introduced pointers to functions, we can implement a more general version. Recall that given a function, $f(x)$, the technique attempts to find a zero of the function by successive iterations of the form:

$$x_{i+1} = x_i - \frac{f(x_i)}{f'(x_i)}.$$

Write a function to implement this technique. The function should have the prototype:

```
double newton(double x_lower, double x_upper,
    double accuracy, void (*f_pt)(double *f_value,
    double *f_derivative, double x));
```

where `x_lower` and `x_upper` are the lower and upper limits of an interval within which a root is known to occur. `f_pt` is a pointer to a function which, given x, calculates $f(x)$ and $f'(x)$, corresponding to `*f_value` and `*f_derivative` respectively. The function, `newton()`, returns a root of $f(x)$ when $|f(x)|$ is within the specified accuracy.

For some functions, the Newton-Raphson technique is very powerful, since it converges quadratically to the root. However, because the method can go badly wrong, you should include code to check whether the iteration has jumped out of the specified interval and also put an upper bound on the number of iterations.

Try your Newton-Raphson implementation for the functions:

(a) $f(x) = e^x + 2^{-x} + 2\cos x - 6$ in the range $1 \le x \le 2$.

(b) $f(x) = x - \cos x$ in the range $0 \le x \le \pi/2$.

In each case, try various values for the accuracy parameter and list successive approximations to the roots. How does the speed of convergence compare with the bisection method described in Section 5.9.2? Try both methods for other functions.

Chapter 8

Classes

Classes are an essential feature of object-oriented programming techniques and can help to control the complexity of application programs. A class is a user-defined type (sometimes called an *abstract data type*[1]) which has its own collection of data, functions and operators. Various levels of data hiding are provided and these help to create an interface to the class which hides its implementation.

8.1 Declaring Classes

The basic syntax for a class declaration is:

```
class class_name {
    // Class body goes here.
};
```

Notice the terminating semi-colon. The `class` keyword introduces the class declaration and `class_name` is the user-defined name for the class. The class body within the braces can consist of variable declarations, together with function definitions and prototypes. Variables, functions etc. declared within a class body are known as *members* of the class. More specifically, variables declared within a class are often called *data members*. It is also possible, by means of overloading, to give operators a special meaning within the context of a class. We leave any discussion of operator overloading until the following chapter.

As a particular example, let us suppose that we are working on a project which uses spheres of various sizes and radii. The project may well use a variety of different shapes, but, in order to concentrate on the C++ language aspects of our project, we will just consider spheres for most of this chapter. We start by defining a `sphere` class:

---

[1]More accurately, a class is an implementation of an abstract data type. A good discussion of this distinction is given in [8].

195

```
class sphere {
    double x_centre, y_centre, z_centre, radius;
};
```

We now have a user-defined type, very much analogous to the fundamental types, such as `int`, `double` etc., but recall that the type `int` does not itself allocate memory for any `int` objects; this is done by defining instances of the type:

```
int i, j, k;
```

In exactly the same way, the **sphere** class does not allocate memory, but rather it declares a type. However, we can define instances of the class and these do allocate memory:

```
sphere sphere1, sphere2, sphere3;
```

Such instances of a class are known as *objects*. These are *the* objects of object-oriented programming. In this example, each object stores its own radius, together with the cartesian coordinates of its centre.

It is possible to define objects by means of the same statement as the class declaration:

```
class sphere {
    double x_centre, y_centre, z_centre, radius;
} sphere1, sphere2, sphere2;
```

but it is usually worth keeping all the class declarations together (in a header file) and separate from objects. The class declaration is an extremely valuable self-documenting feature of C++ and, as such, is best kept as uncluttered as possible.

As well as defining single objects, it is straightforward to define arrays of objects:

```
sphere small_array[10], big_array[100][100];
```

Of course, the same information could be stored without specifying a class, as four separate arrays:

```
x_centre[100][100];
y_centre[100][100];
z_centre[100][100];
radius[100][100];
```

This approach has two disadvantages compared with using classes. Firstly, we have to invent different names for all four variables associated with `sphere1`, `sphere2`, `sphere3`, `small_array`, `big_array` .... This point may seem trivial, but choosing good names makes a major contribution to program readability and eases the task of program maintenance. Secondly, this approach forces us to think in terms of the details of the particular implementation, rather than in terms of broad concepts; instead of thinking in terms of an array of spheres, we would be considering a collection of arrays of coordinates and radii.

8.2 Class Access Specifiers

Our current definition of the `sphere` class has one fundamental problem; we cannot assign values to members of this class. By default, all members of a class are private and private members can only be accessed by function members of the same class. Our declaration of the `sphere` class is equivalent to using the `private` keyword:

```
class sphere {
private:
    double x_centre, y_centre, z_centre, radius;
};
```

However, if all members of the class are private, the class forms an isolated system, which serves no useful purpose.

The keyword, `public`, designates all subsequent members of the class to be public:

```
class sphere {
public:
    double x_centre, y_centre, z_centre, radius;
};
```

In addition to data members, classes can also have *member functions*. Members that are declared `public` can be freely accessed by both member and non-member functions. The keywords, `public` and `private`, are known as *class access specifiers*. A class access specifier is valid until either another class access specifier, or the end of the class, is reached:

```
class my_class {
public:
    // Public members go here.
private:
    // Private members go here.
public:
    // More public members could go here, but it is
    // unusual to repeat access specifiers like this.
};
```

The `public` and `private` keywords can be given in any order within the class body. Some C++ programmers consistently put the `public` members first and there is some motivation for doing this, since it is the `public` members which constitute the class interface.

8.3   Accessing Members

With our present definition of the `sphere class` (including the `public` keyword) we can directly access individual members of the class by using the *member access operator*, which is a single dot:

```
sphere1.x_centre = 2.2;       // Assigns 2.2 to the x_centre
                              // member of the sphere1 object.
sphere1.radius = 10.4;        // Assigns 10.4 to the radius
                              // member of the sphere1 object.
double x = sphere1.x_centre;  // 2.2 is assigned to x.
```

Members of arrays of objects can also be accessed. The following assigns a value to `x_centre` for element 5 in a `sphere` array:

```
sphere many_spheres[10];

many_spheres[5].x_centre = 4.5;
```

Notice that we first find the sphere and then find the required member; that is the syntax is:

```
many_spheres[5].x_centre = 4.5;     // CORRECT.
```

rather than:

```
many_spheres.x_centre[5] = 4.5;     // WRONG!
```

A complete, but very simple, program accessing members is:

```
#include <iostream.hpp>
#include <stdlib.h>                  // for exit()

class sphere {
public:
    double x_centre, y_centre, z_centre, radius;
};

int main()
{
```

```
sphere s;

s.x_centre = 1.1;
s.y_centre = 2.2;
s.z_centre = 3.3;
s.radius = 5.5;

++s.radius;

cout << "x_centre = " << s.x_centre << "\n" <<
    "y_centre = " << s.y_centre << "\n" <<
    "z_centre = " << s.z_centre << "\n" <<
    "radius = " << s.radius << "\n";
return(EXIT_SUCCESS);
}
```

It is also possible to dynamically allocate objects:

```
sphere *a_sphere = new sphere;
sphere *array_of_spheres = new sphere[100];
```

A single object is deallocated in the same way as for a fundamental type:

```
delete a_sphere;
```

The syntax for an array of objects is:

```
delete [100]array_of_spheres;
```

although recent C++ compilers accept:

```
delete [ ]array_of_spheres;
```

The syntax for deleting arrays of objects varies slightly between compilers, so it is worth checking the reference manual for your system. The distinction between deleting an array of a fundamental type and an array of class objects is necessary so that a special member function, known as a destructor, is called for each object of the array.[2]

Exercise:

Compile and run the above program accessing members of a **sphere** object. Modify the program to dynamically allocate an array of three spheres and assign different values to all data members of these objects. You should check the assignments by listing the data members and also delete the array before the program terminates.

---

[2]Destructors are introduced in Chapter 10.

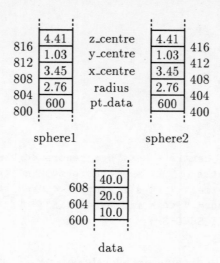

Figure 8.1: Default assignment.

8.4   Assigning Objects

We can assign an object to another object:

```
sphere sphere1, sphere2;

// Assign values to data members of sphere1
// (that is sphere1.x_centre, sphere1.radius etc.)

sphere2 = sphere1;
```

This assignment does a copy of whatever is stored by the data members of **sphere1** to the members of **sphere2**. However, the default assignment operator may not be what is actually required. For instance, the data members could include a pointer to an area of memory used to store data associated with **sphere1**, as shown in Figure 8.1.[3] In this case the **pt** members of both **sphere** objects store the address of the same **data** object. Consequently, changing the values stored in **data** changes the values for both **sphere** objects. It would probably be better if the pointer for **sphere2** pointed to a different area of memory, containing a separate copy of the data values stored in the **data** object. As we will see later, it is possible to overload operators, such as the assignment operator, in order to meet our specific requirements.

---

[3]In Figure 8.1 the numbers outside boxes denote memory addresses and the numbers within boxes represent data stored in memory. (See Figure 6.1.)

Exercise:

Verify that the data stored by `sphere1` is indeed copied to `sphere2` by the default assignment operator.

8.5 Functions and Classes

Functions can access the `public` members of a class by using the class access operator. For instance, a function to return the volume of a sphere could be implemented as:

```
#include <math.h>            // for pow(), PI

double volume(sphere s)
{
    return 4.0 * PI * pow(s.radius, 3) / 3.0;
}
```

which accesses the `radius` member of s as `s.radius`. This function is so simple that we may wish to declare it as inline:

```
#include <math.h>            // for pow(), PI

inline double volume(sphere s)
{
    return 4.0 * PI * pow(s.radius, 3) / 3.0;
}
```

Since the `volume()` function is intimately connected with objects that are spheres, it would be sensible to make the function part of the `sphere` class:

```
#include <math.h>            // for pow(), PI

class sphere {
public:
    double x_centre, y_centre, z_centre, radius;
    double volume(void) { return 4.0*PI*pow(radius,3)/3.0; }
};
```

The function, `volume()`, is now a *member function*, with direct access to data members of the object for which it is invoked, and does not take any argument. For the same reason, the function body uses the variable `radius`, rather than `s.radius`. Indeed, `s.radius` would be incorrect because, within the class definition, the `volume()` function has no access to an object named s. Notice that we have dropped the `inline` keyword; this is because all functions defined (in contrast to declared) within a class are implicitly inline. Also notice that, in order to avoid over-emphasizing member function definitions, we allow a condensed layout style within the class body.

Including complicated function definitions within a class definition would drastically reduce the usefulness of a class as a self-documenting interface. However, the function prototype can be given within the class body and the function definition outside:

```
#include <math.h>                // for pow(), PI

class sphere {
public:
    double x_centre, y_centre, z_centre, radius;
    double volume(void);
};

double sphere::volume(void)
{
    return 4.0 * PI * pow(radius, 3) / 3.0;
}
```

A member function defined outside of the class body is not implicitly inline, but the inline keyword can be added if desired:

```
#include <math.h>                // for pow(), PI

class sphere {
public:
    double x_centre, y_centre, z_centre, radius;
    double volume(void);
};

inline double sphere::volume(void)
{
    return 4.0 * PI * pow(radius, 3) / 3.0;
}
```

It is optional as to whether or not the inline specification is included in the function prototype within the class declaration. Although safer, it could be argued that the inline specifier is an implementation detail that has no place within a class declaration. This approach, which we adopt, is valid provided that the inline function implementation occurs before the function is invoked. As always (see Section 5.3), an inline function implementation belongs in a header (.hpp) rather than source (.cpp) file.

The double colon in the function header is a single token, known as the *scope resolution operator*. This operator signifies that `volume()` is a member of the `sphere` class. Outside the class body, the function header must use the `class_name::`function syntax. A function defined outside any class, such as:

```
double volume(sphere s)
{
    return 4.0 * PI * pow(s.radius, 3) / 3.0;
}
```

is a valid function definition, but not a class member. It is possible to have both a class definition of `volume()` (using the scope resolution operator) and a non-class definition. Indeed, it is possible to have functions with the same name belonging to a number of different classes:

```
double sphere::volume(void)
{
    return 4.0 * PI * pow(radius, 3) / 3.0;
}

double cube::volume(void)
{
    return pow(side, 3);
}
```

Such functions are *not* overloaded since class members have *class* scope. However, if a class has member functions with the same name then the name *is* overloaded, just as with non-member functions.

A function, which is a class member, is accessed in the same manner as a data member; by using the member access operator:

```
sphere s1, s2;
cube s3;

// Assignments to data members of s1, s2, s3.

double vol1 = s1.volume();
double vol2 = volume(s2);
double vol3 = s3.volume();
```

Exercise:

Implement a `cube` class (analogous to the `sphere` class) and assign values to the data members of `s1`, `s2` and `s3`. Check that `vol1`, `vol2` and `vol3` give the correct results.

8.6   Data Hiding

So far, using our **sphere** class has just been a convenient way of collecting related data. Now we dramatically change this situation by introducing data hiding, one of the central concepts of object-oriented programming. The idea is that we should deal with objects, such as spheres, rather than their explicit representation, such as cartesian coordinates; the data associated with an object should only be accessible by means of function calls which hide details of the class implementation.

In fact we already know how to hide the sphere data; what we need are some functions to access that data. A suitable **sphere** class declaration is:

```
class sphere {
public:
    void assign_centre(double x, double y, double z);
    void get_centre(double &x, double &y, double &z);
    void assign_radius(double r);
    void get_radius(double &r);
    double volume(void);
private:
    double x_centre, y_centre, z_centre, radius;
};
```

Notice how the **public** functions provide the class interface and hide details of the class implementation. In fact, we could store the centre in terms of polar coordinates, r, θ and ϕ, without this change being discernible through the interface provided by the **public** functions.

Returning now to the class using a cartesian coordinate representation, suitable implementations for the member functions are:[4]

```
inline void sphere::assign_centre(double x, double y,
    double z)
{
    x_centre = x;
    y_centre = y;
    z_centre = z;
}

inline void sphere::get_centre(double &x, double &y,
    double &z)
{
    x = x_centre;
```

---

[4]It can reasonably be argued that the **volume()** function should not be **inline** since it involves significant computation.

```
    y = y_centre;
    z = z_centre;
}

inline void sphere::assign_radius(double r)
{
    radius = r;
}

inline void sphere::get_radius(double &r)
{
    r = radius;
}

double sphere::volume(void)
{
    return 4.0 * PI * pow(radius, 3) / 3.0;
}
```

In the context of some object-oriented languages (such as Smalltalk), member functions are referred to as *methods*, which send *messages* to objects. An object has a state and the effect of the methods is to access this state. Such terminology is not emphasized in this book, although it is used by some C++ programmers.

It is worth emphasizing again that memory for an object is not defined by the class declaration, but by the object definition itself:

```
    sphere s;
```

Here sufficient memory is assigned to **s** for storing the values of **x_centre** etc. When we invoke a member function, as in:

```
    double vol1 = s.volume();
    s.assign_centre(10, 24, 36):
```

it is the specific memory associated with **s** that is accessed. Moreover, there may be many **sphere** objects, each with its own memory for storing data and access to the *single* copy of the member functions.

Exercise:

Repeat the previous exercise (on page 203) for this new **sphere** class.

8.7   Returning an Object

Previously, we have made frequent use of functions that return a fundamental
type; for instance, the **volume()** functions, defined in this chapter, all return
the type **double**. It is also straightforward for a function to return an object.
Suppose we need a function to return a new sphere, with the same radius as an
existing sphere, but a translated centre. A suitable implementation of such a
function, which should be made a **public** member of the **sphere** class, is:

```
sphere sphere::translated_sphere(double d_x, double d_y,
    double d_z)
{
sphere new_sphere;

new_sphere.x_centre = x_centre + d_x;
new_sphere.y_centre = y_centre + d_y;
new_sphere.z_centre = z_centre + d_z;
new_sphere.radius = radius;

return new_sphere;
}
```

We can invoke this **translated_sphere()** function as follows:

```
sphere s1;

// Assign values to s1.
sphere s2 = s1.translated_sphere(1.1, 2.2, 3.3);
```

Notice that the **translated_sphere()** function is used to assign values to another
sphere object; the function does not translate the original object. We could
achieve translation of the origin of a sphere by using the following **sphere** class
member function:

```
void sphere::translate(double d_x, double d_y, double d_z)
{
    x_centre += d_x;
    y_centre += d_y;
    z_centre += d_z;
}
```

which could be invoked as in:

```
s.translate(1.1, 2.2, 3.3);
```

Now let us examine the `translated_sphere()` function in more detail. The object called `new_sphere` is defined within the function and does not exist outside of the function body. This that means a statement, such as:

```
s2 = s1.translated_sphere(1.1, 2.2, 3.3);
```

creates at least one temporary copy of the `new_sphere` object. Creating these temporary objects is inefficient since only the `s1` and `s2` objects need exist.

In order to overcome this problem of temporary copies, we might be tempted to return a reference object:

```
sphere &sphere::translated_sphere(double d_x, double d_y,
    double d_z)
{
    sphere new_sphere;

    new_sphere.x_centre = x_centre + d_x;
    new_sphere.y_centre = y_centre + d_y;
    new_sphere.z_centre = z_centre + d_z;
    new_sphere.radius = radius;

    return new_sphere;   // WRONG: cannot return a reference
                         //        to a local object.
}
```

Any variation on this theme will fail since `new_sphere` only exists within the scope of the function body and so we cannot return a reference to this object.

Exercise:

Write a program to try out the `translated_sphere()` function, by shifting the centres of a dynamically allocated array of three `sphere` objects. What happens if you replace the correct version of the `translated_sphere()` function by the invalid version which attempts to return a local object?

8.8 Reference Arguments

A valid way of defining a `translated_sphere()` function which does not introduce spurious copies is by means of a `sphere` reference argument:

```
void sphere::translated_sphere(sphere &s, double d_x,
    double d_y, double d_z)
{
```

```
        s.x_centre = x_centre + d_x;
        s.y_centre = y_centre + d_y;
        s.z_centre = z_centre + d_z;
        s.radius = radius;
    }
```

Notice that a member of a reference to an object is accessed in the same way as a member of an object. The formal argument, **s**, is a reference to a **sphere** object and hence no copy of this object is made by the **translated_sphere()** function. An example invoking this function is:

```
    sphere s1, s2;

    // Assignments to s1.

    s1.translated_sphere(s2, 1.1, 2.2, 3.3);
```

The only **sphere** objects are **s1** and **s2**; the function works directly with **s2**, so no temporary copies are made.

Exercise:

Modify the program for the previous exercise so that it uses reference arguments.

8.9   Pointers to Members

An alternative to the reference argument technique, given in the previous section, is to use a pointer to a **sphere** object:

```
    void sphere::translated_sphere(sphere *pt, double d_x,
        double d_y, double d_z)
    {
        (*pt).x_centre = x_centre + d_x;
        (*pt).y_centre = y_centre + d_y;
        (*pt).z_centre = z_centre + d_z;
        (*pt).radius = radius;
    }
```

In this implementation, **pt** is a pointer to the **sphere** type; in other words it is a variable which can store the address of any object of type **sphere**. When the function is invoked, the address of a **sphere** object is passed:

```
sphere s1, s2;

// Assignments to s1.

s1.translated_sphere(&s2, 1.1, 2.2, 3.3);
```

Within the function body, `*pt` is the dereferenced address and hence the object, `s2`. The member access operator, with `*pt` and `x_centre` as operands, therefore modifies the `x` coordinate of the centre of the sphere, `s2`. Notice that the parentheses enclosing `*pt` are necessary because the member access operator binds tighter than the dereferencing operator.[5]

Since accessing a member of an object pointed to by a pointer is a very common requirement, there is a special operator for this purpose, which is known as the *class member access operator* and is represented by a right-pointing arrow. The statement:

```
pt->x_centre = x_centre + d_x;
```

is equivalent to:

```
(*pt).x_centre = x_centre + d_x;
```

The arrow, which is a single token, consists of the minus sign followed by the greater than sign. The `translated_sphere()` function could therefore be rewritten as:

```
void sphere::translated_sphere(sphere *pt, double d_x,
    double d_y, double d_z)
{
    pt->x_centre = x_centre + d_x;
    pt->y_centre = y_centre + d_y;
    pt->z_centre = z_centre + d_z;
    pt->radius = radius;
}
```

Using the class member access operator, rather than the original pointer dereference and member access operator, is simply a notational convenience and has no effect on the way the `translated_sphere()` function is invoked. It is worth emphasizing that, since the class member access operator is a single token, the following is illegal:

```
pt - > x_centre = x_centre + d_x;    // WRONG!
```

Exercise:

Change the program for the previous exercise so that instead of using pass by reference, pointers are used for the function arguments.

---

[5]Recall that Appendix C contains a list giving the precedence and associativity of all operators, including those introduced in this chapter.

8.10   Pointer-to-member Operators[††]

Throughout this section and purely for the purpose of demonstration, we consider a simplified **sphere** class in which the only data member is **public**:

```
class sphere {
public:
    void assign_radius(double r) { radius = r; }
    void get_radius(double &r) { r = radius; }
    double radius;
};
```

There are two fundamental ways in which we can specify an object; we can either use the object itself or else dereference a pointer to an object. For example, in our **sphere** class, we can define a **sphere** object, **s**, and a pointer to a **sphere** object, **pt_s**:

```
sphere s;
sphere *pt_s;
pt_s = &s;              // Address of object assigned to pt_s.
```

There are also two ways in which we can specify members of a class. The obvious method is to use the member directly, such as **assign_radius(10.0)** (for a member function) or **radius** (for a data member). However, we can also dereference a pointer to class members. Such a pointer must be restricted to a particular class and can only point to a particular type of member function or data member. The scope resolution operator, ::, is used to specify the class; for instance:

```
double sphere::*pt;
```

defines a pointer, **pt**, which can point to a data member, of type **double**, belonging to the **sphere** class. In the class defined above, **pt** can only point to the **radius** data member:

```
pt = &sphere::radius;
```

although in some classes there may be many different members which could be pointed to by the same pointer. The combination, ::*, is sometimes known as a *pointer-to-member declarator*.

Recall that, since defining a class does not allocate memory, **pt** does not point to any memory suitable for storing a value for the radius; **pt** is a pointer to a member of a class and *not* to a member of a class object. Statements such as the following are illegal:

```
*pt = 10.0;            // WRONG: incompatible types.
```

It is also possible to point to member functions. The following defines a `sphere` class pointer, `pt_f`, which returns the type, `void`, and has an argument of type, `double`:

```
void (sphere::*pt_f)(double);
```

The first parentheses are necessary because the function call operator, (), has a higher precedence than the dereferencing operator, *. Again, since our current `sphere` class is rather limited, `pt_f` can only point to the `assign_radius()` function:

```
pt_f = sphere::assign_radius;
```

We now have two ways of specifying a `sphere` object (`s` and `*pt_s`) and two ways of specifying a class member (`radius` and `*pt` or `assign_radius()` and `*pt_f`). There are therefore four different ways of accessing object members and each of these methods has its own special binary operator. If we make the definitions:

```
sphere s;
sphere *pt_s;
double sphere::*pt;
double (sphere:: *pt_f)(double);

pt_s = &s;
pt = &sphere::radius;
pt_f = sphere::assign_radius;
```

then the four methods that can be used to access members of the object, `s`, are:

1. The *member access operator* (a single dot) is used when the operands are an object and a member:

```
s.radius = 10.0;        // Access data member.
s.assign_radius(10.0);  // Access member function.
```

This operator was introduced in Section 8.3.

2. The *class member access operator* (a right pointing arrow, `->`) is used when the operands are a pointer to an object and an object member:

```
pt_s->radius = 20.0;        // Access data member.
pt_s->assign_radius(20.0);  // Access function member.
```

We introduced this operator in the previous section.

3. A *pointer-to-member operator*, denoted, .*, is used when the operands are an object and a pointer to a class member:

```
s.*pt = 30.0;              // Access data member.
(s.*pt_f)(30.0);           // Access member function.
```

Notice that the first parentheses are necessary because the function call operator, (), has a higher precedence than the .* operator.

This is the first place that we have used the pointer-to-member operator; it is a single token, consisting of a dot followed by an asterisk. As always, white space is not allowed within the token:

```
s .* pt = 30.0;      // O.K.
s.*pt = 30.0;        // O.K.    Probably the usual style.
s. *pt = 30.0;       // WRONG: White space is not allowed
                     //        within a token.
```

The same notation is used to access members of a reference to an object:

```
sphere &r = s;
r.*pt = 30.0;              // Access data member.
(r.*pt_f)(30.0);           // Access member function.
```

4. A second *pointer-to-member operator*, denoted ->*, is used if the operands are a pointer to an object and a pointer to a class member:

```
pt_s->*pt = 40.0;          // Access data member.
(pt_s->*pt_f)(40.0);       // Access member function.
```

Again, the parentheses are necessary because the function call operator, (), has a higher precedence than the pointer-to-member operator, ->*. This is the first place that we have used this pointer-to-member operator;[6] it is a single token, consisting of a minus sign, greater than sign and an asterisk.

Exercise:

Check the functionality of the four operators considered above by using them to assign different values to `radius` and then print, by means of the `get_radius()` function, the values stored.

---

[6]The usual names given to the four operators considered in this section are slightly confusing. There are two *pointer-to-member* operators, together with the *member access* and the *class member access* operators. The notation used by [7] is *member pointer selector* for −>∗ and *member object selector* for .∗, which seems better but does not have widespread use.

Whereas the member access and class member access operators, . and ->, are used extensively in typical C++ applications, the two pointer-to-member operators, .* and ->*, are less common. It is worth noting that none of these four operators overrides class protection, which is why we have made the radius data member public for this section.

8.11 Scope and Data Protection

We have already seen, in Section 8.5, that functions declared within a class are not visible outside that class, unless the scope resolution operator is used. The same is true for both public and private data members. Consider:

```cpp
#include <iostream.hpp>
#include <stdlib.h>        // for EXIT_SUCCESS

class sphere {
public:
    void assign_centre(double x, double y, double z);
    void get_centre(double &x, double &y, double &z);
    void assign_radius(double r);
    void get_radius(double &r);
    double radius;  // Made public for this example.
private:
    double x_centre, y_centre, z_centre;
};

// Implementation of class member functions go here.

int main()
{
    sphere s;

    s.assign_centre(1.1, 2.2, 3.3);
    s.assign_radius(101.1);
    double x_centre = 0.0;
    double y_centre = 0.0;
    double z_centre = 0.0;
    double radius = 0.0;

    s.get_centre(x_centre, y_centre, z_centre);
    s.get_radius(radius);
    cout << "x_centre = " << x_centre <<
            "\ny_centre = " << y_centre <<
```

```
              "\nz_centre = " << z_centre <<
              "\nradius = " << radius << "\n";

         // The results show that the body of main() does
         // not have visibility of private class members.

         return(EXIT_SUCCESS);
}
```

Although names, such as **x_centre**, are used as members of the **sphere** class, there is no visibility of these names within the body of the function **main()**, where they can safely be reused. In fact a class provides the third kind of scope, the other two being file scope and block scope, as described in Section 5.4.

It is worth pointing out that the concept of **private** class members is intended to encourage safer programming techniques. The **private** access specifier does not provide either secrecy or protection against malicious programming. Once we have the address of an object, a cast to a pointer of a different type would enable us to probe supposedly **private** regions of memory. Of course, there is little purpose in using a sophisticated programming language if the programmer is intent on such subversion.

8.12   Static Members

Each class object has its own set of class data members; every object belonging to our **sphere** class has its own centre coordinates and radius. However, in some circumstances we may want a data member to be common to all objects of a class. For instance, we may want to keep track of the total number of spheres. It would clearly be wasteful if we had to update multiple copies of this number, every time we defined a new **sphere** object. A *static data member* is useful in this situation and a *static member function* is an appropriate way of accessing such data. We now consider these two concepts in more detail.

8.12.1   Static Data Members

As an example of a **static** data member, consider the following suitably modified **sphere** class:[7]

```
class sphere {
public:
     void increment_spheres(int new_spheres);
     int total_spheres(void) { return total; }
```

---

[7]It would be more satisfactory if **total** were incremented with the creation of each **sphere** object, but we have not yet considered the necessary techniques.

```
        // ...
    private:
        static int total;
    };

    inline void sphere::increment_spheres(int new_spheres)
    {
        total += new_spheres;
    }
```

We can access a `static` data member, in the same way as any other data member, by using the member access operator with an object as the left operand. The significant difference is that the same `static` data is seen by all objects:

```
    #include <iostream.hpp>
    #include <stdlib.h>

    int main()
    {
        sphere s1, s2;

        s1.increment_spheres(2);
        cout << "Total number of spheres known to s1 = " <<
            s1.total_spheres() <<
            "\nTotal number of spheres known to s2 = " <<
            s2.total_spheres() << "\n";

        return(EXIT_SUCCESS);
    }
```

The total number of spheres known to the two objects, `s1` and `s2`, is the same in this example. Notice that we did not initialize `total`, since the variable is declared `static` and is therefore initialized to zero by default. A common error is attempting to initialize `static` data within a class declaration:

```
    class sphere {
    public:
        void increment_spheres(int new_spheres);
        int total_spheres(void) { return total; }
    private:
        static int total = 0;        // WRONG!
    };
```

which is illegal, but static data members (even if declared `private`) can be *initialized* by means of the class name and the scope resolution operator:

```
int spheres::total = 10;
```

Notice the emphasis on initialized; we cannot make an assignment to a private `static` member (except within a class member function or `friend`[8]):

```
sphere::total = 10;              // WRONG: total is private.
```

Initialization can only be performed once within a single program. Consequently, the initialization of a `static` data member should be placed in the `.cpp` file which implements the non-`inline` member functions, rather than in the class header file. An example illustrating the initialization of `static` data members is given in Section 8.17.1.

We could, of course, declare `total` to be a global variable instead of making it a member of the `sphere` class. However, the total number of spheres is a property of the class and clearly belongs in the class declaration.

Public `static` data members can be accessed directly by means of the class name and the scope resolution operator, `::`. There is no need for objects of the class to exist since there is always one (and only one) copy of a `static` data member. For the same reason such members can be accessed by pointers to the appropriate type, where the pointers can be defined without using the class name and scope resolution syntax. For example, if we declare:

```
class sphere {
public:
     static int total;
// Other members go here.
};
```

then the following is valid:

```
cout << sphere::total;
```

as is:

```
int *pt = &sphere::total;
cout << *pt;
```

8.12.2   Static Member Functions

In the example given in the previous section, the functions `increment_spheres()` and `total_spheres()` can be invoked for any `sphere` object. This situation is not very satisfactory, since the total number of spheres is a property of the collection of all such objects, rather than any particular instance of the class. Declaring `increment_spheres()` and `total_spheres()` to be `static` member functions is a useful improvement. Static member functions are special in that they can only access `static` data members and need not be invoked by a class object:

---

[8]The idea of a `friend` of a class will be introduced in Section 8.15

```
#include <iostream.hpp>
#include <stdlib.h>      // for EXIT_SUCCESS

class sphere {
public:
    static void increment_spheres(int new_spheres);
    static int total_spheres(void) { return total; }
private:
    static int total;
};

static void sphere::increment_spheres(int new_spheres)
{
    total += new_spheres;
}

int main()
{
    sphere s1, s2;

    sphere::increment_spheres(2);
    cout << "Total number of spheres = " <<
        sphere::total_spheres() << "\n";

    return(EXIT_SUCCESS);
}
```

It is also possible to invoke `static` member functions for particular objects, as in `s1.total_spheres()`, but the `sphere::total_spheres()` notation emphasizes the class aspect.

8.13 Constructor Functions

As with variables of the fundamental types, it is safer to initialize objects rather than to define them with arbitrary values. A class which only has `public` data members:

```
class coordinate {
public:
    double x, y, z;
};
```

can be initialized by a comma-separated list:

```
    coordinate w = {1.0, 2.0, 0.0};
```

but such circumstances are unusual and, in any case, initializers cannot be included in a class declaration. As a change from our **sphere** class, let's consider a complex arithmetic class with real and imaginary data members, **re** and **im**. Such a class cannot be declared by:

```
    class complex {
    private:
        double re = 0.0;        // WRONG!
        double im = 0.0;        // WRONG!
    };
```

However, there is a special kind of function, known as a *constructor function*, (or, more simply, a *constructor*), which is specifically designed for initializing objects. A constructor is declared by giving the class name to a member function:

```
    class complex {
    public:
        complex(double x, double y) { re = x; im = y; }
    private:
        double re, im;
    };
```

With this constructor, objects that are members of the **complex** class can be initialized as follows:

```
    complex u = complex(1.1, 2.2);  // Initializes u data members.
    complex v(1.1, 2.2);            // Initializes v data members.
```

In both examples, the values 1.1 and 2.2 are assigned to the real and imaginary parts respectively, by invoking the constructor function. Notice that the syntax in the second statement does *not* signify that **v** is a function: rather **v** is an object, implicitly invoking the constructor function with arguments 1.1 and 2.2.

Since the only constructor defined for the **complex** class expects two arguments, we cannot declare an uninitialized **complex** object:

```
    complex z;      // WRONG: no suitable constructor defined.
```

However, the constructor function can be modified to provide default initializations:

```
    class complex {
    public:
        complex(double x = 0.0, double y = 0.0) {
            re = x; im = y; }
    private:
        double re, im;
    };
```

If we now have the statement:

```
complex z;
```

then the real and imaginary parts of z are initialized to zero. There are several ways in which this constructor function can be invoked:

```
complex u;                          // Default initialization.
complex v(2.0, 3.0);               // Initialized by 2.0 and 3.0.
complex w = complex(3.0, 4.0);     // Initialized by 3.0 and 4.0.
complex z(2.0);                    // Initialized by 2.0 and 0.0.
complex q = complex(2.0);          // Initialized by 2.0 and 0.0.
```

Notice that, in the above example, the function `complex()` does not have a `return` type; constructors are special functions in that they cannot return a type (not even `void`).

A common error is to attempt to define an object, initialized with default values, by:

```
complex u();          // WRONG: this is a function declaration.
```

In fact, this declares a function, which takes no arguments and returns the `complex` type. However, the following does define (rather verbosely) a `complex` object with the default initialization:

```
complex u = complex();
```

We can overload the constructor function by having more than one member function with the same name as the class name, provided that the function arguments differ. As an example, we may want to initialize a complex object with another object belonging to the same class. This is achieved by the second constructor in the following class declaration:

```
class complex {
public:
    complex(double x=0.0, double y=0.0) { re=x; im=y;}
    complex(const complex &z) { re=z.re; im=z.im; }
private:
    double re, im;
};
```

An example using the two different constructors is:

```
complex u(24.5, 17.6);
complex v(u);
```

In the first statement, the real and imaginary parts of u are initialized to 24.5 and 17.6 respectively. In the second statement, the real and imaginary parts of u are themselves used to initialize v.

A constructor function having a single argument of a *reference* to the class type is a very common requirement and is known as a *copy constructor*. Notice the emphasis on reference; a constructor with the prototype:

```
class_x::class_x(class_x);
```

is illegal, but:

```
class_x::class_x(const class_x &);
```

as in:

```
complex::complex(const complex &z);
```

is both legal and common.

Exercise:

Implement a constructor for the **sphere** class described in Sections 8.12.1 and 8.12.2. The total number of spheres (that is the **static** variable, **total**) should be incremented each time the constructor is invoked. Create various numbers of spheres and check that the **static** **total_spheres()** function gives the correct result.

In order to access the data of **complex** objects, we can introduce the **public** member functions, **real()** and **imag()**, which return the real and imaginary parts of a **complex** object:

```
class complex {
public:
    complex(double x = 0.0, double y = 0.0);
    complex(const complex &z);
    double real(void) { return re;}
    double imag(void) { return im; }
private:
    double re, im;
};

// Inline constructor implementations go here.
```

Our **complex** class is now sufficiently developed for us to try a simple test program. As usual, we put both the class definition and the implementation of **inline** functions in a header file:

```
// source:  complex.hpp
// use:     Defines complex arithmetic class.

#ifndef COMPLEX_HPP
#define COMPLEX_HPP

class complex {
public:
    complex(double x = 0.0, double y = 0.0);
    complex(const complex &z);
    double real(void);
    double imag(void);
private:
    double re, im;
};

inline complex::complex(double x, double y)
{
    re = x;
    im = y;
}

inline complex::complex(const complex &z)
{
    re = z.re;
    im = z.im;
}

inline double complex::real(void)
{
    return re;
}

inline double complex::imag(void)
{
    return im;
}

#endif  // COMPLEX_HPP
```

The following program tests our current version of the **complex** class, by setting:

$$z = 24.5 + 17.6i$$

and printing the real and imaginary parts of **z**:

```
#include <iostream.hpp>
#include <stdlib.h>        // for EXIT_SUCCESS
#include "complex.hpp"

int main()
{
    complex z(24.5, 17.6);

    cout << "Real part = " << z.real() <<
        " Imaginary part = " << z.imag() << "\n";
    return(EXIT_SUCCESS);
}
```

Exercise:

Compile and run the above program. Make modifications so that the copy constructor is also tested.

8.14   Constant Class Objects and Member Functions

We have previously emphasized the desirability of using the **const** specifier to indicate to the compiler that an instance of a fundamental type should not change. Such remarks also apply to instances of classes. For example, we could define:

```
const complex i(0.0, 1.0);
```

A problem now arises if we try to access the real part of **i**, using the **real()** member function:

```
cout << "real part of i = " << i.real();
```

This statement is rejected by the compiler since there is no way of telling from the function prototype whether or not **real()** modifies **i**. Member functions that do not modify any data member can include the **const** specifier at the end of the function prototype:[9]

```
double real(void) const;
```

and before the body of the function implementation:

---

[9]This **const** notation is only possible for member functions and cannot be used for **friend** functions, which are introduced in the next section. This is because only member functions have a hidden pointer, called **this**. The special **this** pointer is introduced in Section 9.1.2.

```
inline double complex::real(void) const
{
    return re;
}
```

Any attempt by a **const** member function to modify member data would be flagged as an error by the compiler. This technique of placing **const** at the end of the function prototype solves the problem, described above, of invoking `i.real()`.

It may be necessary to declare a member function as both **const** and non-**const**. In this case the function is overloaded and which function is actually invoked depends on whether or not the object is defined with the **const** specifier.

8.15 Friend Functions

Our **complex** class is defined to have **private** data (**re** and **im**) and in general this data cannot be accessed by non-member functions. However, a *friend* of a class has access to the data members and member functions of that class, irrespective of any access specifiers. For example, an alternative method for obtaining the real and imaginary parts of the **complex** object is to define **friend** functions, as in:

```
class complex {
    friend double real(const complex &z);
    friend double imag(const complex &z);
// More class declarations go in here.
};

inline double real(const complex &z)
{
    return z.re;
}

inline double imag(const complex &z)
{
    return z.im;
}

// More inline function implementations go in here.
```

`real()` and `imag()` are now **friend**s of the **complex** class, rather than members and can be invoked as in:

```
complex z(24.5, 17.6);

cout << "Real part = " << real(z) <<
    " Imaginary part = " << imag(z) << "\n";
```

Both member and non-member functions provide equally satisfactory techniques for accessing the real and imaginary parts of a `complex` object, although it could be argued that `real(z)` is a more natural syntax than `z.real()`. In fact it is possible to have both definitions in the same class implementation.

Notice that it is worth making these functions `inline` in order to avoid relatively high function call overheads. It is also worth using reference variables, to reduce the call overhead still further, and the `const` keyword, to provide some protection for the member data.

The `friend` keyword indicates that a function has access to the `private` members (data and functions) of a class, but is not a member of that class. A function can be a `friend` of more then one class, or even a member of one class and a `friend` of many classes. Notice that friendship is granted by the class whose `private` members are accessed. One of the special features of constructor functions is that they cannot be declared friends of a class.

It is also possible to declare an entire class to be a `friend` of another class. The statement:

```
class node {
    friend class list;
    // Other declarations.
};
```

declares `list` to be a `friend` of the `node` class and gives `list` access to all members of any `node` object. Both `friend` classes and functions are not affected by access specifiers, such as `public` and `private`, and can be placed anywhere within a class declaration. However, a good convention is to place any `friend` declarations immediately after the class header and before any explicit access specifiers.

Friendship is not transferred to a `friend` of a `friend`. In the following code:

```
class complex {
    friend class complex_vector;
    // Other declarations go here.
private:
    double re, im;
};

class complex_vector {
    friend void print(const complex_vector &v);
```

```
        // Other declarations go here.
private:
    complex x, y, z;
};

void print(const complex_vector &v)
{
    cout << v.x.re;      // WRONG: re is private.
    // etc.
}
```

the `print()` function has access to the `private` members of a `complex_vector` object, but not to the `private` members of any `complex` object. If this restriction did not exist, then granting friendship to one class would open up the entire class implementation to a whole hierarchy of unknown classes and functions.

Exercise:

Write a program which declares an array of ten `complex` objects and uses member function versions of `real()` and `imag()` to assign different values to the real and imaginary parts of each object. Use `friend` versions of these functions to display the values stored.

8.16   Program Structure and Style[†]

Now that we have introduced most of the basic ideas of C++, it is worth making a brief diversion to consider how programs should be structured. The simplest C++ program consists of one file, containing a single function, called `main()`. More realistic programs often contain many thousand lines of code and must be split up into separate files in order to control the complexity. Unlike some languages, C++ does little to enforce any structure on these files, but there are well-established conventions which it is sensible to follow.

8.16.1   Modules

A large program should be split up into a number of source files (with a `.cpp` or equivalent extension), each of which can be compiled independently. Each *module*, as such files are called, usually consists of a number of related function definitions and may use functions defined in other modules. For example, a module may implement all of the non-`inline` functions for a particular class.

Before a program can be executed, the compiled modules must be *linked* both with each other and with the compiled system-provided library functions by means of a special program, known as a *linker.* Linking, in addition to pre-processing and compilation, is usually invoked by a single command which has an option to inhibit one or more of these processes.

In C++, the existence of function overloading makes it particularly important that the argument types of the compiled functions are known. For this reason, *type-safe linking* is used. The compiler *mangles* (that is it modifies) function names in a well-defined way in order to encode information on the number of function arguments and their types. In the case of a member function, the class name is also encoded. Name mangling gives the same unique name to a function which may be declared in many different modules.[10] This means that overloaded functions are resolved on linking rather than on compiling.

However, functions with identical names and arguments that are defined in different modules do not necessarily clash on linking. In general, objects and functions can either have *internal linkage* (the visibility of their names is restricted to one module) or *external linkage* (their names are visible throughout the program). The following have internal linkage:

- `typedef` names (see Appendix D)

- enumerations

- `inline` functions

- objects declared `const`.

whereas external linkage occurs for:

- `static` class members

- non-inline functions

- global (file scope) objects which are not declared `const`.

The default linkage for objects and functions (but nothing else) can be changed by means of the `extern` and `static` specifiers.

Changing linkage using `extern`

The keyword, `extern`, is a specifier which may be used to declare a variable without defining it:

```
extern double pi;
extern sphere s;
extern int &velocity;
```

---

[10]With the exception explained later in this section, a function may only be defined once in a program, but it may be used (and therefore declared) in many modules.

In such cases the name and type of the variable is known to the module, but the definition, which allocates memory, is elsewhere.

It is possible to use the `extern` specifier in a function prototype, for example:

```
extern double sqrt(double z);
```

but this is redundant since the function is necessarily defined 'elsewhere'.

An initialized object which is declared `extern` is in fact a definition. The motivation for such definitions is that a `const` object has internal linkage by default, whereas the `extern` specifier makes the object visible to other modules:

```
extern const double h = 6.6262e-27;   // Planck's constant.
```

Changing linkage using `static`

Functions and global objects have external linkage by default. This may cause problems in large programs, where the same function or object names may be unintentionally reused in different modules. Such multiple definitions would be flagged as errors by the linker. However, the `static` specifier gives internal linkage to an object or function:

```
static int total_iterations;

static void print(void)
{
    // Function body goes here.
}

int main()
{
    // Code goes here.
}
```

which prevents accidental name clashes between different modules. Declaring functions and global variables `static` may also help an optimizing compiler.[11]

It is worth emphasizing that the `static` keyword has three distinct meanings:

- In the above discussion `static` means that visibility is restricted; the `static` specifier changes the linkage of both `total_iterations` and the `print()` function from external to internal.

- A local variable which is declared `static` has permanent storage and its value persists across function calls:

---

[11]A `static` function is not hidden if a file is included, rather than compiled, but including definitions of non-inlined functions is in any case bad style.

```
int sum(int n)
{
    static int grand_total;
    int i, result = 0;
    for (i = 1; i <= n; ++i)
        result += i * i;
    grand_total += result;
    cout << "Total so far = " << grand_total << "\n";
    return result;
}
```

Notice that since `grand_total` is local, it only has visibility within the function body and has internal linkage; the key concept here is *permanent storage*.

- A class data member that is declared `static` is not replicated for each object. Here the use of `static` is analogous to the previous case in that it implies persistence. However, a `static` data member still has external linkage.

8.16.2   Header Files

The proper use of header files can do much to ensure the consistency of classes and functions across modules. Once again C++ does not enforce a particular style, but there are well-established conventions which it is well worth following. C++ header files usually have a `.hpp` (or equivalent) extension, whereas those header files in common with the C programming language use `.h`. A header file is included (by means of the `#include` directive) in the source files for which it is relevant. A large program may have many header files, some of which `#include` other header files and controlling this hierarchy can be a significant task. The example in Section 8.17.1 explains how to use the `#ifndef` directive to avoid the possibility of multiple copies of included files.

In general, header files can and should contain the following:[12]

- Class declarations:

```
class sphere {
public:
    void assign_radius(double r) { radius = r; }
    void get_radius(double &r) { r = radius; }
    double radius;
};
```

---

[12]Note the important distinction between 'define' and 'declare' for variables and functions.

- Function declarations:

```
double sqrt(double);
```

- Inline function definitions:

```
inline void sphere::increment_spheres(int new_spheres)
{
    total += new_spheres;
}
```

- Variable declarations:

```
extern double pi;
```

- Constant definitions:

```
const double ln_pi = 1.14472988584940017;
```

- Enumerations:

```
enum colour {RED, GREEN, BLUE};
```

- Other header files:

```
#include <stdlib.h>
```

- #define directives:

```
#define TRUE  1
#define FALSE 0
```

By contrast, header files should *not* include the following:

- Non-static variable definitions:

```
double relative_velocity;
```

- Non-inline function definitions:

```
int max(int a, int b)
{
    return a >= b ? a : b;
}
```

- Constant array definitions:

```
const float table[] = {0.0, 1.0, 2.0};
```

8.17   Using Classes

Many of the objects that occur in mathematics are obvious candidates for making into classes; the possibilities are endless: vectors, matrices, complex numbers, geometrical objects, quaternions, arbitrary length integer arithmetic and many more. However, most of these classes would benefit considerably from more advanced techniques which are introduced in Chapters 9 and 10. The two examples of classes given here are an array class, which overcomes some of the disadvantages of the built-in subscripting operator, and (as a less blatantly mathematical example) a class for storing weather data.

8.17.1   An Array Class

In this section we consider a self-checking, self-describing one-dimensional array class, which illustrates most of the ideas introduced in this chapter.[13] Let us suppose that this array class has the following design requirements:

- The array must store n values of type `double`, where n is set at run-time.

- The elements of the array are labelled 1 to n, rather than 0 to $n - 1$.

- An array object has a record of its own size and any attempt to access an element outside the array bounds is flagged as a run-time error.

- A tally is kept of the number of initialized array objects.

A suitable class declaration is:

```
// source:    array.hpp
// use:       Defines array class.

#ifndef ARRAY_HPP
#define ARRAY_HPP

#include <iostream.hpp>
#include <stdlib.h>        // for EXIT_SUCCESS

class array {
public:
    array(int size);
    int get_size(void);
    double &element(int i);
    static int number_of_arrays(void);
```

---

[13]The exceptions are the two pointer-to-member operators which are rarely used. (See Section 8.10.)

```
    private:
        int elements;
        static int total;
        double *pt;
    };

    inline int array::get_size(void)
    {
        return elements;
    }

    inline double &array::element(int i)
    {
        if (i < 1 || i > elements) {
            cout << "Array index " << i << " out of bounds\n";
            exit(EXIT_FAILURE);
        }
        return pt[i - 1];
    }

    #endif  // ARRAY_HPP
```

Most of this class declaration is self-documenting. The pointer, **pt**, is the base address of a dynamically allocated array, of sufficient size to store **n** values of type **double**. The **static** variable, **total**, is the total number of arrays that have been initialized. Notice that the entire member data are **private** and only accessible through the member functions. (This is an example of data hiding.) Also of interest is that the function, **element()**, returns a reference and can therefore appear on the left hand side of assignment statements.

A class definition is usually placed in a separate header file and in this case the file is called **array.hpp**. Notice the sequence:

```
    #ifndef ARRAY_HPP
    #define ARRAY_HPP
        // Code in here.
    #endif  // ARRAY_HPP
```

which prevents multiple inclusions of the same file. If **ARRAY_HPP** is not defined, then all of the file is processed and **ARRAY_HPP** is consequently defined. If the preprocessor meets another copy of the include file, then all of the code between the **#ifndef** and **#endif** directives will be omitted. This technique can also be used to avoid multiple definitions in different files. For instance, if **file1.hpp** and **file2.hpp** both contain the statement:

```
    const int TRUE = 1;
```

then a source file that includes both header files would give rise to a compile-time error.

It should also be noted that the **inline** functions are implemented in this header file and *not* in a .**cpp** file. Suitable implementations of the other member functions are as follows:

```
// source:  array.cpp
// use:     Implements array class.


#include <iostream.hpp>
#include <stdlib.h>      // for exit()
#include "array.hpp"


int array::total = 0;            // Included to demonstrate
                                 // technique. (Default is 0)


array::array(int size)
{
    elements = size;
    pt = new double[elements];
    if (pt == NULL) {
        cout << "Failed to allocate array.\n";
        exit(EXIT_FAILURE);
    }
    ++total;
}


int array::number_of_arrays(void)
{
    return total;
}
```

Observe that the only way of accessing an **array** object is through the member function, **element**(), which checks the validity of the array index.

A program which tries out this class is given below:

```
// source:  test.cpp
// use:     Tests array class.


#include <iostream.hpp>
#include <stdlib.h>      // for EXIT_SUCCESS
#include "array.hpp"


int main()
```

```
{
    int array_size = 20;

    // Define an object:
    array x(array_size);

    // Access the array size:
    cout << "The array size is " << x.get_size() << "\n\n";

    // Store some data:
    for (int i = 1; i <= array_size; ++i)
        x.element(i) = i * 25.0;

    // Retrieve some data:
    for (i = 1; i <= array_size; ++i)
        cout << x.element(i) << "\n";

    // Define another object:
    array y(array_size);

    // Now repeat the above, using a pointer to an object:
    array *p = &y;

    // Use static member function to get number of objects:
    cout << "\nNumber of arrays initialized is " <<
        array::number_of_arrays() << "\n";

    // Access the array size:
    cout << "The array size is " << p->get_size() << "\n\n";

    // Store some data:
    for (i = 1; i <= array_size; ++i)
        p->element(i) = i * 250.0;

    // Retrieve some data:
    for (i = 1; i <= array_size; ++i)
        cout << p->element(i) << "\n";

    // Try to go outside of the array bounds:
    p->element(array_size + 1) = 3.142;

    return(EXIT_SUCCESS);
}
```

To test the `array` class, the file, `array.cpp`, is first compiled to give an object file, such as `array.obj`, and then `test.cpp` should be compiled and linked with `array.obj`. You will have to consult your C++ compiler documentation in order to discover the exact commands required. They will probably be something like:

```
c++ -c array.cpp
c++ test.cpp array.obj
```

In fact, most systems will have something resembling the UNIX *make* utility which can be used to simplify program maintenance. For the present example, a file (typically called *makefile*) is created with the following contents:

```
test.exe:   array.obj
    c++ test.cpp  array.obj

array.obj:  array.cpp array.hpp
    c++ -c array.cpp
```

Typing *make* is all that is necessary to keep `test.exe` up to date. Since the exact details of the utility will depend on your system, you should again consult your system manual. However, it is worth emphasizing that using such a utility is almost essential for anything but the simplest program, especially as C++ strongly encourages the use of modules.

Our `array` class still has some weaknesses, all of which can be solved by more advanced techniques:

- The default assignment operator performs a simple copy operation, which is probably not very useful:

  ```
  array x, y;
  x.set_size(10);
  y = x;
  ```

  In this example, `y.pt` points to the same memory as `x.pt`, so that making assignments to the elements of `y` will also change the `x` array.

- The notation:

  ```
  x.elements(i) = 10.0;
  ```

  is rather clumsy; something like:

  ```
  x[i] = 10;
  ```

  would be much better.

- If an array object goes out of scope, the memory is not reclaimed.

8.17.2 A Weather Class

We now implement a class for storing daily weather data, together with associated classes for monthly and yearly records. Similar techniques could be used for storing other data. For instance, an astronomer might want to store data on galaxies, while a geologist might be more interested in mineral specimens. However, before you reach for your keyboard, it is worth pointing out that designing an object-oriented database is a very substantial project and has its own dedicated literature and commercial products.[14] By comparison, what we consider here is very trivial.

Suppose that the design requirements for these weather-related classes are:

- A basic class should have data members for the average temperature, pressure and rainfall for each day. (It is straightforward to add further data members but the current members are sufficient for the purpose of illustration.)

- For simplicity, each month is defined to have thirty days. (Removing this restriction is left as an exercise.)

- Since it is anticipated that the data will be analysed on a monthly and on a yearly basis, separate classes must be provided for storing the weather data for both an entire month and for an entire year.

Suitable class definitions are:

```
// source:      weather.hpp
// use:         Defines weather classes.

#ifndef WEATHER_HPP
#define WEATHER_HPP

const int days_in_month = 30;
const int months_in_year = 12;

class weather_data {
public:
    double temperature;
    double pressure;
    double rainfall;
};

class monthly_weather {
```

---

[14]A C++ implementation of a *relational* database is described in [1], which also has a useful bibliography on object-oriented databases.

```
public:
    void set_daily_weather(int day, const weather_data &data);
    void give_monthly_average(weather_data &data);
private:
    weather_data &daily_average(int day);
    weather_data weather[days_in_month];
};

class yearly_weather {
public:
    yearly_weather(int set_year) { year = set_year; }
    void set_daily_weather(int month, int day,
        const weather_data &data);
    void list_yearly_average(void);
    void list_monthly_averages(void);
private:
    int year;
    monthly_weather &monthly_data(int month);
    monthly_weather weather[months_in_year];
};

#endif  // WEATHER_HPP
```

with the following implementations:

```
// source:      weather.cpp
// use:         Implements weather classes.

#include <iostream.hpp>
#include <stdlib.h>       // for exit()
#include "weather.hpp"

void monthly_weather::set_daily_weather(int day,
    const weather_data &data)
{
    daily_average(day) = data;
}

void monthly_weather::give_monthly_average(weather_data &data)
{
    double temp = 0.0;
    double press = 0.0;
    double rain = 0.0;
    for (int day = 1; day <= days_in_month; ++day) {
```

```cpp
            temp += daily_average(day).temperature;
            press += daily_average(day).pressure;
            rain += daily_average(day).rainfall;
        }
        data.temperature = temp / days_in_month;
        data.pressure = press / days_in_month;
        data.rainfall = rain / days_in_month;
    }


    weather_data &monthly_weather::daily_average(int day)
    {
        if (day < 1 || day > days_in_month) {
            cout << day << " is not a valid day\n";
            exit(EXIT_FAILURE);
        }
        else
            return weather[day-1];
    }


    void yearly_weather::set_daily_weather(int month, int day,
        const weather_data &data)
    {
        monthly_data(month).set_daily_weather(day, data);
    }


    void yearly_weather::list_yearly_average(void)
    {
        double temp = 0.0;
        double press = 0.0;
        double rain = 0.0;
        for (int month = 1; month <= months_in_year; ++month) {
            weather_data data;
            monthly_data(month).give_monthly_average(data);
            temp += data.temperature;
            press += data.pressure;
            rain += data.rainfall;
        }
        temp /= months_in_year;
        press /= months_in_year;
        rain /= months_in_year;
        cout << "Average weather for year " << year <<
            "\nTemperature = " << temp << " (C)  Pressure = " <<
            press << " (mB)  Rainfall = " << rain <<
```

```
                          " (cm)\n\n";
      }

      void yearly_weather::list_monthly_averages(void)
      {
          cout << "month   temperature (C)  Pressure (mB)  " <<
              "Rainfall (cm)\n\n";
          for (int month = 1; month <= months_in_year; ++month) {
              cout << month << "           ";
              weather_data data;
              monthly_data(month).give_monthly_average(data);
              cout << data.temperature << "      " <<
                  data.pressure << "       " << data.rainfall <<
                  "\n";
          }
      }

      monthly_weather &yearly_weather::monthly_data(int month)
      {
          if (month < 1 || month > months_in_year) {
              cout << month << " is not a valid month\n";
              exit(EXIT_FAILURE);
          }
          else
              return weather[month - 1];
      }
```

Appropriate variable names should make the class declarations and implementations reasonably self-documenting, but notice the following features:

- The weather_data class has only public data and no access functions.
  This lack of data hiding is justified because the class is so simple and because
  of the way in which it will be used by other classes.

- All of the data in the monthly_weather class is hidden. The data is stored
  in an array called weather, which is only accessed by means of the helper
  function, daily_average(). This function returns a reference and it is here
  that the days, 1, 2, 3 ... are mapped into the array index which takes the
  values 0, 1, 2, ... Such mappings are a likely source of mistakes but using
  this function has the advantages that:

  - the mapping is done in a single function which means that, elsewhere,
    days take the values 1, 2, 3, ...

  - the daily_average() function checks that it is invoked with a valid
    argument. This is the only place that such checks are performed.

- The `yearly_weather` class data is declared **private**. This data is stored in an array called **weather** which is only accessed by means of the helper function, `monthly_average()`. This function has a similar purpose and similar advantages to the `monthly_weather::daily_average()` function. In particular this implies that months of the year take values 1, 2, 3 ..., rather than 0, 1, 2 ..., which is more typical of indices for built-in C++ arrays.

- Reference arguments are used for **weather_data** in order to save unnecessary copying, with some degree of protection being provided by **const** wherever possible.

- All three classes are defined in a single file (**weather.hpp**) and implemented in a second file (**weather.cpp**); since the classes are very simple and it is only intended that they should be used together, there is no need to use separate files for each class.

- Both the `monthly_weather` and `yearly_weather` classes have data members which are **weather_data** objects. Classes which use another class in this way are said to be *clients*; `monthly_weather` and `yearly_weather` are clients of the **weather_data** class.

A test program for these weather classes is as follows:

```
// source:      test.cpp
// use:         Tests weather classes.

#include <iostream.hpp>
#include <stdlib.h>      // for EXIT_SUCCESS, rand()
#include "weather.hpp"

const int min_temp = -20;
const int max_temp = 20;
const int min_press = 980;
const int max_press = 1100;
const int min_rain = 15;
const int max_rain = 95;

int rand_interval(int start, int end)
{
    float delta =  float(end - start) / RAND_MAX;
    return(start + rand() * delta);
}
```

```cpp
void generate_yearly_weather(yearly_weather &y)
{
    weather_data data;
    for (int month = 1; month <= 6; ++month)
        for (int day = 1; day <= days_in_month; ++day) {
            data.temperature = rand_interval(min_temp,
                max_temp) + month * 2;
            data.pressure = rand_interval(min_press,
                max_press);
            data.rainfall = rand_interval(min_rain, max_rain)
                + month * 5;
            y.set_daily_weather(month, day, data);
        }
    for (; month <= months_in_year; ++month)
        for (day = 1; day <= days_in_month; ++day) {
            data.temperature = rand_interval(min_temp,
                max_temp) + (24 - month * 2);
            data.pressure = rand_interval(min_press,
                max_press);
            data.rainfall = rand_interval(min_rain, max_rain)
                + (60 - month * 5);
            y.set_daily_weather(month, day, data);
        }
}

int main()
{
    yearly_weather y_w(1992);
    generate_yearly_weather(y_w);
    y_w.list_yearly_average();
    y_w.list_monthly_averages();
    return EXIT_SUCCESS;
}
```

Notice that:

- The `generate_yearly_weather()` function is not included in a class definition since is unlikely to be of widespread use.

- The output produced by this test progam is not very well formatted because the same variable may give rise to varying numbers of digits in different months. This deficiency can be overcome by using more sophisticated techniques which are introduced in Chapter 12.

8.18 Summary

- A class is a user-defined data type, complete with its own data, functions and operators:[15]

  ```
  class circle {
      double x_centre, y_centre;
      double area(void);
  };
  ```

- An object is an instance of a class:

  ```
  circle one_circle, many_circles[100];
  ```

- The default assignment operator is a simple copy operator which may inappropriately copy addresses (or other data):

  ```
  circle new_circle = one_circle;
  ```

- Access to members of a class can be declared to be **private** (the default) or public:

  ```
  class circle {
  public:
      double area(void);
      void set_centre(double x, double y);
      void set_radius(double radius) { r = radius; }
      double give_radius(void);
  private:
      double x_centre, y_centre;
      double r;
  };
  ```

  The data members, **x_centre**, **y_centre** and **r** are examples of data hiding.

- A function defined within a class, such as **set_radius()**, is implicitly declared **inline**. The scope resolution operator, ::, is used to define a member function outside the class definition:

  ```
  double circle::give_radius(void) { return r; }
  ```

  Functions defined in this way are not implicitly **inline**.

---

[15]User-defined or, more correctly, overloaded operators are introduced in Chapter 9.

- Reference arguments eliminate unnecessary temporary copies:

```
void circle::translate_circle(circle &c, double d_x,
    double d_y)
{
    c.x_centre = x_centre + d_x;
    c.y_centre = y_centre + d_y;
    c.radius = radius;
}
```

- There are two fundamental ways of specifying an object:

```
circle c;                   // An object.
circle *pt_object;          // A pointer to an object.
```

and two ways of specifying a class member:

```
radius = 10.0;              // A class member.
double circle::*pt_member; // A pointer to a member.
```

Hence, four different operators can be used to access class members:[16]

1. The member access operator:

   ```
   c.radius = 10.0;
   ```

2. The class member access operator:

   ```
   pt_object->radius = 10;
   ```

3. A pointer-to-member operator:

   ```
   c.*pt_member = 10.0;
   ```

4. A second pointer-to-member operator:

   ```
   pt_object->*pt_member = 10.0;
   ```

- There is only one copy of a static data member:

```
class circle {
    // ...
public:
    static int total;
};
```

---

[16]These examples assume that radius is a public member.

All instances of a class have access to this one copy:

```
circle c1, c2;
++c1.total;
++c2.total;
```

- A `static` data member is initialized to zero by default, but can be initialized explicitly:

```
int circle::total = 24;
```

- A `static` member function can only access `static` data and need not be invoked by an instance of a class:

```
class circle {
    // ...
    static int total_circles(void) { return total; }
    static int total;
};
int number_of_circles = circle::total_circles();
```

- A constructor is a member function with the same name as its class. A constructor cannot return a type but can be overloaded:

```
class complex {
// ...
    complex (double x, double y);
    complex (const complex &z);
};
```

For a class, X, a constructor with the prototype, `X::X(const X&)`, is known as a copy constructor.

- If we want to use `const` class objects, then we must define appropriate `const` member functions:

```
inline double complex::real(void) const
{
    return re;
}
```

- A function or class specified to be a `friend` of a class has access to all of the function members and member data, irrespective of any access specifiers:

244 CHAPTER 8. CLASSES

```
class complex {
// ...
    friend double real(const complex &z);
    friend class complex_matrix;
private:
    double re, im;
};
```

8.19 Exercises

1. Improve the **array** class given in Section 8.17.1 by adding a copy constructor. Memory should be dynamically allocated for the new array and the original data elements copied into this memory.

2. Extend the **array** class, which we discussed in Section 8.17.1, to classes for two-dimensional and three-dimensional arrays. In each case write a program to test the new class.

3. Modify the program given in Section 8.17.2 so that weather data is generated for twenty consecutive years. Use the techniques of Section 7.8.2 to sort the yearly averaged data in descending order of the temperature.

4. Modify the constructor in the **yearly_weather** class (discussed in Section 8.17.2) so that it initializes an array whose elements are the number of days in each month, with appropriate allowance being made for a leap year. Use this array to ensure that each **monthly_weather** object has the correct number of **weather_data** items for each month and year.

5. Write a program to measure the time taken to access an element of an object of our array class by means of the member function, **element()**. Compare this time with that for an array which directly uses the built-in subscripting operator, [ ]. What effect does removing the bounds checking from **array::element()** have on this comparison?

   Extend your results to the two and three-dimensional cases.

6. Adapt the classes for storing weather data so that they can store something relevant to your own particular field. For example, an astronomer could start by storing some data on the planets.

Chapter 9

Operator Overloading

In Section 5.6 we introduced the idea of function overloading. Recall that a function is overloaded if there is more than one function with the same name, but the functions have different numbers of arguments or different argument types. Using similar techniques, we can overload the built-in operators (such as assignment, addition, multiplication etc.) so that they perform user-defined operations. This chapter is concerned with the details of how to implement overloaded operators.

9.1   Introducing Overloaded Operators

Operators are overloaded in most languages; that is the meaning of an operator depends on its context. For instance, the operations performed by the binary plus operator, +, on the bits representing two floating point numbers are very different from those for two integers. However, the crucial feature of C++ is that most operators can be given a user-defined meaning. The only operators that cannot be overloaded are:

$$. \qquad .* \qquad :: \qquad ?:$$

and the preprocessor operators, # and ##.

In order to prevent operator overloading getting out of control, there are a number of restrictions:

- An operator can only be overloaded if its operands include at least one class type, or it is a member function. This restriction is necessary so that a non-overloaded operator can be distinguished from its overloaded variant. As a consequence we cannot change the way operators work for the fundamental types; that is we cannot make something like:

```
i = 10 + 20;
```

really mean:

```
i = 20 - 10;
```

Such redefinitions of built-in operators would make programs almost impossible to understand.

- The associativity and precedence of an operator, together with the number of operands, cannot be changed by overloading. Again, if these restrictions were removed, then programs could easily become incomprehensible.

- We cannot introduce new operators (such as ** for exponentiation).

9.1.1   Overloading the Assignment Operator

The assignment operator is rather special in that if we don't define an overloaded assignment operator for a class, then a default definition is provided by the compiler. This default operator simply does a copy of the data members of one object to another. So even the complex class introduced in the previous chapter enables us to do assignments:

```
complex u(24.5, 17.6), v;
v = u;
```

Exercise:

Write a program to demonstrate that the values 24.5 and 17.6 are indeed assigned to the real and imaginary parts of v.

We can explicitly overload the assignment operator by making the following modification to the complex class:

```
class complex {
public:
    void operator=(const complex &z);
// More class declarations go in here.
};

inline void complex::operator=(const complex &z)
{
    re = z.re;
    im = z.im;
}

// More class implementations go in here.
```

This example illustrates the general syntax for overloading operators. In the declaration:

```
void operator=(const complex &z);
```

the `operator` keyword is followed by the operator itself and then parentheses containing the operands. The assignment operator is a binary operator, but only one operand (the second) is given explicitly, since the first operand is implicit. If we have the statement:

```
v = u;
```

for `complex` objects `v` and `u`, then the second operand is `u`. The expressions `z.re` and `z.im`, in the operator implementation, correspond to `u.re` and `u.im` respectively, whereas `re` and `im` (without the class member operator) are the data members of `v`. In other words, because the operator is a *member* function, it has direct access to the member data. Don't forget that, since white space is ignored, the following overloaded operator declarations are equivalent:

```
void operator = (const complex &z);
void operator=(const complex &z);
void operator= (const complex &z);
```

but the second is more usual.

The type which appears as the left-most part of the operator declaration (in this case `void`) is *not* the type of the left operand, but rather the type returned by the operator. Even expressions such as:

```
v = u
```

can return a type. In the above implementation we have chosen the return type to be `void`, but this does not mimic the normal situation for assignment of the fundamental types, as we now demonstrate.

9.1.2 The this Pointer

Consider the following statement for `i` and `j` of type `int`:

```
i = j = 1;
```

The assignment operator associates right to left, so that the first expression to be evaluated is:

```
j = 1
```

the result of which is of type `int` and value 1. It is not just `j` that has the value 1, but also the expression itself. The value of this expression is then assigned to `i`. An analogous situation does not exist for our current definition of the `complex` assignment operator, as can be seen by trying:

```
complex u, v, z(24.5, 17.6);

u = v = z;   // WRONG for the current assignment operator.
```

However, we can mimic the assignment operator for the fundamental types by the following:

```
class complex {
public:
    complex &operator=(const complex &z);
// Class declarations.
};

inline complex &complex::operator=(const complex &z)
{
    re = z.re;
    im = z.im;
    return *this;
}

// More class implementations go in here.
```

which is in fact equivalent to the default operator. In the last statement of the operator function body, we return a dereferenced pointer called this. The pointer, this, is a keyword, which is used by the C++ compiler to point to the object that the function was invoked on.[1] In the expression:

```
u = v;
```

this points to u and:

```
return *this;
```

in fact returns u. Notice that we return a reference, which is permissible here since the reference is to something defined outside the operator function body.

The this pointer can only appear inside the body of a class member function and it is rare to use the pointer explicitly. Since the this pointer is a constant, it cannot be assigned to. The pointer is necessary because, although every instance of a class has its own data, there is only one copy of each member function. However, each non-static member function has its own this pointer which holds the address of the object that the function was invoked on. Static member functions do not have a this pointer since they can only access static data members and there is only one instance of each such data member.

---

[1]Since overloaded operators are actually implemented by function calls, remarks concerning functions also apply to operators. (See Section 9.3 for more details.)

Exercise:

Test the new assignment operator for the `complex` class. In particular, check that the operator behaves correctly for statements such as:

```
u = v = w = z;
```

9.1.3 Overloading the Addition Operator

We would like to be able to write expressions involving the addition of complex objects in a similar way to integer and floating point expressions:

```
z = u + v;
```

This is easily achieved by overloading the binary + operator:

```
class complex {
    friend complex operator+(const complex &z,
        const complex &w);
// More class declarations here.
};

inline complex operator+(const complex &z,
    const complex &w)
{
    return complex(z.re + w.re, z.im + w.im);
}

// More inline function implementations here.
```

where the left and right operands correspond to z and w respectively. We can test this overloaded operator by examining the results of the following code:

```
complex u(1.1, 2.2), v(10.0, 20.0), w;

w = u + v;
cout << "w = " << real(w) << " + i " << im(w) << "\n";
```

Other binary operators, such as -, *, /, && etc. can be implemented in a similar manner.

Exercise:

Implement and test overloaded binary operators for multiplication, *, and equality, ==, for the `complex` class.

The addition operator for the fundamental types has two significant features:

- The operator is symmetric with respect to its operands; that is (u + v) is equivalent to (v + u).

- The operands are not required to be lvalues; that is the expression (u + v) does not assign a value to either u or v.

In order to avoid confusion, an overloaded addition operator should also possess these features.

Most overloaded operators can be defined as either member functions or global functions. Such global functions are usually declared `friend`s. This `friend`ship is not directly connected with operator overloading, but is required whenever the non-member function implementing an overloaded operator needs to access `private` class data. Hence non-member operators are almost always implemented as `friend`s.

To implement the overloaded `complex` addition operator, it is better to use a `friend` rather than a member function. The member function implementation:

```
class complex {
public:
    complex operator+(const complex &v);
    // ...
};
```

has the disadvantage that it is not symmetric with respect to the operands; specifically, an expression, (u + v), would be equivalent to:

```
u.operator+(v);
```

Although an expression such as:

```
u + 10
```

would be valid, the apparently equivalent:

```
10 + u
```

would fail to compile since it is actually:

```
10.operator+(v);          // WRONG!
```

which clearly does not make sense. Similar considerations apply to other *binary* operators, such as -, *, /, && etc.

9.1.4   Overloading the Unary Minus Operator

The minus operator, `-`, in the context:

```
complex u, v(10.0, 20.0);

u = -v;
```

is a unary, rather than binary, operator. For the `complex` class this operator can be implemented by:

```
class complex {
public:
    complex operator-( ) const;
// More class declarations here.
};

inline complex complex::operator-( ) const
{
    return complex(-re, -im);
}

// More inline function implementations here.
```

Here the unary minus operator is defined as a class member operator, rather than a `friend`. For this reason the operator takes no explicit arguments (the parentheses are empty) and the only 'argument' is the hidden `this` pointer. The `const` at the end of the function prototype for the overloaded unary minus operator has a similar significance to `const` in the context of an ordinary member function (see Section 8.14); an object that invokes the operator cannot be changed by it. In the above case an expression, such as `-v`, cannot change the values stored by `v`.

The unary minus operator could alternatively be implemented as a `friend` function:

```
class complex {
// ...
    friend complex - (const complex &z);
};
```

In contrast to binary operators, both member and non-member functions are acceptable ways of overloading the unary minus operator.

Exercise:

Test the above definition of the unary minus operator for the `complex` class.

9.2   User-defined Conversions

The fundamental data types have built-in conversions, which may be either implicit or explicit. In some circumstances, such as:

```
double x = 10;
```

the compiler supplies a cast, which converts 10, of type int, to a double, which is assigned to x. An explicit cast can also be supplied, as in:

```
int i, j;
// Assignments to i and j.
double x = double(i) / double(j);
```

Such conversions are not just a cosmetic change of type; the bit pattern representing 10 is very different from that representing 10.0. Moreover, the built-in conversions are an essential simplification, without which the compiler would have to provide a different implementation of every binary operator for each legal combination of the fundamental types.

It is also possible to perform conversions from a class or fundamental data type to a class. Again, such conversions may be either implicit or explicit, but we must supply functions which specify how the conversions are to be made. There are two ways in which conversions involving classes can be performed: by constructors which accept a single argument and by conversion functions. Before we continue our discussion of operator overloading, we examine these conversions in more detail.

9.2.1   Conversion by Constructors

A constructor, which accepts a single argument, not of the class type, converts that argument to the class type. Such conversions are relatively common. For instance, an example of a constructor that accepts a single argument is:

```
class complex {
public:
    // Additional constructor:
    complex(double x) { re = x; im = 0.0; }
// ...
};
```

In this case the constructor actually has two arguments but one of these has a default value. This constructor can be used to initialize objects in the standard way:

```
complex z = complex(1.2, 4.8);
```

but it can also perform conversions:

```
complex u, v, z;
v = complex(3.6);   // Explicit conversion by constructor.
u = 1.2;            // Implicit conversion by constructor.
z = u + 3 * v;      // Implicit conversion by constructor.
```

The expression for v is consistent with the usual cast syntax (such as int(3.6)) and, indeed, a constructor accepting a single argument is effectively a user-defined cast operator. In the expression for u, the constructor is implicitly used to perform a conversion. Moreover, z is evaluated correctly, even if we have only declared:

```
friend complex operator*(const complex &u, const complex &v);
```

and have not given versions for operands of type double. This is because 3 is converted to double, which is in turn converted to complex by the constructor function.

Exercise:

In Section 8.13 we implemented a constructor with the prototype:

```
complex::complex(double x = 0.0, double y = 0.0);
```

Can this constructor perform conversions for the complex class? Verify your answer by means of a short program.

9.2.2 Conversion Functions††

A constructor accepting a single argument can only convert to its own class and this has two consequences:

- A constructor cannot convert to one of the fundamental types.

- Suppose class Y has been implemented and we define a new class, X. A class X constructor can convert from Y to X, but we must modify class Y in order that a class Y constructor can convert from X to Y. However, changing the source of class Y may be neither feasible nor desirable.

The solution to both of these problems is to use a *conversion function*.[2]
A conversion function is a class member declared as:

---

[2]Since conversion functions are not used elsewhere in this book, you may wish to omit this section.

```
class my_class {
// ...
    operator <type> ();
};
```

where `<type>` is the type returned, which could be either a fundamental type
(or a simple derivation, such as a pointer to a fundamental type) or else a class.
Neither an argument:

```
class my_class {
// ...
    operator double(complex);    // WRONG: cannot specify
                                 //        argument.
};
```

nor the usual syntax for a return type:

```
class my_class {
// ...
    int operator complex();      // WRONG: cannot specify
                                 //        return type.
};
```

can be used. Another restriction is that since conversion functions do not take
arguments they cannot be overloaded.

A conversion function is a user-defined cast operator and can be used in two
distinct ways:

1. **Conversion From a Class to a Fundamental Type**

   Suppose we define a `time` class, which stores the time in hours, minutes
   and seconds. We can define a conversion function which converts a `time`
   object into the `int` type, corresponding to seconds:

   ```
   class time {
   public:
       // Define a constructor:
       time(int h, int m, int s) { hours = h; minutes = m;
           seconds = s; }
       //Define a conversion function:
       operator int() { return(seconds + 60 *
           (minutes + 60 * hours)); }
   private:
       int hours, minutes, seconds;
   };
   ```

An example, using this function is:[3]

```
time t(16, 21, 35); // 16 hours  21 mins.  35 secs.
int s;
s = int(t);            // Time in seconds assigned to s.
```

Exercise:

Write a program to try out the above code fragment. What happens if you comment out the conversion function definition?

2. **Conversion Between Classes**

It is also possible to provide conversion functions which convert between classes. Suppose we define an array class for objects with three elements:

```
class array3 {
public:
    array3(){ data[0] = data[1] = data[2] = 0.0; }
    array3(double x, double y, double z);
    array3 &operator=(const array3 &a);
    double data[3];
};
```

with the following straightforward implementations:

```
array3::array3(double x, double y, double z)
{
    data[0] = x;
    data[1] = y;
    data[2] = z;
}

array3 &array3::operator=(const array3 &a)
{
    data[0] = a.data[0];
    data[1] = a.data[1];
    data[2] = a.data[2];
    return *this;
}
```

An array class, **array2**, for objects with two elements can provide a conversion function from **array2** to **array3**:

---

[3]The (int)t syntax is equivalent to int(t), but the latter is clearer and therefore preferable.

```
class array2 {
public:
    array2(double x, double y);
    array2 &operator=(const array2 &a);
    operator array3();
    double data[2];
};

array2::array2(double x, double y)
{
    data[0] = x;
    data[1] = y;
}

array2 &array2::operator=(const array2 &a)
{
    data[0] = a.data[0];
    data[1] = a.data[1];
    return *this;
}

array2::operator array3()
{
    return array3(data[0], data[1], 1.0);
}
```

If we define an object of the **array2** class:

```
array2 a2(10.0, 20.0);
```

then we can make an explicit conversion to the **array3** class:

```
array3 a3 = array3(a2);
```

Exercise:

Verify that this conversion gives the expected result and then change the initialization statement so that it performs an implicit conversion.

9.2.3   Implicit Conversions[††]

User-defined conversions should be kept simple since they are usually applied implicitly and it may not be obvious which conversions are used.[4] For example, implicit conversions may occur when a function (or operator) call has argument types not exactly matching any defined function with the same name. In principle, it is possible to define a constructor and a conversion function, both of which perform a conversion between the same two types. However, any attempt to perform an implicit conversion between the two types would be ambiguous and would therefore fail.

Not more than one implicit user-defined conversion is applied in any one instance. For example, we could extend the example of the previous section to include an class for objects with four elements:

```
class array4 {
public:
    array4(){ data[0] = data[1] = data[2] = data[3] = 0.0; }
    array4(const array3 &a);
    array4 &operator=(const array4 &a);
    double data[4];
};
```

Since the constructor with a single **array3** argument:

```
array4::array4(const array3 &a)
{
    data[0] = a.data[0];
    data[1] = a.data[1];
    data[2] = a.data[2];
    data[3] = 1.0;
}
```

performs conversions from **array3** to **array4**, we now have the following user-defined conversions:

$$\text{array2} \longrightarrow \text{array3}$$
$$\text{array3} \longrightarrow \text{array4}$$

Given objects, a2, a3 and a4, for the classes, **array2**, **array3** and **array4**, implicit conversions occur for the following statements:

```
a3 = a2;
a4 = a3;
```

---

[4]If you have omitted the previous section you may well wish to omit this one. Any conversions used in this book are indeed kept simple!

However, the statement:

```
a4 = a2;          // WRONG: would need two implicit conversions.
```

is invalid since only one user-defined conversion can be performed implicitly. If this were not so then conversions could get completely out of control.

Conversions are typically applied implicitly in the following circumstances:[5]

1. **Function Arguments**

   A function prototyped as:

   ```
   complex f(complex z);
   ```

   may be invoked by:

   ```
   complex w = f(2.4);
   ```

   The function argument, 2.4, is implicitly converted to a `complex` object and the statement is equivalent to:

   ```
   complex w = f(complex(2.4));
   ```

2. **Function Return Values**

   The body of the function, `f()`, prototyped above, could correctly include the statement:

   ```
   return(x);
   ```

   where `x` has type `double`. This `return` statement would then be equivalent to:

   ```
   return(complex(x));
   ```

3. **Operands**

   If we declare:

   ```
   friend complex operator*(const complex &u,
       const complex &v);
   ```

   then we do not need to declare versions of the * operator with a `double` operand, such as:

---

[5]Notice that in all three examples the required conversion is from `double` to `complex` and therefore must be performed by a constructor rather than a conversion function. However, in other circumstances a conversion function may be appropriate.

```
friend complex operator*(const double &x,
    const complex &v);
```

For example, the expression:

```
complex z = 2.0 * v;
```

has an implicit conversion from `double` to `complex`.

9.3 Operator Function Calls

So far, we have introduced operator overloading in the context of the `complex` class and described user-defined conversion in some detail. We are now ready to return to a more thorough treatment of the subject of operator overloading.

Operator overloading is actually implemented by an *operator function* call. A non-member operator, such as:

```
friend complex operator+(const complex &, const complex &);
```

is a function with the name 'operator+', taking two `complex` arguments and returning the `complex` type. An expression of the form:

```
z = u + v;
```

where `z`, `u` and `v` are all instances of the `complex` class, is directly equivalent to:

```
z.operator=(operator+(u, v));
```

Exercise:

Verify the equivalence between the operator and function call notations by printing `z` for explicit (complex) `u` and `v` in the above expression. Are the outermost parentheses significant in the operator function call? Can white space be inserted around the `=` or `+`?

It is very rare for operator function calls to be invoked explicitly, since the resulting expressions are more cumbersome and less intuitive than their operator counterparts. However, the ability to rewrite expressions in terms of operator function calls (as above) leads to a useful understanding of how overloaded operators really work and this is a prerequiste to actually defining such operators.

Most overloaded operators can be implemented by both non-`static` member functions and non-member functions (which are usually `friends`). One set of exceptions are the assignment, function call, subscripting and class member access operators:

```
=    ( )    [ ]    ->
```

which can only be overloaded by non-`static` member functions. The overloaded class member access operator, `->`, has the additional unique feature in that it is considered to be a unary operator; that is:

```
pt->x
```

is interpreted as:

```
(pt.operator->())->x
```

Consequently, `pt.operator->()` must return something that can be used as a pointer. The other exceptions are the `new` and `delete` operators as these can only be overloaded by `static` member functions. The overloaded `new`, `delete` and member access operators are not considered further since they are only likely to be useful in advanced applications.

9.3.1 Binary Operators

A binary operator is invoked by the expression:[6]

```
A <op> B
```

where A and B are the two operands. This expression is equivalent to:

```
A.operator<op>(B)
```

for a non-`static` member function and

```
operator<op>(A, B)
```

for a non-member function implementation. Whereas the member function has one explicit argument and the hidden `this` pointer, the non-member function has two arguments and no `this` pointer.

As an example, suppose `z` and `w` are instances of the `complex` class, then:

```
z += w;
```

is equivalent to:

```
z.operator+=(w);
```

for the member function, and:

```
operator+=(z, w);
```

for the non-member function. The member function would be declared as:

---

[6]We use `<op>` to denote a generic operator.

```
class complex {
// ...
    complex &operator+=(const complex &z);
};
```

Assuming the data members of the `complex` class are `private`, then the non-member function must be declared a `friend` of the class:

```
class complex {
// ...
    friend complex operator+(const complex &u,
        const complex &v);
};
```

A significant difference between member and non-member binary operators is that for non-member implementations, user-defined conversions may be applied to both operands, whereas for member implementations, user-defined conversions are not applied to the first operand. For example, suppose we declare an (incomplete) `complex` class as:

```
class complex {
public:
    complex(void) { }
    complex(double x, double y = 0.0);
    complex operator+(const complex &z);
    complex &operator=(const complex &z);
 private:
    double re, im;
 };
```

and initialize variables, u, v and x by:

```
complex u(1.0, 2.0), v(3.0, 4.0);
double x = 5.0;
```

Then the statement:

```
z = u + x;
```

is valid because the constructor with the default imaginary argument converts the explicit argument of the 'operator+' function from `double` to `complex`. However, the following statement does not compile:

```
z = x + u;
```

because the user-defined conversion is not applied to the dereferenced hidden `this` pointer. This lack of symmetry for the operands of the addition operator is clearly unsatisfactory and does not occur for a non-member function implementation.

Exercise:

Implement the `complex` class defined above and verify the claims made.

9.3.2   Prefix Unary Operators

A prefix unary member operator is invoked by the expression:

```
<op> A
```

where `A` is the single operand. This expression is equivalent to:

```
A.operator<op>()
```

for a non-`static` member function and

```
operator<op>(A)
```

for a non-member function implementation. Whereas the member function has the hidden `this` pointer and no explicit argument, the non-member implementation has no `this` pointer and a single argument.

As an example, if `z` is an instance of the complex class, then:[7]

```
++z;
```

is invoked by:

```
z.operator++();
```

for the member implementation, and:

```
operator++(z);
```

for the non-member implementation. The member function would be declared as:

```
complex class {
// ...
    complex operator++();
};
```

and the non-member function as:

```
complex class {
// ...
    friend complex operator++(complex &z);
};
```

---

[7]It is not clear how to overload the increment operator for the `complex` class. One possibility is to increment the real part of `complex` objects.

9.3.3 Postfix Unary Operators

The increment and decrement operators have postfix, as well as prefix, variants. These postfix operators can be either non-member functions or non-`static` class members and in both cases are distinguished from their prefix versions by having an extra argument of type `int`.

An expression of the form:

```
A <op>
```

where `<op>` is either `++` or `--`, is equivalent to:

```
A.operator<op>(0)
```

Notice that the function is invoked with an argument of value zero and it is this that distinguishes the postfix from the prefix operators. If `z` is an instance of the `complex` class, then:

```
z++;
```

is invoked by:

```
z.operator++(0);        // Postfix operator.
```

whereas:

```
++z;
```

corresponds to:

```
z.operator++();         // Prefix operator.
```

For the complex class, the postfix `++` member operator would be declared as:

```
class complex {
// ...
    complex operator++(int);
};
```

For a non-member implementation:

```
A <op>
```

is equivalent to:

```
operator<op>(A, 0)
```

The function is invoked with two arguments, the second of which has the value zero. If `z` is a `complex` object, then `z++` is invoked by:

```
    operator++(z, 0);        // Postfix operator.
```

whereas **++z** corresponds to:

```
    operator++(z);           // Prefix operator.
```

The postfix **++** non-member operator would be declared as:

```
class complex {
// ...
    complex complex::operator++(complex &z, int);
};
```

Exercise:

Implement and test overloaded prefix and postfix unary operators for
the **complex** class. The prefix versions should increment and decrement the real part of a **complex** object; the postfix versions should
increment and decrement the imaginary part. Is it a good idea to
overload the operators in this way?

9.4 Some Special Binary Operators

There are three special binary operators, which can only be overloaded by non-
static *member* functions. These are the assignment, subscripting and function
call operators. Since we have already considered the assignment operator in some
detail, we now turn our attention to the subscripting and function call operators.

9.4.1 Overloading the Subscript Operator

As we have already mentioned, the built-in concept of an array in C++ is very
primitive. An array element, **a[i]**, means nothing more than ***(a+i)** and multi-
dimensional arrays, such as **b[i][j][k]**, are merely successive, left to right,
applications of the subscripting operator, **[]**. Moreover, indexing goes from zero
up to one less than the number of elements and no checking is done to ensure
that a program keeps to this range.

The overloaded subscripting operator has the form **A[B]**, where **A** must be a
class object and **B** can have any type. In the function call notation, the expression,
A[B], is equivalent to:[8]

```
    A.operator[](B)
```

---

[8]If white space is inserted within the square brackets of **operator[ ]** it is ignored.

There is no necessity for the overloaded operator to have any connection with the concept of an array; we simply have a function, with the name 'operator[]'. The function has two 'arguments'; the first is the hidden **this** pointer and the second is B, which is not limited to the integral or even fundamental types.

In spite of this freedom of definition, it is advisable to make the overloaded subscripting operator have some connection with its built-in counterpart. As a simple example, suppose we need objects which are one-dimensional arrays and that the index goes from 1 to 3. Also assume that we want any array access to be checked, in case the index goes out of bounds. A suitable class is:

```
#include <stdlib.h>      // for exit()
#include <iostream.hpp>

class array {
public:
    double &operator[](int i);
private:
    double data[3];
};

double &array::operator[](int i)
{
    if (i < 1 || i > 3) {
        cout << "Index = " << i << " out of range\n";
        exit(EXIT_FAILURE);
    }
    return data[i-1];
}
```

Returning a reference for **operator[]** enables us to have **array** objects on the left as well as the right hand side of assignment statements, as the following program demonstrates:

```
#include <iostream.hpp>
int main()
{
    array x;

    // Assign values to elements of the array:
    for (int i = 1; i <= 3; ++i)
        x[i] = 10.0 * i;

    // Test assignment:
    for (i = 1; i <= 3; ++i)
```

```
        cout << "x[" << i << "] = " << x[i] << "\n";

    // Try setting the index out of range:
    x[0] = 3.142;

    return(EXIT_SUCCESS);
}
```

Exercise:

Compile and run this program. Try other array sizes and attempt to access other elements (both valid and invalid).

Use the subscripting operator to improve the **array** class which was introduced in Section 8.17.1.

9.4.2   Overloading the Function Call Operator

The function call operator can also be overloaded. An expression, A(x, y, z), is equivalent to

```
    A.operator()(x, y, z)
```

where A must be a class object, but **x**, **y** and **z** can be of any type. There is no restriction on the number of arguments. For a single argument, the overloaded function call operator can play the same role as the the overloaded subscripting operator.

The function call operator is often used to access the elements of a multi-dimensional **array** class. Suppose we want to extend our example in the previous section to two-dimensional arrays, with the data stored by columns, rather than rows. A suitable class is:

```
#include <stdlib.h>      // for exit()
#include <iostream.hpp>

class array {
public:
    double &operator()(int i, int j);
private:
    double data[3][3];
};

double &array::operator()(int i, int j)
{
```

```
        if (i < 1 || j < 1 || i > 3 || j > 3) {
            cout << "Index out of range:  i = " <<
                i << "  j = " << j <<"\n";
            exit(EXIT_FAILURE);
        }
        return data[j-1][i-1];
    }
```

Notice that the indices are reversed in the return statement for `operator()` in order to implement storage by columns.

A simple test program for this class is:

```
int main()
{
    array x;

    // Assign values to elements of the array:
    for (int i = 1; i <= 3; ++i)
        for (int j = 1; j <= 3; ++j)
            x(i, j) = 10.0 * i * j;

    // Test assignment:
    for (i = 1; i <= 3; ++i)
        for (j = 1; j <= 3; ++j)
            cout << "x(" << i << ", " << j << ") = " <<
                x(i, j) << "\n";

    // Try setting the index is out of range:
    x(0, 2) = 3.142;

    return(EXIT_SUCCESS);
}
```

Exercise:

Compile and run this program. Modify both the class and test program to handle three-dimensional arrays.

9.5 Defining Overloaded Operators

There are some general guidelines that are worth following when defining overloaded operators:

- Overloaded operators should mimic their built-in counterparts; for example:

```
z = u + v;
```

should in some sense correspond to addition for whatever class (or classes) z, u and v belong.

- Operators that have related meanings for fundamental types should do so for their overloaded counterparts. For instance:

```
z += u;
```

should be completely equivalent to:

```
z = z + u;
```

- In general, overloaded operators can be defined as either member functions or global functions (usually **friend**s). The exceptions are that:

$$ = \qquad () \qquad [] \qquad -> $$

must be non-**static** member functions and the operators, **new** and **delete**, must be overloaded by **static** member functions.

If a binary operator for a fundamental type requires an lvalue for the left operand, then the overloaded operator should be declared as a member function. For example, the **+=** operator for the **complex** class should be declared as:

```
class complex {
// ...
    complex &operator+=(const complex &u);
};
```

rather than:

```
class complex {
// ...
    friend void operator+=(complex &u,
        const complex &v);
};
```

In the second case, nonsense statements of the form:

```
1.4 += z;        // WRONG
```

would be accepted by the compiler.

When the operator does not require an lvalue for a fundamental type, the operator should be a global function, rather than a class member. For instance, as discussed in Section 9.1.3, the + operator for the **complex** class should be declared as:

```
class complex {
// ...
    friend complex operator+(const complex &u,
        const complex &v);
};
```

rather than:

```
class complex {
// ...
    complex operator+(const complex &v);
};
```

In contrast to binary operators, member and non-member implementations of unary operators are often equally acceptable. However, as noted previously, one feature distinguishing member and non-member functions is that user-defined conversions are *not* applied to an argument which is effectively the dereferenced hidden **this** pointer.

9.6 Using Overloaded Operators

9.6.1 Complex Arithmetic

In this section we summarize the implementation of a complex arithmetic class; it is left as an exercise to complete the project. First we present the header file for the class:

```
// source:  complex.hpp
// use:     Defines complex arithmetic class.
//          Implements inline functions.

#ifndef COMPLEX_HPP
#define COMPLEX_HPP

#include <iostream.hpp>
#include <math.h>
```

```
class complex {
    friend complex operator+(double x, const complex &v);
    friend complex operator+(const complex &u, double x);
    friend complex operator+(const complex &u,
        const complex &v);
    friend double real(const complex &z);
    friend double imag(const complex &z);
    friend double mod(const complex &z);
    friend complex conj(const complex &z);
    friend complex exp(const complex &z);
public:
    double &real(void);
    double &im(void);

    complex(void) { }
    complex(double r, double i);
    complex(const complex &z);

    complex &operator=(double x);
    complex &operator=(const complex &z);

    complex &operator+=(double x);
    complex &operator+=(const complex &z);

    complex operator-() const;
private:
    double re, im;
};

// friend functions:
inline complex operator+(double x, const complex &v)
{
    return complex(x + v.re, v.im);
}

inline complex operator+(const complex &u, double x)
{
    return complex(u.re + x, u.im);
}

inline complex operator+(const complex &u, const complex &v)
{
```

```
        return complex(u.re + v.re, u.im + v.im);
}

inline double real(const complex &z)
{
        return z.re;
}

inline double imag(const complex &z)
{
        return z.im;
}

inline double mod(const complex &z)
// Modulus of z.
{
        return(sqrt(z.re * z.re + z.im * z.im));
}

inline complex conj(const complex &z)
// Complex conjugate of z.
{
        return complex(z.re, -z.im);
}

inline complex exp(const complex &z)
// Exponential function for complex argument.
{
        double temp = exp(z.re);

        return complex(temp * cos(z.im), temp * sin(z.im));
}

// member functions and operators:
inline double &complex::real(void)
{
        return re;
}

inline double &complex::imag(void)
{
        return im;
}
```

```
inline complex::complex(double r, double i)
{
    re = r;
    im = i;
}

inline complex::complex(const complex &z)
{
    re = z.re;
    im = z.im;
}

inline complex &complex::operator=(double x)
{
    re = x;
    im = 0.0;
    return *this;
}

inline complex &complex::operator=(const complex &z)
{
    re = z.re;
    im = z.im;
    return *this;
}

inline complex &complex::operator+=(double x)
{
    re += x;
    return *this;
}

inline complex &complex::operator+=(const complex &z)
{
    re += z.re;
    im += z.im;
    return *this;
}

inline complex complex::operator-() const
{
return complex(-re, -im);
```

```
}

#endif  // COMPLEX_HPP
```

Notice how, in order in improve efficiency, `complex` arguments are passed as `const complex &z` wherever possible, whereas `double` arguments are passed by value.

Since all functions are `inline`, there is no `complex.cpp` file, although it could reasonably be argued that `mod()` and `exp()` should not be `inline`, as they involve non-trivial computation. A short program which tests this class is as follows:

```cpp
// source:  test.cpp
// use:     Tests complex arithmetic class.

#include <stdlib.h>      // for EXIT_SUCCESS
#include <iostream.hpp>
#include "complex.hpp"

void print(const complex &z)
{
    cout << real(z) << " + i * " << imag(z) << "\n";
}

int main()
{
    complex z1(1, 2), z2(3, 3), z3;
    const complex i(0, 1);

    cout << "z1 = ";
    print(z1);
    cout << "z2 = ";
    print(z2);
    cout << "i = ";
    print(i);

    z3 = z1 + z2;
    cout << "z1 + z2 = ";
    print(z3);

    cout << "1.0 + z1 = ";
    print(1.0 + z1);
    cout << "z1 + 1.0 = ";
    print(z1 + 1.0);
```

```
    cout << "mod(z1) = " << mod(z1) << "\n";

    cout << "conj(z1) = ";
    print(conj(z1));

    cout << "exp(z1) = ";
    print(exp(z1));

    return(EXIT_SUCCESS);
}
```

There is one feature of C++ which would improve this class. We have used:

```
    print(z);
```

to print a complex number, whereas it would be better if this statement were replaced by:

```
    cout << z;
```

Techniques for achieving this are described in Chapter 12.

9.6.2   Strings

In C++, a string simply consists of a **char** array with a string terminator, '\0', Manipulation of such strings is prone to error; for example, a common mistake is to forget that the library function, **strlen()**, does not count the terminator when returning the length of a string. However, a **string** class provides both a safer and a more natural way of manipulating strings. A suitable class declaration is:[9]

```
// source:        string.hpp
// use:           Defines self-describing string class.

#ifndef SELF_DESCRIBING_STRING_HPP
#define SELF_DESCRIBING_STRING_HPP

#include <string.h>      // for memcmp()

class string {
friend string operator+(const string &s1, const string &s2);
friend int operator==(const string &s1, const string &s2);
friend int operator!=(const string &s1, const string &s2);
public:
```

---

[9]Do not confuse **"string.hpp"** with **<string.h>**.

```
        string(void) { characters = 0; pt = NULL; }
        string(const string &s);
        string(char *s);
        string &operator=(const string &s);
        char *char_array (void) const;
        int length(void) const { return characters; }
        void print(void);
    private:
        string(int set_length);
        int characters;
        char *pt;
    };


    inline int operator==(const string &s1, const string &s2)
    {
        if (s1.characters == s2.characters &&
            !memcmp(s1.pt, s2.pt, s1.characters))
            return 1;
        else
            return 0;
    }


    inline int operator!=(const string &s1, const string &s2)
    {
        if (s1.characters == s2.characters &&
            !memcmp(s1.pt, s2.pt, s1.characters))
            return 0;
        else
            return 1;
    }


    #endif  // SELF_DESCRIBING_STRING_HPP
```

A **string** object consists of a **char** array (*without* a string terminator) together with the number of elements in the array, stored by the variable called **characters**. Functions are provided to concatenate **string** objects, test for equality and inequality and to perform assignment. The **char_array()** function returns a pointer to an array which stores a *copy* of the **string** object, s, as a standard C++ null terminated string. This function avoids exposing details of the **string** implementation in circumstances where a ordinary null terminated string is required.

The **string** class can be implemented as follows:

```
    // source:       string.cpp
```

```
// use:           Implements string class.

#include <iostream.hpp>
#include <stdlib.h>      // for exit()
#include "string.hpp"

string::string(const string &s)
{
    characters = s. characters;
    pt = new char[characters];
    if (pt == NULL) {
        cerr << "Failed to allocate string.\n";
        exit(EXIT_FAILURE);
    }
    memcpy(pt, s.pt, characters);
}

string::string(char *s)
{
    characters = strlen(s);
    pt = new char[characters];
    if (pt == NULL) {
        cerr << "Failed to allocate string.\n";
        exit(EXIT_FAILURE);
    }
    memcpy(pt, s, characters);
}

string &string::operator=(const string &s)
{
    delete pt;
    characters = s. characters;
    pt = new char[characters];
    if (pt == NULL) {
        cerr << "Failed to allocate string.\n";
        exit(EXIT_FAILURE);
    }
    memcpy(pt, s.pt, characters);
    return *this;
}

char *string::char_array(void) const
{
```

```
        char *buffer = new char[1 + characters];
        if (buffer == NULL) {
            cerr << "Failed to allocate string.\n";
            exit(EXIT_FAILURE);
        }
        memcpy(buffer, pt, characters);
        buffer[characters] = '\0';
        return buffer;
}


string::string(int set_length)
{
        characters = set_length;
        pt = new char[characters];
        if (pt == NULL) {
            cerr << "Failed to allocate string.\n";
            exit(EXIT_FAILURE);
        }
}


void string::print(void)
{
        for (int i = 0; i < characters; ++i)
            cout << pt[i];
}


// friend function implementation:
string operator+(const string &s1, const string &s2)
{
        int s1_length = s1.length();
        int s2_length = s2.length();
        string new_string(s1_length + s2_length);
        memcpy(new_string.pt, s1.pt, s1_length);
        memcpy(new_string.pt + s1_length, s2.pt, s2_length);
        return new_string;
}
```

A simple program to try out this **string** class is as follows:

```
// source:      test.cpp
// use:         Tests string class.

#include <iostream.hpp>
#include <stdlib.h>        // for EXIT_SUCCESS
```

```cpp
#include "string.hpp"

string f(string s)
{
    string ss;
    ss = s;
    return ss;
}

int main()
{
    // Test string::string(char *s):
    string s1("My first string");

    // Test void string::print(void):
    s1.print();
    cout << "\n";

    // Test int string::length(void):
    cout << "String length: " << s1.length() << "\n";

    // Test string::string(void):
    string s2;

    // Test string &string::operator=(const string &s):
    string s3 = s1;
    cout << "Copied string is: ";
    s3.print();
    cout << "\nWith string length: " <<
        s3.length() << "\n";

    // Test string::string(const string &s)
    // and string::~string():
    string s4 = f(s3);
    cout << "String copied by function is: ";
    s4.print();
    cout << "\nWith string length: " << s4.length() << "\n";

    // Test string operator+(const string &s1,
    //     const string &s2)
    // and  string::string(int set_length):
    string s5(" and this is my second");
```

```
        string s6 = s1 + s5;
        cout << "Adding two strings using +: ";
        s6.print();
        cout << "\nThis new string has length: " <<
            s6.length() << "\n";

        // Test char *string::char_array(const string &s):
        char *pt = s1.char_array();
        cout << "Assigning a 'string' to a char* gives: " <<
            pt << "\n";

        // Test int operator==(const string &s1,
        //    const string &s2):
        cout << "Does string: '";
        s3.print();
        cout << "' == '";
        s4.print();
        cout << "'?\n";
        if (s3 == s4)
            cout << "Yes\n";
        else
            cout << "No\n";
        cout << "Does string: '";
        s3.print();
        cout << "' == '";
        s6.print();
        cout << "'?\n";
        if (s3 == s6)
            cout << "Yes\n";
        else
            cout << "No\n";

        // Test int operator!=(const string &s1,
        //    const string &s2):
        cout << "Does string: '";
        s3.print();
        cout << "' != '";
        s4.print();
        cout << "'?\n";
        if (s3 != s4)
            cout << "Yes\n";
        else
            cout << "No\n";
```

```
    cout << "Does string: '";
    s3.print();
    cout << "' != '";
    s6.print();
    cout << "'?\n";
    if (s3 != s6)
        cout << "Yes\n";
    else
        cout << "No\n";

    return(EXIT_SUCCESS);
}
```

The current implementation of the **string** class has three unsatisfactory features:

- A **string** object is sent to the output stream by using the **print()** function, rather than the **<<** operator. The techniques of Chapter 12 enable the **print()** function to be replaced by an inserter.

- No function is provided for directly reading a **string** object from the input stream. This deficiency can also be overcome by using the techniques of Chapter 12.

- Memory for a string is not reclaimed when the object goes out a scope. It is straightforward to correct this feature by means of a destructor function which is introduced in the next chapter.

9.7   Summary

- All of the built-in C++ operators can be overloaded, with the exception of:

  .   .*   ::   ? :

  and the preprocessor operators, **#** and **##**.

- The associativity, precedence and number of operands of an overloaded operator cannot be changed by overloading:

  ```
  z = u ! v;          // WRONG!
  ```

- With few exceptions, an overloaded operator can be either a non-member function (usually a **friend**):[10]

---

[10]The exceptions are described in Section 9.3.

```
class X {
// ...
    friend X operator+(const X &u, const X &v);
};
```

or a member function:

```
class complex {
// ...
    complex &operator+=(const complex &u);
};
```

- Overloaded operators, when implemented as member functions, can also use the `const` specifier, as in:

```
class complex {
// ...
    complex operator-() const;
};
```

- A constructor accepting a single argument, not of the class type, performs a conversion to the class:

```
class complex {
// ...
    complex(const double &x);
};
```

```
complex z = 1.414;          // Implicit conversion.
complex w = complex(0.707); // Explicit conversion.
```

- A conversion function takes the form:

```
class complex {
// ...
    operator double();
};
```

Neither a `return` type nor argument can be specified.

- Operator overloading is implemented by an operator function. Member functions have an implicit argument, which is the hidden **this** pointer. The relationship between an operator and the corresponding function call notation is summarized in Table 9.1.

Operator	Function call	
	Member	Non-member
A <op> B	A.operator<op>(B)	operator<op>(A, B)
<op> A	A.operator<op>( )	operator<op>(A)
A <op>	A.operator<op>(0)	operator<op>(A, 0)

Table 9.1: Operator Function Calls.

9.8   Exercises

1. What are the difficulties in trying to implement a class for two-dimensional arrays by overloading the subscripting, rather than function call, operator.

2. Further improve our `array` class (originally given in Section 8.17.1) by adding an overloaded assignment operator. Memory should be dynamically allocated for the new elements and the original data copied into this memory.

3. Extend and test the complex arithmetic class, described in Section 9.6.1, as far as you can. Some of the many omissions are subtraction, multiplication and division, together with the elementary functions for complex arguments.

4. In the `complex` arithmetic class, implemented in Section 9.6.1, there is neither a constructor accepting a single argument nor a conversion function. Consequently, explicit operators must be defined for each possible operation performing mixed arithmetic. Implement the alternative technique of only defining operators for `complex` arguments and relying on implicit conversion. Write a program which tests the modified class as thoroughly as you can. What are the relative merits of the two techniques?

Chapter 10

Constructors and Destructors

In this chapter we consolidate our previous discussion of constructor functions and introduce destructor functions. A constructor is invoked whenever an object is created and a destructor is invoked whenever an object is destroyed. Constructors are often invoked by the compiler, rather than as an explicit part of a user-supplied statement; destructors are also often invoked by the compiler but almost never as an explicit part of a user-supplied statement.

Constructors are necessary because objects can be created throughout a program, often implicitly and with their initial data unknown at compile-time. A user-defined constructor can initialize object data and this may include storing the address of dynamically allocated memory. Constructors are also often used to open files.

If there is no user-defined constructor, then a simple `public` default which takes no arguments is supplied by the compiler. If at least one constructor is defined for a class, but all the constructors must take arguments, then objects of this class cannot be defined without being initialized. Such a class prevents the otherwise common error of using objects which have not been initialized.

Constructors are usually `public`. However, making all constructors `private` for a particular class means that only member functions and friends can create objects of the class. A class which has no `public` constructors is known as a *private class* and can be useful if objects of one class are only ever used as clients of another.[1]

A destructor is called when an object goes out of scope, or a program terminates normally, and is used to cleanup before an object is destroyed. Often there is no need for a user-defined destructor since the default is perfectly adequate. However, if a constructor dynamically allocates memory, then a destructor should be defined in order that this memory can be returned to the heap when the memory is no longer required. Another common use of a destructor is to close a file which has been opened by a constructor. Since destructors are invoked implicitly

---

[1]To ensure there are no `public` constructors, a `private` copy constructor must be defined or else the compiler will provide a `public` default.

283

by the compiler, such a file is usually closed as its associated object goes out of scope, rather than as a result of a user-supplied statement.

10.1   More on Constructor Functions

10.1.1   Dynamic Memory Management

A common requirement is for the storage needed by an object to be allocated at run-time. For example, we may have a matrix class, which could include functions to perform the usual multiply, add and inversion operations. A typical program using this class might ask the user to enter the size of the matrix to be created:

```
cout << "Enter number of rows: ";
cin >> rows;
cout << "Enter number of columns: ";
cin >> columns;

matrix m(rows, columns);        // Create matrix.
```

Rather than statically allocating sufficient memory for matrices up to a certain size, the **matrix** class could have a constructor which uses the **new** operator to dynamically allocate memory:[2]

```
#include <stdlib.h>             // for exit()

class matrix {
public:
    matrix(int rows, int columns);
    double *p;                  // Address of data.
    int m, n;                   // m x n matrix.
};

matrix::matrix(int rows, int columns)
{
    m = rows;
    n = columns;
    p = new double[m * n];
    if (p == NULL ) {
        cout << "Cannot allocate matrix.\n";
        exit(EXIT_FAILURE);
    }
}
```

---

[2]For simplicity we make all the data members **public** in the current discussion.

Notice that the constructor assigns the address of dynamically allocated memory to the pointer, p. That is the constructor does *not* dynamically allocate the matrix object (whose data members are m, n and p) but rather initializes the object after memory for m, n and p has been allocated. The above function initializes a matrix; a second constructor would be needed to copy a matrix:[3]

```
#include <string.h>           // for memcpy()

matrix::matrix(matrix &a)
{
    m = a.m;
    n = a.n;
    p = new double[m * n];
    if (p == NULL) {
        cout << "Cannot allocate matrix.\n";
        exit(EXIT_FAILURE);
    }
    memcpy(p, a.p, m * n * sizeof(double));
}
```

10.1.2   Assignment and Initialization

In C++ it is important to distinguish between assignment and initialization since they are implemented by different functions. An assignment is implemented by an assignment operator, whereas an initialization is performed by a constructor. In either case the compiler supplies defaults if necessary.

Assignment implies that an object already exists and its data members are changed through an assignment statement:

```
int x;
x = 10;           // 10 is assigned to x.
complex u, v(1.1, 2.2);
u = v;            // Assignment to u.
```

An assignment is a copy operation which, with one exception, takes place whenever we use the = symbol. The exception is that use of the = symbol within a declaration is an initialization.

An initialization can occur in the following circumstances:

- when an object is declared, as in the statements:

---

[3]A class often requires three types of constructor. The third type of constructor for this class would convert an object of another type into a matrix; for instance, we might want to convert an array into a matrix.

```
complex z(1.1, 2.2);
matrix m(4, 5);
complex z = 1.1;
int x = 10;
```

- when an object is passed by value as a function argument. For instance, if a function:

```
void f(complex z)
{
    // function body.
}
```

is invoked by:

```
f(u);
```

then z is initialized rather than assigned to.

- when an object is returned by value from a function:

```
complex f(complex z)
{
    complex u;
    // Assignment to u.
    return u;        // Implicit temporary is initialized.
}
```

If an object is passed by reference in a function argument or return value, then there is no assignment. For many objects, such as large matrices, this is important since large (and unnecessary) copying operations may be avoided.[4]

Exercise:

To illustrate the difference between assignment and initialization, implement functions for the following version of the complex class:

```
class complex {
    friend complex operator+(const complex &u,
        const complex &v);
public:
```

---

[4]However, remember that it is *not* possible to return a reference to a local non-static object.

```
        complex(double x = 0.0, double y = 0.0);
        complex(const complex &z);
        complex &operator=(const complex &z);
        double re, im;
    };
```

As each function is invoked, it should insert an identifying message in the output stream. Use these implementations to write a program which enables you to distinguish initializations from assignments in the code fragment:

```
complex u;
u = complex(2.0, 3.0);
complex v(1.0, 7.0);
complex z;
z = u + v;
```

Repeat the exercise with other operators, such as +=.

10.1.3 Member Objects with Constructors

The data members of a class are not restricted to the fundamental types; members can themselves be instances of another class:

```
class data {
public:
    data(const complex &z1, const complex &z2);
private:
    complex u, v;
};
```

In this example, the member objects have constructors that take no arguments. Since the complex() constructors are called before the data() constructor, this means that the member objects may be first initialized to zero and then be assigned the values z1 and z2. For instance, the constructors may take the form:

```
complex::complex(void)
{
    re = 0.0;
    im = 0.0;
}

data::data(const complex &z1, const complex &z2)
```

```
{
    u = z1;
    v = z2;
}
```

This sequence of initialization followed immediately by assignment is not very efficient, particularly for large or much used data structures. However, if we have a constructor taking arguments for the member objects, such as:

```
complex::complex(const complex &z)
{
    re = z.re;
    im = z.im;
}
```

then an alternative syntax for the **data()** constructor is:

```
data::data(const complex &z1, const complex &z2) : u(z1),
    v(z2)
{
    // The constructor body goes in here.
}
```

This directly calls the copy constructor for u and v and the **complex(void)** constructor is not invoked. In general, the colon is followed by a comma separated list of constructors taking arguments. This list, which is followed by the constructor body, can only occur in a constructor definition and not a declaration:

```
data::data(const complex &z1, const complex &z2) : u(z1),
    v(z2);  // WRONG: prototype cannot have constructor list.
```

The order in which the constructors are invoked is not influenced by this list since the rule is that the constructors for member objects are invoked first, in the order in which they are declared within the class, and then the constructor for the class is invoked.[5]

Exercise:

Modify the **complex()** and **data()** constructors so that they insert identifying messages in the output stream when they are called. Write short programs to demonstrate that:

1. If the **data()** constructor has the implementation:

---

[5]Destructors, which are introduced in the next section, are called in the reverse order.

```
data::data(const complex &z1, const complex &z2)
{
    // The constructor body goes here.
}
```

then u and v are first initialized to zero and then assigned the values of z1 and z2.

2. The data() constructor with the prototype:

```
data::data(const complex &z1, const complex &z2)
    : u(z1), v(z2)
{
    // The constructor body goes here.
}
```

does not first initialize u and v to zero, but rather invokes the copy constructor for the complex class.

10.2 Destructor Functions

A destructor is a class member function with the name ~X, where X is the name of the class; for instance:

```
class matrix {
public:
    matrix(int rows, int columns);
    ~matrix();          // Declares destructor function.
    double *p;          // Address of data.
    int m, n;           // m x n matrix.
};
```

There is often no need to declare a destructor: the complex class is a typical example; memory is allocated when a complex object is defined and deallocated when the object goes out of scope:

```
complex f(void)
{
    complex z;  // Memory allocated for z.
    // ...
    return z;
}              // z goes out of scope; memory is deallocated.
```

However, our matrix class is very different. Each time the matrix(m, n) constructor is called, the new operator allocates sufficient memory to store an m × n matrix. When the `matrix` object goes out of scope this memory is not deallocated, resulting in a gradual 'memory leakage' which can cause unnecessary exhaustion of the available heap. The solution to this problem is to define a destructor which uses the delete operator to release memory back to the heap:

```
inline matrix::~matrix() { delete p; }
```

Notice that the destructor deletes the memory whose address is stored by the pointer, `p`; the constructor does *not* actually delete the `matrix` object, since this consists of the three data members, `m`, `n` and `p`.

Destructors are rather special functions; a destructor takes no arguments, does not have a return type (not even `void`) and cannot be declared `static`.[6] Since a destructor cannot have any arguments, it cannot be overloaded. Destructors are called implicitly:

```
matrix f(void)
{
    matrix m(5, 6);
    // ...
    return m;
}                    // ~matrix() called implicitly
                     // as m goes out of scope.
```

It is usually neither necessary nor desirable for the programmer to explicitly invoke a destructor; doing so typically results in an attempt to `delete` memory that has already been deleted and the consequence is a corrupted heap. One of the few cases where it may be necessary to explicitly invoke a destructor is when an object has been placed at a specific address by means of the `new` operator. The implementation of such cases is not straightforward due to the fact that ~ is the unary bitwise complement operator, which is introduced in Chapter 13, and examples demonstrating how to explicitly invoke destructors are given in [2] and [7].

10.3   Creating and Destroying Objects[††]

It is sometimes useful to know at what point objects are created and destroyed during the execution of a program. Of particular interest is the creation and destruction of *temporary* objects. The lifespan and even the existence of such objects depends on the particular C++ compiler being used.

---

[6]The fact that a destructor takes no arguments *can* of course be indicated by using a `void` argument.

Suppose we need a class capable of manipulating vectors of any dimension. Our initial design for a **vector** class has constructor and destructor functions, together with overloaded assignment, addition and subscripting operators:[7]

```
#include <iostream.hpp>
#include <string.h>       // for memcpy()
#include <stdlib.h>       // for exit()

class vector {
    friend vector operator+(const vector &u,
        const vector &v);
public:
    vector(int elements);
    vector(vector &a);
    ~vector();
    vector &operator=(const vector & v);
    double &operator[](int i);
private:
    double *p;   // Address of memory to hold data.
    int n;       // Number of elements in vector.
};

vector::vector(int elements)
{
    n = elements;
    p = new double[n];
    if (p == NULL) {
        cout << "Cannot allocate vector.\n";
        exit(EXIT_FAILURE);
    }
    cout << "constructor invoked: address " <<
        p << "\n";
}

vector::vector(vector &v)
{
    n = v.n;
    p = new double[n];
    if (p == NULL) {
        cout << "Cannot allocate vector.\n";
        exit(EXIT_FAILURE);
```

---

[7]Note the distinction between an **array** and a **vector** class; there is no concept of *adding* **array** objects.

```
    }
    memcpy(p, v.p, n * sizeof(double));
    cout << "copy constructor invoked: address " <<
        p << "\n";
}


vector::~vector()
{
    cout << "destructor invoked: address " <<
        p << "\n";
    delete p;
}


vector operator+(const vector &u, const vector &v)
{
    if (u.n != v.n) {
        cout << "Cannot add vectors:\n" <<
            "\tdifferent numbers of elements\n";
        exit (EXIT_FAILURE);
    }
    vector w(u.n);
    double *pt_w = w.p;
    double *pt_u = u.p;
    double *pt_v = v.p;
    double *pt_end = pt_w + u.n;
    while (pt_w < pt_end)
        *pt_w++ = *pt_u++ + *pt_v++;
    return w;
}


vector & vector::operator=(const vector &v)
{
    if (n != v.n) {
        cout << "Cannot assign:\n" <<
            "\tdifferent numbers of elements\n";
        exit (EXIT_FAILURE);
    }
    memcpy(p, v.p, n * sizeof(double));
    return *this;
}


double & vector::operator[](int i)
{
```

```
        return *(p+i);
    }
```

We can now observe objects being created and destroyed in a simple program:

```
    int main()
    {
        const int elements = 5;
        vector p(elements), q(elements);

        // Assign values to p and q:
        for (int i = 0; i < elements; ++i) {
            p[i] = i + 1;
            q[i] = 2 * i + 1;
        }

        {
            vector r(elements);

            r = p + q;

            // Check one result:
            cout << "r[4] = " << r[4] << "\n";
        }   // r goes out of scope.

        vector s(p);
        p = s + q;

        return(EXIT_SUCCESS);
    }   // p, q and s go out of scope.
```

The output obtained from this program is given in Table 10.1.

As a second example, we could introduce a simple function, which manipulates vector objects:

```
    vector f(vector p, double k, int m)
    {
        vector q(m);

        for (int i = 0; i < m; ++i)
            q[i] = k + p[i];

        return q;
    }
```

constructor invoked:	address :0000624C	*p created*
constructor invoked:	address :0000667C	*q created*
constructor invoked:	address :000066A8	*r created*
constructor invoked:	address :000066D4	*w created by + operator*
r[4] = 14		
destructor invoked:	address :000066D4	*w destroyed*
destructor invoked:	address :000066A8	*r destroyed*
copy constructor invoked:	address :000066A8	*s created*
constructor invoked:	address :000066D4	*w created by + operator*
destructor invoked:	address :000066D4	*w destroyed*
destructor invoked:	address :000066A8	*r destroyed*
destructor invoked:	address :0000667C	*q destroyed*
destructor invoked:	address :0000624C	*p destroyed*

Table 10.1: Calling Constructors and Destructors.

```
int main()
{
    const int elements=5;

    vector x(elements), y(elements);

    for (int i = 0; i < elements; ++i)
        x[i] = i + 1;

    y = f(x, 10.0, elements);

    for (i = 0; i < elements; ++i)
        cout << "y[" << i << "] = " << y[i] << "\n";

    return(EXIT_SUCCESS);
}
```

Table 10.2 lists the output obtained from this program.

Exercise:

How does the output change if you insert `exit(EXIT_SUCCESS)` before the `return(EXIT_SUCCESS)` statement in the above program? What conclusions can you draw from your observations?

It is also possible to initialize a `static` object by a constructor:

```
const int elements = 5;
```

```
    vector x(elements);

    int main()
    {
        // ...
    }
```

Note that, since `exit()` causes the destructor to be invoked for a `static` object, it is not a good idea to invoke `exit()` in a destructor: the result would be an infinite loop.

constructor invoked:	address :00006526	*x created*
constructor invoked:	address :00006956	*y created*
copy constructor invoked:	address :00006988	*q created by f()*
constructor invoked:	address :000069B4	*temporary created by return*
destructor invoked:	address :00006988	*q destroyed*
y[0] = 11		
. . .		
destructor invoked:	address :000069B4	*temporary destroyed*
destructor invoked:	address :0000695C	*y destroyed*
destructor invoked:	address :0000652C	*x destroyed*

Table 10.2: Constructors and Destructors Invoked by a Function Call.

10.4 Using Constructors and Destructors

A common requirement in many applications is the manipulation of lists. The data stored in an item of a list is frequently large (perhaps information on a galaxy or the complete record of a student) and the number of data items is often not known until run-time. Moreover, the number of items may even change during program execution. An array is not an appropriate data structure for such problems, but a suitable alternative is a *linked list*. Linked lists are good examples of constructors and destructors in use.

10.4.1 Singly Linked Lists

For simplicity we first consider a singly linked list. This consists of a number of *nodes*, with each node storing a data item and the address of the next node in the list. The address of the first node is known as the *head* of the list. A typical list is shown in Figure 10.1.

It is convenient to have separate classes for the nodes and lists:

Figure 10.1: Singly linked list.

```
// source:  slist.hpp
// use:     Defines singly linked list class.

#ifndef SLIST_HPP
#define SLIST_HPP

#include <stdio.h>          // for NULL

typedef int DATA_TYPE;
const int TRUE = 1;
const int FALSE = 0;

class node {
    friend class list;
public:
    DATA_TYPE data;
private:
    node *next;
};

class list {
public:
    list(void);
    ~list();
    void push(DATA_TYPE new_data);
    void pop(DATA_TYPE &old_data);
    int is_not_empty(void);
private:
    node *head;
};

inline int list::is_not_empty(void)
{
    if (head == NULL)
        return FALSE;
    else
        return TRUE;
```

```
}

#endif  // SLIST_HPP
```

The following points are worth noting for the `node` class:

- The `node` class declares the entire `list` class (not just a single function) to be a `friend`. This means that the `list` functions have access to all member functions of the `node` class and to all data members of `node` objects.

- For simplicity, the data stored by a `node` object is a single `int`; in practice this would be replaced by a large data structure, perhaps the data on some physical observation or a standard component for an engineering project. Each time we change `DATA_TYPE`, the `node` and `list` classes must be recompiled, which is contrary to the spirit of code reusability in object-oriented programming. *Class templates* are a recent extension to C++ which overcome this problem. However, until templates are widely available, the simplest approach is to use a typedef to globally define `DATA_TYPE`.[8]

- The data member, called `next`, stores the address of the next node. Notice that it is legal to declare a pointer to `node` within the `node` class declaration, but it is not legal to declare another `node` object within the `node` class:

```
class node {
    // ...
    node another_node;      // WRONG!
};
```

This is because within a class definition the class is considered to be declared, but not defined.

- The `node` class has no user-defined constructors or destructor. This is because `node` objects do not dynamically allocate memory, initialize other objects or open files.

Note the following comments concerning the `list` class:

- The `list` class uses the notation of a *stack*; that is we can add data to the head of the list (`push()`) and remove data from the head (`pop()`). There is no way of accessing data further down the stack, except by popping the entire stack. A stack is a 'last in first out' (LIFO) list and is traditionally drawn vertically, as shown in Figure 10.2. (In fact this is the only difference between Figures 10.1 and 10.2.)

---

[8]If you do have access to a compiler which implements templates, Appendix A explains how to make the necessary modifications to `list` and `node`.

- The `list` class has a user-defined constructor and destructor. The constructor is needed because we want the head of an empty list to be set to NULL. A destructor is required so that all dynamically allocated memory is returned to the heap when a `list` object goes out of scope.

- Since the `list` class does not have `node` data members, but rather a pointer to a `node`, the class could be compiled separately, provided it had access to a `node` class declaration:

  ```
  class node;
  ```

  This technique is known as a *forward class declaration*.

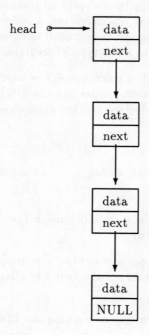

Figure 10.2: A stack.

Suitable class implementations are given below:

```
// source:   slist.cpp
// use:      Implements singly linked list class.

#include "slist.hpp"
```

```
list::list(void)
{
    head = NULL;
}

list::~list()
{
    node *pt;

    while (head != NULL) {
        pt = head;
        head = head->next;
        delete pt;
    }
}

void list::push(DATA_TYPE new_data)
{
    node *pt = new node;
    pt->next = head;
    head = pt;
    pt->data = new_data;
}

void list::pop(DATA_TYPE &old_data)
{
    if (head != NULL) {
        old_data = head->data;
        node *pt = head;
        head = head->next;
        delete pt;
    }
}
```

The following program pushes values onto the stack and then prints the results obtained by popping the stack:

```
// source:  test.cpp
// use:     Tries out singly linked list class.

#include "slist.hpp"
#include <iostream.hpp>
#include <stdlib.h>      // for EXIT_SUCCESS
```

```
int main()
{
    list s;
    DATA_TYPE j;

    for (int i = 1; i <= 5; ++i)
        s.push(10 * i);
    while (s.is_not_empty()) {
        s.pop(j);
        cout << j << "\n";
    }
    return(EXIT_SUCCESS);
}
```

Notice that we do not pop the stack by doing something like:

```
for (int i = 1; i <= 5; ++i) {
    s.pop(j);
    cout << j << "\n";
}
```

The list, s, has a state (either it is empty or it is not) so the best technique is to obtain the object's state from the object itself.

Returning to our test program, we could try replacing the loop which prints the contents of the stack by a function call:

```
print(s);
```

where the print() function is defined by:

```
void print(list t)
{
    DATA_TYPE j;

    while (t.is_not_empty()) {
        t.pop(j);
        cout << j << "\n";
    }
}
```

This is a disaster. The problem is that, since the t in the function header:

```
void print(list t)
```

is a formal argument, a default copy constructor is invoked, which performs a simple copy of the original list. Unfortunately both lists contain the address of the same dynamically allocated memory. As an item of the list is popped, the memory is deallocated. This is of no consequence as we return from `print()`, since `t` is empty but, when `s` goes out of scope, the destructor attempts to deallocate memory which is already deallocated and the result is a corrupted heap.

A possible solution to the above problem is to define `print()` with a reference argument since this involves no copying:[9]

```
void print(list &t)
{
    // Same function body as before.
}
```

However, this does not prevent us from inadvertently implementing other functions which lead to similar corrupted heap disasters. The lesson to be drawn is that when designing a class we should provide all functions for which inappropriate defaults could be supplied, *even* if we do not envisage using them. For an arbitrary class, X, there are three such functions:

X::X(const X &)	copy constructor
X::operator= (const &X)	assignment operator
X:: ˜X()	destructor

In some circumstances, invoking the copy constructor or assignment operator may actually constitute an error if, for example, only one instance of a class is supposed to exist. Such errors can be trapped by:

```
X &X::operator=(const X &x)
{
    cout << "No assignment implemented for class X\n";
    exit(EXIT_FAILURE);
    return *this;
}
```

This should be a `private` member of the class, X, so that as many errors as possible are trapped at compile-time.

Exercise:

Implement an appropriate copy constructor and assignment operator for the `list` class.

---

[9]Notice that the data is discarded as it is printed. This is a feature of any stack and can be overcome by introducing a function which traverses a list rather than popping the stack.

10.4.2 Doubly Linked Lists

Singly linked lists are of limited use since they can only be scanned efficiently in one direction. By contrast, doubly linked lists can be scanned in either direction with equal efficiency and only require the extra overhead of one additional pointer for each node. Simple node and doubly linked lists classes are given below:

```cpp
// source     dlist.hpp
// use:       Defines doubly linked list class.

#ifndef DLIST_HPP
#define DLIST_HPP

typedef int DATA_TYPE;
#include <iostream.hpp>
#include <stdlib.h>      // for exit()
#include <stdio.h>       // for NULL

class node {
    friend class dlist;
public:
    DATA_TYPE data;
private:
    node *next, *last;
};

class dlist {
public:
    dlist(void);
    ~dlist();
    void add_head();
    void delete_head(void);
    node *forward(void);
    node *backward(void);
    void set_cursor_head(void);
    void set_cursor_tail(void);
    node *cursor_position(void);
private:
    node *head, *tail, *cursor;
};

inline node *dlist::forward(void)
{
    node *pt = cursor;
```

```
        if (cursor != NULL)
            cursor = cursor->next;
        return pt;
    }


    inline node *dlist::backward(void)
    {
        node *pt = cursor;
        if (cursor != NULL)
            cursor = cursor->last;
        return pt;
    }


    inline void dlist::set_cursor_head(void)
    {
        cursor = head;
    }


    inline void dlist::set_cursor_tail(void)
    {
        cursor = tail;
    }


    inline node *dlist::cursor_position(void)
    {
        return cursor;
    }


    #endif  // DLIST_HPP
```

Each node has a pointer to the next node (**next**) and a pointer to the previous node (**last**), as shown in Figure 10.3. The list has a pointer to **head** and **tail**, in addition to a cursor. The cursor is useful for list manipulations, such as sorting, and can be moved backwards (**backward()**) and forwards(**forward()**) along the list. These last two functions also return the address of the node before the cursor was moved. There are two other functions which manipulate the cursor position (**set_cursor_head()**, **set_cursor_tail()**) and a function to give the current position (**cursor_position()**).

The **dlist** class implementation, for those functions that are not **inline**, is as follows:

```
    // source:     dlist.cpp
    // use:        Implements doubly linked list class.
```

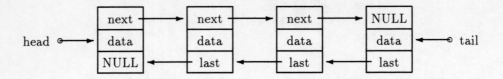

Figure 10.3: Doubly linked list.

```cpp
#include "dlist.hpp"
#include <iostream.hpp>
#include <stdlib.h>        // for exit()
#include <stdio.h>         // for NULL

dlist::dlist(void)
{
    head = NULL;
    tail = NULL;
    cursor = NULL;
}

dlist::~dlist()
{
    node *pt;

    while (head != NULL) {
        pt = head;
        head = head->next;
        delete pt;
    }
}

void dlist::add_head(void)
{
    node *pt = new node;
    if (pt == NULL) {
        cout << "Failed to allocate node.\n";
        exit(EXIT_FAILURE);
    }
    if (head == NULL) {
        tail = pt;
    }
    else
```

```
        head->last = pt;
    pt->next = head;
    pt->last = NULL;
    head = pt;
    cursor = pt;
}


void dlist::delete_head(void)
{
    if (head == NULL)
        return;
    node *pt = head;
    head = head->next;
    if (head != NULL)
        head->last = NULL;
    cursor = head;
    delete pt;
}
```

These functions are straightforward generalizations of those for singly linked lists. Notice that we have had to make a choice as to where the cursor points after some of these operations.

A simple test program is:

```
// source:    test.cpp
// use:       Tests doubly linked list class.

#include "dlist.hpp"
#include <iostream.hpp>
#include <stdlib.h>       // for EXIT_SUCCESS

void print_forward(dlist &s)
{
    node *pt;

    s.set_cursor_head();
    cout << "head -> ";
    while ((pt = s.forward()) != NULL) {
        cout << pt->data << " -> ";
    }
    cout << "NULL\n";
}


void print_backward(dlist &s)
```

```
{
    node *pt;

    s.set_cursor_tail();
    cout << "tail -> ";
    while ((pt = s.backward()) != NULL) {
        cout << pt->data << " -> ";
    }
    cout << "NULL\n";
}

int main()
{
    // Create an empty list:
    dlist s;

    // Put some items in the list:
    for (int i = 1; i <= 5; ++i) {
        s.add_head();
        (s.cursor_position())->data = 10 * i;
    }

    // Print the list:
    print_forward(s);

    // Delete an item:
    s.delete_head();

    // Print the new first item:
    cout << "Head of list is now " <<
        (s.cursor_position())->data << "\n";

    // Print the list backwards:
    print_backward(s);

    return(EXIT_SUCCESS);
}
```

As with the singly linked list example, changing &s to s in the function headers
for print_forward() and print_backward() invokes an inappropriate default
copy constructor.

Exercise:

Modify the copy constructor and assignment operator which you provided for the **list** class so that they are suitable for the **dlist** class.

10.5   Summary

- A constructor is invoked whenever an object is created. A class typically requires (or would benefit from) a user-defined constructor or destructor when there is initialization, dynamic memory allocation or file manipulation.

- A destructor is a class member function with the name of the class, prefixed by the tilde symbol:

```
class matrix {
    // ...
    ~matrix();
};
```

A destructor cannot have an argument, return a type or be declared **static**.

- It is very rare to explicitly invoke a destructor.

10.6   Exercises

1. Provide a destructor for the **string** class described in Section 9.6.2.

2. Replace the function header for **print_forward()** in Section 10.4.2 by the following (inappropriate) version:

```
void print_forward(dlist s)
```

and add statements to the relevant **dlist** functions so that the addresses of **node** objects are printed as they are created and destroyed. Run the test program for **dlist** and work out exactly where **node** objects are created and destroyed.

3. Modify the **dlist** class (given in Section 10.4.2) to include the following functions:

   - Add or delete a node at the tail:

```
void add_tail(void);
void delete_tail(void);
```

- Add a node before or after the current cursor position:

  ```
  void add_before(void);
  void add_after(void);
  ```

- Delete the node at the current cursor position:

  ```
  void delete_node(void);
  ```

(You will have to decide where the cursor should be placed after these operations.)

4. Implement a sorting algorithm (either a bubble sort or a more efficient technique) using your modified `dlist` class of the previous exercise.[10]

5. Change the `node` class, used by `dlist`, so that the data consists of instances of `weather_data` class. (See Section 8.17.2.) Write a function to sort a doubly linked list of weather data according to the total daily rainfall.

6. An instructive, but complicated, application of linked lists occurs in the implementation of a sparse matrix class. A much simpler, but related, problem is a sparse vector class. Use the `dlist` class to design and implement a sparse vector class. Each node should store the index of a component of a vector, together with the component itself, as a `double`. The list should be sorted on the basis of the index.

   Use overloaded operators to access individual vector components and to implement the addition of two vectors. You should also write a function which returns the dot product of two vectors.

---

[10]Almost any sorting algorithm is better than a bubble sort. For example, try a *merge sort* as described in [18].

Chapter 11

Single Inheritance

11.1 Derived Classes

One of the fundamental techniques in object-oriented programming is the use of *inheritance*. Inheritance is a way of creating new classes which extend the facilities of existing classes by including new data and function members, as well as (in certain circumstances) changing existing functions. The class which is extended is known as the *base class* and the result of an extension is known as the *derived class*;[1] the derived class *inherits* the data and function members of the base class.

Inheritance allows a class to be extended rather than modified. For a well-designed base class, only the base class interface rather than the implementation need be known. This avoids recompiling the base class and even means that a class can be extended without the source for its implementation being available. Moreover, both the base and derived classes can be used by a program. Without inheritance, the source for the original class would have to be modified. Consequently, either the original class would no longer be available, or else there would be code for two separate classes with the associated problem of maintaining consistency.

Inheritance also facilitates having consistent interfaces for a whole hierarchy of related classes. The same function interface may be used by objects of different classes, with the implementation of the function depending on the type of object by which it is invoked. In effect, this is a switch which depends on the object type but it is implemented automatically by the compiler, rather than by complicated control statements in the code.

Any class can be a base class. As an example, suppose we have a project involving general two-dimensional shapes, together with related objects, such as

---

[1]Some authors use *superclass* and *subclass* (which are taken from the language, Simula) instead of base class and derived class. Other authors find the terms confusing and they are not used in this book.

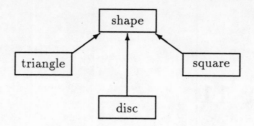

Figure 11.1: Classes derived from **shape**.

discs, squares, triangles etc. A **shape** class might take the form:

```
class shape {
public:
    int i_d;
    float x, y;
    material_type material;
};
```

where **i_d** is an identifying number for a particular shape and **x** and **y** are its position coordinates. The shape could be manufactured from various substances, which are defined by an enumeration:

```
enum material_type {WOOD, STEEL, ALUMINIUM, PLASTIC};
```

The syntax for defining a class, **disc**, which is derived from **shape**, is:

```
class disc : public shape {
public:
    float radius(void) { return disc_radius; }
private:
    float disc_radius;
};
```

Other classes, such as **square** and **triangle** can be derived from **shape** in a similar manner to **disc**. The relationship between such classes is often clarified by a *directed acyclic graph* (or DAG),[2] as shown in Figure 11.1. A common convention, followed here, is to place the base class at the top of the diagram, with the arrows flowing from the derived classes towards the base class. Notice that a derived class possesses a 'kind of' relationship with respect to its base class; that is a **disc** object is a 'kind of' **shape**. Therefore it is both meaningful and useful to assign a derived class object to an instance of the base class:

---

[2]A DAG is a graph in which the arcs have a direction, but there are no closed loops.

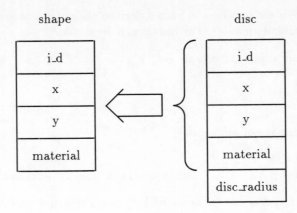

Figure 11.2: Assigning data for a `disc` object to a `shape` object.

```
shape s;
disc d;

s = d;
```

since this corresponds to a truncation of data. (See Figure 11.2.) However, the assignment, without an explicit cast, of a base class object to an instance of a derived class is illegal since in general some data members will have no base class counterparts.

The single colon in the first line of the `disc` class declaration is used to separate the derived class, `disc`, from the base class, `shape`. The derived class possesses all of the member functions and data specified in its own class definition, together with all those of the base class; inheritance therefore adds attributes to a base class. By default, all members of a base class are `private` in the derived class, but this can be overridden by putting an access-specifier before the base class in the derived class declaration; in this example we have specified `public`. It is a useful piece of defensive programming to always include the access-specifier, since a common error is to forget that the default is `private`. Member access privileges are considered in more detail in Section 11.6. However, it is important to realise that placing `public` before the base class in a class declaration does *not* permit a derived class to access the `private` members of a base class.

It is usually desirable that names given to members (particularly data members) of a derived class are different from those of a base class. However, in some cases there may be duplication of names and, in such situations, the concept of *dominance* often resolves any potential ambiguity.[3] If a class member name

---

[3]Duplication of names is particularly likely in a complicated class hierarchy where the classes

(either function or data) occurs in both a derived class and a base class, then the derived class name dominates. For instance, if we declare:

```
class disc : public shape {
public:
    int i_d;
};
```

then the following is not ambiguous:

```
disc d;
d.i_d = 100;          // Derived class member accessed.
```

The base class member can be accessed by using the scope resolution operator, ::, together with the base class name:

```
d.shape::i_d = 10;   // Base class member accessed.
```

Exercise:

Verify that, on your system, dominance does indeed resolve the potential access ambiguity for the two variables, i_d.

It is quite common for a derived class to provide its own implementation of a base class function. Dominance then ensures that the derived class function is called for derived class objects. The base class function is *hidden* rather than overloaded, even if the argument types differ:

```
class shape {
public:
    float give_area(void) { return area; }
private:
    float area;
};


class disc : public shape {
public:
    float give_area(float radius) {
        return(3.142 * radius * radius); }
private:
    float radius;
};

disc d;
```

---

may be the work of different programmers. (See Section 11.4 and Chapter 14.)

```
cout << d.give_area(10.0);      // Uses function defined
                                // in derived class.
cout << d.give_area();          // WRONG: attempts to use
                                // function defined in base
                                // class.
```

It might be supposed that `give_area()` is overloaded and that `d.give_area()` invokes the base class function. What actually happens is that the derived class function hides the base class version, so that invoking `d.give_area()` is a compile-time error since the function has the wrong number of arguments. It is not the class definitions that are in error, but rather the attempt to invoke the base class function. This can be corrected by using:

```
cout << d.shape::give_area();   // Uses function defined
                                // in base class.
```

Now that we have introduced inheritance, we can distinguish the three ways in which a class is able to use other classes:

1. An object may contain objects which are instances of other classes. For example, the `monthly_weather` class, described in Section 8.17.2, has elements that are instances of the `weather_data` class:

```
class weather_data {
public:
    double temperature;
    double pressure;
    double rainfall;
};

class monthly_weather {
private:
    weather_data weather[days_in_month];
    // Other members go here.
};
```

A `monthly_weather` object is said to be a *client* of the `weather_data` class; it is not a 'kind of' `weather_data` object.

2. A class may use a pointer to an object of the same or another class. For example, a `node` class object has a pointer to a `node` object:

```
class node {
    friend class list;
public:
```

```
      DATA_TYPE data;
private:
      node *next;
};
```

A `node` object does not contain another `node`, which is in any case illegal, but rather accesses the data of another `node`.

3. A class may be derived from another class. For example, an instance of the `disc` class is a 'kind of' `shape`;

```
class disc : public shape {
public:
      float radius(void) { return disc_radius; }
private:
      float disc_radius;
};
```

but in no sense does a `disc` object use a `shape` object.

11.2   virtual **Functions**

A common requirement is for objects corresponding to different derived classes to respond differently to the same function call. This behaviour is known as *polymorphism* and we have already seen how it may be achieved through a derived class which provides its own implementation of a base class function. However, the exact kind of object on which a function acts may not be known at compile-time. For example, we may want to have an array of various derived `shape` objects, such as `squares`, `discs`, `triangles` etc., which are chosen at run-time. It would then be convenient if we could invoke different `give_area()` functions for different kinds of elements in the array. All this can be achieved by using `virtual` functions.

A function is declared `virtual` by including the `virtual` keyword, as in:

```
class shape {
public:
      virtual float give_area(void) { return area; }
private:
      float area;
};
```

The function must be a non-`static` class member and the `virtual` specifer can *only* occur within a class body. A common error is to attempt to define an `inline` `virtual` function by:

```
inline virtual float shape::give_area(void)
    { return area; }                                    // WRONG!
```

Such functions are often useful but are correctly defined as in:

```
inline float shape::give_area(void) { return area; } // O.K.
```

as it is sufficient to declare a function virtual in the base class for it to be virtual everywhere.

The virtual specifier in the shape class has no effect unless a derived class also defines a give_area() function:

```
class disc : public shape {
public:
    virtual float give_area(void) { return(3.142 * radius
        * radius); }
private:
    float radius;
};
```

Notice that both the return type and function arguments are identical in the two versions of give_area(). However, the situation here is subtly different from the duplication of names discussed in Section 11.1. To appreciate this distinction and to see the true significance of virtual functions, consider the following:

```
shape *pt;
shape s;
disc d;
pt = &s;
cout << pt->give_area();
pt = &d;
cout << pt->give_area();
```

The first point to notice is that a base class pointer can store the address of a derived class object; in this case pt is first used to store the address of a shape object and then a disc object. The second point is that the statements which output the areas of the different kinds of object are identical. This is because if a virtual function is invoked through a pointer then which of the functions is actually called depends on the class of the object pointed to; whereas the first statement involving give_area() calls the shape function, the second statement calls the disc version. This is how virtual functions can be used to implement polymorphism and is an important feature of object-oriented programming in C++.[4] The role of virtual functions is crucial; for non-virtual functions the

---

[4]Some authors, such as [2], describe the effect of virtual functions by saying that the derived class function **overrides** the base class version. However, you should understand that overriding is not the same as dominance; there is more to virtual functions than the mere hiding of base class names!

base class pointer in the above code would invoke the same shape version of the give_area() function in both statements.

Exercise:

Write a short program to confirm that whether the statement:

```
cout << pt->give_area()
```

invokes the shape or disc versions of give_area() depends on the kind of object pointed to by pt. What happens if the virtual specifier is removed from either one or both class declarations?

In the previous example there was no need to include the virtual specifier in the derived disc class declaration and we could alternatively use:

```
class disc : public shape {
public:
    float give_area(void) { return(3.142 * radius * radius); }
private:
    float radius;
};
```

since the give_area() function is implicitly virtual due to the declaration within the shape class. However, including the keyword may actually be useful since it clearly indicates, without examining the base class, that the function is virtual.

There are two subtleties involving virtual functions which are worth mentioning:

- A function declared in a derived class and a base class cannot differ only by the return type if the base class function is virtual:

```
class shape {
public:
    virtual float give_area(void) { return area; }
private:
    area;
};

class disc : public shape {
public:
    double give_area(void) { return(3.142 * radius *
        radius); } // WRONG: only differ by return type.
private:
    float radius;
};
```

In this example the second declaration cannot hide the first, since only the **return** types differ. But neither can the second declaration be **virtual** since the **return** types *do* differ. As a result, the two declarations are inconsistent and there is a compile-time error.

- If a **virtual** function is invoked through a pointer, then the access level is determined by the function declaration in the class corresponding to the pointer and not to the function actually invoked. In the code fragment:

```
class shape {
public:
    virtual float give_area(void) { return area; }
private:
    area;
};

class disc : public shape {
private:
    virtual float give_area(void) { return(3.142 *
        radius * radius); }
    float radius;
};

disc d;
shape *pt = &d;
cout << pt->give_area(); // O.K.
```

the pointer successfully invokes **disc::give_area()**, even though the latter is **private**. This is because **pt** is of type pointer to **shape** and the function, **shape::give_area()**, *is* public. By contrast, the following code:

```
disc *p;
cout << p->give_area();  // WRONG: give_area() is private
```

fails to compile since **disc::give_area()** *is* **private**. This may appear to be a minor hole in the access protection mechanism but is consistent with the fact that which **virtual** function is actually invoked through a pointer is a run-time decision.

Exercise:

By introducing **public** functions to assign values to **area** and **radius** in **shape** and **disc** objects, verify that the **disc** version of **give_area()** is indeed invoked by the statement:

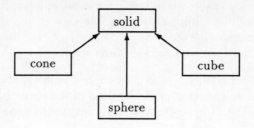

Figure 11.3: Classes derived from `solid`.

```
cout << pt->give_area();
```

in the above code.

11.3   Abstract Classes and Pure virtual Functions

Suppose we have an project involving solids such as cubes, spheres, cones etc. Corresponding to each type of solid there is an appropriate equation for the volume and surface area. Moreover, suppose that we want to consider a collection of different kinds of solids and to perform calculations such as summing their volumes and surface areas. This project is an obvious candidate for inheritance; that is we could have a `solid` base class with derived `cone, sphere` and `cube` classes, as shown in Figure 11.3. Furthermore, if the `solid` class has `virtual` member functions for calculating the volume and surface area, then polymorphism can be used to find the total area and volume for a collection of `solid` objects. Ignoring the `cone` class for the sake of simplicity, suitable classes are:

```
#include <math.h>        // for PI

class solid {
public:
    virtual double volume(void);
    virtual double surface(void);
};

class sphere : public solid {
public:
    double volume(void) {return(4.0 * PI * r * r * r / 3.0);}
    double surface(void) {return(4.0 * PI * r * r);}
```

```
        void set_radius(double radius) { r = radius; }
private:
        double r;
};

class cube : public solid {
public:
        double volume(void) { return(side * side * side); }
        double surface(void) { return(6.0 * side * side); }
        void set_side(double length_of_side) {
                side = length_of_side; }
private:
        double side;
};
```

Notice that we have implemented member functions for the sphere and cube classes but not for the solid class. The problem is that the two member functions must return a value of type double, but without knowing the particular kind of solid it is not possible to calculate what this value should be. Returning an arbitrary volume and surface area is not very satisfactory; it would be much better if solid were an *abstract class*. That is it should be possible for the solid class to be used as a base class without implementing every member function, but it should not be possible to have instances of the class.

An abstract class is declared by including at least one member which is a *pure virtual function*:

```
class X {
public:
        virtual void f(int i) = 0;  // A pure virtual function.
        // More members.
};
```

A pure virtual function is denoted by the strange 'f() = 0' syntax. This does not indicate that the function is numerically zero, but rather that it is not defined. An abstract solid class can therefore be declared by:

```
class solid {
public:
        virtual double volume(void)=0;  // Pure virtual function.
        virtual double surface(void)=0; // Pure virtual function.
};
```

and this avoids the problem of how to implement these member functions.

An example of the sphere and cube classes in use is:

```
    sphere s;

    s.set_radius(2.0);
    cout << "Volume of sphere = " << s.volume() << "\n";
    cout << "Area of sphere = " << s.surface() << "\n";

    cube c;

    c.set_side(2.0);
    cout << "Volume of cube = " << c.volume() << "\n";
    cout << "Area of cube = " << c.surface() << "\n";
```

There a few restrictions on abstract classes:

- It is not possible to have instances of an abstract class since the class has at least one undefined function:

```
    solid s;          // WRONG: solid is an abstract class.
```

- An abstract class cannot be an argument type:

```
    void f(solid s);          // WRONG!
```

- An abstract class cannot be a function return type:

```
    solid f(void);          // WRONG!
```

- An abstract class cannot be the type of an explicit conversion:

```
    x = solid(y);          // WRONG!
```

All of these restrictions are very reasonable since an abstract class has at least one undefined function. However, a pointer to an abstract class *is* legal:

```
    solid *pt;               // O.K.
```

as is a reference to an abstract class:

```
    double f(solid &s);      // O.K.
```

The reason why these are both legal and potentially useful is that a pointer to an abstract class can point to an instance of a derived class.

As an example of references to an abstract class, suppose we want to write a function which returns the total volume of two objects derived from the solid class. These objects may be instances of either the sphere or cube class, or even other classes (derived from solid) that we have not yet considered. A suitable implementation uses solid reference arguments:

```
double volume_of_two_solids(solid &s1, solid &s2)
{
    return (s1.volume() + s2.volume());
}
```

whereas non-reference arguments would necessitate four separate overloaded functions for just the **sphere** and **cube** classes. An example of calling the above function is:

```
cube c;
c.set_side(2.0);
sphere s;
s.set_radius(3.0);
cout << "Volume of 2 solids = " <<
    volume_of_two_solids(c, s) << "\n";
```

Notice how one reference argument is a **sphere** whereas the other is a **cube**.

More realistically, we may want a function which returns the volume of a list of **solid** objects:

```
double total_volume(solid *pt[], int solids)
{
    double vol = 0.0;
    for (int i = 0; i < solids; ++i)
        vol += pt[i]->volume();
    return vol;
}
```

To use this function it is convenient to set up an array of pointers to **solid** objects (the type of the first argument in **total_volume()**), as in:

```
cube c1, c2;
c1.set_side(2.0);
c2.set_side(4.0);
sphere s1, s2;
s1.set_radius(3.0);
s2.set_radius(5.0);
solid *pt[4];
pt[0] = &s1;
pt[1] = &s2;
pt[2]= &c1;
pt[3] = &c2;
cout << "Total volume = " << total_volume(pt, 4) << "\n";
```

Again notice how the array can store the addresses of different kinds of objects and how the **volume()** function appropriate to the particular object is invoked automatically.

A pure **virtual** function is inherited as a pure **virtual** function. In the following, the derived class, **cone**, is also an abstract class, since **cone::surface()** is a pure **virtual** function.

```
class cone : public solid {
public:
    double volume(void) { return(PI * r * r * h / 3.0); }
    void set_radius(double radius) { r = radius; }
    void set_height(double height) { h = height; }
private:
    double r, h;
};
```

Exercise:

Modify the **cone** class to include a definition of the **surface()** function and then let **total_volume()** act on a list of **sphere**, **cube** and **cone** objects. Likewise, implement and test a **total_surface()** function.

11.4   Class Hierarchies

A derived class can be the base class for another class. For instance, we can use the **sphere** class, which was derived from the **solid** class, as a base class for a class of coloured spheres (**c_sphere**):

```
#include <stdlib.h>      // for exit()

enum colour {red, orange, yellow, green, blue, indigo,
    violet};

class c_sphere : public sphere {
public:
    void set_colour(const colour &col) { c = col; }
    void print_colour(void);
private:
    colour c;
};

void c_sphere::print_colour(void)
```

```
    {
        switch (c) {
        case red:
            cout << "red\n";
            break;
        case orange:
            cout << "orange\n";
            break;
        case yellow:
            cout << "yellow\n";
            break;
        case green:
            cout << "green\n";
            break;
        case blue:
            cout << "blue\n";
            break;
        case indigo:
            cout << "indigo\n";
            break;
        case violet:
            cout << "violet\n";
            break;
        default:
            cout << "Invalid colour\n";
            exit(EXIT_FAILURE);
        }
    }
```

The **solid** class is known as an *indirect base class* of the **c_sphere** class and the resulting class *hierarchy* is shown in Figure 11.4.

A simple example of using the **c_sphere** class is:

```
c_sphere s[7];

for (int i = 0; i < 7; ++i) {
    s[i].set_radius(i + 10.0);
}
s[0].set_colour(red);
s[1].set_colour(orange);
s[2].set_colour(yellow);
s[3].set_colour(green);
s[4].set_colour(blue);
s[5].set_colour(indigo);
```

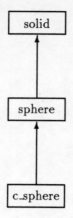

Figure 11.4: A simple class hierarchy.

```
s[6].set_colour(violet);
for (i = 0; i < 7; ++i) {
    cout << "sphere " << i << " has colour ";
    s[i].print_colour();
    cout << "The volume is " << s[i].volume() << "\n\n";
}
```

Notice that `volume()` is declared as a pure `virtual` function in the `solid` class, with the appropriate definition for the special case of a sphere being given in the `sphere` class. The `set_radius()` and `set_colour()` functions are defined in the `sphere` class and `c_sphere` classes respectively.

The `enum colour` statement could alternatively be placed inside the class declaration:

```
class c_sphere : public sphere {
public:
    enum colour {red, orange, yellow, green, blue,
        indigo, violet};
    void set_colour(const colour &col) { c = col; }
    void print_colour(void);
private:
    colour c;
};
```

Enumerations defined within a class have the scope of that class and are only accessible outside of this scope by using the explicitly qualified name:

```
c_sphere s;
s.set_colour(c_sphere::red);
```

Such enumerations obey the same access rules as other class members; in this particular case colour is public. Placing an enumeration within a class declaration is consistent with the idea of data hiding and means that we can use the same enumeration names for different classes. For example, the permissible colours may be different for different types of solids.

Our print_colour() function illustrates one of the main problems with conventional procedural languages. The function has a **switch** statement which depends crucially on the allowed colours. If we decide to add another colour to the enumeration, then we must change the **switch** statement. For the current example this change is simple but in a complicated program there may be many functions containing **switch** statements, all of which need modifying when the permissible data changes. The distributed nature of these changes can make maintaining such code a huge problem. However, the problem is much reduced by using object-oriented techniques. As a trivial example, we could define a pure abstract **coloured_sphere** class and use this to derive **red_sphere** and **blue_sphere** classes:

```
class coloured_sphere : public sphere {
public:
    virtual void print_colour(void) = 0;
};

class red_sphere : public coloured_sphere {
public:
    void print_colour(void) { cout << "red\n"; }
};

class blue_sphere : public coloured_sphere {
public:
    void print_colour(void) { cout << "blue\n"; }
};
```

Defining a pointer to the **coloured_sphere** base class enables us to store the address of the derived class objects:

```
red_sphere r_s;
blue_sphere b_s;
coloured_sphere *pt = &r_s;

pt->print_colour();
pt = &b_s;
pt->print_colour();
```

Notice that which function is actually called is determined by the type of object
that the function is invoked on, rather than by a **switch** statement. In fact the
type may not even be known until run-time. Type resolution of this form is called
dynamic or *late binding* and is one the major contributions of object-oriented
programming.[5] The significant feature is that extending an existing data type
only involves defining an extra class, as in:

```
class green_sphere : public coloured_sphere {
public:
    void print_colour(void) { cout << "green\n"; }
};
```

rather than modifying **switch** statements in what may be a large number of
functions. The changes are all in one place and manifest, rather than scattered
and buried.

Since any class may be the base class for any number of derived classes,
class hierarchies can get very complicated. We can get a glimpse of the possible
complication by adding a class for heavy spheres (an **h_sphere** class):

```
class h_sphere : public sphere {
public:
    void set_mass(double mass) { m = mass; }
    double mass(void) { return m; }
private:
    double m;
};
```

The resulting class hierarchy is shown in Figure 11.5

Exercise:

In Figure 11.5, replace the **c_sphere** class by our **coloured_sphere**
class, which avoids using the **switch** statement, and construct the
appropriate class hierarchy diagram.

---

[5]Which non-virtual function should be invoked is known at compile-time. This is called
static or *early binding*. Dynamic binding should not be confused with polymorphism. Polymorphism means that the same function interface can perform different actions on different
objects. Polymorphism may indeed be implemented by means of dynamic binding but in some
circumstances the compiler may be able to decide which function to invoke (that is the binding
may be static).

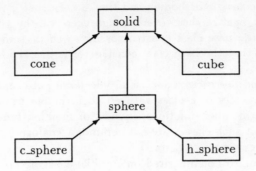

Figure 11.5: A complicated class hierarchy.

11.5 Constructors and Destructors

Constructors are rather special member functions and, in particular, constructors are not inherited and cannot be declared `virtual`. The compiler may generate a default or a constructor may be user-defined, in which case it must call the *direct* base class constructor. This is achieved by a constructor definition containing a colon followed by the base class constructor immediately before the constructor body:[6]

```
class sphere {
public:
    sphere(double radius) { r = radius; }
    double r;
};

class coloured_sphere : public sphere {
public:
    virtual void print_colour(void) = 0;
    coloured_sphere(double radius) : sphere(radius){}
};

class red_sphere : public coloured_sphere {
public:
    void print_colour(void) { cout << "red\n"; }
    red_sphere(double radius) : coloured_sphere(radius){}
};
```

---

[6]This is the same syntax as described in Section 10.1.3 for member objects with constructors.

Notice the empty constructor bodies and that a constructor is required for the abstract `coloured_sphere` class, even though there can be no instances of the class. In general, the base class constructor may well do something useful and the general rule is that the base class constructor is invoked before that of the derived class.

Constructors and destructors are usually declared `public`, but they can also be `private`. Instances of a class with all constructors `private` can only be created by `static` member functions, friends, or member functions invoked by existing objects, but such classes are not common. Analogous restrictions apply to classes with a `private` destructor.

Destructors are also not inherited but, unlike constructors, they can be declared `virtual` and it is often useful to do so. The following code illustrates what can go wrong when a base class destructor is not declared `virtual`:

```
class data {
public:
    data(int m) { p1 = new double[m]; }
    ~data() { cout << "p1\n"; delete p1; }
private:
    double *p1;
};

class more_data : public data {
public:
    more_data(int m, int n) : data(m) { p2 = new double[n]; }
    ~more_data() { cout << "p2\n"; delete p2; }
private:
    double *p2;
};
```

Creating and attempting to destroy an instance of the derived class, as in:

```
data *pt = new more_data(10, 20);
delete pt;
```

only invokes the base class destructor. Declaring `~data()` to be `virtual` solves this problem.

Exercise:

In what order are the `data` and `more_data` destructors invoked? Verify your answer by means of a program.

As a general rule it is usually worth declaring a base class destructor `virtual`. In fact, the only reason for not doing so is when the slightly increased object size is unacceptable.

11.6 Member Access and Inheritance

All of the derived classes considered so far can access the `public` (but not the `private`) base class members. For many applications this 'all or nothing' approach is very appropriate. However, C++ has techniques for obtaining a greater variation of access privilege and it is to these techniques that we now turn.

11.6.1 Access Specifiers[†]

The members of a class can have three levels of access: `public`, `protected` and `private`:

```
class A {
public:
    int a;
private:
    int b;
protected:
    int c;
};
```

We have already made use of the `public` and `private` specifiers. The reason we have not previously met the `protected` access-specifier is that it is only relevant when we have a derived class.

The effect of the *protected* access-specifier, used in the declaration of the **shape** class, is intermediate between the `public` and `private` specifiers. A `protected` member can be accessed by member functions and friends of the class, as well as by certain derived classes. In general, a derived class can be specified to have a `public` or `private` base class so the effect of `<access_specifier>` in:

```
class X : <access_specifier> A {
// Declarations.
};
```

is as follows:

- If `<access_specifier>` is public:

    `public` members of A are `public` members of X.

    `protected` members of A are `protected` members of X.

    `private` members of A are `private` members of X.

- If `<access_specifier>` is private:

> `public` members of A are `private` members of X.
>
> `protected` members of A are `private` members of X.
>
> `private` members of A are `private` members of X.

Effectively, a `protected` member is `private` in most circumstances, except that it is accessible to a derived class when `<access_specifier>` is public. Notice that `private` members of a base class remain `private` and are not accessible to members of a derived class. This restriction is necessary since otherwise a derived class would be a trivial way of getting round class access restrictions.

As an example, suppose we modify our **shape** class (on page 310) so that the members have the following access privileges:[7]

```
class shape {
public:
    int i_d;
protected:
    float x, y;
private:
    material_type material;
};
```

Then with the same `disc` class as on page 310, the following demonstrates the various ways in which we can attempt to access data members:

```
shape s;
s.i_d = 204;              // O.K.
s.material = WOOD;        // WRONG: material is private.
s.x = 54.37;             // WRONG: x is protected;

disc d;
d.i_d = 100;             // O.K.
d.material = STEEL;      // WRONG: material is private.
d.y = -71.3;            // WRONG: y is protected.
cout << d.x_coord();    // O.K. function has access to
                        // protected member, x.
```

As mentioned previously, constructors and destructors are usually declared `public`, but can also be `private`. In fact they can also be declared `protected`. Instances of a class with all constructors `protected` can only be created by friends, members and derived classes; such classes are therefore useful when we don't want clients to construct objects. Analogous restrictions apply to classes with a `protected` destructor.

---

[7]This class declaration is *only* for illustration since there is no way of accessing the variable, `material`.

11.7 Access Declarations††

Occasionally it may be necessary to adjust the derived class access to a specific member of a base class.[8] This can be achieved by using the scope resolution operator, ::, in what is known as an *access declaration*:

```
class square : private shape {
public:
    shape::i_d;
protected:
    shape::x;
    shape::y;
};
```

Notice that no type can be specified in an access declaration. For example, we could attempt to derive a **square** class from the **shape** class, but the following is incorrect:

```
class square : private shape {
public:
    int shape::i_d;      // WRONG: cannot specify type.
};
```

Since the member's type is declared in the base class, this restriction is entirely reasonable.

The purpose of an access declaration is to weaken the restriction imposed by the access specifier in the derived class header. For this reason, an access declaration can only appear in the **public** or **protected** part of a derived class. There are two other restrictions which can be illustrated by means of the **shape** class given on page 330:

- An access declaration cannot grant access to a member of the base class which could not otherwise be made accessible:

  ```
  class disc : public shape {
  public:
      shape::material;      // WRONG: cannot increase access.
  };
  ```

  If this restriction did not exist, then any **private** or **protected** member of a class could be made **public** by means of a trivial derived class. This would make the entire idea of a class access restriction almost worthless.

---

[8]Since the author has never had occasion to make such adjustments, the reader could be forgiven for skipping this section!

- An access declaration cannot restrict access to the base class member:

```
class square : public shape {
protected:
    shape::i_d;              // WRONG: cannot restrict access.
};
```

It is not just the access to data members that can be modified; an access declaration can also be used for member functions:

```
class shape {
public:
    float give_area(void) { return area; }
protected:
    void set_area(float a) { area = a; }
private:
    float area;
};

class square : private shape {
public:
    shape::give_area;
protected:
    shape::set_area;
};
```

Notice that, since neither a return type nor arguments can be given in the access declaration for a function, it is impossible to distinguish overloaded functions. This has several implications:

- A derived class cannot both overload a base class member function and adjust the access of that function:

```
class shape {
protected:
    void set_area(float a);
};

class square : private shape {
protected:
    void set_area(double side);
    shape::set_area;          // WRONG!
};
```

- The access to overloaded base class functions cannot be changed if these functions have different base class access:

```
class shape {
public:
    void set_area(float a);
private:
    void set_area(int i);
};

class square : private shape {
public:
    shape::set_area;       // WRONG: overloaded functions
                           // have different access.
};
```

- The access to different overloaded functions with the same name cannot be modified independently:

```
class shape {
public:
    void set_area(float a);
    void set_area(int i);
};

class square : private shape {
public:
    shape::set_area;       // Both overloaded functions
                           // are public.
};
```

11.7.1   Friendship and Derivation

In Section 8.15 we introduced the idea of an entire class being a friend of another class. A friend class and a derived class both have special privileges to access members of another class. However, friendship should not be confused with derivation. A friend class has access to *all* members of a class which has granted friendship. In the example:

```
class node {
    friend class list;
    // Other members go here.
```

```
private:
    node *next;
};

class list {
    // Members go here.
};
```

the `list` class has access to the `private` member, called `next`. By contrast, the `coloured_sphere` class has no access to the `private` member, r, of the `sphere` class:

```
class sphere {
public:
    sphere(double radius) { r = radius; }
protected:
    static int spheres;
private:
    double r;
};

class coloured_sphere : public sphere {
public:
    virtual void print_colour(void) = 0;
    coloured_sphere(double radius) : sphere(radius){}
};
```

although it does have access to `protected` and `public` members.

Friendship is *not* inherited. If the class, `superlist`, is a `friend` of `list`:

```
class list {
    friend class superlist;
    // Members go here.
};

class superlist {
    // Members go here.
};
```

then `superlist` has no access to any `private` or `protected` members of the `node` class. In this particular case the `next` member of the `node` class is not accessible. If this restriction did not exist, then granting friendship to one class would open up the entire class implementation to an arbitrary hierarchy of derived classes. As a general rule if classes need access to the members of an indirect base class then `protected` access rather than friendship is the appropriate technique.

11.8 Using Single Inheritance

11.8.1 A Bounds Checked Array Class

In Section 8.17.1 we implemented a primitive self-describing, self-checking `array` class. This class was improved in subsequent exercises and further improvements can now be made by introducing destructors and `virtual` functions. The most fundamental change that we make is to remove the bounds checking from the `array` class and to introduce a derived class, called `checked_array`, which takes over this role:

```
// source:    array.hpp
// use:       Defines array class.

#ifndef ARRAY_HPP
#define ARRAY_HPP

#include <iostream.hpp>
#include <stdlib.h>      // for EXIT_SUCCESS
#include <string.h>      // for memcpy()

class array {
public:
    array(int size);
    array(const array &x);
    ~array() { delete pt; }
    array &operator=(const array &x);
    virtual double &operator[](int index);
    int get_size(void);
protected:
    int n;
    double *pt;
};

class checked_array : public array {
public:
    checked_array(int size) : array(size) { }
    double &operator[](int index);
private:
    void check_bounds(int index);
};

// inline array class implementations:
```

```
inline int array::get_size(void)
{
    return n;
}

inline double &array::operator[](int index)
{
    return pt[index - 1];
}

// inline checked_array class implementations:

inline double &checked_array::operator[](int index)
{
    check_bounds(index);
    return array::operator[](index);
}

inline void checked_array::check_bounds(int index)
{
    if (index < 1 || index > n) {
        cout << "Array index " << index << " out of bounds\n";
        exit(EXIT_FAILURE);
    }
}
```

```
#endif  // ARRAY_HPP
```

In total, the improvements made to the original **array** class are:

- An assignment operator and copy constructor are supplied since otherwise defaults would be generated by the compiler. Because an **array** object has a pointer to dynamically allocated memory, these defaults would not work correctly.

- A destructor is introduced to delete the dynamically allocated memory.

- Instead of the **element()** function we overload the subscripting opera-tor, which is declared **virtual** so that dynamic binding can be invoked. Overloading the function call operator would provide an equally natural interface.

The **checked_array** class, which is derived from the **array** class, has the following features:

- A constructor must be defined since constructors are not inherited. The new constructor simply calls the base class constructor and has an empty body.

- A new subscripting operator is defined. This operator invokes the base class function, which is safer than having two independent implementations.

- A function such as `check_bounds()` is sometimes called a *helper function* since it is only used internally by the `checked_array` class.

For efficiency, some of the smaller and much used functions are implemented `inline`. Implementation of the remaining functions is straightforward:

```
// source:  array.cpp
// use:     Implements array class.

#include <iostream.hpp>
#include <stdlib.h>      // for exit()

#include "array.hpp"

array::array(int size)
{
    n = size;
    pt = new double[n];
    if (pt == NULL) {
        cout << "Failed to allocate array.\n";
        exit(EXIT_FAILURE);
    }
}

array::array(const array &x)
{
    n = x.n;
    pt = new double[n];
    if (pt == NULL) {
        cout << "Failed to allocate array.\n";
        exit(EXIT_FAILURE);
    }
    memcpy(pt, x.pt, n * sizeof(double));
}

array &array::operator=(const array &x)
{
```

```
        delete pt;
        n = x.n;
        pt = new double[n];
        if (pt == NULL) {
            cout << "Failed to allocate array.\n";
            exit(EXIT_FAILURE);
        }
        memcpy(pt, x.pt, n * sizeof(double));
        return *this;
    }
```

The following program tries out the **array** and **checked_array** classes:

```
// source:   test.cpp
// use:      Tests array class.

#include <iostream.hpp>
#include <stdlib.h>        // for EXIT_SUCCESS

#include "array.hpp"

double sum(const array &a, int first_index, int last_index)
{
    double result = a[first_index];
    for (int i = first_index + 1; i <= last_index; ++i)
        result += a[i];
    return result;
}

int main()
{
    const int n = 10;

    // Define an object:
    checked_array x(n);

    // Access the array size:
    cout << "The array size is " << x.get_size() << "\n\n";

    // Store some data:
    for (int i = 1; i <= n; ++i)
        x[i] = i * 25.0;

    // Retrieve some data:
```

```
    for (i = 1; i <= n; ++i)
        cout << x[i] << "\n";

    // Define another object using copy constructor:
    checked_array y = x;

    // Check the array size:
    cout << "The array size is " << y.get_size() << "\n\n";

    // Check that the copy is identical:
    for (i = 1; i <= n; ++i)
        if (x[i] != y[i])
            cout << "x[" << i << "] != y[" << i << "]\n";

    // Define another object with half the size
    // but no bounds checking:
    array z(n/2);

    // Check the array size:
    cout << "The array size is " << z.get_size() << "\n\n";

    // Try out the assignment operator:

    z = x;

    // Check the array size:
    cout << "The array size is " << z.get_size() << "\n\n";

    // Check that the copy is identical:
    for (i = 1; i <= n; ++i)
        if (z[i] != x[i])
            cout << "z[" << i << "] != x[" << i << "]\n\n";

    // Find sum for z[i], going out of bounds:
    cout << "The sum for z[i] = " << sum(z, 0, n) << "\n\n";

    // Find sum for x[i], going out of bounds:
    cout << "The sum for x[i] = " << sum(x, 0, n) << "\n\n";

    return(EXIT_SUCCESS);
}
```

Of particular interest is the `sum()` function. Since this function accepts a *reference* to an `array` object, the function body can manipulate both derived and base class objects; which overloaded subscripting operator gets invoked depends on the type of object that is passed as the function argument.

Putting the bounds check in a derived class has the advantage that we can choose to either have checked or unchecked arrays. We could also achieve this by having two distinct classes rather than using inheritance. However, this would complicate program maintenance, in addition to making it more difficult to mix checked and unchecked arrays.[9]

Exercise:

Try running the test program. Describe and explain what happens in the following circumstances:

1. The `virtual` specifier is omitted from the base class declaration for the subscripting operator.

2. The `sum()` function is changed so that the `array` argument is passed by value.

11.8.2   A Menu Class

As mentioned previously, a common method of 'driving' a program is to use a menu. In this section we develop a general menu class. Typically a user initiates a program which displays a list of options, as shown below:

```
Options:
    0    Exit menu
    1    Jacobi iteration
    2    Weighted Jacobi iteration
    3    Gauss-Seidel iteration
Select option:
```

A *menu* consists of a number of items, which we call *options*. An option may either be a menu, which itself has a list of options, or an *action*. An action does some specific task, such as setting the value of a parameter, running another program, opening a file, etc. When an action is completed, it may either invoke a menu or perform some other task, such as return to the operating system. This discussion leads naturally to the idea of having three classes, as shown in Figure 11.6.

Suitable definitions for the three classes are given below:

---

[9]It could be argued that it is the client that should provide error checking rather than the class. A detailed discussion of this point is given in [8].

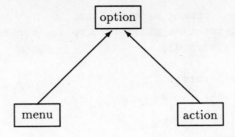

Figure 11.6: Classes for menus.

```
// source:        menu.hpp
// use:           Defines menu classes.

#ifndef MENU_HPP
#define MENU_HPP

#include <stdlib.h>        // for NULL
#include "string.hpp"

class option {
public:
    option(const string &option_label) {
        label = option_label; }
    virtual void activate(void) = 0;
protected:
    string label;
};

class menu : public option {
public:
    menu(const string &menu_label, int max_number_of_options);
    ~menu();
    void set_option(option *op_pt);
    void activate(void);
private:
    option **option_list;
    int options, max_options;
};

class action : public option {
public:
```

```
        action(const string &action_label,
            void (*function_pt)(void), option *option_pt = NULL);
        void activate(void);
    private:
        void (*f_pt)(void);
        option *op_pt;
    };
```

```
    #endif   // MENU_HPP
```

Notice how use is made of the **string** class, introduced in Section 9.6.2. The **option** class is an abstract base class and, as such, we cannot define instances of the class. However, the two derived classes inherit the properties of this base class; they all have an **activate()** function and a 'label'. These derived classes also add their own data and member functions on top of those provided by the base class.

The **option_list** data member of the **menu** class is used to store the address of a dynamically allocated array of **option** pointers. The class also has data members to hold the size of this array (**max_options**) and the number of options set (**options**). The **set_option()** member function is used to assign an **option** address to an element of the array.

The **action** class has a pointer to the function which invokes the action (**f_pt**) and a pointer to an option (**op_pt**) which may be invoked after the action has completed.

Suitable class implementations are given by:

```
// source:        menu.cpp
// use:           Implements menu classes.

#include <stdlib.h>            // for NULL
#include <iostream.hpp>
#include "menu.hpp"

menu::menu(const string &menu_label,
    int max_number_of_options) : option(menu_label)
{
    max_options = max_number_of_options;
    if (max_options <= 0) {
        cout << "Error in menu(): options = " <<
            max_options <<"\n";
        exit(EXIT_FAILURE);
    }
    else {
        option_list = new menu *[max_options];
```

```
            if (option_list == NULL) {
                cout << "Heap allocation failed for " <<
                    "option_list\n";
                exit(EXIT_FAILURE);
            }
        }
        options = 0;
    }


menu::~menu()
{
    delete option_list;
}


void menu::set_option(option *op_pt)
{
    if (options < max_options) {
        option_list[options] = op_pt;
        ++options;
    }
    else {
        cerr << "Attempt to set " << options + 1 <<
            " menu options\nOnly " << max_options <<
            " options are allowed.\n";
        exit(EXIT_FAILURE);
    }
}


void menu::activate(void)
{
    int i, choice;

    do {
        cout << "\n";
        label.print();
        cout << "\n";
        for (i = 0; i < options; ++i) {
            cout << i << "\t";
            (option_list[i]->label).print();
            cout << "\n";
        }
        cout << "Select option:  ";
        cin >> choice;
```

```
        } while (choice < 0 || choice >= options);
        option_list[choice]->activate();
}

    action::action(const string &action_label,
        void (*function_pt)(void),
        option *option_pt) : option(action_label)
    {
        f_pt = function_pt;
        op_pt = option_pt;
    }

    void action::activate(void)
    {
        f_pt();
        op_pt->activate();
    }
```

The `menu` constructor initializes the `option_list` pointer to sufficient dynam-ically allocated memory to store addresses for the maximum number of options and also initializes the current number of options to zero. Notice the way in which the base class, `option()`, constructor is called.

Initialization of the `action` data members, `f_pt` and `op_pt`, is carried out by the `action` constructor, which also invokes the base class constructor. The value stored by `op_pt` is the address of either an `action` or `menu` object.

The `menu::activate()` function lists the menu items, accepts a menu choice and activates that particular option. Since the `option_list[ ]` array holds addresses of both `action` and `menu` objects, which `activate()` function is invoked depends on the object type. This is a run-time decision and another example of dynamic binding. It is:

```
    option_list[choice]->activate();
```

in the `menu::activate()` function which replaces the notorious `switch` state-ment.

The `action::activate()` function is very simple. Since no choice is involved, the appropriate function for the particular action is first invoked and then the option pointed to by `op_pt` is activated; it is this that allows us to do some-thing after the action has terminated, such as going to a menu or exiting to the operating system.

A simple example demonstrating these classes in use is as follows:

```
    // source:      test.cpp
    // use:         Tests menu.
```

```
#include <iostream.hpp>
#include <stdlib.h>          // for EXIT_SUCCESS
#include "menu.hpp"

void to_system(void);
void create_multi_grid(void);
void run_V_cycle(void);
void run_W_cycle(void);
void delete_multi_grid(void);

void to_system(void)
{
    cout << "Returning to system.\n";
    exit(EXIT_SUCCESS);
}

void create_multi_grid(void)
{
    cout << "Multi-grid created.\n";
}

void run_V_cycle(void)
{
    cout << "A single V-cycle has been run.\n";
}

void run_W_cycle(void)
{
    cout << "A single W-cycle has been run.\n";
}

void delete_multi_grid(void)
{
    cout << "The multi-grid has been deleted.\n";
}

int main()
{
    const int top_menu_options = 2;
    const int grid_menu_options = 3;
    // Define menus:
    menu top_menu("Top menu:", top_menu_options);
```

```
menu grid_menu("Multi-grid menu:", grid_menu_options);
// Set options for top menu:
top_menu.set_option(new action("Return to system",
    to_system));
top_menu.set_option(new action("Create multi-grid",
    &create_multi_grid, &grid_menu));
// Set options for multi-grid menu:
grid_menu.set_option(new action("Delete multi-grid",
    delete_multi_grid, &top_menu));
grid_menu.set_option(new action("Run V-cycle multi-grid",
    run_V_cycle, &grid_menu));
grid_menu.set_option(new action("Run W-cycle multi-grid",
    run_W_cycle, &grid_menu));
// Start the menu system:
top_menu.activate();
return EXIT_SUCCESS;
}
```

For simplicty the functions do not actually do very much; they only send messages to the output stream declaring which action they should have performed. A typical session is shown below; bold face type represents entries typed in by the user and italics are used for the results of a particular action:

Top menu:
0   Return to system
1   Create multi-grid
Select option: **1**

Multi-grid created.

Multi-grid menu:
0   Delete multi-grid
1   Run V-cycle multi-grid
2   Run W-cycle multi-grid
Select option: **1**

A single V-cycle has been run.

Multi-grid menu:
0   Delete multi-grid
1   Run V-cycle multi-grid
2   Run W-cycle multi-grid
Select option: **2**

A single W-cycle has been run.

Multi-grid menu:
0   Delete multi-grid
1   Run V-cycle multi-grid
2   Run W-cycle multi-grid
Select option: **0**

The multi-grid has been deleted.

Top menu:
0   Return to system
1   Create multi-grid
Select option: **0**

Returning to system.

The structure of this menu system is shown in Figure 11.7. The single ovals contain descriptions of particular options that can be activated; the two double ovals represent menus that are presented to the user. Execution of the program causes `top_menu` to be activated and a list of options to be displayed. In the above case the user chooses option 1 which in turn invokes the `create_multi_grid()` function and then causes the `grid_menu` options to be presented. The user next chooses option 1, which invokes the `run_V_cycle()` function and then returns to the same `grid_menu`. Eventually option 0 of `top_menu` is chosen and the program terminates.

It is possible to build a complicated system of many sub-menus and options by simply adding more statements to the function, `main()`. It is dynamic binding which causes either a `menu` or `action` object to be activated as a result of a run-time decision by the user; the member functions for the `option, action` and `menu` classes remain unchanged.

Exercise:

Compile and run this example of using a menu. Try adding more sub-menus with different options.

11.9   Summary

- A class, `X`, is declared to be derived from a base class, `A`, by the statement:

```
class X : public A {
public:
```

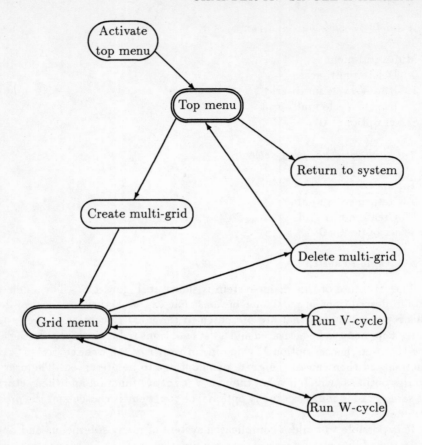

Figure 11.7: A typical menu system.

```
      int x;
private:
      int y;
protected:
      int z;
};
```

The **public** access specifier before the base class, **A**, overrides the **private** default. **Protected** members of a class *may* be accessed by a derived class, whereas **private** members can never be accessed by a derived class.

- A derived class has the members given in its declaration, in addition to all of the members of the base class. (However, note that the latter members may not be accessible.)

- The scope resolution operator, `::`, can be used to access a member declared in the base class:

```
class A {
public:
    int v;
};

class X : public A {
public:
    int v;
};

X x;
x.v = 1;    // Access v declared in class X.
x.A::v = 2; // Access v declared in class A.
```

- The scope resolution operator can also be used to adjust the derived class access to a specific base class member:

```
class X : private A {
public:
    A::a;
};
```

- Which `virtual` function is invoked through a pointer or reference depends on the type of object:

```
class A {
public:
    virtual void f(void) { cout << "Class A\n"; }
};

class X : public A {
public:
    void f(void) { cout << "Class B\n"; }
};

A a;
X x;
A *pt = &a;
```

```
pt->f();      // Invokes A::f()
pt = &x;
pt->f();      // Invokes X::f()
```

- The declaration of an abstract class must contain a pure **virtual** function:

```
class solid {
public:
    virtual double volume(void) = 0;
};
```

A reference or pointer to an abstract class is allowed but an instance of an abstract class is illegal.

- A derived class can be the base class for another derived class:

```
class A {
    // ...
};

class B : public A {
    // ...
};

class C : public B {
    // ...
};
```

Class A is an indirect base class of C, whereas B is a direct base class of C.

- An enumeration defined within a class has the scope of that class:

```
class coloured_cone : cone {
public:
    enum colour {red, yellow, blue};
};
```

- Constructors cannot be declared **virtual** and are not inherited. A derived class should define its own constructor and call the base class constructor if necessary:

```
class checked_array : public array {
public:
    checked_array(int size) : array(size){}
};
```

11.10   Exercises

1. The current version of our `menu` class uses a constructor which dynamically allocates sufficient memory for a specified number of options. Implement an alternative version using a linked list. (See Section 10.4.1.) Initially the list should be empty, with nodes being added by the `set_option()` function.

2. Use the `menu` class to drive a test program for one of the previous classes that we have developed. Suitable examples are the weather data (Section 8.17.2) and complex arithmetic (Section 9.6.1) classes.

3. Implement an overloaded `!=` operator for the array class which we developed in Section 11.8.1. If `x` and `y` are arrays, then `x != y` must return TRUE or FALSE, as appropriate. You should provide both an unchecked `virtual` function for the `array` class and a bounds checked function for the `checked_array` class.

4. Use the doubly linked list of Section 10.4.2 as the base class for a sparse vector class which provides the same methods as Exercise 6 of Chapter 10.

Chapter 12

Input and Output

12.1 Introduction

Input and output (I/O) are not part of the C++ language, but these facilities are provided by a library of classes. This library is not yet completely standardized. Early releases of C++ compilers implemented the stream library, described in the first edition of [10], whereas most recent compilers implement what is often referred to as the *iostream library*;[1] this is the library currently submitted to the ANSI C++ committee and described in the second edition of [10]. It is also the I/O library described in this chapter. However, since present compilers may vary slightly, you should consult the C++ reference manual for your particular system.

The I/O library provides a strongly typed and very safe system for performing input and output operations; errors either get trapped at compile-time or set error flags associated with the I/O library objects. This library is an excellent example of a C++ application and consists of a hierarchy of derived classes.[2] The nine main classes that are directly relevant to the user are as follows:

- generic input and output classes declared in `<iostream.hpp>`:

output:	`ostream` class
input:	`istream` class
input and output:	`iostream` class

- file based input and output classes declared in `<fstream.hpp>`:

---

[1]A rather confusing point is that one of the classes in this library is actually called *iostream*. To avoid any possible ambiguity, the terminology, I/O library is used in this chapter.

[2]The library actually uses multiple inheritance which is not introduced until Chapter 14. For the current discussion it is only necessary to realize that a derived class can have more than one base class.

output: `ofstream` class
input: `ifstream` class
input and output: `fstream` class

- in memory input and output classes declared in `<strstream.hpp>`:

output: `ostrstream` class
input: `istrstream` class
input and output: `strstream` class

Since these classes are all *derived* classes, they have a common basic public interface, together with additional features peculiar to each class. For instance, the `iostream` class has both `ostream` and `istream` as base classes. Much insight into the structure of the library can be gained from constructing an inheritance diagram, as suggested in Exercise 1 of this chapter.

There are several predefined objects which are instances of two of the classes belonging to the library:

- `cin` is an instance of the `istream` class and is the standard input stream (typically the keyboard).

- `cout` is an instance of the `ostream` class and is the standard output stream (typically the screen).

- `cerr` is an instance of the `ostream` class. It is the standard error stream (typically the screen) and is effectively unbuffered.

- A buffered version of `cerr`, called `clog`, may also be defined.

Data is inserted in an output stream by using the binary *insertion operator*, `<<` (also known as an *inserter*):

```
cout << "The value of x is " << x;
```

Data is removed from an input stream by means of the binary *extraction operator*, `>>` (also known as an *extractor*):

```
cin >> x;
```

12.2   Generic Input and Output Classes

We begin by considering the input and output stream classes, which are defined in `<iostream.hpp>`, and illustrate the techniques involved by means of the familiar `cin` and `cout` objects.

12.2.1 Output

Throughout this book we have used the insertion operator to send data to the standard output stream. This operator is overloaded for all of the fundamental types; as a simple example we can list the addresses of elements of an array:

```
#include <iostream.hpp>

double x[10];
for (int i = 0; i < 10; ++i)
    cout << "Address of element " << i <<
        " is " << (x + i) << "\n";
```

Notice that the insertion operators can be concatenated. An alternative for long strings is to use the backslash, \, to continue the string to the next line:

```
cout << "This is a long sentence which is given solely to\
demonstrate how to continue long strings.\n";
```

The output appears without the backslash, of course. This technique is not common because white space at the start of the second line *is* significant and this is incompatible with most layout styles for C++ programs. A better method is to use the fact that adjacent string constants are concatenated:

```
cout << "This long sentence demonstrates a better way "
        "to continue long strings by using concatenation";
```

The `ostream` object, `cout`, provides buffered output.[3] This is usually more efficient than unbuffered output, but may sometimes be inconvenient. For instance, if we are trying to debug a program, we might try sending the values of some crucial variables to `cout`. However, if the messages are still stuck in a buffer when disaster strikes, then we may not get any output. The `flush()` function overcomes this problem, by *flushing* data from the appropriate stream buffer:

```
// Forgot to set max_error.

// Put in a debug statement:
cout << "max_error: " << max_error;
cout.flush();

while (max_error > error) {
    // Solve differential equation.
}
```

---

[3] `cout` is actually an object of a class derived from `ostream`, but this detail can be ignored for the current discussion. A similar remark applies to `cin` and the `istream` class.

The `flush()` function is unnecessary (but harmless) in the following situation:

```
cout << "Input the start time: ";
cout.flush();
cin >> t;
```

since `cout` is *tied* to `cin`; that is the `cout` buffer is automatically flushed before any attempt is made to extract data from `cin`.

The object, `cerr`, is similar to `cout`, except that it is the standard error stream (usually the screen) and is flushed after each insertion. The flushing has the advantage that critical error messages cannot get stuck in a buffer:

```
if (n != m)
    cerr << "Cannot invert matrix: " <<
         "matrix is not square\n";
```

The library provides special flags, known as *manipulators*, each of which performs a particular action on a stream. For instance, in the statement:

```
cout << "The value of t is " << t << endl;
```

`endl` is a manipulator which inserts a new line and flushes the buffer. Some manipulators change the state of a stream without inserting any data; an example is the statement:

```
cout << hex;
```

where the manipulator, `hex`, results in all subsequent insertions of integers being in hexadecimal format. We discuss other format manipulators later in this chapter.

There are a few features of the insertion operator which could initially cause some confusion. Consider the code fragment:

```
#include <iostream.hpp>
char array[] = "A message.";
char *string = "Another message.";

cout << "Base address of char array is: " << array <<
    "\nValue of char pointer is: " << string;
```

The result is:

```
Base address of char array is: A message.
Value of char pointer is: Another message.
```

In contrast to the other fundamental types, if the right operand of an insertion operator has the type `char*`, then a string, rather than the value of an address, is inserted. A cast to `void*` produces the address stored by the pointer and:

```
cout << "Base address of char array is: " <<
    (void *)array <<
    "\n value of char pointer is: " <<
    (void *)string;
```

typically gives the (hexadecimal) result:

```
00273DE0
00003BBF
```

Another feature of the insertion operator is that statements such as:

```
cout << "i || j is: " << i || j;
```

should be rewritten with parentheses as:

```
cout << "i || j is: " << (i || j);
```

since the insertion operator has a higher precedence than the logical OR operator. (See Chapter 13 and Appendix C.) Insertion expressions involving other low precedence operators also need parentheses and analogous remarks apply to the extraction operator.

Unformatted Output

Single characters can be inserted in an output stream by means of the put() library function:

```
cout.put('C');
```

The put() function can be concatenated, as can any function which returns a reference to an appropriate class object:

```
cout.put('C').put('+').put('+');
```

but statements of this form are cumbersome and usually unnecessary.

There is also a write() function, with the prototype:

```
ostream &ostream::write(const void *buffer, size_t n);
```

which inserts n bytes, starting from the address stored in buffer:

```
char buffer[3] = {'C', '+', '+'};
cout.write(buffer, 3);
```

12.2.2 Input

We are already familiar with using an input stream. For instance:

```
#include <iostream.hpp>
cin >> i;
```

extracts the value of i from the input stream, `cin`. Extraction operators can be concatenated; the expression:

```
cin >> i >> j >> k;
```

extracts i, then j, then k, from `cin`. Since white space is ignored, typing:

```
1    2    3
```

and

```
1
2    3
```

both assign the same values to i, j and k. Notice that statements such as:

```
cin >> i, j, k;       // WRONG!
```

superficially look alright and even compile, but do not have the desired effect since only i is assigned to.

The extraction operator is overloaded for all of the fundamental types; for example:

```
#include <iostream.hpp>

char buffer[128];
cout << "Input a string: " << endl;
cin >> buffer;
cout << "You input: " << buffer;
```

Note that characters are extracted from the `cin` stream until white space is encountered, so that input of the form:

```
This is a message.
```

results in the output:

```
This
```

Unformatted Input

There are three `istream` functions that can be used to perform unformatted input. These functions just extract bytes from an input stream, without regard to what the data represents.

- We can use the function, prototyped as:

```
int istream::get(void);
```

to extract and return a single character from an input stream:

```
#include <iostream.hpp>

int c;
cout << "Input a string:\n";
c = cin.get();
if (c != '\n') {
    cout << "Your string contains the characters:\n" <<
        char(c)  << "\n";
    while ((c=cin.get()) != '\n')
        cout << char(c) << "\n";
}
```

Notice that `get()` returns the type `int`, rather than `char`.

- The function prototyped as:

```
istream &istream::getline(char *buffer, int length,
    char delimiter);
```

attempts to extracts up to `length-1` characters from an input stream, but stops if the character stored in `delimiter` is extracted. The string terminator is appended to the characters extracted. For example, using the code:

```
#include <iostream.hpp>

const int length = 128;
char buffer[length];

cout << "Input a short sentence:\n";
cin.getline(buffer, length, ' ');
cout << cin.gcount() << " characters read:  " <<
    buffer << endl;
```

with the input:

How many Mersenne primes are now known?

gives the output:

4 characters read: How

This example uses the istream::gcount() function, which returns the number of characters actually extracted and can be used *immediately* after invoking any of the unformatted input functions (get(), getline() or read()). Notice that the count includes the delimiting character, ' ', which is also inserted in the output stream.

- The function prototyped as:

  istream &istream::read(void *buffer, size_t n);

  is the converse of the ostream::write() and attempts to extract n bytes of data from an input stream and place them in the array with base address given by buffer:

  ```
  #include <iostream.hpp>

  const int length = 10;
  char buffer[length + 1];
  cin.read(buffer, length);
  cout << buffer;
  ```

  Notice that '\n' counts as a character, so that typing:

  ```
  12345
  67
  890
  ```

  gives the output:

  ```
  12345
  67
  8
  ```

As an example of unformatted input, a common requirement is for a program to prompt the user to answer a question, such as:[4]

---

[4]A humane program would also accept variations on the theme YES, Yes, etc.

```
char c;
do {
    cout << "Do you want to continue? (Enter Y or N) ";
    cin >> c;
} while (c != 'Y' && c != 'N');
```

Unfortunately, incorrect replies of the form, 'perhaps', send us spinning many times round the do while loop. Our program should remove all of the incorrect characters for each attempted reply and the following code achieves this:

```
int i;
do {
    cout << "Do you want to continue? (Enter Y or N) ";
    i = cin.get();
    while (cin.get() != '\n') {
        ;          // Do nothing!
    }
} while (char(i) != 'Y' && char(i) != 'N');
```

An alternative approach is:

```
const int length = 128;
char buff[length];
do {
    cout << "Do you want to continue? (Enter Y or N) ";
    cin.getline(buff, length, '\n');
} while (buff[0] != 'Y' && buff[0] != 'N');
```

Exercise:

Both code fragments, given above, are not completely satisfactory since they also accept input, such as 'Newton-Raphson' or 'Y-chromosome', as correct. Modify the second version so that only sensible inputs, such as 'YES', 'Y', 'Yes', 'NO', 'N' and 'No' are accepted.

12.2.3 User-defined Types

As an example of input and output with a user-defined type, consider the complex class, defined in Section 9.6.1. Overloaded insertion and extraction operators can be defined by:

```
ostream &operator<<(ostream &os, const complex &z)
{
    os << '(' << z.re << ',' << z.im << ')';
```

```
        return os;
    }

istream &operator>>(istream &is, complex &z)
{
        is >> z.re >> z.im;
        return is;
}
```

Notice that both operators must be declared friends of the `complex` class and that the operators also return the appropriate class object, making operator concatenation possible. More sophisticated implementations would carry out error checking and ensure that formatting states of the streams are appropriately set.

Exercise:

Implement insertion and extraction operators for the array class described in Section 11.8.1.

12.3   File Input and Output

This section describes how to perform input and output on a file, which is typically stored on a disc. Such operations are often crucial to numerical applications which process very large amounts of experimental data or produce complicated simulations.

The I/O library class used for output[5] from a program to a file is `ofstream`, so to open a file for output only, we must define an `ofstream` object:

```
#include <fstream.hpp>

ofstream my_file("example.dat");
```

In the above statement, `example.dat` is the name of the file. Notice that the header file, `<fstream.hpp>` (which in turn includes `<iostream.hpp>`) is required for all operators and functions concerned with file input and output.

Before attempting to use a file, it is always worth testing whether the file has been opened successfully:

---

[5]Notice the potential source of confusion. Opening a file for output means output from the application program; that is *input* to the file! The compiler will reject any attempt to perform an insertion to a file only open for input.

```
#include <stdlib.h>      // for exit()

if (!my_file) {
    cerr << "Failed to open my_file\n";
    exit(EXIT_FAILURE);
}
```

Data can subsequently be inserted in this stream:

```
my_file << "This is an example file.\n" <<
    "The approximate value of pi is " <<
    3.142 << "\n";
```

When the `ofstream` object goes out of scope, a destructor flushes the buffer and closes the file. The file can also be closed explicitly:

```
my_file.close();
```

in which case any necessary flushing is done automatically.

To open a file only for input to the program, we need to create an `ifstream` object:

```
#include <fstream.hpp>
#include <stdlib.h>      // for exit()

ifstream file("example.dat");
if (!file) {
    cerr << "Failed to open file\n";
    exit(EXIT_FAILURE);
}
const int length = 128;
char buffer[length];
file.getline(buffer, length, '\n');
cout << "The first string is:\n\t" << buffer << "\n";
file.getline(buffer, length, '\n');
cout << "The second string is:\n\t" << buffer << "\n";
```

Running the above code gives the result:

```
The first string is:
    This is an example file.

The second string is:
    The approximate value of pi is 3.142
```

Exercise:

Check that the above output is produced by your system.

Creating an `fstream` object, opens a file for both input and output. The following code writes data to a file and then reads from the file; notice that no `flush()` is needed before reading from the file:

```
fstream file("temp.dat");
if (!file) {
    cerr << "Failed to open file\n";
    exit(EXIT_FAILURE);
}
const int length = 10;
for (int i = 0; i < length; ++i)
    file << (100.0 * i) << " ";
// Perhaps do some work here.
// Go to start of file:
file.seekg(0);
double x;
for (i = 0; i < length; ++i) {
    file >> x;
    // Check what was stored:
    cout << x << " ";
}
```

This is the first time that we have come across the `seekg()` function and it requires some explanation. The file has an associated pointer which points to the position from which the next byte can be obtained.[6] The relative postion of the pointer can be changed by means of the `seekg()` function and, as in this example, `seekg(0)` positions the pointer at the start of the file.

The previous examples use formatted input and output. (Try examining the files, `example.dat` and `temp.dat`, with an editor.) However, if data only needs to be read by a subsequent program (rather than displayed on a terminal for instance) it is much more efficient to use unformatted file I/O; the three file stream classes are the same, but we use different functions (namely `write()` and `read()`). For example, we could use unformatted I/O for a file that is open for both input and output:

```
fstream file("scratch.dat");
if (!file) {
    cerr <<"Failed to open file\n";
    exit(EXIT_FAILURE);
```

---

[6]The **g** in **seekg** stands for get.

```
    }
    const int length = 20;
    double buffer_1[length];
    double buffer_2[length];
    // Create some data:
    for (int i = 0; i < length; ++i)
        buffer_1[i] = 100.0 * i;
    file.write(buffer_1, length * sizeof(double));
    // Perhaps do some work here.
    // Go to start of file:
    file.seekg(0);
    file.read(buffer_2, length * sizeof(double));
    // Check what was stored:
    for (i = 0; i < length; ++i) {
        cout << buffer_2[i] << "\n";
    }
```

Now try examining the file, `scratch.dat`, with your editor!

Assigning Streams

Data inserted in the `cout` and `cerr` streams is often sent to the screen by default, whereas it may be more convenient to send one or other of the streams to a separate disc file. Fortunately the `cout`, `cin`, `cerr` and `clog` (if applicable) streams are defined so that assignment is possible. For example, the following sends all subsequent error messages to 'error.dat':

```
    ofstream error_file("error.dat");
    if (!error_file) {
        cerr << "Failed to open error_file\n";
        exit(EXIT_FAILURE);
    }
    cerr = error_file;
    cerr << "This is an example error file.\n";
```

12.4 Formatting

It is particularly important to be able to control formatting in numerical applications; the results of one calculation may only be significant to 1 decimal place, whereas another calculation may be accurate to 14 places. Each object derived from one of the `<iostream.hpp>` classes has a format state which determines how data is formatted. The default format state can be changed by means of either manipulators or functions:

```
#include <math.h>          // for PI, LN2
#include <iostream.h>

cout << PI;
```

gives:

```
3.141593
```

Using the `precision()` member function:

```
cout.precision(10);
cout << PI;
```

changes the above result to:

```
3.1415926536
```

This change persists for subsequent insertions. For instance:[7]

```
cout << LN2;
```

gives:

```
0.6931471806
```

A manipulator can be used to specify scientific notation, so that:

```
cout << scientific << LN2;
```

gives the result:

```
6.9314718056e-1
```

An equivalent, but more obscure, way of setting the scientific flag is:

```
cout.setf(ios::scientific, ios::floatfield);
```

where `ios` is the **virtual** base class for all of the `iostream` library classes. A manipulator can also change the format to fixed point, as in:

```
cout << fixed << 10000.0 * LN2;
```

which gives:

```
6931.4718055995
```

It is possible to control how integers are formatted. By default the radix for integers is 10, but integers can also be represented in octal:

---

[7]LN2 is ln 2 and is also defined in <math.h>.

```
    cout << oct << 15;
```

giving:

```
    17
```

or hexadecimal:

```
    cout << hex << 15;
```

giving:

```
    f
```

Formatting can be set for input to a program, as well as output. The following program illustrates writing the (decimal) number, 255, to a file using decimal, hexadecimal and octal formats. The three numbers are then read by setting the cin stream to the correct format. The final extraction incorrectly takes the decimal representation as if it were octal. (For some values this would fail, of course.)

```cpp
#include <fstream.hpp>
#include <stdlib.h>      // for exit()

int main()
{
    fstream file("scratch.dat");
    if (!file) {
        cerr << "Failed to open file\n";
        exit(EXIT_FAILURE);
    }
    int i = 255;
    file << i << " " << hex << i << " " << oct << i << dec;

    file.seekg(0);
    int j;
    file >> j;
    cout << "Value in decimal is: " << j << "\n";
    file >> hex >> j;
    cout << "Value in hexadecimal is: " << j << "\n";
    file >> oct >> j;
    cout << "Value in octal is: " << j << "\n";

    file.seekg(0);
    file >> j;
    cout << "Incorrect value in decimal is: " << j << "\n";
```

```
        return(EXIT_SUCCESS);
    }
```

Notice that the syntax for changing the format of any stream is similar, although the:

```
    file >> hex;
```

notation is less natural than:

```
    cout << hex;
```

The latter actually *looks* like we are sending a message to an object.

> **Exercise:**
> List the file, `scratch.dat`, and verify that the values it contains are consistent with the output sent to the screen by this program.

12.5   Stream Condition

Each object derived from one of the `<iostream.hpp>` classes has an associated condition state, indicating whether or not an error has occurred. There are four possible states:

good No error has occurred.

eof (end-of-file) No more data could be inserted or extracted.

fail An error has occurred, but the stream is probably usable if the error state is cleared.

bad A serious error has occurred and the stream is probably not usable.

There are also four functions which test for these states:

good() returns TRUE if no errors have occurred.

eof() returns TRUE if an end-of-file was encountered.

fail() returns TRUE if an operation has failed. This includes an `eof` or `bad` error.

bad() returns TRUE if there has been a serious failure.

The logical NOT operator is overloaded so that, if we have a file called `my_file`, then `!my_file` gives the same result as `my_file.fail()`. We have already used this notation to test opening a file.

The error state can be reset to **good** by invoking the `clear()` function:

```
my_file.clear();
```

but this would probably not be useful if the condition was bad.

Exercise:

In order to demonstrate the various possible condition states, edit a file called, `input.dat`, so that it contains the single floating point number, 1e1. Now compile and run the following program:

```
#include <fstream.hpp>
#include <stdlib.h>        // for exit()

int main()
{
    ifstream file("input.dat");
    if (!file) {
        cerr << "Failed to open file\n";
        exit(EXIT_FAILURE);
    }
    double x;

    file.seekg(1024);
    cout << "\nThe condition states are:\n" <<
        "\tgood is: " << file.good() <<
        "\teof is: " << file.eof() <<
        "\tfail is: " << file.fail() <<
        "\tbad is: " << file.bad() << "\n\n";
    file >> x;
    cout << "Data read was: " << x <<
        "\nThe condition states are:\n" <<
        "\tgood is: " << file.good() <<
        "\teof is: " << file.eof() <<
        "\tfail is: " << file.fail() <<
        "\tbad is: " << file.bad() << "\n\n";

    file.clear();

    file >> x;
```

```
cout << "Data read was: " << x <<
    "\nThe condition states are:\n" <<
    "\tgood is: " << file.good() <<
    "\teof is: " << file.eof() <<
    "\tfail is: " << file.fail() <<
    "\tbad is: " << file.bad() << "\n\n";

return(EXIT_SUCCESS);
}
```

Notice that all of the error states are set and any attempt to clear the `file` stream is futile.

Now delete the `file.seekg(1024)` statement, which attempts to position the `get` pointer past the end-of-file marker, and try running the program with different data in `input.dat`. Suggestions are: 1e1, 1e500, 1e1 2.4, Z, etc. You could also try changing `x` from `double` to other types.

12.6   In Memory Input and Output

It is sometimes useful to treat an area of memory as a file, so that we can perform formatted insertion or extraction.[8] Such files can be created for input, output, or both input and output and there is a different class for each of these three cases. The classes are called `istrstream`, `ostrstream` and `strstream` respectively. To use objects of these classes, the `<strstream.hpp>` include file (which in turn includes `<iostream.hpp>`) is required.[9]

As a simple example, suppose we want to create a sequence of disc files with related names. This could be achieved by inserting the various parts of a particular file name into an `ostrstream` object:

```
#include <fstream.hpp>
#include <strstream.hpp>
#include <stdlib.h>      // for exit()

const int  length = 32;
// Define memory to be used by ostrstream object:
char name[length];
ostrstream file_name(name, length);
```

---

[8]There would be no point in doing unformatted operations.

[9]The exact name of the header file varies for different systems; in particular, since MS-DOS does not accept long file names an alternative (such as `<sstream.hpp>`) must be used.

```
        if (!file_name) {
            cerr << "Failed to create file_name\n";
            exit(EXIT_FAILURE);
        }
        fstream *file[5];
        for (int i = 1; i <= 5; ++i) {
            // Move pointer to start of ostrstream object:
            file_name.seekp(0);
            file_name << "matrix" << i << ".dat" << ends;
            file[i] = new fstream(name);
            if (!file[i]) {
                cerr << "Failed to create " << name << "\n";
                exit(EXIT_FAILURE);
            }
        }
    }
```

In this example, the **ostrstream** constructor uses the statically allocated memory of **name** with the specified length, but another constructor which dynamically allocates memory is also defined in the library. Since we are using the **ostrstream** class, **file_name** is only open for output (from the program). Inserting data into the **file_name** stream does *not* place a string terminator in the **name**[] array; in the above code we do this by inserting the manipulator, **ends**.

Notice that we do not attempt to create the five **fstream** objects by the statement:

```
        fstream file[i](name);
```

which gives a compiler error. Instead we define an array of five pointers of type, **fstream**, and then assign the address of a dynamically created **fstream** object to each element of the array. This is the first time we have met the **seekp()** function. The **ostrstream** file, called **file_name**, has an associated pointer which points to the position where the next byte can be put.[10] The relative position of the pointer can be changed by means of the **seekp()** function and, in this example, **seekp(0)** positions the pointer at the start of the file.

Exercise:

Using the above code fragment, write two programs which open seven disc files corresponding to the seven days of the week. The first program should write different amounts of known data to the files, with each file storing its own record of the quantity of data stored. The second program should read data from the seven files and check that it is correct.

---

[10]The **p** in **seekp** stands for put.

12.7 Using the I/O Library

As an example of the I/O library in use, we present a much simplified version of
the program which was used to generate the index for this book. This version of
the code falls into three parts:

1. The header file, ind.hpp, declares an index_list class. An instance of this
   class is a sorted list of index entries:

```
// source:       ind.hpp
// use:          Defines index making class.

#ifndef INDEX_HPP
#define INDEX_HPP

#include <stdio.h>       // for NULL
#include <fstream.hpp>   // for ofstream

class index_list {
public:
    index_list(char *file_name);
    void get_entries(void);
private:
    void insert_entry(char *string);
    // Data:
    char *input_file_name;
    char *output_file_name;
    ofstream *output_file;
    int items_input;
};

#endif   // INDEX_HPP
```

2. The index_list class is implemented in the file, ind.cpp:

```
// source:       ind.cpp
// use:          Implements index making class.

#include <string.h>  // for strlen(), strcpy(), strcat()
#include <stdlib.h>  // for exit()
#include <iostream.hpp>
#include "ind.hpp"
```

```cpp
// index_list implementations:

index_list::index_list(char *file_name)
{
    int name_length = strlen(file_name);
    input_file_name = new char[name_length + 5];
    if (input_file_name == NULL) {
        cerr << "\nindex_list::index_list() failed to" <<
            " allocate input file name.\n";
        exit(EXIT_FAILURE);
    }
    strcpy(input_file_name, file_name);
    strcat(input_file_name, ".idx");
    output_file_name = new char[name_length + 5];
    if (output_file_name == NULL) {
        cerr << "\nindex_list::index_list() failed to" <<
            " allocate output file name.\n";
        exit(EXIT_FAILURE);
    }
    strcpy(output_file_name, file_name);
    strcat(output_file_name, ".ind");
}


void index_list::get_entries(void)
{
    ifstream input_file(input_file_name);
    if (!input_file) {
        cerr << "\nindex_list::index_list failed to" <<
            " open " << input_file_name << "\n";
        exit(EXIT_FAILURE);
    }
    output_file = new ofstream(output_file_name);
    if (!output_file) {
        cerr << "\nindex_list::index_list failed to" <<
            " open " << output_file_name << "\n";
        exit(EXIT_FAILURE);
    }

    const int buffer_length = 128;
    items_input = 0;
    char buffer[buffer_length];
    while (1) {
        input_file.getline(buffer, buffer_length, '\n');
```

```
        if (input_file.eof()) {
            input_file.close();
            break;
        }
        ++items_input;
        int last_character = input_file.gcount() - 1;
        if (last_character) {
            buffer[last_character] = '\0';
            insert_entry(buffer);
        }
    }
    output_file->close();
    cout << "\nTotal items input from <" <<
        input_file_name << ">: " <<
        items_input << "\n\n";
}


void index_list::insert_entry(char *string)
{
    *output_file << string << "\n";
}
```

The constructor has as its argument the name of the file (without an extension) containing the unsorted index data. The constructor then creates an input file name (with an `.idx` extension) and an output file name (with a `.ind` extension). The function, `get_entries()`, opens the input file and reads one line at a time of index data. The data on each line has the typical form:[11]

    \indexentry{cin@{\tt cin}}{3}

and is extracted from the `input_file` stream by the `istream::getline()` function. The `istream::gcount()` function returns the number of characters extracted by each invocation of `getline()`. This enables us to replace the new line character, `'\n'`, by the string terminator, `'\0'`, and to reject any line containing no other characters. After each line has been read, it is processed by the `insert_entry()` function. Eventually an `end-of-file` is detected by the `ios::eof()` function and the input file is closed.

The `insert_entry()` function given here is just a 'stub'; it merely sends each (unsorted) line to the output file. In practice, the function would

---

[11]For the background to this application, see [16].

invoke a hierarchy of objects which would sort the entries alphabetically
(as items, sub-items and sub-sub-items).

It is worth emphasizing that the output file is opened in `get_entries()`,
rather than `insert_entry()`, since this avoids opening the file every time
a non-blank line is read. The identifier, `index_list::output_file`, is
a pointer to an `ofstream` object, which is dynamically allocated by the
`get_entries()` function. Dereferencing `output_file` enables other member functions to insert data in the `output_file` stream. One subtlety is
that we must explicitly invoke the `close()` function for `output_file` since
dynamically created streams are not automatically flushed when a program
terminates.

3. Finally, the file, `index.cpp`, is the driver for the index list sorting program:

```
// source:       index.cpp
// use:          Driver for index making program.

#include <stdlib.h>       // for EXIT_SUCCESS
#include <iostream.hpp>
#include "ind.hpp"

main(int argc, char *argv[])
{
    if (argc != 2) {
        cout << "Usage:  index <file name>\n";
        exit(EXIT_FAILURE);
    }
    index_list ind(argv[1]);
    ind.get_entries();

    return(EXIT_SUCCESS);
}
```

The program accepts a string (the data file name) as the command line
argument and uses this to create an `index_list` object. The data file is
then processed by `get_entries()`.

Exercise:

Our simplified version of the index sorting program has the effect of
merely removing blank lines from a text file. Try processing a text
file of your choice. (A suitable example would be `ind.cpp`.) What
happens if a data file contains very long lines? Explain this.

Further develop the program so that entries are sorted into alphabetic
order.

12.8   Summary

- Input and output streams are declared in the header file, `<iostream.hpp>`.

- The standard input stream, `cin`, is a predefined `istream` object.

- The standard output, `cout`, and standard error, `cerr`, streams are predefined `ostream` objects.

- The insertion operator, `<<`, is used to insert data into an output stream. The operator can be overloaded for a user-defined class, `X`, by a `friend` function with the prototype:

  ```
  ostream &operator<<(ostream &os, const X &obj);
  ```

- The extraction operator, `>>`, is used to extract data from an input stream. The operator can be overloaded for a user-defined class, `X`, by a `friend` function with the prototype:

  ```
  istream &operator>>(istream &is, X &obj);
  ```

- The `flush()` function is used for flushing a buffered output stream, such as `cout`:

  ```
  cout.flush();
  ```

- A manipulator changes the state of a stream, without necessarily inserting or extracting data:

  ```
  cout << hex;
  ```

- The functions, `put()` and `write()`, are used for unformatted insertion into an output stream:

  ```
  cout.put('C');
  char buffer[3] = {'C', '+', '+'};
  cout.write(buffer, 3);
  ```

- The functions, `get()` and `getline()`, are used for unformatted extraction from an input stream:

  ```
  int c = cin.get();
  cin.getline(buffer, length, '$');
  ```

gcount() counts the number of characters extracted by such operations.

- File I/O uses the classes declared in **<fstream.hpp>**. For example, to open a file for output (*from* a program) use the **ofstream** constructor:

      ofstream output_file("file.data");

- Always check that the file has been successfully opened:

      if (!output_file)
          cerr << "Failed to open file.\n";

- Use **close()** to explicitly close a file:

      output_file.close();

- The function, **seekg()**, changes the position of the **get** pointer, associated with a file open for input:

      input_file.seekg(0);

- The function, **seekp()**, changes the position of the **put** pointer, associated with a file open for output:

      output_file.seekp(0);

- The default format state for a stream can be changed by functions:

      cout.precision(10);

  or manipulators:

      cin >> oct;

- The condition of a stream is tested by the **good()**, **eof()**, **fail()** and **bad()** functions.

- A stream can be created for in memory (formatted) input and/or output. The relevant classes are defined in **<strstream.hpp>**.

- There are many details of the I/O Library which are not discussed in this chapter. Consult the reference manual for your particular system to obtain more information.

12.9   Exercises

1. Using information given in the reference manual for your C++ compiler, construct an inheritance diagram for the I/O library classes.

2. Explain the result of the following code:

```
#include <iostream.hpp>
double x = 128.0;
cout.write(x, sizeof(x));
```

3. Using the techniques learnt in this chapter, modify the `activate()` function for the `menu` class discussed in Section 11.8.2 so that the function handles incorrect user-supplied values for `choice`, such as 'which one?'.

4. By assigning `cin` and `cout`, modify the alphabetic sort program, developed in Section 7.8.2, so that it reads the data from a file and writes the results to a different file.

5. Modify the extraction operator for the `complex` class given in Section 12.2.3 so that complex numbers are assumed to be in the form, `(x, y)`. The operator should skip white space and set an appropriate error flag if incorrect characters are extracted. Do not make any assumptions concerning the formatting state of the input stream.

6. Implement insertion and extraction operators for the `string` class, described in Section 9.6.2.

7. For the `list` class (developed in Section 10.4.1) replace the `print()` function by an inserter.

8. Implement an inserter for a two-dimensional self-describing array class. (See Chapter 8.) For small arrays, your operator should produce output in the style:

$$\begin{bmatrix} 1 & 4 & 7 \\ 2 & 3 & 0 \\ 9 & 1 & 5 \end{bmatrix}$$

whereas for large arrays the required style is:

```
row 0:
    1  3  2  7  8  9  ...

row 1:
    0  9  2  1  4  6  ...
```

Ensure that the output is appropriately formatted, irrespective of the initial format setting for the output stream.

9. Design and implement a class so that objects can store an arbitrary length, signed integer. Implement an appropriate inserter and extractor.

10. Modify the weather data classes, given in Section 8.17.2, so that the data for an entire year is stored on a disc file. Use unformatted I/O and overload the insertion and extraction operators.

11. Use the I/O library to output a *neatly* formatted calendar of the form:

		January					February			
Sun		5	12	19	26		2	9	16	23
Mon		6	13	20	27		3	10	17	24
Tue		7	14	21	28		4	11	18	25
Wed	1	8	15	22	29		5	12	19	26
Thu	2	9	16	23	30		6	13	20	27
Fri	3	10	17	24	31		7	14	21	28
Sat	4	11	18	25		1	8	15	22	29

Chapter 13

Bitwise Operations[††]

In this chapter we are concerned with the manipulation of single bits, each one of which can only store a value of zero or one. Explicit bitwise operations are not common in numerical applications. However, such operations are sometimes used to reduce memory requirements and it is also important to understand how the fundamental data types are represented, together with the limitations that this imposes on our calculations.

13.1 Bitwise Operators

There are six bitwise operators, as shown in Table 13.1, and these operators only operate on integral types; their precedence and associativity are given in

Logical operators	
bitwise complement	~
bitwise AND	&
bitwise exclusive OR	^
bitwise OR		

Shift operators	
left shift	<<
right shift	>>

Table 13.1: Bitwise Operators.

Appendix C. The complement operator, ~, is unary, but all the other operators are binary. Throughout this chapter, these operators are illustrated by using 16 bit integers, but it should be understood that some features of bit operations are compiler dependent. Also the way in which the 'sign bit' is handled for some bitwise operations can depend on the particular compiler, so it is safer to use the unsigned types for such operations where possible.

13.1.1   Bitwise Complement

The *bitwise complement* (or *one's complement*) operator, ~, changes all of the
ones in the operand to zero and all of the zeros to ones. For example, if **x** is
represented by:

    1 0 1 1 1 1 0 0 0 0 0 0 1 1 1 1

then ~**x** is represented by:

    0 1 0 0 0 0 1 1 1 1 1 1 0 0 0 0

Notice that ~**x** is an expression; that is the value of **x** itself remains unchanged.

13.1.2   Bitwise AND

The bitwise AND operator, **&**, compares the two operands bit by bit. If both bits
are set, the result is 1, otherwise the result is 0. For example, if **x** is represented
by:

    1 0 1 1 1 1 0 0 0 0 0 0 1 1 1 1

and **y** by:

    1 1 1 1 0 0 0 0 1 1 1 0 1 0 1 0

then **x & y** is:

    1 0 1 1 0 0 0 0 0 0 0 0 1 0 1 0

Notice that it is important not to confuse **&** with **&&**. The expression, **x && y**,
gives the integer one if at least one bit in each of **x** and **y** is set, which is not
necessarily the case for **x & y**.

13.1.3   Bitwise Exclusive OR

The bitwise exclusive OR operator, ^, compares the two operands bit by bit. If
either, but not both, bits are set, then the result is 1, otherwise it is 0. If **x** is
represented by:

    1 0 1 1 1 1 0 0 0 0 0 0 1 1 1 1

and **y** by:

    1 1 1 1 0 0 0 0 1 1 1 0 1 0 1 0

then **x ^ y** is:

    0 1 0 0 1 1 0 0 1 1 1 0 0 1 0 1

13.1.4 Bitwise Inclusive OR

The bitwise inclusive OR operator, |, compares the two operands bit by bit. If either bit is set, then the result is 1, otherwise it is 0. If **x** is represented by:

    1 0 1 1 1 1 0 0 0 0 0 0 1 1 1 1

and **y** by:

    1 1 1 1 0 0 0 0 1 1 1 0 1 0 1 0

then **x** | **y** is:

    1 1 1 1 1 1 0 0 1 1 1 0 1 1 1 1

Be careful not to confuse | with ||. The expression, **x** || **y**, gives one if any bit of **x** or **y** is set, which is very different from the result for **x** | **y** given above.

13.1.5 Shift Operators

The *left shift* operator, <<, shifts the bits in the left operand to the left by the number of bits specified in the right operand. If **x** is represented by:

    1 0 1 1 1 1 0 0 0 0 0 0 1 1 1 1

then **x** << 3 is:

    1 1 1 0 0 0 0 0 0 1 1 1 1 0 0 0

The vacated bits are always filled with zeros.

The *right shift* operator, >>, shifts the bits in the left operand to the right by the number of bits specified in the right operand. If the left operand has an **unsigned** type or is not negative, then the vacated bits are filled by zeros, otherwise the filling is dependent on the compiler. If **x** is an **unsigned** type, represented by:

    1 0 1 1 1 1 0 0 0 0 0 0 1 1 1 1

then **x** >> 3 is:

    0 0 0 1 0 1 1 1 1 0 0 0 0 0 0 1

Notice that both **x** >> 3 and **x** << 3 are expressions; the value of **x** (or equivalently, the bit pattern) does not change. To shift the bits in **x**, we must make an assignment:

```
x >>= 3;
```

At this stage, you may be worried that these shift operators are the same as those used by the `iostream` library. But the fundamental operators, as defined by both the C and C++ languages, are actually the left and right shift operators. These operators are simply overloaded by the `iostream` library. In fact, we have been using overloaded operators from our very first C++ program! The only consequence of this overloading is that the `iostream` operators must have the same associativity and precedence as the left and right shifts. This is why, for example, successive items can be sent to the output stream:

```
cout << "Output " <<
    "More output " <<
    "Yet more output";
```

and occasionally parentheses are needed to overcome the built-in precedence or associativity:

```
cout << (x && y);
```

13.1.6   Bitwise Assignment Operators

All of the bitwise operators, with the exception of the bitwise complement, have an associated assignment operator:

`<<=`	`>>=`	`&=`	`^=`	`|=`

For instance, the statement:

```
i <<= 4;
```

is equivalent to:

```
i = i << 4;
```

These operators introduce nothing new and are simply shorthand for a bitwise operation on a variable, followed by an assignment to the same variable. However, recall that if we overload an operator, then the corresponding assignment operator is not necessarily defined. For example, we have made much use of the overloaded left shift operator to insert objects in the output stream:

```
cout << "The answer to everything is " << 47;
```

but the `iostream` library does not overload the `<<=` operator. In general we are free to overload an assignment operator in such a way that its meaning is unrelated to the associated overloaded bitwise operator, but this would clearly be very confusing.

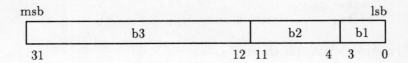

Figure 13.1: An example of bit-fields.

13.2 Bit-fields

A *bit-field* is a class member with a width specified in bits:

```
class packed {
    int b1:4;
    int b2:8;
    int b3:20;
};
```

where each statement of the form:

```
int b1:4;
```

is a *field declaration*. In this example a bit-field of 4 bits is declared for `b1`. Bit-fields can be accessed using the usual class member notation:

```
packed p;
p.b2 = '\0';
```

For the class declared above, the bit-fields may be packed into a single 32 bit word, as shown in Figure 13.1.[1] However, such details are dependent on the compiler and the assumptions underlying any use of bit-fields should be carefully documented.

Bit-fields are sometimes used to access particular, system dependent, memory locations, such as for memory mapped I/O drivers or to save on storage. However, using bit-fields to reduce storage requirements is often misguided. Different compilers pack the bit-fields into words in different ways and this may even result in a waste of space. Moreover, there is usually a performance overhead in accessing bit-fields, so it is possible end up with a slower program that uses more memory!

Bit-fields can be of any integral type. The main restrictions are:

- The address-of operator cannot be applied to bit-fields:

---

[1] We use the convention that the *least significant bit* (lsb) is shown on the right and the *most significant bit* (msb) is on the left. The bits are labelled upwards from zero (corresponding to the least significant bit in a word).

```
    packed p;
    &p.b1;                // WRONG:   cannot use &.
```

- Pointers to bit-fields are not legal.

- References to bit-fields are not allowed.

These restrictions are all very reasonable, since memory is addressable in bytes rather than bits.

Having introduced bit-fields, we won't meet them again in this book; they are best forgotten until you need to implement something like a memory mapped I/O driver.

13.3   Unions

A *union* is a special class in which the data members have overlapping memory locations:

```
union U {
    char c;
    int i;
    float f;
    double d;
};
```

A storage scheme for this `union` is given in Figure 13.2. (Assumptions have been made about the number of bits required to store the different data types.)

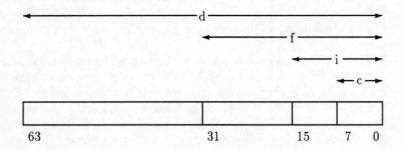

Figure 13.2: An example of a `union`.

The main motivation for unions is to reduce memory requirements. For example, if you need to store an `int` and a `float` in the same application and are certain that you don't need to store them at the same time, then a `union` will save memory:

```
union int_float {
    int i;
    float f;
};
```

The members of a `union` are accessed in the same way as other class members:

```
int_float x;

x.i = 10;
cout << x.i << "\n";
x.f = 3.142;
cout << x.f;
```

Notice that there is no conversion between the two data types; the bits are interpreted as an `int` for `x.i` and as a `float` for `x.f`. Also, members of a `union` are `public` by default. Such members can be declared `private`, but this is not particularly useful.

Our simple `int_float` example doesn't save much memory, but if we have large objects, such as large arrays, then the saving can be significant. Unlike bit-fields, accessing the members of a `union` does not incur high overheads.

It is not necessary for a `union` to be named; an *anonymous union* is a `union` without a name:

```
void g(void)
{
    union {
        int i;
        float f;
    };
    i = 10;
    // ...
    f = 3.142;
    // ...
}
```

An anonymous `union` simply makes the members occupy the same memory and such unions have rather restricted usage. As the above example illustrates, member names must be used directly, without a member operator. Anonymous unions cannot have member functions and, if global, must be declared `static`.

A named `union` can have member functions, including constructors and destructors:

```
union int_float {
    int i;
```

```
    float f;
    int_float(int j) { i = j; }
    int_float(float x) { f = x; }
};

int_float x(1);        // x.i = 1
int_float y(3.142f);   // y.f = 3.142
```

There are many restrictions on unions:

- A `virtual` function is not allowed as a member of a union.

- A `union` cannot be a base class.

- A `union` cannot be a derived class.

- Data members cannot be `static`.

- If a data member is an instance of a class, then that class must not have constructors, destructors or a user-defined assignment operator.

These restrictions do not detract from the fundamental idea of a `union` as a low-level construct for saving memory.

13.4   Using Bitwise Operators

13.4.1   A Bit Array Class

A fairly common requirement is to store a large array of data, each element of which can only be zero or one. An obvious space-saving device is to store each data item as a single bit, but it would be convenient to be able to access all of the data via an array-like notation. In this section we describe a simple *bit array* class. The header file for such a class is given below:

```
// source:    b_array.hpp
// use:       Defines bit array class.

#ifndef BIT_ARRAY_HPP
#define BIT_ARRAY_HPP

class bit_array {
public:
    bit_array(unsigned max_length);
    ~bit_array() { delete data; }
    void set(unsigned position);
```

```cpp
        void clear(unsigned position);
        void set(void);
        void clear(void);
        void display(void);
        int operator[](unsigned position);
        unsigned length(void) { return max_bits; }
    private:
        unsigned *data;
        unsigned max_bits;
        static unsigned bits_per_word;
        unsigned max_words(void) const;
        unsigned max_bytes(void) const;
};

inline unsigned bit_array::max_bytes(void) const {
    return(max_words() * sizeof(*data));
}


#endif  // BIT_ARRAY_HPP
```

Objects of the `bit_array` class store data items as single bits. Individual bits can be set (`set(unsigned)`) or cleared (`clear(unsigned)`) and the subscripting operator, `[ ]`, is overloaded to return TRUE or FALSE, depending on whether or not a bit is set. The number of bits that can be stored by an object is given by the `length()` function. Notice that a small number of bits may be wasted since `max_length` is not rounded up to an integral number of the basic storage type (`unsigned`).

The `bit_array` class can be implemented as follows:

```cpp
// source:   b_array.cpp
// use:      Implements bit array class.

#include <stdlib.h>      // for exit(), NULL, system()
#include <iostream.hpp>
#include <limits.h>      // for CHAR_BIT
#include <string.h>      // for memset()
#include "b_array.hpp"

const int TRUE = 1;
const int FALSE = 0;
const unsigned BIT_MASK = 1;

unsigned bit_array::bits_per_word=CHAR_BIT*sizeof(unsigned);
```

```
bit_array::bit_array(unsigned max_length)
{
    max_bits = max_length;
    data = new unsigned[max_words()];
    if (data == NULL) {
        cerr << "Failed to allocate bit_array.\n";
        exit(EXIT_FAILURE);
    }
}

void bit_array::set(unsigned position)
{
    if (position >= max_bits) {
        cerr << "bit_array set(" << position <<
            ") out of range\n";
        exit(EXIT_FAILURE);
    }
    unsigned word = position / bits_per_word;
    unsigned bit = position % bits_per_word;
    data[word] |= (BIT_MASK << bit);
}

void bit_array::clear(unsigned position)
{
    if (position >= max_bits) {
        cerr << "bit_array clear(" << position <<
            ") out of range\n";
        exit(EXIT_FAILURE);
    }
    unsigned word = position / bits_per_word;
    unsigned bit = position % bits_per_word;
    data[word] &= ~(BIT_MASK << bit);
}

void bit_array::set(void)
{
    memset(data, ~0, max_bytes());
}

void bit_array::clear(void)
{
    memset(data, 0, max_bytes());
}
```

```
void bit_array::display(void)
{
    const unsigned display_width = 80;
    system("cls");              // Clears screen for MS-DOS
    for (unsigned i = 0; i < max_bits; ++i) {
        if (!(i % display_width))
            cout <<"\n";
        if (operator[](i))
            cout << "x";
        else
            cout << ".";
    }
    cout << endl;
}

int bit_array::operator[](unsigned position)
{
    if (position >= max_bits) {
        cerr << "bit_array [" << position <<
            "] out of range\n";
        exit(EXIT_FAILURE);
    }
    unsigned word = position / bits_per_word;
    unsigned bit = position % bits_per_word;
    if (data[word] & (BIT_MASK << bit))
        return TRUE;
    else
        return FALSE;
}

unsigned bit_array::max_words(void) const
{
    unsigned result = max_bits / bits_per_word;
    if (max_bits % bits_per_word)
        ++result;
    return result;
}
```

Notice that the static variable, bit_array::bits_per_word, is initialized (*not* assigned to) in this file. The constant, CHAR_BIT, which is defined in <limits.h>, is the number of bits for a char type. Since the sizeof operator gives the size of an object in units of char (that is, sizeof(char) is defined to be one), the expression for `bits_per_word` is entirely independent of the particular compiler being used. In the context of the `bit_array` class, we define a word to be the basic unit of storage for the `unsigned` type.

Turning now to the `set(unsigned)` function, the variable called `word` gives the element of the array of type `unsigned` which stores a particular data item and `bit` gives the position within that word, as shown in Figure 13.3. The `BIT_MASK` constant has the single lowest bit set. A *mask* is an object that can be used to pick out particular bits from another object. In the `set(unsigned)` function we want to extract a single bit from an `unsigned` object. This can be achieved by left shifting `BIT_MASK` and taking the inclusive bitwise OR of the result with the `unsigned` object. An example is given in Figure 13.4.

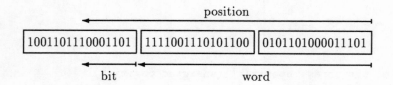

Figure 13.3: Accessing an element of a `bit_array` object.

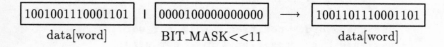

Figure 13.4: Using BIT_MASK to set a bit.

Implementation of the `clear(unsigned)` function is similar to the implementation of `set(unsigned)`. The complement of the left-shifted `BIT_MASK` gives a mask which is all ones, except for a single zero in the required position. A bitwise AND then clears (sets to zero) the corresponding bit in an element of the `data` array, as shown in Figure 13.5.

Figure 13.5: Using BIT_MASK to clear a bit.

The `display()` function shows the current state of a `bit_array` object. An `x` marks a set bit and a dot is used to denote a cleared bit. `display()` uses the ANSI C library function, `system()`, which causes the operating system to execute the function's argument. In this program, the MS-DOS command, cls, is used to clear the screen. An appropriate command should be substituted if the program is run under a different operating system. Since display() is a class member, the function notation can be used to invoke the bit_array operator:

```
operator[](i)
```

Valid alternatives are:

```
this->operator[](i)
```

and:

```
(*this)[i]
```

The following example stores an alternating series of bit_array elements and then displays the data:

```
// source:     test.cpp
// use:        Tries out bit_array class.

#include <stdlib.h>      // for EXIT_SUCCESS, atoi()
#include <iostream.hpp>
#include "b_array.hpp"

// function prototype:
void wait(void);

void wait(void)
{
    cout << "\nHit <Enter> to continue." << endl;
    cin.get();
}

int main(int argc, char *argv[])
{
    if (argc != 2) {
        cerr << "Usage:  test <length>\n";
        exit(EXIT_FAILURE);
    }
    unsigned bits = atoi(argv[1]);
    bit_array b(bits);
    for (unsigned i = 0; i < bits; ++i)
        if (i % 2)
            b.set(i);
```

```
            else
                b.clear(i);
        cout << "bit array set\n" <<
            "Array length available = " << b.length() << endl;
        wait();
        b.display();
        wait();
        b.clear();
        b.display();
        wait();
        b.set();
        b.display();
        wait();
        return(EXIT_SUCCESS);
}
```

Exercise:

Try modifying this program so that more interesting bit data is stored, such as data which appears as a disc when the `display()` function is invoked.

13.4.2   The Sieve of Eratosthenes

An interesting application of the `bit_array` class is to implement the Sieve of Eratosthenes, which finds all primes up to some specified maximum. Suppose we want to find the primes up to 20. The technique consists of writing down all the integers from 2 to 20 and striking out every second integer after 2. We then strike out every third integer after 3, every fourth integer after 4 and so on, as shown in Figure 13.6. Those integers that are not struck out are prime. Of course, in practice we would probably be interested in very large prime numbers and the technique is only limited by the available memory.

The following implements the Sieve of Eratosthenes using our `bit_array` class:

```
// source:     primes.cpp
// use:        Implements the Sieve of Eratosthenes
//             using the bit_array class.

#include <stdlib.h>      // for EXIT_SUCCESS, atoi()
#include <math.h>        // for sqrt()
#include <iostream.hpp>
#include "b_array.hpp"
```

2	3	4	5	6	7	8	9	10	11	12	13	14	15	16	17	18	19	20
·		×		×		×		×		×		×		×		×		×
	·					×	×			×			×		×			
			·					×		×			×		×	×		×
					·					×				×		×		×
									·	×						×		
											·	×						
													·			×		
															·			×

Figure 13.6: The Sieve of Eratosthenes. (A dot indicates the start of a sweep through the integers and a cross marks integers that are struck out.)

```cpp
// function prototypes:
void wait(void);
void list_primes(bit_array &b);

void wait(void)
{
    cout << "\nHit <Enter> to continue." << endl;
    cin.get();
}

void list_primes(bit_array &b)
{
    const unsigned display_height = 24;
    unsigned primes_displayed = 1;

    unsigned i_max = b.length();
    system("cls");
    for (unsigned i = 0; i < i_max; ++i) {
        if (b[i]) {
            cout << 2 * i + 3 << "\n";
            if (primes_displayed % display_height)
                ++primes_displayed;
            else {
                primes_displayed = 1;
                cout.flush();
                wait();
                system("cls");
            }
        }
    }
```

```
        }
    }

    int main(int argc, char *argv[])
    {
        if (argc != 2) {
            cerr << "Usage:  primes <largest integer>\n";
            exit(EXIT_FAILURE);
        }
        unsigned max_int = atoi(argv[1]);
        // Only store odd numbers:
        unsigned bits = (max_int - 1) / 2;
        bit_array b(bits);
        b.set();
        unsigned max_m = sqrt(max_int);

        // These 2 loops are the Sieve of Eratosthenes:
        for (unsigned m = 3; m <= max_m; m += 2) {
            unsigned max_n = max_int / m;
            for (unsigned n = m; n <= max_n; n += 2)
                b.clear(m * n / 2 - 1);
        }

        cout << "Bit array set for primes:\n";
        b.display();
        wait();
        cout << "Primes between 3 and " << max_int << ":\n";
        list_primes(b);
        wait();
        return(EXIT_SUCCESS);
    }
```

The performance of the two loops in `main()` corresponding to the Sieve could be improved, but the version given here makes it easier to understand the algorithm. In any case, a number of techniques have already been used to speed up the program:

- Only odd integers are stored since we know that no even integer (apart from two) is prime.

- If we are searching for all primes up to m, then we know that integers greater than $\sqrt{m}$ cannot divide m, so we only need to consider sweeps through the integers which start at values less than $\sqrt{m}$.

- If, on a given sweep through the integers, we are striking out all those divisible by n, then we only need to start at n^2 because smaller multiples of n will already have been struck out.

13.4.3 Bit Representation of Integral Types

Bitwise operations enable us to investigate how the basic data types are stored on different systems. The following program gives the bit pattern for the **unsigned** type:

```cpp
// source:     bits.cpp
// use:        Prints representation in bits
//             for the unsigned type.

#include <stdlib.h>      // for EXIT_SUCCESS
#include <limits.h>      // for CHAR_BIT
#include <iostream.hpp>

void print_bits(unsigned i)
{
    unsigned bit_mask = 1U << (CHAR_BIT*sizeof(unsigned)-1);
    for (int j = 0; j < sizeof(unsigned); ++j) {
        for (int k = 0; k < CHAR_BIT; ++k) {
            if (i & bit_mask)
                cout << "1";
            else
                cout << "0";
            bit_mask >>= 1;
        }
        cout << " ";
    }
    cout << "\n";
}

int main()
{
    print_bits(0);
    print_bits(1);
    print_bits(-1);
    print_bits(32760);
    print_bits(-32760);
    return(EXIT_SUCCESS);
}
```

The `print_bits()` function constructs a mask with only the most significant (left-most) bit initially non-zero. A bitwise AND of the mask and the function argument detects whether or not the left-most bit is set. Progressively right-shifting the mask enables us to test the remaining bits.

The `print_bits(unsigned)` function also works for `signed int` if a two's complement representation is used, since conversion occurs with no change in the bit pattern. To understand this comment a brief diversion must be made to consider what is meant by a two's complement representation.

There are several ways of representing signed integers and two's complement is one of the most popular. For a positive integer, n, the most significant bit is 0 and the other bits take the expected form for a positive integer. To represent $-n$ we do the following:

- Find the binary representation of n.

- Take the bitwise complement.

- Add 1.

The consequence of these operations is that the most significant bit is always 1 for a negative integer. As an example consider -59 where, for the three stages listed above, we get:

        0000 0000 0011 1011

        1111 1111 1100 0100

        1111 1111 1100 0101

Typical bit patterns obtained on a particular system (using 16 bits to represent the `unsigned` type) are given in Table 13.2. Notice how all of the bits are set for -1; this is because two's complement arithmetic is being used.

Decimal number	Bit pattern
0	00000000 00000000
1	00000000 00000001
-1	11111111 11111111
32760	01111111 11111000
-32760	10000000 00001000

Table 13.2: Bit Patterns Given by `print_bits(unsigned)`.

Exercise:

Use the `print_bits()` function to give the bit patterns for the largest and smallest integers that can be represented on your system by the `unsigned` and `int` types.

We can easily convert the `print_bits(unsigned)` function to accept an **unsigned long** argument:

```
void print_bits(unsigned long i)
{
    unsigned long bit_mask = 1LU
        << (CHAR_BIT * sizeof(unsigned long) - 1);
    for (int j = 0; j < sizeof(unsigned long); ++j) {
        for (int k = 0; k < CHAR_BIT; ++k) {
            if (i & bit_mask)
                cout << "1";
            else
                cout << "0";
            bit_mask >>= 1;
        }
        cout << " ";
    }
    cout << "\n";
}
```

Notice that it is 1LU, rather than 1, that is left-shifted. (Why is this important?) Typical results on a system using 32 bits to represent the **unsigned long** type are given in Table 13.3.

Decimal number	Bit pattern
1	00000000 00000000 00000000 00000001
-1	11111111 11111111 11111111 11111111
2000000000	01110111 00110101 10010100 00000000
-2000000000	10001000 11001010 01101100 00000000

Table 13.3: Bit Patterns Given by `print_bits(unsigned long)`.

13.4.4   Bit Representation of Floating Point Types

The way in which floating point numbers are represented varies between compilers. However, many systems use what is known as the 'IEEE Standard for Binary Floating Point Arithmetic'.[2] The following discussion is restricted to systems conforming to the IEEE Standard, with the **float** type represented by 32 bits and **double** by 64 bits. Both of these values are the minimum acceptable under the Standard.

---

[2]ANSI/IEEE Std 745-1985, published by the Institute of Electrical and Electronics Engineers, Inc.

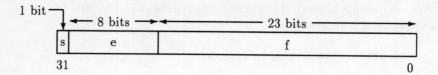

Figure 13.7: The bit structure for a `float`.

A floating point number can be written in binary form as:[3]

$$x = (-1)^s 2^E (b_0.b_1 b_2 \ldots b_{p-1})$$

To be definite, we start by restricting our discussion to the `float` type, where p has the value of 24. There are three distinct parts to the binary representation of a floating point number:

The sign bit

The parameter, s, is a single bit, known as the *sign bit*. A floating point number is positive or negative, depending on whether s takes the value 0 or 1.

The exponent

Rather than storing the *exponent*, E, a *biased exponent* is used. That is, the exponent is shifted by a constant, known as the *bias*, so that the value actually stored is not negative. For the representation being considered here, the biased exponent, e, is defined by:

$$e = E + 127.$$

In this case the bias is 127 and the biased exponent, e, is stored as 8 bits.

The significand

The b_i's are single bits which can take the values 0 and 1. The sequence of b_i's is known as the *significand* and consists of b_0 followed by a binary point and a *fractional* part (b_1 to b_{23}), which we will label as f. The value of b_0 is implicit, which means that only s, e and f are stored, as shown in Figure 13.7. (We adopt the convention of showing the least significant bits on the right.)

Combinations of the values of e and f are used to store five different types of information:

---

[3]It is a sobering thought that there is an infinity of floating point numbers which cannot be represented on any computer, since the sequence of b_i's is finite and the range of E is limited.

1. If $0 < e < 255$ then what is known as a *normalized* number is stored and this has the value given by:[4]

$$x = (-1)^s 2^{e-127} (1.f)$$

Notice that b_0 is implicitly 1 and that f may or may not be zero.

2. If $e = 0$ and $f \neq 0$, then what is known as a *denormalized* number is stored and this has the value given by:

$$x = (-1)^s 2^{-126} (0.f)$$

Notice that in this case b_0 is implicitly 0, rather than 1, and that 2 is raised to a fixed power. Denormalized numbers extend downwards the range of numbers that can be stored by a fixed length word. However, as the number gets smaller, f fills from the left with zeros and the precision decreases; in the limiting case only one bit is significant.

3. If $e = 0$ and $f = 0$, then zero is stored:

$$x = (-1)^s 0$$

4. If $e = 255$ and $f = 0$, then signed infinity is stored:[5]

$$x = (-1)^s \infty$$

5. If $e = 255$ and $f \neq 0$, then what is known as a *NaN* (Not a Number) is stored. A NaN is the result of an invalid floating point operation, such as $0 \times \infty$ or $0 \div 0$. Once created, NaNs propagate through a computation and may appear in your (incorrect) final results.

It would be nice to be able to print bit patterns for the floating types. This is slightly complicated by the fact that bitwise operators only act on the integral types. However, an anonymous union enables us to store a **float** and then to treat it as an **unsigned long**:[6]

```
void print_bits(const float &x)
{
    union {
        unsigned long i;
```

---

[4]In this discussion a number written as (1.f) or (0.f) is in binary notation.

[5]A signed infinity is generated when the magnitude of a floating point number exceeds that which can be represented by the particular type.

[6]We assume that an **unsigned long** has the same number of bits as a **float**. If this is not true on your system, then you should make the necessary simple modifications to **print_bits(float)**.

```
        float y;
    };
    y = x;
    unsigned long bit_mask = 1LU
        << (CHAR_BIT * sizeof(unsigned long) - 1);
    for (int j = 0; j < sizeof(unsigned long); ++j) {
        for (int k = 0; k < CHAR_BIT; ++k) {
            if (i & bit_mask)
                cout << "1";
            else
                cout << "0";
            bit_mask >>= 1;
        }
        cout << " ";
    }
    cout << "\n";
}
```

However, this groups the bit pattern in terms of bytes, which are not easy to interpret. Some simple modifications (which we leave as an 'exercise for the student') would enable us to separate out the s, e and f terms and some typical results are given in Table 13.4.

Exercise:

Show mathematically that the bit patterns given in Table 13.4 are correct.

Floating point number	Bit pattern
0.0	0 00000000 00000000000000000000000
1.0	0 01111111 00000000000000000000000
2.0	0 10000000 00000000000000000000000
1×10^{-7}	0 01100111 10101101011111110010101
-10.0	1 10000010 01000000000000000000000

Table 13.4: Bit Patterns Given by `print_bits(float)`.

The representation of the type **double** is very similar to **float**, except that e and f are assigned additional bits, as shown in Figure 13.8. The biased exponent is represented by 11 bits, with a bias of 1023:

$$e = E + 1023$$

and the fractional part has 52 bits. Clearly a **double** has a much greater range and precision than a **float**.

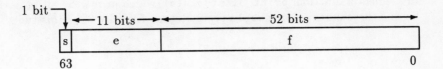

Figure 13.8: The bit structure for a `double`.

13.5 Summary

- The bitwise logical operators are, ~, &, ^ and |.

- Don't confuse & with &&, or | with ||.

- The left shift operator is denoted by, <<, and the right shift operator by, >>.

- A bit-field is a class member with a specified width in bits. Bit-fields are very compiler dependent and their use often carries a high performance penalty.

- A union is a class in which data members have overlapping memory locations:

```
union int_float {
    int i;
    float f;
};
```

13.6 Exercises

1. Implement a copy constructor, assignment operator and != operator for our bit-array class (Section 13.4.1).

2. Modify the Sieve of Eratosthenes program (Section 13.4.2) to make it perform as fast as you are able. (You should get some ideas from [12] and Figure 13.6.) Your changes could also include removing range checking from the `bit_array` class.

3. Calculate the *theoretical* maximum and minimum normalized numbers that can be represented by the `float` type on your system. Verify your answers by using the `print_bits(float)` function.

   How many decimal places are significant for a normalized `float` and what is the smallest denormalized `float` on your system? Again, calculate these numbers and then verify them using `print_bits(float)`.

4. Implement a function, `print_bits(double)`, which prints the bit patterns for the three parts of the `double` type. Repeat Exercise 3 for this type.

Chapter 14

Multiple Inheritance

As has already been emphasized, inheritance is a natural technique to use when we have a 'kind of' relationship; for instance, a cube is a 'kind of' solid and a triangle is a 'kind of' shape. Sometimes, we would like to construct a derived class with more than one base class. Simple examples abound in the natural world. For instance, if we classify animals into carnivores and herbivores, then we will probably also need an omnivores class which is derived from both of these, as shown in Figure 14.1. In fact many hierarchical classification systems lead to

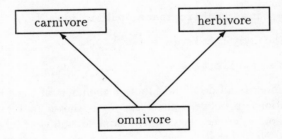

Figure 14.1: Multiple inheritance.

this type of relationship.[1] The ability to have a derived class with more than one base class is known as *multiple inheritance* and is the subject of this chapter.

14.1 Derived Classes

In Chapter 11 we introduced the idea of a derived class, such as `disc`, depending on a single base class:

```
class shape { // ... };
```

[1]See [7] for a detailed class hierarchy based on animals in a zoo.

```
class disc : public shape { // ... };
```

Multiple inheritance consists, syntactically, of replacing the base class by a list of base classes, known as a *derivation list*.   As an example, suppose we are working on a project in special relativity. Since space and time transform differently, it would be natural to have a `time` class and a separate `space` class:[2]

```
class time {
public:
    double t;
    void translate(time a);
};

class space {
public:
    double x, y, z;
    void rotate(const space &s);
};
```

However, an *event* is a point in the four-dimensional (x, y, z, ct) space[3] so we also need a `space_time` class:

```
class space_time : public space, public time { // ... };
```

In this example, the derivation list is:

```
public space, public time
```

and `space_time` inherits all data and function members of the `time` and `space` classes. The relationship between these classes is shown in Figure 14.2. The access restrictions on a derived class are the same for multiple inheritance as for single inheritance. Notice that in order for both `time` and `space` to be `public` base classes, we *must* repeat the `public` specifier. A common mistake is to write the derivation list as:

```
public space, time
```

with the assumption that `public` also applies to `time`. However, since no access specifier is given for `time`, the access defaults to `private`. Even if a `private` base class is intended, it is worth including the access specifier.

Exercise:

Either

---

[2]Most of the classes given in this chapter are only for illustration; for instance, it would normally be very unusual to have `public` data members.

[3]c is the speed of light, which is often set equal to 1 in the physics literature.

If you have some knowledge of special relativity, try using multiple inheritance to implement a `space_time` class, as in Figure 14.2. What are the transformations that could be performed on objects belonging to each of the three classes? What member functions are required?

or

Implement the classes shown in Figure 14.1. The data for each base class should include a list of typical items that are eaten, with items chosen from two enumerations corresponding to the two base classes. Provide functions to list what is eaten by a particular animal. Is there any difficulty in having a data member to store the name of the particular species of carnivore, herbivore or omnivore?

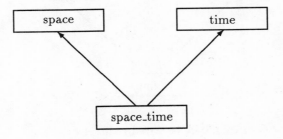

Figure 14.2: Derivation of a `space_time` class.

Now suppose we are developing a geometrical application in two dimensions. An obvious class is one whose objects represent points:

```
class point {
public:
    double x, y;
};
```

and since a straight line can join two points, we may be tempted to declare:

```
class line : public point, public point {
    // ...
};              // WRONG: repeated base classes are not allowed.
```

but we cannot have a repeated base class in a derivation list since there would be no way of distinguishing members of the repeated class. However, multiple base classes can themselves have the same base class:

```
class point_1 : public point { // ... };

class point_2 : public point { // ... };

class line : public point_1, public point_2 { // ... };
```

as shown in Figure 14.3. A base class of another base class is known as an *indirect*

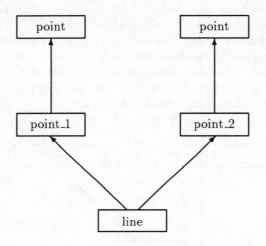

Figure 14.3: A repeated indirect base class.

base class; for example, `point` is an indirect base class of `line`. The inheritance diagram (Figure 14.3) shows one class (`point_1` or `point_2`) between `line` and each copy of `point`, but there is no limit on the possible number of classes between an indirect base class and a derived class.

14.2 Virtual Base Classes

If an indirect base class is used more than once, we may not want to have two or more copies of the class. For example, suppose we are considering solids of various shapes and materials. We may want to have a general `solid` class with `sphere` and `plastic_solid` as derived classes. A `plastic_sphere` class could then be derived from the `sphere` and `plastic_solid` classes. However, it would clearly be inappropriate for a `plastic_sphere` object to have two copies of the `solid` data member. Such multiple copies can be avoided by using the `virtual` specifier before the indirect base class:

```
class solid {
```

```
public:
    int i_d;
};

class sphere : virtual public solid { // ... };

class plastic_solid : virtual public solid { // ... };

class plastic_sphere : public sphere, public plastic_solid {
    // ...
};
```

The class hierarchy is shown in Figure 14.4. There is only one copy of the `i_d`

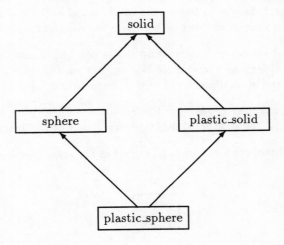

Figure 14.4: A virtual base class.

data member of the `solid` class, which can therefore be accessed unambiguously:

```
plastic_sphere s;
```

```
s.i_d = 1;
```

Notice that the indirect base class, `solid`, is an ordinary class, with the **virtual** specifier only occurring at the next level.[4] Also, specifying **virtual** has no effect on the `sphere` and `plastic_solid` classes.

An indirect base class can be both **virtual** and non-**virtual**, as in:

---

[4]The **virtual** keyword, used in the context of an indirect base class, is rather different from the idea of a **virtual** function; the `solid` class could also contain **virtual** functions. The relative order of **virtual** and **public** is of no consequence.

```
class A { // ... };

class W : public A { // ... };

class X : virtual public A { // ... };

class Y : virtual public A { // ... };

class Z : public A { // ... };

class P : public W, public X, public Y, public Z { // ... };
```

for which the class hierarchy is shown in Figure 14.5. Notice that:

- If the derived class is to have **public** access to each base class, then the **public** access specifier must be repeated for each base class.

- The order of classes in a derivation list is not important. The order may effect such things as the storage layout, but in any case this is compiler dependent and should not be of any concern to the C++ programmer.

- There is no **virtual** keyword in the declaration of the class **P**; this keyword only occurs at the next level, in the declarations of the **X** and **Y** classes.

- There are three, rather than four, copies of the data members of class **A**.

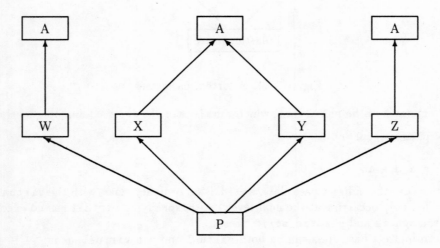

Figure 14.5: An indirect base class which is both **virtual** and non-**virtual**.

Exercise:

Use multiple inheritance and `virtual` indirect `point` base classes to implement a `triangle` class. The data members of all classes should be either `private` or `protected` and consequently suitable access functions must be provided. Also provide functions to calculate both the area and perimeter of a `triangle` object.

14.3 Constructors and Destructors

As we remarked in Section 11.5, constructors and destructors are not inherited and the derived class constructor usually calls the base class constructor. The additional feature with multiple inheritance is that the derived class constructor can call a list of base class constructors. Only the *direct* base classes (as distinct from the indirect base classes) can normally be members of this list. The one exception is that `virtual` base classes can be included. The classes forming the hierarchy shown in Figure 14.4 can be modified to provide a simple example:

```
class solid {
public:
    int i_d;
    solid(int identifier) { i_d = identifier; }
};

class sphere : virtual public solid {
public:
    double r;
    sphere(int identifier, double radius) : solid(identifier)
        { r = radius; }
};

class plastic_solid : virtual public solid {
public:
    double rho;
    plastic_solid(int identifier, double density) :
        solid(identifier) { rho = density; }
};

class plastic_sphere : public sphere, public plastic_solid {
public:
    plastic_sphere(int identifier, double density,
        double radius) : sphere(identifier, radius),
```

```
        plastic_solid(identifier, density) { }
};
```

The constructors, `sphere()` and `plastic_solid()`, both initialize the `solid` base class, which is clearly unsatisfactory since we cannot initialize the same object twice. However, including the `solid()` constructor in the initialization list:

```
class plastic_sphere : public sphere, public plastic_solid {
public:
    plastic_sphere(int identifier, double density,
        double radius) : solid(identifier),
        sphere(identifier, radius),
        plastic_solid(identifier, density) { }
};
```

overcomes this problem since a `virtual` base class is initialized by its *most* derived class (in this case `plastic_sphere()`).

14.4   Member Access Ambiguities

Part of the motivation for multiple inheritance is to reuse existing classes. However, the base classes may well have members with the same names. As for single inheritance, potential ambiguities are often resolved by the concept of dominance; that is names in the derived class *dominate* those of the base classes. For example, suppose we modify our `point` and `line` classes to contain a function to print the coordinates and we also (perhaps unwisely) use `x` and `y` for the storing the mid-point coordinates of a line:

```
class point {
public:
    double x, y;
    void print_coords(void) { cout << "point is (" <<
        x << ", " << y << ")\n"; }
};

class point_1 : public point {
public:
    void print_coords(void) { cout << "point_1 is (" <<
        x << ", " << y << ")\n"; }
};

class point_2 : public point {
public:
    double x, y;
```

```
    void print_coords(void) { cout << "point_2 is (" <<
        x << ", " << y << ")\n"; }
};

class line : public point_1, public point_2 {
public:
    double x, y;
    void print_coords(void) { cout << "mid-point is (" <<
        x << ", " << y << ")\n"; }
};
```

then the following are valid ways of accessing data members of the class:

```
line my_line;

my_line.x = 10;            // Member of line class.
my_line.point_1::x = 50.0;  // Member of point_1 class.
my_line.point_2::y = 45.0;  // Member of point_2 class.
```

Member functions with duplicate names are accessed in a similar manner and the three different functions can be invoked as follows:

```
line my_line;

my_line.print_coords();         // Invokes line function.
my_line.point_1::print_coords(); // Invokes point_1 function.
my_line.point_2::print_coords(); // Invokes point_2 function.
```

Exercise:

By assigning different values to all of the data members of a `line` object, verify the above statements concerning which `print_coords()` functions are invoked.

Use of a `virtual` base class is another way in which potential ambiguities are resolved since there is only one instance of that base class within a derived class object. The `plastic_sphere` class, which we discussed in Section 14.2, is an example of this. However, for `virtual` base classes there is also a potential access privilege ambiguity. Suppose, for some obscure reason, we decide to make `solid` a `private` base class of `plastic_solid`:

```
class solid {
public:
    int i_d;
};
```

```
class sphere : virtual public solid {
};

class plastic_solid : virtual private solid {
};

class plastic_sphere : public sphere, public plastic_solid {
};
```

The `plastic_sphere` class can access the `public` member of `solid` via `sphere`, but not via `plastic_solid`. This ambiguity is resolved by the rule that the `public` access path always dominates.

14.5   Using Multiple Inheritance

One of the primary reasons for introducing multiple inheritance is to control the complexity that occurs in very large applications. This makes it difficult to find realistic examples that can be explained within a few pages; a description of carnivore, herbivore and omnivore classes is unlikely to convince an engineer of the true power of C++. What follows is a semi-realistic example, but you will only come to really appreciate multiple inheritance when writing large applications.

In this section we consider a set of *controller* classes. A `controller` base class:

```
// source:        control.hpp
// use:           Defines controller class.

#ifndef CONTROLLER_HPP
#define CONTROLLER_HPP

#include "string.hpp"

class controller {
public:
    virtual void input(double set_data) { }
    virtual void output(double &give_data) { }
    virtual void display(void);
protected:
    controller(double set_max_data, const string &set_label,
        int set_scale_length);
    int cursor, scale_length;
    double max_data, data;
```

```
    string label;
};
```

```
#endif  // CONTROLLER_HPP
```

determines the interface for this set of classes. An object of an appropriate derivative of this `controller` class accepts a controlling value via the `input()` function, displays this value using the `display()` function and produces a controlled output by means of the `output()` function. Such a controller could be used for anything from a hi-fi system to a power station. All three `controller` functions could take many different forms. For example, the volume control on a hi-fi system might accept inputs from 0 to 100 (in some arbitrary units) whereas inputs from −50 to +50 would be more appropriate for the stereo balance control. The output may be any function of the input; two obvious examples are linear and logarithmic outputs.

For some applications there may be many different types of controller but, rather than design each controller from scratch, we can use multiple inheritance to mix and match the various controller classes, as shown in Figure 14.6. The

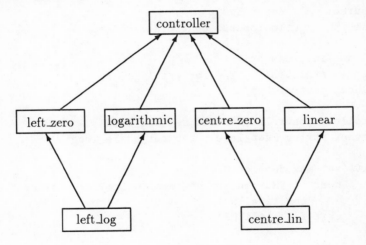

Figure 14.6: Controller classes.

`controller` base class ensures a uniform interface, but it is not intended that we should be able to create instances of this class. A number of derived classes, such as `left_zero` and `centre_zero`, implement specific `input()` functions, corresponding to the various kinds of input that may be appropriate for a particular project. A number of other classes, such as `log` and `linear`, implement different versions of the `output()` function. Again, it is not intended that objects of any of these classes can be created. However, one class from each of the sets of

input and output classes can be used as bases for the required controller classes;
`left_log` and `centre_lin` are the examples shown in Figure 14.6. Instances of
such classes *can* indeed be created.

The `controller` class has already been listed. The main points worthy of
note are:

- The `input()` and `output()` functions are declared to be `virtual` rather
  than *pure* `virtual` since no derived class provides implementations for both
  of them.

- The one and only constructor has **protected** access which ensures that
  a `controller` object cannot be created. This is a very desirable restriction since the class does not provide satisfactory implementations for the
  `input()` and `output()` functions.

- Use is made of the `string` class which was initially described in Section 9.6.2
  and improved in the exercises of Chapters 10 and 12.

The `controller` class implementation is straightforward:

```
// source:      control.cpp
// use:         Implements controller class.

#include <iostream.hpp>
#include <stdlib.h>        // for exit()
#include "control.hpp"

controller::controller(double set_max_data,
    const string &set_label, int set_scale_length)
{
    if (set_max_data <= 0.0) {
        cerr << "Maximum input to a controller must be " <<
            "positive.\n";
        exit(EXIT_FAILURE);
    }
    max_data = set_max_data;
    label = set_label;
    scale_length = set_scale_length;
    data = 0.0;       // Default initial value.
}

/*
The following function displays the value of data on an
analogue scale. The cursor is set by the input() function:
```

```
                       -------------
                       |     *     |
                       -------------
                           label
*/
void controller::display(void)
{
    cout << "\n";
    // Draw upper edge:
    for (int i =- 2; i <= scale_length; ++i)
        cout << "-";
    // Draw left edge:
    cout << "\n|";
    // Step to cursor position:
    for (i = 0; i < cursor; ++i)
        cout << " ";
    // Draw cursor:
    cout << "*";
    // Step to right edge:
    while (i++ < scale_length)
        cout << " ";
    // Draw right edge:
    cout << "|\n";
    // Draw lower edge:
    for (i =- 2; i <= scale_length; ++i)
        cout << "-";
    cout << "\n";
    // Shift label to centre of display:
    int offset = (scale_length + 3 - label.length()) / 2;
    if (offset < 0)
        offset = 0;
    for (i = 0; i < offset; ++i)
        cout << " ";
    cout << label << endl;
}
```

Notice how the insertion operator is used to send a **string** object to the output stream; this assumes that you have done Exercise 6 of Chapter 12.

The class for a controller accepting values from zero up to a positive maximum (called **max_data** in the **controller** base class) is as follows:

```
// source:      left.hpp
// use:         Defines left_zero controller class.
```

```
#ifndef LEFT_ZERO_HPP
#define LEFT_ZERO_HPP

#include "control.hpp"

class left_zero : virtual public controller {
public:
    void input(double set_data);
protected:
    left_zero(double set_max_data, const string &set_label,
            int set_scale_length) :
        controller(set_max_data, set_label,
            set_scale_length) { }
};

#endif   // LEFT_ZERO_HPP
```

with the implementation:

```
// source:      left.cpp
// use:         Implements left_zero controller class.

#include "left.hpp"

void left_zero::input(double set_data)
{
    if (set_data <= 0.0)
        data = 0.0;
    else if (set_data >= max_data)
        data = max_data;
    else
        data = set_data;
    // Calculate cursor position (0.5 ensures rounding):
    cursor = (data * scale_length) / max_data + 0.5;
}
```

Note the following:

- The `left_zero` class has a `controller` base class which is `virtual`. This is because `left_log` objects should only have one copy of the data members of the `controller` class, as shown in Figure 14.6.

- The constructor is `protected` so that `left_zero` objects cannot be created. The base class constructor is specifically invoked since constructors are not inherited.

- The input() function ensures that only valid values are stored by the data variable, no matter what numbers are actually input.

The class for a controller which accepts input values between +max_data and −max_data is similar to the previous class:

```
// source:      centre.hpp
// use:         Defines centre_zero controller class.

#ifndef CENTRE_ZERO_HPP
#define CENTRE_ZERO_HPP

#include "control.hpp"

class centre_zero : virtual public controller {
public:
    void input(double set_data);
protected:
    centre_zero(double set_max_data, const string &set_label,
            int set_scale_length) :
        controller(set_max_data, set_label,
            set_scale_length) { }
};

#endif  // CENTRE_ZERO_HPP
```

and has the implementation:

```
// source:      centre.cpp
// use:         Implements centre_zero controller class.

#include "centre.hpp"

void centre_zero::input(double set_data)
{
    if (set_data <= -max_data)
        data = -max_data;
    else if (set_data >= max_data)
        data = max_data;
    else
        data = set_data;
    // Calculate cursor position (0.5 ensures rounding):
    cursor = 0.5 * (data + max_data) * scale_length /
        max_data + 0.5;
}
```

Note that:

- The `controller` base class is `virtual` so that each `centre_lin` object only has one copy of the data members of `controller`.

- The constructor is `protected` which ensures that no `centre_zero` objects can be created. Since constructors are not inherited the base class constructor is explicitly invoked.

- The `input()` function ensures that only values between −`max_data` and +`max_data` are stored by the `data` variable.

The class for a controller giving a linear output is completely defined by the following header file:

```
// source:       lin.hpp
// use:          Defines linear controller output class.

#ifndef LINEAR_HPP
#define LINEAR_HPP

#include "control.hpp"

class linear : virtual public controller {
public:
    void output(double &give_data) { give_data = data; }
protected:
    linear(double set_max_data, const string &set_label,
            int set_scale_length) :
        controller(set_max_data, set_label,
            set_scale_length) { }
};

#endif  // LINEAR_HPP
```

Observe that:

- As for the `centre_zero` class, the `controller` base class is `virtual` and the `protected` constructor invokes the base class constructor.

- In order to avoid a comparatively large function call overhead, the `output()` function is implemented `inline`.

A controller class giving a logarithmic output is likewise very simple:

```
// source:      log.hpp
// use:         Defines logarithmic controller output class.

#ifndef LOG_HPP
#define LOG_HPP

#include <math.h>        // for log()
#include "control.hpp"

class logarithmic : virtual public controller {
public:
    void output(double &give_data) { give_data = log(1.0 +
        data); }
protected:
    logarithmic(double set_max_data, const string &set_label,
            int set_scale_length) :
        controller(set_max_data, set_label,
            set_scale_length) { }
};

#endif  // LOG_HPP
```

From these four base classes we could construct four derived classes. Two of these classes are shown in the inheritance diagram given in Figure 14.6 and the appropriate code is as follows:

```
// source:      left_log.hpp
// use:         Defines controller class with left-zero
//              display & logarithmic output.

#ifndef LEFT_LOG
#define LEFT_LOG

#include "left.hpp"
#include "log.hpp"

class left_log : public left_zero, public logarithmic {
public:
    left_log(double set_max_data, const string &set_label,
            int set_scale_length) :
        left_zero(set_max_data, set_label,
            set_scale_length),
        logarithmic(set_max_data, set_label,
            set_scale_length),
```

```
            controller(set_max_data, set_label,
                set_scale_length) { }
    };

    #endif  // LEFT_LOG
```

and

```
    // source:       c_lin.hpp
    // use:          Defines controller class with centre-zero
    //               display & linear output.

    #ifndef CENTRE_LIN
    #define CENTRE_LIN

    #include "centre.hpp"
    #include "lin.hpp"

    class centre_lin : public centre_zero, public linear {
    public:
        centre_lin(double set_max_data, const string &set_label,
                int set_scale_length) :
            centre_zero(set_max_data, set_label,
                set_scale_length),
            linear(set_max_data, set_label, set_scale_length),
            controller(set_max_data, set_label,
                set_scale_length) { }
    };

    #endif  // CENTRE_LIN
```

Notice that for both of these derived classes the `public` constructors invoke the
direct and indirect base classes, although in fact the `controller` data is only
initialized once. (See Section 14.3.) Since the constructors are `public`, we can
create `left_log` and `centre_lin` objects.

A very simple program using the controller classes is as follows:

```
    // source:       test.cpp
    // use:          Tests controller classes.

    #include <iostream.hpp>
    #include <stdlib.h>                // for EXIT_SUCCESS
    #include "left_log.hpp"
    #include "c_lin.hpp"
```

```
int main()
{
    double x, y, z;

    left_log controller_1(100, "volume", 10);
    cout << "\n";
    centre_lin controller_2(100, "balance", 10);
    cout << "\n";

    cout << "Input value to be displayed: ";
    cin >> x;
    controller_1.input(x);
    controller_2.input(x);

    controller_1.display();
    controller_2.display();

    controller_1.output(y);
    controller_2.output(z);
    cout << "controller_1 output = " << y <<
        "\ncontroller_2 output = " << z << endl;

    return(EXIT_SUCCESS);
}
```

which can be compiled and linked by using a sequence of system dependent commands, such as:

```
c++ -c string.cpp
c++ -c control.cpp
c++ -c left.cpp
c++ -c centre.cpp
c++ test.cpp control.obj left.obj centre.obj string.obj
```

where `string.cpp` is given in Section 9.6.2. As mentioned in Section 8.17.1, something resembling the UNIX *make* utility is invaluable for projects which have multiple source files.

Exercise:

Compile and run the above program.

The `display()` function used by this program is portable but rudimentary. Use the graphics library for your system to produce a more sophisticated display.

Of course this discussion of controller classes uses some very powerful language features to implement what are really very simple requirements. However, in a real application area, such as chemical engineering or power generation, object-oriented techniques would help to reduce software complexity and to increase maintainability.

14.6   Summary

- A class is declared to depend on multiple base classes by using a derivation list:

```
class X : public A, public B, public C {
    // ...
};
```

- A direct base class cannot be repeated:

```
class X : public A, public A { };        // WRONG!
```

- An indirect base class can be repeated:

```
class A : public P { };
class B : public P { };
class X : public A, public B { };
```

- A derived class has only one copy of a `virtual` indirect base class:

```
class A : virtual public P { };
class B : virtual public P { };
class X : public A, public B { };
```

- Except for `virtual` indirect base classes, only direct base classes can occur in a constructor initialization list.

- If the same member name occurs in multiple base classes, or in a base class and a derived class, then the derived class dominates. In such cases, the base class names can be accessed by using the scope resolution operator.

14.7 Exercises

1. A `line` class could either have two `point` member objects or it could be derived from two indirect `point` base classes. Implement both approaches and examine their relative merits.

2. Our `controller` classes do not define copy constructors or overloaded assignment operators. Is this of any consequence? If so, define *suitable* copy constructors and overloaded assignment operators.

3. By developing the `controller` classes, described in Section 14.5, create treble, base, volume and balance controllers for a hi-fi system. Should the system have its own class? If so, would it be better for this `hi_fi` class to be derived from the controller classes or to be a client of them?

   (Your hi-fi system should have an array of `controller` pointers and dynamically create objects for the specific derived classes.)

4. Suppose we now decide to upgrade the hi-fi system, built in the previous exercise, so that it has a remote controller. This controller can only issue ±1 to indicate whether a particular parameter should be increased or decreased. Make whatever changes are necessary to the `input()` functions, using the + and − keys to issue 'increase' or 'decrease' commands.

Chapter 15

C++ Applications

This final chapter describes two projects written in C++; the first demonstrates how to solve a simple partial differential equation and the second is an example of a simulation. These examples cover two very common application areas; other applications are suggested as exercises.

15.1 Finite Difference Techniques

Our first project is to develop a class for solving differential equations by means of finite difference techniques. For simplicity we only consider Laplace's equation in two dimensions:

$$\frac{\partial^2 \phi(x,y)}{\partial x^2} + \frac{\partial^2 \phi(x,y)}{\partial y^2} = 0$$

since the generalization to other problems is straightforward. Details of the finite difference method are given in many standard texts, including [17]. Essentially the x-y space is replaced by a regular two-dimensional grid, as shown in Figure 15.1. Consequently $\phi(x,y)$ becomes $\phi_{i,j}$ (i and j are integers) and the deriva-

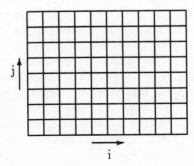

Figure 15.1: Two-dimensional grid.

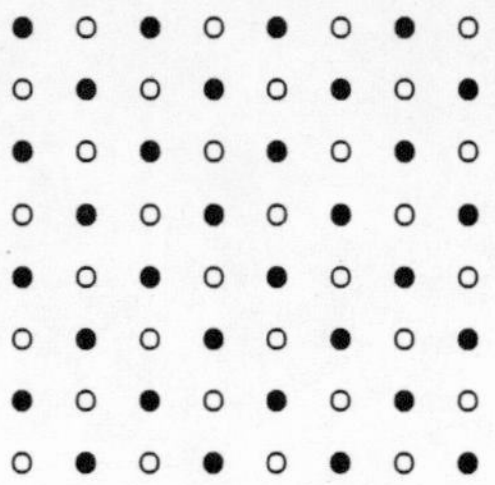

Figure 15.2: Red-black labelling of grid points.

tives are replaced by differences between the values of ϕ at neighbouring grid points. Initially the boundaries of the grid are set to specified constant values and all other points are either set to some arbitrary value or a suitable estimate.

Various update schemes can be used and for Laplace's equation they typically involve successively replacing $\phi_{i,j}$ by:

$$(\phi_{i-1,j} + \phi_{i+1,j} + \phi_{i,j-1} + \phi_{i,j+1})/4$$

The Jacobi technique is the simplest scheme and consists of using values of $\phi_{i\pm1,j\pm1}$ obtained from the previous sweep to update $\phi_{i,j}$. This scheme therefore requires two $\phi_{i,j}$ arrays. By contrast, the Gauss-Seidel technique uses the most recent $\phi_{i\pm1,j\pm1}$ values to perform the update and therefore only requires a single $\phi_{i,j}$ array. It is the Gauss-Seidel technique that we use here.

It is possible to update the grid points by sweeping across the rows and down the columns. However, a more symmetric variant of the Gauss-Seidel method is to use a chequer-board, or red-black, update scheme. Imagine that the points of the grid are alternately coloured red or black, in a similar manner to a chequer-board. This is illustrated in Figure 15.2, where the open circles correspond to red grid points and the bullets correspond to black points. Updating the red points only requires information from the black points and *vice versa*. Consequently a sweep through the red points can be performed in any order, as can a sweep through the black points. Apart from being more symmetric, this technique is suitable for solving very large problems on computers with insufficient memory to store the entire grid data. Since the update can be performed in any order, it is straightforward to split the grid into blocks, with each block just able to fit in the computer's main memory. A single block can be read from disc and all the points within the block updated before returning the blocks to disc. This process is repeated until the entire grid is updated. The technique is also very appropriate for distributed memory parallel computers.

15.1.1   Array Classes

One advantage of C++ is that it encourages the development of reusable code and a scientist or engineer will soon acquire a library of useful classes. Likely candidates for inclusion in this library are array classes, which we now use as the basis for an implementation of the Gauss-Seidel method. It is straightforward to extend the one-dimensional array class described in Section 11.8.1 to two dimensions:

```
// source:      array.hpp
// use:         Defines array class.

#ifndef ARRAY_HPP
#define ARRAY_HPP

#include <iostream.hpp>

class array { // rows & columns are numbered 1, 2, ...
public:
    array(int set_rows, int set_columns);
    array(const array &a);
    virtual ~array() { delete pt;}
    array &operator=(const array &a);
    double &operator()(int row, int col);
    int number_of_rows(void) { return rows; }
    int number_of_columns(void) { return columns; }
protected:
    int rows, columns;
    double *pt;
};

// inline array class implementations:

inline double &array::operator()(int row, int col)
{
    return pt[(row - 1) * columns + col - 1];
}

#endif  // ARRAY_HPP
```

Notice that array indices start at one rather than zero and that, as a precautionary measure, the destructor is declared `virtual`.

A suitable `array` class implementation is:

```
// source:      array.cpp
```

```
// use:          Implements array class.

#include <iostream.hpp>
#include <stdlib.h>      // for exit()
#include <string.h>      // for memcpy()

#include "array.hpp"

array::array(int set_rows, int set_columns)
{
    rows = set_rows;
    columns = set_columns;
    pt = new double[rows * columns];
    if (pt == NULL) {
        cout << "Failed to allocate array.\n";
        exit(EXIT_FAILURE);
    }
}

array::array(const array &a)
{
    rows = a.rows;
    columns = a.columns;
    pt = new double[rows * columns];
    if (pt == NULL) {
        cerr << "Failed to allocate array.\n";
        exit(EXIT_FAILURE);
    }
    memcpy(pt, a.pt, rows * columns * sizeof(double));
}

array &array::operator=(const array &a)
{
    delete pt;
    rows = a.rows;
    columns = a.columns;
    pt = new double[rows * columns];
    if (pt == NULL) {
        cerr << "Failed to allocate array.\n";
        exit(EXIT_FAILURE);
    }
    memcpy(pt, a.pt, rows * columns * sizeof(double));
    return *this;
```

```
    }
```

Notice that, although we don't anticipate using them in this project, we do define
a copy constructor and an assignment operator. Failure to make these definitions
may lead to incorrect defaults being accidentally invoked in a later project.

A bounds-checked array class takes the form:

```
// source:        c_array.hpp
// use:           Defines bounds checked array class.

#ifndef C_ARRAY_HPP
#define C_ARRAY_HPP

#include <iostream.hpp>
#include "array.hpp"

class checked_array : public array {
public:
    checked_array(int set_rows, int set_columns) :
        array(set_rows, set_columns) { }
    checked_array(const checked_array &a) :
        array(a) { }
    checked_array &operator=(const checked_array &a);
    double &operator()(int row, int col);
};


#endif   // C_ARRAY_HPP
```

with the implementation:

```
// source:        c_array.cpp
// use:           Implements checked array class.

#include <iostream.hpp>
#include <stdlib.h>      // for exit()

#include "c_array.hpp"

checked_array &checked_array::operator=(const checked_array
    &a)
{
    this->array::operator=(a);
    return *this;
```

```
    }

    double &checked_array::operator()(int row, int col)
    {
        if (row < 1 || row > rows) {
            cerr << "Row index of block = " << row <<
                " which is out of bounds\n";
            exit(EXIT_FAILURE);
        }
        if (col < 1 || col > columns) {
            cerr << "Column index of block = " << col <<
                " which is out of bounds\n";
            exit(EXIT_FAILURE);
        }
        return array::operator()(row, col);
    }
```

Since constructors and the assignment operator are not inherited, suitable functions are included in the `checked_array` class. However, no destructor is defined since a satisfactory default is provided by the compiler. Both of the functions in `c_array.cpp` invoke base class implementations. This is safer than reimplementing the functions since it reduces the possibility of inconsistencies arising due to subsequent modifications. Notice that the `operator()(int,int)` function is not declared `virtual` in the `array` base class. This is because we do not anticipate using mixed `array` and `checked_array` objects and static binding is more efficient than the dynamic binding associated with `virtual` functions.

15.1.2   Grid Class

A two-dimensional grid class, implementing the Gauss-Seidel solver for Laplace's equation, can easily be derived from the checked array class:

```
    // source:       c_grid.hpp
    // use:          Defines checked grid class.

    #ifndef C_GRID_HPP
    #define C_GRID_HPP

    #include <iostream.hpp>
    #include "c_array.hpp"

    class checked_grid : public checked_array {
    public:
        checked_grid(int set_rows, int set_columns);
```

```
        checked_grid(const checked_grid &a) :
            checked_array(a) { }
        checked_grid &operator=(const checked_grid &a);
        virtual void update(void);
};
```

```
#endif  // C_GRID_HPP
```

with the implementation:

```
// source:       c_grid.cpp
// use:          Implements checked grid class.

#include <iostream.hpp>
#include <stdlib.h>          // for exit()
#include <math.h>            // for fabs()

#include "c_grid.hpp"
const int TRUE = 1;
const int FALSE = 0;

checked_grid::checked_grid(int set_rows, int set_columns) :
    checked_array(2 * (set_rows / 2), 2 * (set_columns / 2))
{
    // Force even number of grid points in rows and columns.
    // This is useful for very large problems in which the
    // grid is split into blocks. This constructor would
    // create one of these blocks:
    if (set_rows % 2)
        cerr << "Red-black grid has been truncated to " <<
            "even rows.\n";
    if (set_columns % 2)
        cerr << "Red-black grid has been truncated to " <<
            "even columns.\n";
}

checked_grid &checked_grid::operator=
    (const checked_grid &a)
{
    this->array::operator=(a);
    return *this;
}

void checked_grid::update(void)
```

```cpp
// Update the grid points for Laplace's equation.
// See the following explanation together with that at
// the start of Section 15.1.
{
    static int red = FALSE;
    int row, col;
    if (red) {
        // Update red points:
        for (row = 2; row < rows; row += 2) {
            for (col = 2; col < columns; col += 2) {
                (*this)(row, col) =
                    0.25 * ((*this)(row - 1, col)
                    + (*this)(row + 1, col)
                    + (*this)(row, col - 1)
                    + (*this)(row, col + 1));
            }
        }
        for (row = 3; row < rows; row += 2) {
            for (col = 3; col < columns; col += 2) {
                (*this)(row, col) =
                    0.25 * ((*this)(row - 1, col)
                    + (*this)(row + 1, col)
                    + (*this)(row, col - 1)
                    + (*this)(row, col + 1));
            }
        }
        red = FALSE;
    }
    else {
        // Update black grid points:
        for (row = 2; row < rows; row += 2) {
            for (col = 3; col < columns; col += 2) {
                (*this)(row, col) =
                    0.25 * ((*this)(row - 1, col)
                    + (*this)(row + 1, col)
                    + (*this)(row, col - 1)
                    + (*this)(row, col + 1));
            }
        }
        for (row = 3; row < rows; row += 2) {
            for (col = 2; col < columns; col += 2) {
                (*this)(row, col) =
                    0.25 * ((*this)(row - 1, col)
```

```
                          + (*this)(row + 1, col)
                          + (*this)(row, col - 1)
                          + (*this)(row, col + 1));
            }
        }
        red = TRUE;
    }
}
```

This class implements the red-black variant of the Gauss-Seidel method. Notice that the constructor ensures that only grids with an even number of rows and columns can be created. This is an important simplifying restriction if the red-black update scheme is to be used for problems where the entire grid is too large to be stored in the main memory associated with a single processor.

Although the `check_grid::update()` function looks rather involved it merely implements the substitution:

$$(\phi_{i-1,j} + \phi_{i+1,j} + \phi_{i,j-1} + \phi_{i,j+1})/4 \longrightarrow \phi_{i,j}$$

for the red-black grid shown in Figure 15.2. Whenever the `update()` function is invoked it alternately updates either the red or black points. In either case the odd and even rows must be considered separately since odd and even rows have different sequences of red-black points; more specifically, if odd rows start with black points then even rows start with red points (and vice versa). Within the `update()` function, grid values are accessed by means of the notation:

```
(*this)(row, col);
```

although an equivalent alternative is:

```
operator()(row, col);
```

Neither notation is a particularly natural way of accessing what are really array elements.

15.1.3 Testing the Laplace Equation Solver

Our `menu` class again provides a convenient way of developing and testing the array and grid classes. The code to demonstrate using the grid class is as follows:

```
// source:      test.cpp
// use:         Tests Laplace equation solver.

#include <iostream.hpp>
#include <stdlib.h>              // for NULL, exit()
```

```cpp
#include "menu.hpp"
#include "c_grid.hpp"

// Function prototypes:
void to_system(void);
int rand_interval(int start, int end);
void define_grid(void);
void fill_grid(void);
void display_grid(void);
void update_grid(void);
void delete_grid(void);

static checked_grid *pt_checked_grid;

void to_system(void)
{
    cout << "Returning to system\n";
    exit(EXIT_SUCCESS);
}

inline int rand_interval(int start, int end)
// Returns a random integer in the range start to end:
{
    float delta =  float(end - start) / RAND_MAX;
    return(start + rand() * delta);
}

void define_grid(void)
// Prompts user for grid parameters and creates grid:
{
    int rows, columns;
    cout << "Enter grid size (<rows> <columns>): ";
    cin >> rows >> columns;
    cout << "Creating a " << rows << " x " << columns <<
        " array" << endl;
    pt_checked_grid = new checked_grid(rows, columns);
    if (pt_checked_grid == NULL) {
        cerr << "Failed to allocate red-black grid.\n";
        exit(EXIT_FAILURE);
    }
}

void fill_grid(void)
```

```
// Assigns random values to interior points of the grid
// and non-random values to the boundary points:
{
    int rows = pt_checked_grid->number_of_rows();
    int columns = pt_checked_grid->number_of_columns();

    // Set top and bottom:
    for (int col = 1 ; col <= columns; ++col) {
        (*pt_checked_grid)(1, col) = 0.0;
        (*pt_checked_grid)(rows, col) = 0.0;
    }

    // Set sides:
    for (int row = 2; row < rows; ++row) {
        (*pt_checked_grid)(row, 1) = 0.0;
        (*pt_checked_grid)(row, columns) = 0.0;
    }

    // Set other points:
    for (row = 2; row < rows; ++row)
        for (col = 2; col < columns; ++col)
            (*pt_checked_grid)(row, col) =
                rand_interval(0, 100);
}


void display_grid(void)
// Displays values at points on grid:
{
    const int max_columns = 18; // Adjust for screen width.
    int rows = pt_checked_grid->number_of_rows();
    int columns = pt_checked_grid->number_of_columns();
    if (columns > max_columns) {
        cerr << "Two many columns to display\n";
    }
    else {
        // Control formatting to ensure proper display:
        cout.width(4);
        cout << stickywidth;
        cout << leftjust;
        cout << "\n";
        for (int row = 1; row <= rows; ++row) {
            for (int col = 1; col <= columns; ++col) {
                cout << int((*pt_checked_grid)(row, col));
```

```
            }
            cout << "\n";
        }
        cout << endl;

        // Reset formatting to default:
        cout << defaults;
    }
}

void update_grid(void)
// Carry out requested number of updates on the grid:
{
    int iterations;
    cout << "Enter number of iterations: ";
    cin >> iterations;
    for (int i = 0; i < iterations; ++i)
        pt_checked_grid->update();
}

void delete_grid(void) { delete pt_checked_grid; }

int main()
{
    menu top_menu("Top menu", 2);
    menu test_menu("Test 2-dimensional grid class", 4);

    // Set options for main menu:
    top_menu.set_option(new action("Define 2-dimensional "
        "red-black grid", define_grid, &test_menu));
    top_menu.set_option(new action("Return to system",
        to_system));

    // Set options for sub-menu:
    test_menu.set_option(new action("Initialize grid",
        fill_grid, &test_menu));
    test_menu.set_option(new action("Display grid",
        display_grid, &test_menu));
    test_menu.set_option(new action("Update grid",
        update_grid, &test_menu));
    test_menu.set_option(new action("Delete grid",
        delete_grid, &top_menu));
```

```
    // Start menu system:
    top_menu.activate();
    return(EXIT_SUCCESS);
}
```

In order to compile and link the various files, something like the following sequence of commands should be appropriate:

```
c++ -o array.obj -c array.cpp
c++ -o c_array.obj -c c_array.cpp
c++ -o c_grid -c c_grid.cpp
c++ -o menu.obj -c menu.cpp
c++ -o string.obj -c string.cpp
c++ test.cpp array.obj c_array.obj c_grid.obj menu.obj \
    string.obj
```

Notice that we need the **menu** class of Section 11.8.2 which in turn uses the **string** class of Section 9.6.2. (The \ in the final command may be used to continue long lines but this depends on the operating system.)

Exercise: Compile and run this Gauss-Seidel solver. Try using the display option after successive updates. What do you observe?

The display_grid() function uses some new features of the I/O library and these require explanation. The statement:

```
cout.width(4);
```

sets the field width for the **cout** stream to four characters and:

```
cout << stickywidth;
```

implies that this specification will hold for all subsequent insertions, rather than just the next one. These characters are left-justified owing to the inclusion of:

```
cout << leftjust;
```

The result is a well structured display for integers of one, two or three digits, with the remainder of the field being padded by blanks. The format flags are reset to their default values by the statement:

```
cout << default;
```

Also notice that the fill_grid() function sets all of the grid boundary points to 0 and the internal points to a random number between 0 and 100. With these initial conditions, the exact solution to Laplace's equation is zero everywhere. It is therefore very easy to see how well values at the grid points tend towards the correct solution after each update.

15.1.4   Exercises

All of the following exercises refer to the array and grid classes:

1. Modify the test program to provide menus which try out the checked and unchecked arrays.

2. For situations in which the boundary conditions are zero, the normalized absolute value of $\phi_{i,j}$, summed over the internal points:

$$E \equiv (internal\ points)^{-1} \sum_{i,j} |\ \phi_{i,j}\ |$$

   is a reasonable measure of the error. Write a function to plot a graph of E against the number of updates. What is the most significant feature of the graph?[1]

3. Replace the `update()` function by a pointer version that does no bounds-checking and accesses array elements directly, rather than via the overloaded function call operator. Make this new version as efficient as you can and compare the times taken to update a 100×100 grid with the original technique.

4. Extend the two-dimensional solver to three-dimensions.

15.2   A Simulation

15.2.1   Outline of Project

A large class of typical C++ applications involves displaying the results of measurements or events. Moreover, a frequent requirement is to simulate such results. Examples include air-traffic control, flight-deck simulators and central-heating systems. Here we consider a weather-station simulation. The aim is to present the results of measurements in the form shown in Figure 15.3, with the additional feature of colour if available. For the purpose of simulation, random weather data is generated at fixed time intervals. Of course, similar techniques could be used to present the results of measurements in other diverse fields of interest, ranging from chemical engineering to particle physics.

---

[1]A very accessible explanation is given in [13]. You can see the same effect by using the `display_grid()` function to give the values of $\phi_{i,j}$ after successive updates.

15.2.2   Graphics

The display shown in Figure 15.3 can only be obtained by explicitly controlling the smallest individual element of the screen image, known as a *pixel*.[2] Pixel manipulations are not part of the C++ language and are usually provided by a non-standard library. Such libraries are excellent candidates for object-oriented techniques. The code in the following sections uses the library supplied with the Zortech compiler but it should be straightforward to modify this code for other C++ compilers.

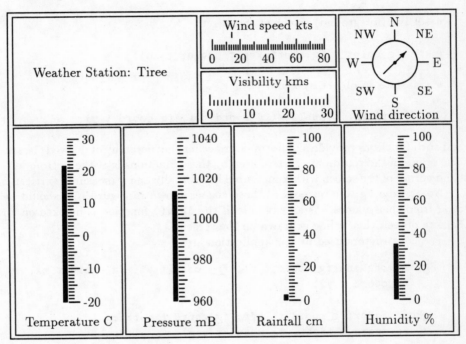

Figure 15.3: Weather station display.

In order to understand some parts of the weather station simulation, it is necessary to briefly consider the Zortech graphics library.[3] This library requires the header file, `<fg.hpp>`, for class declarations. The same file also declares the type `fg_coord_t`, which is used to specify the position of an object on the screen in terms of pixels, and the type `fg_color_t`, which is used for an object's colour. Those classes belonging to the Zortech library which are relevant to the current application are shown in Figure 15.4.

---

[2]The word, pixel, is derived from picture element.

[3]The Zortech graphics library is copyright Symantec Corporation. Portions of the library are described here with the permission of Symantec Corporation.

The `Fg` class is an abstract base class whose members include functions to:

- draw an object:

    ```
    void Fg::draw(void);
    ```

- erase an object:

    ```
    void Fg::erase(void);
    ```

- set the (foreground) colour of an object:

    ```
    fg_color_t Fg::setforeg(fg_color_t col);
    ```

- translate an object by **x** and **y**:

    ```
    void Fg::translate(fg_coord_t x, fg_coord_t y);
    ```

and such functions provide a uniform interface for the hierarchy of derived classes. The origin of the coordinate system used by these functions is at the bottom left-hand corner of the screen with **x** measured horizontally and **y** measured vertically.

Apart from `Fg`, the purpose of those classes shown in Figure 15.4 should be clear from their names. As an example, if the `draw()` function is invoked on an `FgLine` object, then a line is drawn on the screen.

The constructors used by our application are:

```
FgLine::FgLine(fg_coord_t x1, fg_coord_t y1, fg_coord_t x2,
    fg_coord_t y2);

FgBox::FgBox(fg_coord_t left, fg_coord_t bottom,
    fg_coord_t right, fg_coord_t top);

FgFillBox::FgFillBox(fg_coord_t left, fg_coord_t bottom,
    fg_coord_t right, fg_coord_t top);

FgString::FgString(fg_coord_t x, fg_coord_t y, char *string);

FgCircle::FgCircle(fg_coord_t x, fg_coord_t y,
    fg_coord_t radius);
```

Some of the classes have additional member functions of the form `set...()`; for example, `setstring(char *string)` is a member of the `FgString` class and is used to set an `FgString` object to hold a copy of the specified (null terminated) `string`.

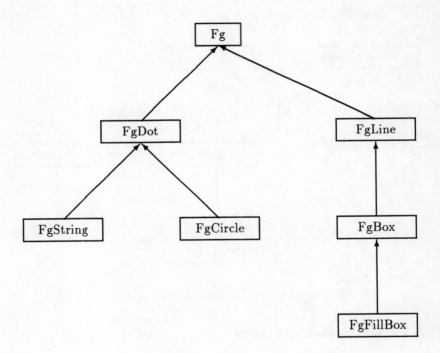

Figure 15.4: Graphics classes.

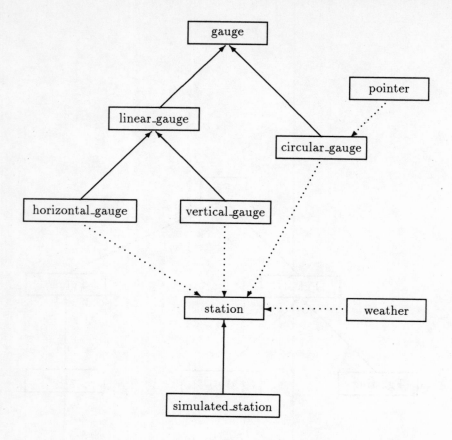

Figure 15.5: Classes used in the simulation.

15.2.3 Class Declarations

The classes used by this project are depicted in Figure 15.5.[4] The weather data
is stored by a **weather** class object and the **weather** class is declared as:

```
// source:        weather.hpp
// use:           Defines weather class.

#ifndef WEATHER_HPP
#define WEATHER_HPP
```

---

[4]As usual, solid lines denote class hierarchies. Dotted lines show classes that are used (rather
than inherited) by other classes; the arrow on a dotted line points towards the client.

```
class weather {
public:
    float temperature, pressure, rainfall, humidity;
    float visibility, wind_direction, wind_speed;
};


#endif  // WEATHER_HPP
```

Public data members are appropriate for this simple class since little is to be gained by hiding the data.

The weather station displays data members of the **weather** class, such as **temperature**, **pressure** etc. by means of gauges. The minimum requirements for each gauge are a label, the smallest and largest values to be displayed and the number of intervals into which the scale is to be divided. A **display()** function accepts and displays a single item of data. A suitable **gauge** class is:

```
// source:      gauge.hpp
// use:         Defines gauge class.

#ifndef GAUGE_HPP
#define GAUGE_HPP

#include "string.hpp"

class gauge {
public:
    gauge(const string &label, int data_minimum, int data_maximum,
        int divisions);
    virtual void display(float data) = 0;
protected:
    int max, min, div;
    string name;
};


#endif  // GAUGE_HPP
```

Since this is an abstract class we cannot create **gauge** objects. However, we can create objects belonging to the (direct or indirect) derived **horizontal_gauge**, **vertical_gauge** and **circular_gauge** classes and such objects give rise to the display shown in Figure 15.3. Notice that the **gauge** class in turn makes use of the **string** class, which was developed in Section 9.6.2 and improved in the exercises of Chapters 10 and 12. As can be seen from Figure 15.3, the horizontal and vertical gauges have much in common and therefore code duplication can be avoided by declaring a **linear_gauge** class:

```
// source:        l_gauge.hpp
// use:           Defines linear_gauge class.

#ifndef LINEAR_GAUGE_HPP
#define LINEAR_GAUGE_HPP

#include <fg.hpp>          // for graphics
#include "gauge.hpp"

class linear_gauge : public gauge {
public:
    linear_gauge(const string &label, int data_minimum,
        int data_maximum, int divisions,
        fg_coord_t set_left, fg_coord_t set_bottom,
        fg_coord_t set_right, fg_coord_t set_top);
    virtual ~linear_gauge(void);
    virtual void display(float data) = 0;
    void initialize(void);
    fg_coord_t cursor_position(float data);
protected:
    // Bounding coordinates of gauge:
    fg_coord_t left, bottom, right, top;

    // Bottom left-hand coordinates of label:
    fg_coord_t x_label, y_label;

    // Difference between coordinates of
    // fine graduations of scale:
    fg_coord_t x_shift, y_shift;
    float cursor_scaling;
    fg_coord_t cursor_zero;
    FgFillBox *pt_cursor;
    FgString *pt_graduation_label;

    // Lines for making scale graduations:
    FgLine *pt_main_graduation, *pt_medium_graduation;
    FgLine *pt_fine_graduation;
};

#endif  // LINEAR_GAUGE_HPP
```

This is again an abstract class and consequently we are not be able to create
linear_gauge objects. The constructor specifies the location of the four corners

of a derived class object, such as the vertical and horizontal gauges shown in
Figure 15.3.

The `horizontal_gauge` class is derived from `linear_gauge` and declared in
the header file, `<horiz.hpp>`:

```
// source:      horiz.hpp
// use:         Defines horizontal gauge class.


#ifndef HORIZONTAL_GAUGE_HPP
#define HORIZONTAL_GAUGE_HPP


#include <fg.hpp>        // for graphics
#include "l_gauge.hpp"


class horizontal_gauge : public linear_gauge {
public:
    horizontal_gauge(const string &label, int data_minimum,
        int data_maximum, int divisions,
        fg_coord_t set_left, fg_coord_t set_bottom,
        fg_coord_t set_right, fg_coord_t set_top);
    void display(float data);
};


    #endif  // HORIZONTAL_GAUGE_HPP
```

Notice that no attempt is made to explicitly invoke the base class destructor;
although destructors are not inherited, the base class destructor is invoked implicitly.

The declaration of the `vertical_gauge` class closely resembles that given for
the `horizontal_gauge`:

```
// source:      vert.hpp
// use:         Defines vertical gauge class.


#ifndef VERTICAL_GAUGE_HPP
#define VERTICAL_GAUGE_HPP


#include <fg.hpp>        // for graphics
#include "l_gauge.hpp"


class vertical_gauge : public linear_gauge {
public:
    vertical_gauge(const string &label, int data_minimum,
        int data_maximum, int divisions,
```

```
            fg_coord_t set_left, fg_coord_t set_bottom,
            fg_coord_t set_right, fg_coord_t set_top);
        void display(float data);
    };


    #endif  // VERTICAL_GAUGE_HPP
```

The `circular_gauge` class declaration differs from the other derived **gauge** classes since it is displayed within a square (rather than rectangular) box on the screen:

```
    // source:      circ.hpp
    // use:         Defines circular gauge class.


    #ifndef CIRCULAR_GAUGE_HPP
    #define CIRCULAR_GAUGE_HPP


    #include <fg.hpp>        // for graphics
    #include "gauge.hpp"
    #include "pointer.hpp"


    class circular_gauge : public gauge {
    public:
        circular_gauge(const string &label, int data_minimum,
            int data_maximum, int divisions, fg_coord_t left,
            fg_coord_t bottom, fg_coord_t right);
        ~circular_gauge(void) { delete pt_pointer; }
        void display(float data);
    private:
        pointer *pt_pointer;
        float theta;          // Angle between the pointer
                              // and the zero reference line.
    };


    #endif  // CIRCULAR_GAUGE_HPP
```

The `circular_gauge` uses a **pointer** object to generate the arrow shown in the 'Wind direction' display of Figure 15.3. This class is declared by:

```
    // source:      pointer.hpp
    // use:         Defines pointer class for circular gauge.


    #ifndef POINTER_HPP
    #define POINTER_HPP
```

```
#include <fg.hpp>          // for graphics

class pointer {
public:
    pointer(fg_coord_t x_centre, fg_coord_t y_centre,
        fg_coord_t radius);
    ~pointer(void);
    void draw(float theta);      // 0 <= theta < 2 * pi
    void erase(void);
private:
    fg_coord_t x0, y0;           // Centre of pointer.
    fg_coord_t r;                // Half length of pointer.
    FgLine *pt[3];               // Segments of pointer.
    FgCircle *pt_circle;         // Marks centre of pointer.
};

#endif   // POINTER_HPP
```

We now have all the ingredients for a weather station:

```
// source:        station.hpp
// use:           Defines weather_station class.

#ifndef WEATHER_STATION_HPP
#define WEATHER_STATION_HPP

#include "weather.hpp"
#include "gauge.hpp"
#include "string.hpp"

class weather_station {
public:
    weather_station(const string &station_name);
    ~weather_station(void);
    void input(const weather &new_data);
    void display(void);
protected:
    string name;
    weather data;          // Current data.
    weather max, min;      // Limits on data.
    int number_of_gauges;
    gauge **pt_gauge;
};
```

```
#endif  // WEATHER_STATION_HPP
```

However, since we don't have access to real pressure gauges etc., we define a derived class which generates its own weather:

```
// source:      sim_sta.hpp
// use:         Defines simulated_weather_station class.

#ifndef SIMULATED_WEATHER_STATION_HPP
#define SIMULATED_WEATHER_STATION_HPP

#include "station.hpp"

class simulated_weather_station : public weather_station {
public:
    simulated_weather_station(const string &station_name);
    void generate_weather(int days);
};

#endif  // SIMULATED_WEATHER_STATION_HPP
```

15.2.4   Utilities

The class implementations are simplified by introducing the functions prototyped in:

```
// source:      utils.hpp
// use:         Defines utilities.

#ifndef UTILS_HPP
#define UTILS_HPP

#include <stdlib.h>     // for rand()

// Return a random integer in the range start to end:
inline float rand_interval(int start, int end)
{
    float delta =  float(end - start) / RAND_MAX;
    return(start + rand() * delta);
}

// Wait for seconds:
void pause(int seconds);
```

```
        // Check dynamic memory allocation (pt != NULL):
        void check_allocation(void *pt, char *function_name);

        // Write message to error file and exit:
        void error(char *message);

        #endif  // UTILS_HPP
```

and the non-inline implementations are given by:

```
        // source:        utils.cpp
        // use:           Implements utilities.

        #include <stdlib.h>      // for exit()
        #include <fstream.hpp>
        #include <time.h>        // for time()
        #include "utils.hpp"

        extern ofstream *pt_error_file;

        void pause(int seconds)
        {
            time_t end_time, start_time;
            time(&end_time);
            end_time += seconds;
            do {
                time(&start_time);
            } while (start_time < end_time);
        }

        void check_allocation(void *pt, char *function_name)
        {
            if (pt == NULL) {
                *pt_error_file << "Heap allocation failed in: " <<
                    function_name << "\n";
                pt_error_file->close();
                exit(EXIT_FAILURE);
            }
        }

        void error(char *message)
        {
            *pt_error_file << message << "\n";
```

```
        pt_error_file->close();
        exit(EXIT_FAILURE);
    }
```

The `ofstream` pointer, `pt_error_file`, holds the address of an `ofstream` object which is created in the function, `main()`, and is used to record any error messages.

15.2.5   Class Implementations

The abstract `gauge` class has the following simple constructor:

```
// source:       gauge.cpp
// use:          Implements gauge class.


#include "gauge.hpp"
#include "utils.hpp"

gauge::gauge(const string &label, int data_minimum,
    int data_maximum, int divisions)
{
    name = label;
    max = data_maximum;
    min = data_minimum;
    div = divisions;
}
```

Notice how the **string** class gives rise to concise (and safer) code.

The file implementing the `linear_gauge()` class is listed next. Notice how the constructor uses the object-oriented graphics library in a very natural way by sending messages to objects; for example, a box is created, coloured green and then drawn:

```
// source:       l_gauge.cpp
// use:          Implements linear_gauge class.


#include <sstream.hpp>
#include "l_gauge.hpp"
#include "utils.hpp"

linear_gauge::linear_gauge(const string &label,
    int data_minimum, int data_maximum, int divisions,
    fg_coord_t set_left, fg_coord_t set_bottom,
    fg_coord_t set_right, fg_coord_t set_top) :
    gauge(label, data_minimum, data_maximum, divisions)
```

```
{
    left = set_left;
    bottom = set_bottom;
    right = set_right;
    top = set_top;
}

linear_gauge::~linear_gauge(void)
{
    delete pt_cursor;
    delete pt_graduation_label;
    delete pt_main_graduation;
    delete pt_medium_graduation;
    delete pt_fine_graduation;
}

void linear_gauge::initialize(void)
{
    // Draw boundary:
    FgBox box(left, bottom, right, top);
    box.setforeg(FG_GREEN);
    box.draw();

    // Draw gauge label:
    char *pt_string = name.char_array();
    FgString display_string(x_label, y_label, pt_string);
    display_string.setforeg(FG_GREEN);
    display_string.draw();
    delete pt_string;

    // Create stream for in memory formatted writes
    // in order to label the main scale divisions:
    const int buffer_size = 8;
    char buffer[buffer_size];
    ostrstream file(buffer, buffer_size);

    // Draw and label the main scale divisions:
    float cursor_increment = float(max - min) / div;
    for (int i = 0; i <= div; i += 10) {
        pt_main_graduation->draw();
        pt_main_graduation->translate(10 * x_shift,
            10 * y_shift);
        file.seekp(0);
```

```
        file << min + i * cursor_increment << ends;
        pt_graduation_label->setstring(buffer);
        pt_graduation_label->draw();
        pt_graduation_label->translate(10 * x_shift,
            10 * y_shift);
    }

    // Draw the intermediate scale divisions:
    for (i = 5; i <= div; i += 10) {
        pt_medium_graduation->draw();
        pt_medium_graduation->translate(10 * x_shift,
            10 * y_shift);
    }

    // Draw the fine scale divisions:
    for (i = 1; i <= div; ++i) {
        if (i % 5) {
            pt_fine_graduation->draw();
            pt_fine_graduation->translate(x_shift, y_shift);
        }
        else {
            pt_fine_graduation->translate(x_shift, y_shift);
            continue;
        }
    }
}


fg_coord_t linear_gauge::cursor_position(float data)
{
    fg_coord_t position;
    if (data <= min)
        position = 0;
    else if (data >= max)
        position = (max - min) * cursor_scaling;
    else
        position = (data - min) * cursor_scaling;
    pt_cursor->erase();
    return position;
}
```

When an object is created, any base class constructors are called before the constructor for the class to which an object belongs. For example, the `linear_gauge` constructor is called before the constructor for a `vertical_gauge` object. This means that much of the common code for setting up vertical and horizontal gauges resides in the `initialize()` function rather than the `linear_gauge` constructor.

The code implementing the `horizontal_gauge` class is as follows:

```
// source:      horiz.cpp
// use:         Implements horizontal gauge class.

#include <sstream.hpp>
#include "horiz.hpp"
#include "utils.hpp"

horizontal_gauge::horizontal_gauge(const string &label,
    int data_minimum, int data_maximum, int divisions,
    fg_coord_t set_left, fg_coord_t set_bottom,
    fg_coord_t set_right, fg_coord_t set_top) :
    linear_gauge(label, data_minimum, data_maximum, divisions,
    set_left, set_bottom, set_right, set_top)
{
    // Set position of label:
    x_label = left + 65;
    y_label = top - 20;

    // Set distance between fine divisions:
    fg_coord_t left_right_margin = 40;
    x_shift = (right - left - left_right_margin) / divisions;
    y_shift = 0;

    // Create FgString for numbering larger divisions:
    cursor_zero = left + left_right_margin / 2;
    pt_graduation_label = new FgString(cursor_zero - 7,
        bottom + 10, " ");
    check_allocation(pt_graduation_label,
        "horizontal_gauge::horizontal_gauge()");
    pt_graduation_label->setforeg(FG_WHITE);

    // Create graduations:
    fg_coord_t y = bottom + 30;
    pt_main_graduation = new FgLine(cursor_zero, y,
        cursor_zero, y + 20);
    check_allocation(pt_main_graduation,
        "horizontal_gauge::horizontal_gauge()");
    pt_medium_graduation = new FgLine(cursor_zero + 5 *
        x_shift, y, cursor_zero + 5 * x_shift, y + 15);
```

```
        check_allocation(pt_medium_graduation,
            "horizontal_gauge::horizontal_gauge()");
        pt_fine_graduation = new FgLine(cursor_zero + x_shift, y,
            cursor_zero + x_shift, y + 10);
        check_allocation(pt_fine_graduation,
            "horizontal_gauge::horizontal_gauge()");

        // Create the cursor:
        cursor_scaling = x_shift * divisions / (data_maximum
            - data_minimum);
        pt_cursor = new FgFillBox(cursor_zero, bottom + 52,
            cursor_zero, bottom + 62);
        check_allocation(pt_cursor,
            "horizontal_gauge::horizontal_gauge()");
        pt_cursor->setforeg(FG_YELLOW);
        initialize();
    }

    void horizontal_gauge::display(float data)
    {
        pt_cursor->setleft(cursor_zero + cursor_position(data));
        pt_cursor->setright(cursor_zero + cursor_position(data));
        pt_cursor->draw();
    }
```

Many of the integer values occuring in the implementation of this and subsequent classes correspond to screen coordinates. These values are appropriate for a 600 × 800 pixel display and will need scaling for any other display size.[5] Minor adjustments may also need to be made to the position of text on the screen because of differing font sizes.

Implementing the `vertical_gauge` involves no new techniques and is very similar to the `horizontal_gauge` class.

```
    // source:        vert.cpp
    // use:           Implements vertical gauge class.

    #include <sstream.hpp>
    #include "vert.hpp"
    #include "utils.hpp"

    vertical_gauge::vertical_gauge(const string &label,
```

---

[5]It would not be difficult to introduce parameters representing general horizontal and vertical scalings, but this would increase the amount of code still further.

```
                int data_minimum, int data_maximum, int divisions,
                fg_coord_t set_left, fg_coord_t set_bottom,
                fg_coord_t set_right, fg_coord_t set_top) :
                linear_gauge(label, data_minimum, data_maximum, divisions,
                set_left, set_bottom, set_right, set_top)
      {

          // Set position of label:
          x_label = left + 55;
          y_label = bottom + 2;

          // Set distance between fine divisions:
          x_shift = 0;
          fg_coord_t top_bottom_margin = 40;
          y_shift = (top - bottom - top_bottom_margin) / divisions;

          // Create FgString for numbering larger divisions:
          fg_coord_t x_centre = (left + right) / 2;
          pt_graduation_label = new FgString(x_centre + 40,
              bottom + 17, " ");
          check_allocation(pt_graduation_label,
              "vertical_gauge::vertical_gauge()");
          pt_graduation_label->setforeg(FG_WHITE);

          // Create graduations:
          cursor_zero = bottom + 25;
          fg_coord_t x = x_centre + 10;
          pt_main_graduation = new FgLine(x, cursor_zero, x + 20,
              cursor_zero);
          check_allocation(pt_main_graduation,
              "vertical_gauge::vertical_gauge()");
          pt_medium_graduation = new FgLine(x, cursor_zero + 5 *
              y_shift, x + 15, cursor_zero + 5 * y_shift);
          check_allocation(pt_medium_graduation,
              "vertical_gauge::vertical_gauge()");
          pt_fine_graduation = new FgLine(x, cursor_zero + y_shift,
              x + 10, cursor_zero + y_shift);
          check_allocation(pt_fine_graduation,
              "vertical_gauge::vertical_gauge()");

          // Create the cursor:
          cursor_scaling = y_shift * divisions / (data_maximum
              - data_minimum);
          const fg_coord_t thickness = 5;
```

```
        pt_cursor = new FgFillBox(x_centre - thickness,
            cursor_zero, x_centre + thickness, cursor_zero);
        check_allocation(pt_cursor,
            "vertical_gauge::vertical_gauge()");
        pt_cursor->setforeg(FG_YELLOW);
        initialize();
    }

    void vertical_gauge::display(float data)
    {
        pt_cursor->settop(cursor_zero + cursor_position(data));
        pt_cursor->draw();
    }
```

It is worth noting how the **vertical_gauge** constructor invokes the direct base
class **initialize()** function and **display()** invokes the **cursor_position()**
function.

The **circular_gauge** implementation follows a similar pattern to the previous
two gauges:[6]

```
    // source:        circ.cpp
    // use:           Implements circular gauge class.

    #include <math.h>
    #include "circ.hpp"
    #include "utils.hpp"

    circular_gauge::circular_gauge(const string &label,
        int data_minimum, int data_maximum, int divisions,
        fg_coord_t left, fg_coord_t bottom, fg_coord_t right) :
        gauge(label, data_minimum, data_maximum, divisions)
    {
        fg_coord_t gauge_width = right - left;
        fg_coord_t gauge_height = gauge_width;
        fg_coord_t top = bottom + gauge_height;

        // Draw boundary:
        FgBox box(left, bottom, right, top);
        box.setforeg(FG_GREEN);
        box.draw();

        // Draw gauge label:
```

---

[6]Figure 15.3 does not show the full detail of graduations for a **circular_gauge** object.

```
char *pt_string = label.char_array();
FgString display_string(left + 45, bottom + 5, pt_string);
display_string.setforeg(FG_GREEN);
display_string.draw();
display_string.setforeg(FG_WHITE);
delete pt_string;

// Draw scale and label main divisions:
fg_coord_t x_centre = left + gauge_width / 2;
fg_coord_t y_centre = 10 + bottom + gauge_height / 2;
fg_coord_t inner_radius = (gauge_width - 90) / 2;
FgCircle circle(x_centre, y_centre, inner_radius);
circle.setforeg(FG_RED);
circle.draw();
fg_coord_t outer_radius = inner_radius + 15;
fg_coord_t string_radius = inner_radius + 25;
FgLine line(0, 0, 0, 0);      // Don't draw this line!
line.setforeg(FG_WHITE);
for (int i = 0; i < 4; ++i) {
    double sin_theta = sin(0.5 * PI * i);
    double cos_theta = cos(0.5 * PI * i);
    line.setx1(x_centre + inner_radius * sin_theta);
    line.setx2(x_centre + outer_radius * sin_theta);
    line.sety1(y_centre + inner_radius * cos_theta);
    line.sety2(y_centre + outer_radius * cos_theta);
    line.draw();
    display_string.setx(x_centre - 5 + string_radius *
        sin_theta);
    display_string.sety(y_centre - 7 + string_radius *
        cos_theta);
    switch (i) {
    case 0:
        display_string.setstring("N");
        break;
    case 1:
        display_string.setstring("E");
        break;
    case 2:
        display_string.setstring("S");
        break;
    case 3:
        display_string.setstring("W");
        break;
```

```
        default:
            error("Error in circular gauge.");
        }
        display_string.draw();
    }
    if (divisions >= 8) {
        outer_radius -= 5;
        for (i = 0; i < 4; ++i) {
            double theta = PI * (0.25 + 0.5 * i);
            double sin_theta = sin(theta);
            double cos_theta = cos(theta);
            line.setx1(x_centre + inner_radius * sin_theta);
            line.setx2(x_centre + outer_radius * sin_theta);
            line.sety1(y_centre + inner_radius * cos_theta);
            line.sety2(y_centre + outer_radius * cos_theta);
            line.draw();
            display_string.setx(x_centre - 5 + string_radius *
                sin_theta);
            display_string.sety(y_centre - 7 + string_radius *
                cos_theta);
            switch (i) {
            case 0:
                display_string.setstring("NE");
                break;
            case 1:
                display_string.setstring("SE");
                break;
            case 2:
                display_string.setstring("SW");
                break;
            case 3:
                display_string.setstring("NW");
                break;
            default:
                error("Error in circular gauge.");
            }
            display_string.draw();
        }
        if (divisions >= 16) {
            outer_radius -= 5;
            for (i = 0; i < 8; ++i) {
                double theta = PI * (0.125 + 0.25 * i);
                double sin_theta = sin(theta);
```

```
                    double cos_theta = cos(theta);
                    line.setx1(x_centre + inner_radius *
                        sin_theta);
                    line.setx2(x_centre + outer_radius *
                        sin_theta);
                    line.sety1(y_centre + inner_radius *
                        cos_theta);
                    line.sety2(y_centre + outer_radius *
                        cos_theta);
                    line.draw();
                }
            }
        }

        // Create pointer:
        pt_pointer = new pointer(x_centre, y_centre,
            inner_radius - 5);
        check_allocation(pt_pointer,
            "circular_gauge::circular_gauge()");
    }

    void circular_gauge::display(float data)
    {
        if (data > 360.0 || data < 0.0)
            error("Invalid argument for circular_gauge::"
                "display()");
        else if (data == 360.0)
            theta = 0.0;
        else
            theta = data * PI / 180.0;
        pt_pointer->erase();
        pt_pointer->draw(theta);
    }
```

as does the pointer class:

```
    // source:      pointer.cpp
    // use:         Implements pointer class. This is used by
    //              circular gauge. The pointer is an arrow with
    //              a small circle indicating the centre of the
    //              pointer.

    #include <math.h>
    #include <fg.hpp>        // for graphics
```

```cpp
#include "pointer.hpp"
#include "utils.hpp"

pointer::pointer(fg_coord_t x_centre, fg_coord_t y_centre,
    fg_coord_t radius)
{
    // Centre coordinates of the arrow:
    x0 = x_centre;
    y0 = y_centre;

    // The half-length of the arrow:
    r = radius;

    // Create arrow shaft:
    pt[0] = new FgLine(0,0,0,0);

    // Create lines for arrow head:
    pt[1] = new FgLine(0,0,0,0);
    pt[2] = new FgLine(0,0,0,0);
    for (int i = 0; i < 3; ++i)
        check_allocation(pt[i], "pointer::pointer");

    // Create small circle at centre of arrow:
    pt_circle = new FgCircle(x0, y0, 3);
    check_allocation(pt_circle, "pointer::pointer");
}

pointer::~pointer(void)
{
    for (int i = 0; i < 3; ++i)
        delete pt[i];
    delete pt_circle;
}

void pointer::draw(float theta)
{
    // Set coordinates for arrow shaft:
    double sin_theta = sin(theta);
    float x1 = x0 - r * sin_theta;
    float x2 = x0 + r * sin_theta;
    double cos_theta = cos(theta);
    float y1 = y0 - r * cos_theta;
    float y2 = y0 + r * cos_theta;
```

```
        pt[0]->setx1(x1);
        pt[0]->sety1(y1);
        for (int i = 0; i < 3; ++i) {
            pt[i]->setx2(x2);
            pt[i]->sety2(y2);
        }

        // Set coordinates for parts of arrow head:
        pt[1]->setx1(x2 - 8 * sin(theta + 0.25 * PI));
        pt[1]->sety1(y2 - 8 * sin(0.25 * PI - theta));
        pt[2]->setx1(x2 - 8 * sin(theta - 0.25 * PI));
        pt[2]->sety1(y2 - 8 * sin(0.75 * PI - theta));

        // Draw arrow:
        for (i = 0; i < 3; ++ i)
            pt[i]->draw();

        // Draw small circle around centre of arrow:
        pt_circle->draw();
}

void pointer::erase(void)
{
    for (int i = 0; i < 3; ++i)
        pt[i]->erase();
}
```

The `station` class implementation is as follows:

```
// source:        station.cpp
// use:           Implements weather_station class.

#include <fg.hpp>            // for graphics
#include <sstream.hpp>
#include "station.hpp"
#include "utils.hpp"
#include "vert.hpp"
#include "circ.hpp"
#include "horiz.hpp"

weather_station::weather_station(const string &station_name)
{
    name = station_name;
    if (fg_init() == FG_NULL)
```

```
        error("Failed to initialize graphics board.");

    // Set maximum and minimum possible values for
    // observations:
    max.temperature = 30;
    max.pressure = 1020;
    max.rainfall = 100;
    max.humidity = 100;
    max.visibility = 30;
    max.wind_direction = 360;
    max.wind_speed = 80;
    min.temperature = -20;
    min.pressure = 980;
    min.rainfall = 0;
    min.humidity = 0;
    min.visibility = 0;
    min.wind_direction = 0;
    min.wind_speed = 0;

    // Draw bounding box:
    FgBox box(2, 0, 796, 598);
    box.setforeg(FG_GREEN);
    box.draw();

    // Draw box for station name:
    box.setleft(9);
    box.setright(337);
    box.setbottom(394);
    box.settop(592);
    box.draw();

    // Create gauges:
    number_of_gauges = 7;
    pt_gauge = new(gauge *[number_of_gauges]);
    check_allocation(pt_gauge,
        "weather_station::weather_station()");
    const fg_coord_t top_v_gauge = 387;
    const fg_coord_t bottom_v_gauge = 7;
    pt_gauge[0] = new vertical_gauge("Temperature C",
        min.temperature, max.temperature,
        max.temperature - min.temperature,
        9, bottom_v_gauge, 199, top_v_gauge);
    pt_gauge[1] = new vertical_gauge("Pressure mB",
```

```
            min.pressure, max.pressure,
            max.pressure - min.pressure,
            206, bottom_v_gauge, 396, top_v_gauge);
        pt_gauge[2] = new vertical_gauge("Rainfall cm",
            min.rainfall, max.rainfall,
            (max.rainfall - min.rainfall) / 2,
            403, bottom_v_gauge, 593, top_v_gauge);
        pt_gauge[3] = new vertical_gauge("Humididty %",
            min.humidity, max.humidity,
            (max.humidity - min.humidity) / 2,
            600, bottom_v_gauge, 790, top_v_gauge);
        pt_gauge[4] = new circular_gauge("Wind direction",
            min.wind_direction, max.wind_direction, 16,
            592, 394, 790);
        pt_gauge[5] = new horizontal_gauge("Wind speed kts",
            min.wind_speed, max.wind_speed,
            (max.wind_speed - min.wind_speed) / 2,
            345, 497, 585, 592);
        pt_gauge[6] = new horizontal_gauge("Visibility kms",
            min.visibility, max.visibility,
            max.visibility - min.visibility,
            345, 394, 585, 489);
        for (int i = 0; i < number_of_gauges; ++i)
            check_allocation(pt_gauge[i],
                "weather_station::weather_station()");

        // Draw station name:
        string s = string("Weather Station: ") + station_name;
        char *pt_string = s.char_array();
        FgString s3(70, 485, pt_string);
        s3.setforeg(FG_WHITE);
        s3.draw();
        fg_flush();
        delete pt_string;
}


weather_station::~weather_station(void)
{
        for (int i = 0; i < number_of_gauges; ++i)
            delete pt_gauge[i];
        delete pt_gauge;
}
```

```
void weather_station::input(const weather &new_data)
{
    data = new_data;
}


void weather_station::display(void)
{
    pt_gauge[0]->display(data.temperature);
    pt_gauge[1]->display(data.pressure);
    pt_gauge[2]->display(data.rainfall);
    pt_gauge[3]->display(data.humidity);
    pt_gauge[4]->display(data.wind_direction);
    pt_gauge[5]->display(data.wind_speed);
    pt_gauge[6]->display(data.visibility);
    fg_flush();
}
```

The `weather_station` constructor uses two functions which are specific to the Zortech graphics library. The `fg_init()` function initializes the graphics board and `fg_flush()` ensures that any outstanding draw instructions are completed.

The `simulated_weather_station` class is only concerned with generating weather data:

```
// source:       sim_sta.cpp
// use:          Implements simulated_weather_station class.

#include "sim_sta.hpp"
#include "utils.hpp"

simulated_weather_station::
    simulated_weather_station(const string &station_name) :
    weather_station(station_name) { }

// Generate weather every 6 hours for specified days:
void simulated_weather_station::generate_weather(int days)
{
    for (int day = 0; day < days; ++day) {
        data.temperature = rand_interval(min.temperature,
            max.temperature);
        data.pressure = rand_interval(min.pressure,
            max.pressure);
        data.rainfall = rand_interval(min.rainfall,
            max.rainfall);
        data.humidity = rand_interval(min.humidity,
```

```
                    max.humidity);
            data.visibility = rand_interval(min.visibility,
                max.visibility);
            data.wind_direction =
                rand_interval(min.wind_direction,
                max.wind_direction);
            data.wind_speed = rand_interval(min.wind_speed,
                max.wind_speed);
            display();
            pause(2);        // Wait for 2 seconds.
        }
    }
```

Having implemented these classes, it is now straightforward to simulate a weather station:

```
// source:        test.cpp
// use:           Simulates weather station.

#include <stdlib.h>       // for exit(), atoi()
#include <fstream.hpp>
#include "sim_sta.hpp"
#include "utils.hpp"

ofstream *pt_error_file;

int main(int argc, char *argv[])
{
    if (argc != 2) {
        cout << "Usage: test <days>" << endl;
        exit(EXIT_FAILURE);
    }
    pt_error_file = new ofstream("weather.err");
    if (pt_error_file == NULL) {
        cerr << "Failed to open: weather.err\n";
        exit(EXIT_FAILURE);
    }
    int days = atoi(argv[1]);
    simulated_weather_station station("Tiree");
    station.generate_weather(days);
    pt_error_file->close();
    return EXIT_SUCCESS;
}
```

Notice that we have not used the `weather_station::input()` function, which would be required for real data, since the weather station simulation generates its own data and, due to inheritance, a `simulated_weather_station` object has access to `weather_station` data.

Exercise:

Make whatever modifications are necessary for the above code to be consistent with the graphics library available with your compiler and then compile and run the weather station simulator.

15.2.6   Exercises

In order to reduce the amount of code, many desirable features have been omitted from the weather station implementation. These omissions can be rectified by the following exercises:

1. Assignment operators and copy constructors are only defined for those weather station classes for which they are absolutely necessary. Since such omissions may cause problems if these classes are used in another project, implement and test appropriate assignment operators and copy constructors.

2. Maximum and minimum values for the `weather` data are built into the `weather_station` constructor. Add functions so that these default values can be changed if necessary.

3. The weather station implementation is only suitable for a 600 × 800 screen display. Make modifications so that the code can handle any screen dimensions.

4. The `error()` function implemented in `utils.cpp` is rather harsh. Make modifications so that different actions are invoked which are appropriate to the severity of the error.

Additional exercises concerning the weather station classes are:

6. Use similar techniques to perform a different simulation, such as a flight-deck.

7. Modify the `controller` classes of Section 14.5 to use the more sophisticated graphical techniques exemplified in the classes derived from `gauge`.

15.3   Projects

The following are open-ended projects which are intended to encourage you to explore using C++ in more complicated examples than have been presented in this book:

1. Matrices are of fundamental importance for many branches of science and engineering. Construct a `matrix` class such that the operators `*`, `+`, `-`, `=`, `+=` etc. are overloaded. The operators should check for consistency between the sizes of their operands and your class should provide bounds-checked access to matrix elements by overloading the function call operator. Try using both `double` and `complex` data types, making use of `templates` if possible.

2. Implement a square matrix class where the elements are themselves square matrices which are stored on disc. All matrix operations should automatically read the necessary sub-matrices and you should assume that there is only sufficient memory available to hold a few of these sub-matrices in memory at any one time.

3. Design and implement a class for performing arithmetic on arbitrary length signed integers. The class should include addition, subtraction, multiplication, division, insertion and extraction operators.[7] A large variety of ideas in number theory can be illustrated by using such a class, for instance:

   (a) If $p_1, p_2, \ldots p_n$ are the first n primes, write a program to check whether or not:

   $$N \equiv p_1 p_2 p_3 \ldots p_n + 1$$

   is prime for $n = 1, 2, 3, \ldots$

   (b) The integer:

   $$M_p \equiv 2^p - 1$$

   with p prime, is known as the p*th Mersenne* number. For certain p, M_p is prime. Find as many Mersenne primes as you can.

   Many more number theory applications, suitable for this class, can be found in [12].

4. Design and implement a class to perform arithmetic on rational numbers. Your class will presumably store a rational number as a numerator and denominator and also provide a function to find the greatest common divisor.

---

[7]Simple algorithms for multiple precision arithmetic are given in [12], whereas [15] provides more sophistication.

Provide another rational number class which uses your arbitrary length integer arithmetic class to perform *multiprecision* arithmetic. How would you handle expressions involving objects from *both* classes.

Appendix A

Templates

Templates, which are also called *parameterized types*, are a recent addition to the C++ language.[1] Consider a function which returns the maximum of two integers:

```
int max(int a, int b)
{
    return(a > b ? a : b);
}
```

A straightforward substitution of `double` for `int` would produce a function suitable for arguments of type `double`. Similar substitutions could be performed for any other fundamental or derived type for which a greater than operator is defined. For instance, the operator may be implemented for classes such as `complex` or `string`. It is clearly tedious to implement many closely related functions; what is needed is a function for a generic type and this can be achieved by using a template.

The general syntax for a template is:

```
template <template_argument_list> declaration
```

where `declaration` may refer to either a function or class. As an example, a *function template* returning the maximum of two values is:[2]

```
template <class X> X max(X a, X b)
{
    return(a > b ? a : b);
}
```

Assuming that the greater than operator is defined for the `complex` class, then the following would be valid:

---

[1]This description is confined to an appendix because templates are currently only available for a few compilers. However, templates are undoubtably useful in many scientific applications.

[2]Note that throughout this appendix the < > pair is an essential part of the syntax.

471

```
complex z(2.0, 3.4), w(1.0, 4.5);
cout << max(z, w);
```

as would:

```
cout << max(mod(z), mod(w));
```

However, there must be an exact match between argument types for the functions invoked and those functions that can be generated from the template, so that the statements:

```
cout << max(1, 3.4);          // WRONG!
cout << max(3.4, z);          // WRONG!
```

are incorrect.

Now consider the declaration for a one-dimensional array class:

```
class array {
public:
    array(int size);
    array(const array &a);
    ~array() { delete pt; }
    double &operator[](int index);
    array &operator=(const array &a)
private:
    int n;
    double *pt;
};
```

This class is suitable for storing elements of type double. However, simple changes would make the class equally suitable for storing many other types, such as int, complex, list, matrix .... Rather than modifying the code, a *class template* can be used to specify how an array class is to be constructed with elements of an type, X:

```
template <class X> class array {
public:
    array(int size);
    array(const array<X> &a);
    ~array() { delete pt; }
    X &operator[](int index);
private:
    int n;
    X *pt;
};
```

X does not have to be the name of a user-defined class; it can also be the name of a fundamental or derived type. Notice that a class template does not actually declare a class; a compiler can only generate a class declaration if the template is used with the parameter, X, replaced by a known type; as in:

```
array<double> x(20);
array<complex> z(10);
```

Here the compiler would generate classes with the names `array<double>` and `array<complex>`.

Another obvious candidate for using templates is the linked list class introduced in Section 10.4.1:

```
template <class X> class node {
    friend class list<X>;
public:
    X data;
private:
    node<X> *next;
};

template <class X> class list {
public:
    list(void);
    ~list();
    void push(X new_data);
    void pop(X &old_data);
    int is_not_empty(void);
private:
    node<X> *head;
};
```

Notice how a **friend** to a class template is *not* implicitly a template, so we must use `list<X>`, rather than `list`, within the **node** class declaration.

Member functions for a class template are implicitly function templates, so the `push()` function belonging to the `list<X>` class can be implemented by:

```
template <class X> list<X>::push(X new_data)
{
    node<X> *pt = new node<X>;
    pt->next = head;
    head = pt;
    pt->data = new_data;
}
```

Note that the constructor implementation is:

```
template <class X> list<X>::list(void)
{
    head = NULL;
}
```

rather than:

```
template <class X> list<X>::list<X>(void)    // WRONG!
{
    head = NULL;
}
```

You should now be able to convert many of the classes described in this book to use templates; some suggestions are:

- Section 10.4.1, the singly linked list class.

- Section 10.4.2, the doubly linked list class.

- Section 11.8.1, the array class.

- Section 15.3, the matrix class.

Appendix B

The ASCII Character Codes

decimal	octal	hex.	meaning	decimal	octal	hex.	meaning
0	0	0	null	28	34	1c	FS
1	1	1	SOH	29	35	1d	GS
2	2	2	STX	30	36	1e	RS
3	3	3	ETX	31	37	1f	US
4	4	4	EOT	32	40	20	space
5	5	5	ENQ	33	41	21	!
6	6	6	ACK	34	42	22	"
7	7	7	bell	35	43	23	#
8	10	8	backspace	36	44	24	$
9	11	9	horizontal tab	37	45	25	%
10	12	a	new line	38	46	26	&
11	13	b	vertical tab	39	47	27	'
12	14	c	form feed	40	50	28	(
13	15	d	carriage return	41	51	29	)
14	16	e	SO	42	52	2a	*
15	17	f	SI	43	53	2b	+
16	20	10	DLE	44	54	2c	,
17	21	11	DC1	45	55	2d	-
18	22	12	DC2	46	56	2e	.
19	23	13	DC3	47	57	2f	/
20	24	14	DC4	48	60	30	0
21	25	15	NAK	49	61	31	1
22	26	16	SYN	50	62	32	2
23	27	17	ETB	51	63	33	3
24	30	18	CAN	52	64	34	4
25	31	19	EM	53	65	35	5
26	32	1a	SUB	54	66	36	6
27	33	1b	escape	55	67	37	7

decimal	octal	hex.	meaning	decimal	octal	hex.	meaning
56	70	38	8	92	134	5c	\
57	71	39	9	93	135	5d	]
58	72	3a	:	94	136	5e	^
59	73	3b	;	95	137	5f	_
60	74	3c	<	96	140	60	`
61	75	3d	=	97	141	61	a
62	76	3e	>	98	142	62	b
63	77	3f	?	99	143	63	c
64	100	40	@	100	144	64	d
65	101	41	A	101	145	65	e
66	102	42	B	102	146	66	f
67	103	43	C	103	147	67	g
68	104	44	D	104	150	68	h
69	105	45	E	105	151	69	i
70	106	46	F	106	152	6a	j
71	107	47	G	107	153	6b	k
72	110	48	H	108	154	6c	l
73	111	49	I	109	155	6d	m
74	112	4a	J	110	156	6e	n
75	113	4b	K	111	157	6f	o
76	114	4c	L	112	160	70	p
77	115	4d	M	113	161	71	q
78	116	4e	N	114	162	72	r
79	117	4f	O	115	163	73	s
80	120	50	P	116	164	74	t
81	121	51	Q	117	165	75	u
82	122	52	R	118	166	76	v
83	123	53	S	119	167	77	w
84	124	54	T	120	170	78	x
85	125	55	U	121	171	79	y
86	126	56	V	122	172	7a	z
87	127	57	W	123	173	7b	{
88	130	58	X	124	174	7c		
89	131	59	Y	125	175	7d	}
90	132	5a	Z	126	176	7e	~
91	133	5b	[	127	177	7f	delete

Table B.1: The ASCII Character Codes. (Infrequently used non-printing codes are given abbreviations which are not explained here.)

Appendix C

Operator Precedence and Associativity

Table C.1 lists the available C++ operators and also gives the sections where they are first introduced. All of the operators within a group in this table have the same precedence and associativity and a higher precedence than a group further down the table.[1]

Within an expression, operators with the higher precedence are evaluated first. If the resulting expression contains operators with the same precedence, then these are evaluated right to left, or left to right, according to their associativity. For instance, in the expression:

```
6 + 3 * 4 / 3 + 2
```

the * and / operators have the same highest precedence. Since they are necessarily in the same group, they also have the same left to right associativity. Therefore 3 * 4 is evaluated first, giving 4 (rather than 3) for the expression 3 * 4 / 3. The whole expression then reduces to:

```
6 + 4 + 2
```

which is evaluated, left to right, giving the final result of 12.

There are so many different operators in C++ that it is not worth learning the associativity and precedence of all of them; for the less well used operators either consult Table C.1 or else use parentheses.

---

[1]The precedence of operators shown in this table is consistent with [10]. Some compilers exhibit minor differences for a few of the more obscure operators, but hopefully such inconsistencies will disappear when the ANSI C++ Standard is published.

Operator		Associativity	Section first defined
`::`	scope resolution	left to right	8.5
`()`	function call	left to right	5.1
`[]`	subscripting		6.2
`sizeof`	size		3.4.1
`.`	member access		8.3
`->`	class member access		8.9
`++`	increment	right to left	3.1.5
`--`	decrement		3.1.5
`-`	unary minus		3.1.6
`type()`	cast		3.3.2
`!`	logical negation		4.2
`&`	address-of		6.1.1
`*`	dereference		6.1.2
`new`	allocate		7.6.1
`delete`	deallocate		7.6.2
`~`	one's complement		13.1.1
`->*`	pointer-to-member	left to right	8.10
`.*`	pointer-to-member		8.10
`*`	multiplication	left to right	3.1.2
`/`	division		3.1.3
`%`	modulus		3.1.4
`+`	addition	left to right	3.1
`-`	subtraction		3.1
`<<`	left shift	left to right	13.1.5
`>>`	right shift		13.1.5
`>`	greater than	left to right	4.1
`>=`	greater than or equal to		4.1
`<`	less than		4.1
`<=`	less than or equal to		4.1
`==`	equal	left to right	4.3
`!=`	not equal		4.3

	Operator	Associativity	Section first defined
&	bitwise AND	left to right	13.1.2
^	bitwise XOR	left to right	13.1.3
|	bitwise OR	left to right	13.1.4
&&	logical AND	left to right	4.2
||	logical OR	left to right	4.2
? :	conditional operator	left to right	4.11
=	assignment	right to left	3.1
+=			3.4.3
-=			3.4.3
*=			3.4.3
/=			3.4.3
%=			3.4.3
<<=			13.1.6
>>=			13.1.6
&=			13.1.6
^=			13.1.6
|=			13.1.6
,	comma	left to right	4.9

Table C.1: Operator Precedence and Associativity.

Appendix D

Differences between C and C++

The basic premiss underlying this book is that C++ can be learnt from scratch, rather than as an adjunct to C. However, you may have to reuse existing code written in C. The aim of this Appendix is to highlight some of the differences between the two languages. Exception handling is a recent extension to the C++ language; exceptions are not considered in this book, but details are given in [10] and [2].

There are also some differences between the original, 1978, edition of [6] and the ANSI C standard; these differences are discussed in many references, including [6]. Here we concentrate on the major differences between ANSI C and C++.[1]

Features only available in C++

The following features are only available in C++:

- Support is provided for object-oriented programming. Classes can be defined and these can have data hiding, member functions, virtual functions, overloaded operators, derived classes, friend functions, friend classes, constructors, destructors, ... (See chapters 8 to 15 for numerous examples.)

- Function names can be overloaded:

  ```
  int square(int i);
  double square(double x);
  ```

- The inline specifier can be used to suggest that the compiler directly substitutes the function body:

  ```
  inline int square(int i) { return i * i; }
  ```

---

[1]Since the assumption is that you will mainly program in C++ rather than C, this Appendix only highlights the major differences. More complete discussions are given in [2] and [7].

481

- Reference variables can be declared:

```
int i;
int &j = i;
```

Function arguments can be passed by reference:

```
void print(list &my_list);
```

and functions can return a reference:

```
double &element(object &v, int i, int j);
```

- The `new` and `delete` operators perform dynamic memory management:

```
double *pt = new double[1000];
// ...
delete pt;
```

- Unions can be anonymous:

```
union i_f {
    int i;
    float f;
};
```

- Objects can be declared anywhere within a block:

```
int length;
length = 1000;
vector v(length);
```

- Comments can be denoted by `//`:

```
// This is a comment.
```

- Although not part of the language, the standard `iostream` library overloads operators to perform type-safe I/O:

```
cout << "Enter dimension: " << flush;
cin >> dim;
```

Unemphasized features common to C and C++

There are some features, common to C and C++, which have not been described in detail because they have been superseded by features available in C++:

- The `#define` preprocessor directive is often used to implement complicated macros in C programs and examples occur in many of the header files for the standard C libraries. The C++ technique of declaring `inline` functions provides a safer alternative.

- Structures are widely used in C and are like *very* restricted classes which can only have `public` data members:

  ```
  struct complex {
      double re, im;
  };

  struct complex z;
  z.re = 11.11;
  z.im = -2.13;
  ```

  Structures have not been introduced since classes give a uniform notation.

- Dynamic memory management is performed in C by library functions (such as `malloc()`) rather than the `new` and `delete` operators. The C++ operators are safer and more convenient.

- Although not part of the language, input and output are carried out by standard library functions, such as `scanf()` and `printf()`. The C++ `iostream` library provides a safer, more convenient and object-oriented technique.

- Using the ellipsis in a function prototype, as in:

  ```
  void results(...);
  ```

  indicates that the function has an unknown number of arguments. Since any type checking is lost it is best to avoid defining such functions if it is at all possible.

Some incompatibilities between C and C++

There are some very minor differences of interpretation between statements that are valid C and C++:

- In C++, 'x' has the type char, whereas in C it has the type, int. As a consequence, sizeof('x') is equal to sizeof(char) in C++ and sizeof(int) in C.

- In C++, an empty argument list in a function declaration means that there are no arguments (as does void), whereas in C it indicates unknown arguments.

- A C++ structure, struct, is a synonym for a class in which all of the members are public by default. Since a C++ structure *can* have function members, it is a significant extension of the C construct.

- The default linkage of an identifier, preceded by the const specifier, is static in C++ and extern in C. The defaults can be overridden by an explicit extern or static specifier.

- A C++ compiler 'mangles' function names (in a well defined way) in order to provide type-safe linkage. This means that object code resulting from a C compiler will not link with code from a C++ compiler. The simplest solution may be to recompile the C modules using the same C++ compiler. The alternative is to use a linkage directive in the C++ code:

  ```
  extern "C" double old_C_function(double x);
  ```

  which prevents name mangling for this particular function. There is an alternative form of the linkage directive for more than one function:

  ```
  extern "C" {
      double old_C_function(double x);
      int ancient_C_function(char *pt);
  }
  ```

Bibliography

[1] Grady Booch. *Object-Oriented Design with Applications.* Benjamin-Cummings, Redwood City, California, 1991.
This book is about design, rather than language, and is not specifically on C++, although there is some discussion of C++. It is recommended reading when you have mastered most of the contents of *C++ for Scientists, Engineers and Mathematicians* and are designing large applications using object-oriented techniques.

[2] Margaret A. Ellis and Bjarne Stroustrup. *The Annotated C++ Reference Manual.* Addison-Wesley, Reading, Massachusetts, 1990.
This is very much a reference manual rather than a tutorial. It is the basis for the proposed ANSI C++ Standard and is a good, authoritative source of information on the details of C++ and why various features of the language are defined as they are. It is certainly not an easy book for the beginner.

[3] Keith E. Gorlen, Sanford M. Orlow, Perry S. Plexico. *Data Abstraction and Object-Oriented Programming in C++.* John Wiley & Sons, Chichester, 1990.
There is some description of C++ here, but this work mainly concerns the design of object-oriented applications and, in particular, use of the NIH class library.

[4] Andrew Koenig. *C Traps and Pitfalls.* Addison-Wesley, Reading, Massachusetts, 1989.
A very readable description of some of the features of C that can trap the programmer. Most of the examples are also relevant to C++; those that are not serve to demonstrate what you are missing.

[5] Al Kelly and Ira Pohl. *A Book On C.* Benjamin/Cummings, Menlo Park, California, 1984.
This is an excellent introduction to C and is recommended if you need to use those aspects of C++ that are included to provide backward compatibility with C.

[6] Brian W. Kernighan and Dennis M. Ritchie. *The C Programming Language.*
Prentice-Hall, Englewood Cliffs, New Jersey, 1988.
Some may find the style rather terse, but this is the standard reference on
the C programming language.

[7] Stanley B. Lippman. *C++ Primer, Second Edition.* Addison-Wesley, Reading, Massachusetts, 1991.
This is a very readable tutorial approach to learning C++, although it would
be quite hard for anyone lacking a knowledge of C. There is no special emphasis on numerical applications.

[8] Bertrand Meyer. *Object-oriented Software Construction.* Prentice Hall, London, 1988.
Here is a wealth of useful ideas on object-oriented design. Example code
fragments use the author's own language, Eiffel, but much of the book is
relevant to C++.

[9] James T. Smith. *C++ for Scientists and Engineers.* McGraw-Hill, New Y-
ork, 1991.
A description of useful application packages rather than the language itself.
The applications include complex arithmetic, elementary functions, vector
and matrix algebra, together with the solution of linear and non-linear alge-
braic equations.

[10] Bjarne Stroustrup. *The C++ Programming Language, Second Edition.*
Addison-Wesley, Reading, Massachusetts, 1991.
A very readable introduction with lots of useful insights by the designer of
the language. Chapters on design and development are particularly interesting and there is also a description of exception handling, which we have
not considered. The first edition describes the stream library, which may
still be implemented by older compilers. There is no emphasis on numerical
applications and a knowledge of C is assumed.

The following references provide the background for many of the applications
that appear in this book. With one exception, they are not directly relevant to
C++ and some of them are quite specialized:

[11] Milton Abramowitz and Irene A. Segun. *Handbook of Mathematical Functions.* Dover Publications, New York, 1968.
A standard source of formulas and graphs for a large variety of mathematical
functions.

[12] R.B.J.T. Allenby and E.J. Redfern. *Introduction to Number Theory with
Computing.* Edward Arnold, London, 1989.

This is a delightful introduction to number theory and a useful background to some of our programming examples.

[13] William L. Briggs. *A Multigrid Tutorial.* Society for Industrial and Applied Mathematics, Philadelphia, Pennsylvania, 1987.
An illuminating introduction to an important technique that has now pervaded many areas of numerical methods.

[14] E. Atlee Jackson. *Perspectives of Nonlinear Dynamics, Volume 1.* Cambridge University Press, Cambridge, 1989.
Contains a useful description of the logistic map, together with many references.

[15] Donald E. Knuth. *The Art of Computer Programming, Volume 2, Seminumerical Algorithms.* Addison-Wesley, Reading, Massachusetts, 1981.
Not easy reading, but a classic work in its field.

[16] Leslie Lamport. LaTeX: *A Document Preparation System.* Addison-Wesley, Reading, Massachusetts, 1986.
This is the background to one of the applications (and was used in the preparation of this book).

[17] William H. Press, Brian P. Flannery, Saul A. Teukolsky, William T. Vetterling. *Numerical Recipes in C, The Art of Scientific Computing.* Cambridge University Press, Cambridge, 1989.
This is an excellent and very readable source of information on numerical techniques.

[18] Robert Sedgewick. *Algorithms in C.* Addison-Wesley, Reading, Massachusetts, 1990. Another good source of algorithms, with more emphasis on non-numerical techniques than [17]. There is also a C++ version: *Algorithms in C++.* Addison-Wesley, Reading, Massachusetts, 1992.

Index

! *see* logical negation operator
!= *see* inequality operator
" *see* string
see preprocessor operator
see preprocessor operator
% *see* modulus operator
%= *see* assignment operator
&
    see address operator
    see bitwise AND operator
    see reference declarator
&& *see* logical AND operator
&= *see* assignment operator
()
    see function call operator
    see parentheses
*
    see dereferencing operator
    see indirection operator
    see multiplication operator
*= *see* assignment operator
+
    see addition operator
    see unary plus operator
++ *see* increment operator
+= *see* assignment operator
, *see* comma operator
−
    see subtraction operator
    see unary minus operator
−− *see* decrement operator
− = *see* assignment operator
− > *see* class member access operator
− >* *see* pointer-to-member operator
. *see* member access operator
.* *see* pointer-to-member operator
... *see* ellipsis

/ *see* division operator
/* */ *see* comment
// *see* comment
/= *see* assignment operator
:
    see access specifier
    see field declaration
    see label specifier
:: *see* scope resolution operator
::* *see* pointer-to-member declarator
;
    see separator
    see statement terminator
< *see* less than operator
<<
    see inserter
    see insertion operator
    see left shift operator
<<= *see* assignment operator
<= *see* less than or equal operator
= *see* assignment operator
> *see* greater than operator
>= *see* greater than or equal operator
>>
    see extraction operator
    see extractor
    see right shift operator
>>= *see* assignment operator
?: *see* conditional expression operator
[ ]
    see square brackets
    see subscripting operator
\
    see backslash
    see escape sequence
\" *see* double quote
\' *see* single quote

489

\? *see* question mark
\\ *see* escape sequence, backslash
\a *see* alert
\b *see* backspace
\f *see* form feed
\n *see* new line
\r *see* carriage return
\t *see* horizontal tab
\v *see* vertical tab
^ *see* bitwise exclusive OR operator
^= *see* assignment operator
{}
    see block
    see braces
    see class declaration
    see **enum** declaration
    see function body
    see initialization list
| *see* bitwise inclusive OR operator
|= *see* assignment operator
|| *see* logical OR operator
~ *see* bitwise complement operator

a.out 2
Abramowitz, Milton 486
abstract class 318 - 322
    constructor for 328
abstract data type 195
access declaration 331 - 333
actual argument of function 83
ada 12
addition
    matrix 182 - 187
addition operator 33, 478
address 117
address-of
    operator 117 - 118, 478
alert 14
Allenby, R.B.J.T. 486
allocating memory dynamically 169 - 175
alphabetic sort 187 - 191, 378
alternative returns 56
anonymous **union** 387, 482
ANSI 4
argc 160
argument *see* function argument

arguments to **main()** 160 - 163
argv 160
arithmetic
    complex 218 - 225, 269 - 274, 282
    floating point 33
    integer 21, 23
    pointer 127 - 130
        addition 127
        relational operation 129
        subtraction 128
    two's complement 398
array
    and pointers 127 - 131
    as function argument 156 - 160
    base address 127, 131, 135
    bounds checked class 335 - 340, 351
    element 125
    index 125
        negative 132
    initialization 136 - 137
    multi-dimensional 133 - 136, 139 -
        141
        and pointers 135 - 136
    of objects 196, 198
    of pointers 139 - 141
    one-dimensional 125 - 127
    ragged 143 - 145, 177
    size 125
    sizeof 138 - 139
    storage map 135
    subscript 125
array class 230 - 234, 244, 266, 282, 429
    - 432, 435
asm 12
assignment
    integer 21
    of stream 365
assignment operator 39 - 40, 479
    bitwise 384
    floating point 32
    integer 21
    overloaded 259
    overloading 246 - 247
        default 246
assignment vs. initialization 285 - 287

associativity of operators 477
    floating point 33
    integer 26 - 29
    logical 45
atoi() 161
auto 12, 95 - 98
automatic storage 95 - 98

backslash 14
    for string continuation 355
backspace 14, 475
bad condition 368
bad() 368
base address of an array 127, 131, 135
base class 309
    indirect 408
    initialization list 411
    virtual 408 - 411, 413
bell 14, 475
benchmark
    Savage 104 - 106
Bessel function 113
bias 400
biased exponent 400
binary operator 26
    overloaded 260 - 262
binding
    dynamic 326
    early 326
    late 326
    static 326
bisection
    root finding 106 - 109, 112, 166, 194
bit 9
    array class 388 - 394
    least significant 385
    mask 392
    most significant 385
    representation
        floating point types 399 - 402
        integral types 397 - 399
bit array
    class 403
bit-field 385 - 386
bitwise
    AND operator 382, 479
    complement operator 382, 478
    exclusive OR operator 382, 479
    inclusive OR operator 383, 479
    operators 381 - 384
block 50 - 51, 96
    empty 50
Booch, Grady 485
boolean type 45
brace
    empty 86
braces 28, 50, 53, 55, 82, 195
bracket 28
branch statement 51 - 56
break 12, 57, 64
Briggs, William L. 487
bubble sort 190, 193, 308
byte 9

C macro 483
C structure 483
C++
    differences from C 481 - 484
    incompatibilities with C 483
carriage return 14, 475
case 12, 58
cast 37, 254, 478
    pointer 133
catch 12
cerr 354
changing linkage
    using **extern** 226
    using **static** 227
char 12, 30
character 9
    constant 14 - 15
character set 9
    ASCII 475
cin 4, 24, 354
class
    abstract 318 - 322
    access declaration 331 - 333
    access specifier 197 - 198, 329 - 330
    arbitrary length integer arithmetic 469
    array 429 - 432
    assignment operator

default 200
base 309
bit array 388 - 394, 403
bounds checked array 335 - 340, 351
client of 239
complex 218 - 225, 269 - 274, 282,
    286, 378
  addition by operator function 259
  addition operator 249
  assignment operator 246, 248
  conversion by constructor 253
  input and output 361
  unary minus operator 251
controller 414 - 424, 425
declaration 195 - 197
derivation list 406
derived 309
forward declaration 298
friend vs. derived 333
grid 432 - 435
inheritance hierarchy 322 - 326, 378
istream 358 - 361
list 378
matrix 284
member 195
member access operator 209, 211,
    478
menu 340 - 347, 351, 378, 435
ostream 355 - 357
private 283
rational arithmetic 469
scope 203, 214
shape 310, 330
sparse vector 308, 351
sphere 195
string 274 - 280, 307, 378
template 297, 472
using classes 313 - 314
vector 291 - 294
weather 351
weather_data 379
weather_data 235 - 240, 244, 308
class member access operator
  overloaded 259
class scope 94

class 12
clear() 369
client 313
client of a class 239
clock() 105
CLOCKS_PER_SEC 105
clog 354
comma 136
comma operator 66 - 67, 479
comment 2, 9, 105, 482
compilation
    conditional 72 - 74
compiling a C++ program 1
complex arithmetic 218 - 225, 246, 269
        - 274, 282, 286
complex class 218 - 225, 269 - 274, 282,
        286, 361, 378
compound statement 50 - 51
concatenation of string constants 15
conditional compilation 72 - 74
conditional expression operator 68, 479
const 12, 40 - 41, 222, 226, 251
constant 13 - 15
    character 14 - 15
    expression 13, 14
    floating point 14
    hexadecimal 13
    integer 13
    octal 13
    string 15
constructor 217 - 220, 284 - 289
    access specifier for 328, 330
    base class initialization list 411
    default 283
    for abstract class 328
    function 217 - 220
    not inherited 327
    not virtual 327
    overloading 219
continue 12, 64
control structure 45 - 79
controller classes 414 - 424, 425
conversion
    by constructor 252 - 253
    explicit *see* cast

function 253 - 256
    implicit 257 - 259
    user-defined 252 - 259
copy constructor 220
cout 2, 354
<ctype.h> 103

DAG 310
dangling **else** trap 54
    preprocessor directives 73
data hiding 204 - 205
data member 195
database 235
deallocation
    array of user-defined objects 199
    user-defined objects 199
declarator
    reference 177, 179 - 182, 482
declare vs. define 20
decrement operator 25 - 26, 33, 478
default 12, 58
default
    constructor 283
    destructor 283
    function argument 89 - 91
#define 16, 69, 70 - 72, 120, 483
define vs. declare 20
definition hiding 50
delete 12, 169 - 177, 476, 478, 482, 483
denormalized number 401
dereferencing operator 119, 478
derivation list 406
derived class 309
    function hidding 312
    multiple inheritance 405
derived type 19
destructor 289 - 290
    access specifier for 328, 330
    base class 328, 447
    default 283
    explicit call 290
    virtual 328
directed acyclic graph 310
directives 69
division
    integer 23

    by zero 23
    truncation 23
    operator 23, 33, 478
do 12, 62 - 63
dominance 311, 412
double 3, 12, 31, 32 - 34
double quote 14, 15
doubly linked list 302 - 307, 351
duplicate names 412
dynamic
    binding 326
    memory management 169, 284 - 285
        user-defined objects 199

e *see* exponent
early binding 326
element of array 125
#elif 69
ellipsis 483
Ellis, Margaret A. 485
else 12
#else 69
empty argument list in C 484
#endif 69, 231
endl 356
ends 371
enum 12, 74, 324
    declaration 74
enumeration 74 - 76, 226
    defined with class scope 324
    type 74
      scope of 75
    unnamed 76
    variable 75
enumerator 74
    scope of 75
eof condition 368
eof() 368
equality operator 49 - 50, 478
    incorrect use of 52
#error 69
escape 475
escape sequence 14
    alert 14
    backslash 14
    backspace 14

bell 14
carriage return 14
double quote 14
form feed 14
hexadecimal constant 14
horizontal tab 14
new line 14
octal constant 14
question mark 14
single quote 14
vertical tab 14
exception handling 481, 486
exit() 101
EXIT_FAILURE 101
EXIT_SUCCESS 101
exponent 14, 32, 400
extern 12, 226, 484
external linkage 226
extraction operator 25, 354
extractor 354

factorial function 82, 92, 101
fail condition 368
fail() 368
FALSE 53
fg_color_t 441
fg_coord_t 441
Fibonacci sequence 78, 93
Fibonnaci sequence 93
field declaration 385
file
    extension
        header file 2
        source code 2
    input and output 362 - 365
    scope 95
finite difference 427 - 440
    Gauss-Seidel method 428
    Jacobi method 428
    red-black scheme 428
fitting data 141 - 143
fixed point format 366
Flannery, Brian P. 487
float 12, 31, 34
    bit representation 399
<float.h> 43, 103

floating point
    constant 14
    conversion 36
    overflow 33
    type 31 - 35
        bit representation 399 - 402
    underflow 33
    variable 3
for 12, 60 - 62
form feed 14
formal argument of function 82
    unused 88 - 89
format control 365 - 368
FORTRAN 33, 126
fortran 12
forward class declaration 298
fractional part 32
free store 169
friend 12
    class 224
    function 223 - 225
    not inherited 334
    of a friend 224
fstream class 353, 364
<fstream.hpp> 353, 362
function 81 - 115
    actual argument 83
    argument
        default 89 - 91
        empty list 85
        pointer 154 - 155
        reference 177 - 179, 207 - 208, 482
        type conversion 258
        void 85
    body 82
    call 83
        operator 478
        operator overloading 266 - 267
    constructor 217 - 220
    declaring function 86
    definition 81 - 84
    formal argument 82
    friend 223 - 225
    header 82
    helper 337

inline 93 - 94, 202, 481, 483
invoking 81 - 84
main() 100
mathematical 103
member 197, 201
overloading 98 - 100, 481
    ambiguity resolution 99
pointer to 163 - 168
prototype 86
pure virtual 318 - 322
return type conversion 258
template 471
unused formal argument 88 - 89
virtual 314 - 318
    overridding of 315
function call operator
    overloaded 259
fundamental type 19 - 35

gcount() 360
generic pointer type 132
get() 359
getline() 359
global object
    initialization 97
global scope 95
good condition 368
good() 368
Gorlen, Keith E. 485
goto 12, 65 - 66
greater than operator 45, 478
greater than or equal operator 45, 478
grid classes 432 - 435

header file 3, 70, 86, 102, 228 - 229
heap 169
helper function 337
hex 356, 367
hexadecimal constant 13, 14
horizontal tab 14, 475
Horner's method 112
huge 12

I/O library 353, 482
identifier 11
    with embedded double underscore 11

with leading underscore 11
with trailing underscore 12
IEEE floating point standard 33, 399
if 12, 51 - 54
if else 54 - 56
#if 69
#ifdef 69
#ifndef 69, 231
ifstream class 353, 363
implicit conversion 257 - 259
in memory formatting 370 - 371
#include 69, 70
include file *see* header file
increment operator 25 - 26, 33, 478
index of array 125
indirect base class 323, 408
indirection operator 119
inequality operator 49 - 50, 478
infinity
    signed 401
inheritance 309
    multiple 405 - 425
        derivation list 406
    single 309 - 351
initialization 38 - 39
    list 136
    object
        public data members 217
    of array 136 - 137
    of global objects 97
    of member object having a construc-
        tor 287
    of static objects 96
    static data member 215
inline 12, 202
inline function 93 - 94, 202, 226, 481,
        483
input
    for files 362 - 365
    for user-defined types 361 - 362
    stream 4, 24
    unformatted 359 - 361
inserter 354
insertion operator 2, 22, 354
int 12, 20 - 22

integer
    addition 21
    assignment 21
    constant 13
    division 23
        by zero 23
        truncation 23
    multiplication 23
    overflow 22
    part 32
    subtraction 21
    underflow 22
integral
    conversion 36
    promotion 36
    widening 36
integral type 20 - 31
    bit representation 397 - 399
    character 20
    integer 20
internal linkage 226
INT_MAX 22
INT_MIN 22
ios class 366
iostream class 353
<iostream.hpp> 2, 353, 354
istream class 353, 354, 358 - 361
istrstream class 370
iteration statements 59 - 63

Jackson, E. Atlee 487

Kelly, Al 485
Kernighan, Brian W. 486
keyword 12 - 13
Knuth, Donald E. 487
Koenig, Andrew 485

l *see* long, long double
label
    case 58
    default 58
Lamport, Leslie 487
Laplace's equation 427
late binding 326
least significant bit 385

left shift operator 383, 478
Legendre polynomial 114
less than operator 45, 478
less than or equal operator 45, 478
lexical basis of C++ 9 - 18
library 1
<limits.h> 20, 22, 43, 103
#line 69
linkage
    C and C++ 484
    external 226
    internal 226
    type-safe 226, 484
linked list
    double 302 - 307, 351
    single 295 - 301
linker 226
linking
    C++ code 1
Lippman, Stanley B. 486
list
    LIFO 297
    stack 297
list class 378
literal 13 - 15
LN2 366
logical
    AND operator 47 - 49, 479
    negation operator 47 - 49, 478
    OR operator 47 - 49, 479
logistic map 115
long 12, 29
    bit representation 399
long double 31, 34 - 35
long int 29
lvalue 40
    unmodifiable 131, 152

macro 71
main() 2, 100
    arguments to 160 - 163
make utility 234, 423
malloc() 483
manipulator 356
    endl 356
    fixed 366

hex 356, 367
oct 366
scientific 366
mathematical functions 103
<math.h> 4, 103
matrix
   addition 182 - 187
   class 284
   multiplication 4
maximal munch 17
member 195
   access
      ambiguities 412
      operator 198, 203, 211
   data 195
      static 214 - 216
   function 197, 201
      const 222 - 223
      static 216 - 217
   object
      with constructor 287
   object selector 212
   pointer selector 212
member access
   operator 478
memcpy 189
memory
   addressing 117
menu class 340 - 347, 351, 378, 435
Mersenne
   number 469
   prime 469
messages 205
methods 205
Meyer, Bertrand 486
module 70, 225 - 228
modulo arithmetic 30
modulus operator 24 - 25, 33, 478
Monte Carlo technique 112
most significant bit 385
multi-dimensional array 133 - 136, 139 - 141
   and pointers 135 - 136
multiple assignments 39
multiple inheritance 405 - 425

derivation list 406
multiplication
   integer 23
   operator 33, 478
      floating point 33

name mangling 226, 484
NaN 33, 401
far 12
negative array index 132
nested comments 10
   alternative to 74
new 12, 169 - 177, 478, 482, 483
new line 14, 475
Newton-Raphson 79, 194
normalized number 401
Not a Number 33, 401
not equal operator 49 - 50, 478
null 475
   pointer 125, 171
   statement 67
NULL 125, 171
numerical integration 79

object 196
   initialization
      auto 96
      static 96
object-oriented xviii, 6, 88
   database 235
oct 366
octal constant 13, 14
ofstream class 353, 362
one's complement operator 382, 478
one-dimensional array 125 - 127
operands
   order of evaluation of 68 - 69
   type conversion 258
operator 15 - 16
   addition 33
   address-of 117 - 118
   assignment 39 - 40
   associativity 45, 477
   binary 26
   bitwise 381 - 384
      AND 382

assignment 384
    complement 382
    exclusive OR 382
    inclusive OR 383
class member access 211
comma 66 - 67
conditional expression 68
const 251
decrement 25 - 26, 33
    postfix 26
    prefix 26
delete 260, 482, 483
dereferencing 119
division 33
equality 49 - 50
extraction 25
function 259 - 264
    explicit call 259
greater than 45
greater than or equal 45
increment 25 - 26, 33
    postfix 25
    prefix 25
indirection 119
insertion 2
left shift 383
less than 45
less than or equal 45
logical
    AND 47 - 49
    negation 47 - 49
    OR 47 - 49
member access 198, 203, 211
modulus 33
multiplication 33
new 260, 482, 483
not equal 49 - 50
one's complement 382
overloading 245 - 282
    general guidelines 267, 269
    restriction to non-**static** members 259, 268
    restriction to **static** members 260, 268
    restrictions 245

pointer-to-member 210 - 213
    precedence 45, 477
    relational 45 - 47
    right shift 383
    scope resolution 203, 210
    sizeof 37
    subscripting 125
        overloading 336
    subtraction 33
    unary 27
    unary minus 27, 33
    unary plus 27
    which cannot be overloaded 245
operator 12
Orlow, Sanford M. 485
ostream class 353, 354, 355 - 357
ostrstream class 370
output
    for files 362 - 365
    for user-defined types 361 - 362
    unformatted 357
overload 12
overloaded
    assignment operator 246 - 247, 259
        default 246
    binary operator 260 - 262
    class member access operator 259
    constructors 219
    delete operator 260
    function 98 - 100, 481
        ambiguity resolution 99
    function call operator 259, 266 - 267
    new operator 260
    operators 245 - 282
        general guidelines 267, 269
        restriction to non-**static** members 259, 268
        restriction to **static** members 260, 268
        restrictions 245
    subscripting operator 259, 264 - 266, 336
    unary operator
        postfix 263 - 264
        prefix 262

overridding of `virtual` function 315

parameterized types 471
parentheses 28, 83, 86, 168
parse 9
Pascal 86
`pascal` 12
pass by reference 83, 177, 482
pass by value 83
PI 113
pixel 441
Plexico, Perry S. 485
Pohl, Ira 485
pointer 119 - 123
    and arrays 127 - 131
    arithmetic 127 - 130
        addition 127
        relational operation 129
        subtraction 128
    as function argument 154 - 155
    conversion 133
    to an array 139
    to function 163 - 168
    to member 208 - 209
    to pointer 122
    to undeclared memory 123 - 124
pointer-to-member
    declarator 210
    operator 210 - 213, 478
pointers and multi-dimensional arrays
        135 - 136
polymorphism 314, 326
postfix
    ++ operator 25
        overloaded 263 - 264
    -- operator 26
        overloaded 263 - 264
`pow()` 165
`#pragma` 69
precedence of operators 477
    floating point 33
    integer 26 - 29
    logical 45
`precision()` 366
prefix
    ++ operator 25

        overloaded 262
    -- operator 26
        overloaded 262
preprocessor 16, 69 - 74
    directive 69
        `elif` 72
        `else` 72
        `endif` 72, 231
        `if` 72
        `ifndef` 231
    operator 69
Press, William H. 487
prime numbers 113, 161, 394, 403
`printf()` 483
`private` 12, 197, 329
    class 283
programming style 16 - 17, 225 - 229
`protected` 12, 329, 406
prototype 4
`ptrdiff_t` 42, 128
`public` 12, 197, 329, 414
pure `virtual` function 318 - 322
`put()` 357

quadratic equation 3, 45, 55, 56, 73
question mark 14
Quicksort 193

ragged array 143 - 145, 177
`rand()` 113, 148
`rand()` 103
`RAND_MAX` 113, 148
`read()` 360
recursion 91 - 93, 107
Redfern, E.J. 486
reference
    argument 177 - 179, 207 - 208, 482
    declarator 177, 179 - 182, 482
    pass by 177
    `return` 179 - 181, 482
    variable 181 - 182
`register` 12, 41
relational database 235
relational operators 45 - 47
remainder operator 24 - 25
`return` 12, 82

for an object 206 - 207
int default 85
reference 179 - 181, 207, 482
type 84 - 86
value 91
Riemann ζ function 165
right shift operator 383, 478
Ritchie, Dennis M. 486
root finding
    by bisection 106 - 109, 112, 166, 194
    Newton-Raphson 79, 194
rvalue 40

Savage benchmark 104 - 106
scanf() 483
scientific format 366
scope 50 - 51, 94 - 95
    of enumeration type 75
    and data protection 213 - 214
    class 94, 203, 214
    file 95
    global 95
    of enumerators 75
    resolution operator 203, 210, 478
Sedgewick, Robert 487
seekg() 364
seekp() 371
Segun, Irene A. 486
separator 11
shape class 310, 330
shift operators 383 - 384
short 12, 29 - 30
short int 29 - 30
Sieve of Eratosthenes 394 - 397, 403
sign bit 400
signed 12
signed char 30
signed infinity 401
significand 400
Simula 309
single inheritance 309 - 351
single quote 14
singly linked list 295 - 301
size of array 125
size_t 42, 103
sizeof 12, 37, 38, 478

array 138 - 139
sizeof(char) in C 484
size_t 38
Smalltalk 205
Smith, James T. 486
sort 193
    alphabetic 187 - 191
    bubble 190, 193, 308
sparse vector class 308, 351
specifier
    auto 95 - 98
    class access 197 - 198
      private 197
      protected 329
      public 197
    const 40 - 41
    inline 202
    register 41
    static 95 - 98
    storage class 41
    type 40
    volatile 41
sphere class 195
sqrt() 4
square brackets 28, 125, 133, 152
square root 4
stack 92, 297
    checking 92
    overflow 92
standard functions 101 - 104
standard library 101 - 104
    mathematical functions 103
    rand() 103
    string manipulation 103
    system() 103
    timing functions 103
standard output stream 2
statement
    label 65
    terminator 2
static 12, 227, 484
    class member 226
    data member 214 - 216
    initialization of 97
    member function 216 - 217

storage 95 - 98
static binding 326
`<stddef.h>` 103
`<stddef.h>` 38
`<stdio.h>` 103
`<stdlib.h>` 101, 103
storage class specifier 41
storage map 135
`strcat()` 153
`strcmp()` 191
`strcpy()` 152
stream assignment 365
stream condition 368 - 370
    bad 368
    eof 368
    fail 368
    function
      `bad()` 368
      `eof()` 368
      `fail()` 368
      `good()` 368
    good 368
`<strstream.hpp>` 370
string 2, 151 - 154
    constant 15
      concatenation 15
    continuation 355
    functions 103
    terminator 151
string class 274 - 280, 307, 378
`<string.h>` 103, 152
`strlen()` 189
Stroustrup, Bjarne xvii, 485, 486
strstream class 354, 370
`<strstream.hpp>` 354
`struct` 12, 483, 484
structure *see* **struct**
subclass 309
subscript of array 125
subscripting
    operator 125, 478
      overloading 259, 264 - 266, 336
subtraction
    integer 21
    operator 33, 478

floating point 33
superclass 309
`switch` 12, 56 - 58, 326
    disadvantage of 325
`system()` 103

`template` 12, 297, 471 - 474
Teukolsky, Saul A. 487
`this` 12, 247 - 249
`throw` 12
`<time.h>` 103, 105
token 9
top-down design 182
translator 1
trapezoidal rule 79
TRUE 53
`try` 12
two's complement arithmetic 398
type 19
    character 30 - 31
    checking 19
    conversion 35
    demotion 36
    derived 19
    floating point 31 - 35
    int 20 - 22
    promotion 35
    specifier 40
    user-defined 195
type-safe linking 226, 484
`typedef` 12, 42 - 43, 120, 168, 226

u *see* **unsigned**
unary operator 27
    postfix 25
      overloaded 263 - 264
    prefix 25
      overloaded 262
    minus 27, 33, 478
    plus 27
`#undef` 69
unformatted input 359 - 361
unformatted output 357
`union` 12, 386 - 388
    anonymous 387, 482
UNIX

make utility 234, 423
unsigned 12, 30
    addition 30
    bit representation 397
    subtraction 30
unsigned char 30
unused formal argument of function 88
    - 89

vector class 291 - 294
vertical tab 14, 475
Vetterling, William T. 487
virtual 12
    base class 408 - 411, 413
    function 314 - 318
        overridding of 315

void 12, 85
void* 132 - 133
volatile 12, 41

weather class 351
weather_data class 379
weather_data class 235 - 240, 244, 308
while 12, 59 - 60
white space 9, 11
widening
    integral 36
write() 357

Zortech 441
zero 125
    divide by 23, 33